TH

In memory of Edward Smakman

THE PROBLEM OF EVIL

A Reader

Edited by Mark Larrimore

Princeton University

Blackwell
Publishing

BLACKWELL PUBLISHING
350 Main Street, Malden, MA 02148-5020, USA
9600 Garsington Road, Oxford OX4 2DQ, UK
550 Swanston Street, Carlton, Victoria 3053, Australia

First published 2001 by Blackwell Publishing Ltd

11   2010

Library of Congress Cataloging-in-Publication Data

The problem of evil : a reader / edited by Mark Larrimore.
    p. cm.
Includes bibliographical references and index.
ISBN 978-0-6312-2013-8 (hbk. : alk. paper) ISBN 978-0-6312-2014-5 (pbk. : alk. paper)
1. Theodicy.   2. Good and evil.   I. Larrimore, Mark J. (Mark Joseph), 1966–
BL216.P76   2001
214—dc21

                                                                    00-009180

A catalogue record for this title is available from the British Library.

Set in 10.5 on 12.5 pt Bembo
by Best-set Typesetter Ltd, Hong Kong

For further information on
Blackwell Publishing, visit our website:
www.blackwellpublishing.com

Contents

Acknowledgments

The editor and publishers gratefully acknowledge the following for permission to reproduce material:

Anselm of Canterbury, "On the Fall of the Devil" from *The Major Works* (eds. Brian Davies and G. R. Evans) (Oxford University Press, Oxford, 1998)

St Thomas Aquinas, "Summa Theologica" from *Summa Theologica: Complete English Edition in Five Volumes* (trans. Fathers of the English Dominican Province) (Christian Classics, Allen, Tex., 1981 [1948])

Auden, W. H. "Musee des Beaux Arts" from *Selected Poems, New Edition* (ed. Edward Mendelson) (Vintage Books, New York, 1979, reprinted by permission of Random House Inc.)

St. Augustine, *Concerning the City of God, against the Pagans* (trans. Henry Bettenson) (Penguin, Harmondsworth, 1984)

Barth, Karl, *Church Dogmatics* (trans. G. W. Bromily and R. J. Ehrlich) (T. & T. Clark Ltd, Edinburgh, 1960)

Bayle, Pierre, *Historical and Critical Dictionary: Selections* (trans. Richard H. Popkin) (Bobbs-Merrill Inc., Indianapolis [The Library of Liberal Arts] 1965)

Boethius, *The Consolation of Philosophy* (trans. V. E. Watts) (Penguin, Harmondsworth, 1969)

Calvin, John, *Institutes of the Christian Religion* (Library of Christian Classics) (ed. John T. McNeill. Used by permission of Westminster John Knox Press, Philadelphia, 1960 and T. T. Clark Ltd, Edinburgh)

Chaucer, Geoffrey, "The Oxford Scholar's Tale" from *The Canterbury Tales* (trans. David Wright) (Penguin, Harmondsworth, 1985)

Cohen, Hermann, *The Religion of Reason out of the Sources of Judaism* (trans. Simon Kaplan) (Frederick Ungar, New York, 1972)

Conway, Anne, *The Principles of the Most Ancient and Modern Philosophy* (trans. Allison P. Coudert and Taylor Corse) (Cambridge University Press, Cambridge, 1996)

Cudworth, Ralph, *The True Intellectual System of the Universe* (1820)

Du Bois, W. E. B., "A Litany at Atlanta" *The Independent* (Oct. 11, 1906)

Donne, John, "Batter my heart, three-personed God" from *The Norton Anthology of English Literature* (ed. M. H. Abrams) 6th ed. (W. W. Norton, Inc., New York 1993)

Dostoyevsky, Fyodor, *The Brothers Karamazov* vol. 4 (Rebellion) (trans. Constance Garnett) (The Modern, Library, New York, n.d.)

Eckhart, Meister, *Sermons and Treatises* (trans. M. O'C. Walshe) (Dorset Element Books, Longmead, Shaftesbury, 1989)

Emerson, Ralph Waldo, "The Tragic" from *Natural History of Intellect and other papers* (*Emerson's Works* XII) (Riverside Press, Cambridge, 1893)

Epictetus, "Encheiridion" from Gerard Boter, ed., *The Encheiridion of Epictetus and Its Three Christian Adaptations: Transmission and Critical Editions* (Brill Academic Publishers, Leiden, Boston, Koln, 1999)

Freud, Sigmund, *The Future of an Illusion* (trans. James Strachey) Copyright © 1961 by James Strachey, renewed 1989 by Alix Strachey. Used by permission of W.W. Norton & Company, Inc.

Hegel, Georg Wilhelm Friedrich, "The Philosophical History of the World" from *Hegel: Lectures on the Philosophy of World History* (trans. H. B. Nisbet) (Cambridge University Press, Cambridge, 1975)

Heidegger, Martin, *An Introduction to Metaphysics* (trans. Ralph Manheim) (Yale University Press, New Haven, 1959)

Hick, John, *Evil and the God of Love* (rev. ed.) (Harper Collins Inc., New York, 1977)

Hildegard of Bingen, *The Letters of Hildegard of Bingen* vol. 1 eds. Joseph L. Baird & Radd K. Ehrman, trans. Joseph L. Baird & Radd K. Ehrman, copyright © 1994 by Oxford University Press, Inc. Used by permission of Oxford University Press Inc.

Hobbes, Thomas, *Leviathan* (ed. Richard Tuck) (Cambridge University Press, Cambridge, 1991)

Hopkins, Gerard Manley, "Thou art indeed just, Lord" from *The Norton Anthology of English Literature*, 6th ed. (ed. M. H. Abrams) (W. W. Norton Inc., New York, 1993)

Hume, David, *Dialogues Concerning Natural Religion* (ed. Richard H. Popkin) (Hackett Publishing Company, Inc., Indianapolis, 1980, reprinted by permission of Hackett Publishing Company, Inc. All rights reserved).

Irenaeus, "Against Heretics" from *The Ante-Nicene Christian Library*, vol. 9 (trans. Rev. Alexander Roberts & James Donaldson) (T. & T. Clark Ltd, Edinburgh, 1869)

James, William, *The Varieties of Religious Experience: A Study in Human Nature* (Penguin, 1982 [facsimile reprint of 1902 edition])

Jones, William, *Is God a White Racist? A Preamble to Black Theology* (Beacon Press, Boston, 1998)

Jung, C. G., *Aion: Researches into the Phenomenology of the Self* (2nd ed.) (trans. R. F. C. Hull) (Bollingen Series XX) Copyright © 1959 by Princeton University Press. Reprinted by permission of Princeton University Press.

Keats, John, *The Letters of John Keats: A New Selection* (ed. Robert Gittings) (Oxford University Press, Oxford, 1970)

Kempis, Thomas à, *The Imitation of Christ* (Everyman's Library, Dutton, New York, 1960)

Lactantius, "The Wrath of God (De ira dei)" from *The Minor Works* (trans. Sister Mary Frances McDonald, OP) (The Fathers of the Church: A New Translation, vol. 54) (Catholic University of America Press, Washington, DC 1965)

Leibniz, G. W., *Theodicy: Essays on the Goodness of God, the Freedom of Man, and the Origin of Evil* (trans. E. M. Huggard) (Open Court Publishing, Chicago and La Salle, 1985)

Levinas, Emmanuel, "Useless Suffering" from *The Provocation of Levinas: Rethinking the Other* (trans. Richard Cohen, eds. Robert Bernasconi and David Wood) (Routledge, London and New York, 1988)

Lewis, C. S. *The Problem of Pain*, copyright © C. S. Lewis Pte. Ltd. 1940. Extract reprinted by permission.

Lucretius, *On the Nature of the Universe* (trans. R. E. Latham, revised by John Godwin) (Penguin, Harmondsworth, 1994)

Luther, Martin, "Prefaces to the Books of the Bible" from *Works of Martin Luther* vol. VI (Trans. C. M. Jacobs) (A. J. Holman & The Castle Press, 1932)

Kant, Immanuel, "On the miscarriage of all philosophical trials in philosophy" from *Immanuel Kant, Religion and Rational Theology* (trans. George di Giovanni, eds. Allen W. Wood and George di Giovanni) (Cambridge University Press, Cambridge, 1996)

Maimonides, Moses, *The Guide of the Perplexed* (trans. Schlomo Pines) (Chicago, 1963)

Malebranche, Nicolas, *Dialogues on Metaphysics and on Religion* (ed. Nicholas Jolley, trans. David Scott) (Cambridge University Press, Cambridge, 1997)

Malthus, Thomas Robert, "An Essay on the Principle of Population IV" from *An Essay on the Principle of Population: The Sixth Edition* (1826) with variant readings from the second edition (1803)

Mill, John Stuart, *An Examination of Sir William Hamilton's Philosophy, and of The Principal Philosophical Questions Discussed in his Writings* (ed. J. M. Robson) (University of Toronto Press, Toronto and Buffalo, 1979)

Milton, John, *Paradise Lost,* 1667, revised 1674.

Nietzsche, Friedrich, *On the Genealogy of Morality: A Polemic* (trans. Maudemarie Clark & Alan J. Swensen) (Hackett Publishing Company Inc., Indianapolis and Cambridge, 1998, reprinted by permission of Hackett Publishing Company Inc., all rights reserved)

Noddings, Nel, *Women and Evil* (University of California Press, Berkeley, 1989, copyright © 1989 The Regents of the University of California)

Norwich, Julian of, "Showings, Long Text" from *Revelations of Divine Love* (trans. Elisabeth Spearing) (Penguin, Harmondsworth, 1998)

Ovid, *Metamorphoses* (trans. A. D. Melville) (Penguin, Harmondsworth 1986)

Plato, "Timaeus" from *The Collected Dialogues* (trans. Benjamin Jowett, Edith Hamilton, Cairns Huntington) [Bollingen Series LXXI] Copyright © 1961 by Princeton University Press. Reprinted by permission of Princeton University Press.

Plotinus, *The Enneads* (Providence First Treatise) (trans. Stephen MacKenna) (Penguin, Harmondsworth, 1991)

Pseudo-Dionysius Areopagit, "On the Divine Names" and "Mystical Theology" from *The Divine Names and Mystical Theology* (trans. John D. Jones) (Marquette University Press, Milwaukee, 1980)

Rousseau, Jean-Jacques, "Letter from J. J. Rousseau to Mr de Voltaire, August 18, 1756" from *Discourse on the Origins of Inequality (Second Discourse) Polemics, and Political Economy (The Collected Writings of Rousseau,* vol. 3) (eds. Roger D. Masters and Christopher Kelly, trans. Judith R. Bush, Roger D. Masters, Christopher Kelly, and Terence Marshall) (University Press of New England/Dartmouth College, Hanover and London, 1992)

Royce, Josiah, "The Problem of Job" in *Studies of Good and Evil* (D. Appleton & Co., New York, 1906 [1898])

Schelling, F. W., "Philosophical Investigations into the Essence of Human Freedom and Related Matters" from *Philosophy of German Idealism* (trans. Priscilla Hayden-Roy, ed. Ernst Behler) [The German Library, vol. 23] (Continuum, New York, 1987)

Schopenhauer, Arthur, *The World as Will and Representation* (trans. E. F. J. Payne) (Dover Publications, New York, 1958)

Seneca, Lucius Annaeus, "To Lucilius on Providence" from *Moral Essays* (trans. John W. Basore) (Harvard University Press, Cambridge, Mass., 1928, 1932, 1935, reprinted by permission of the publishers and the Loeb Classical Library)

Serenity Prayer, quoted in Richard Wightman Fox, *Reinhold Niebhur: A Biography* (Pantheon Books, New York, 1985)

Sextus Empiricus, "Outlines of Pyrrhonism" from *The Skeptic Way, Sextus Empiricus's Outlines of Pyrrhonism* by Benson Mates, trans. by Benson Mates, copyright © 1996 by Benson Mates. Used by permission of Oxford University Press, Inc.

Soelle, Dorothee, *Suffering* (trans. Everett R. Kalin) (Augsburg Fortress, Philadelphia, 1975)

Spinoza, Baruch, "Ethics I, Appendix" from *The Ethics and Selected Letters* (trans. Samuel Shirley) (Hackett Publishing Company Inc., Indianapolis and Cambridge, reprinted by permission of Hackett Publishing Company Inc., all rights reserved)

Voltaire, "The Lisbon Earthquake: An Inquiry into the Maxim, 'Whatever is, is Right'" from *The Portable Voltaire* (trans. Tobias Smollett and others, ed. Ben Ray Redman) (Penguin, Harmondsworth, 1949)

Weil, Simone, "The Love of God and Affliction" from *Waiting for God* (trans. Emma Craufurd) (Harper & Row, New York, 1951)

The publishers apologize for, and will be pleased to correct at the earliest opportunity, any errors or omissions in the above list.

While the idiosyncrasies of this reader are mine, its strengths owe to others. I'm grateful for help and inspiration from Amakusa Kazunori, Marilyn McCord Adams, Leora Batnitzky, Beth Eddy, John Gager, Bob Gibbs, Jennifer Herdt, Richard Johnston, George Kateb, Shaun Marmon, Pratap Mehta, Ohba Takeshi, Victor Preller, Al Raboteau, Patrick Riley, Jerry Schneewind, Jeff Stout, Terrence Tilley, Candace West and Cornel West. Special thanks to Alex Wright for proposing this volume, to Hannah Schell for indispensable research and editorial assistance, and to the sterling team at Blackwell, especially Cameron Laux and Joanna Pyke.

Introduction:
Responding to Evils

This book assembles materials for a religious studies approach to the problem of evil in the west. Philosophical readers tend to present the "problem of evil" as a perennial issue, and perhaps the clearest challenge reason poses to faith: evil is "the rock of atheism," as Hans Küng (quoting Georg Büchner) has put it. Yet the experience of evils – as victim or participant or spectator – can lead in many directions; atheism is just one of them. Many people have lost faith because of suffering or evil, but others have found their way deeper into religious traditions, or found their way from one religious tradition to another.

Rather than seeing the encounter with evils as the door between belief and unbelief, it is perhaps better to see it as one of the main stimuli for religious change – changes in the affiliations of individuals (and occasionally communities), and also, as a result, in religious systems of myth, thought, and practice. The history of efforts to respond effectively to evils is largely a history of redefinition, amplification, modification, or subversion of inherited traditions.

Evil is a *practical* problem. Even the person who is a witness to evils finds her sense of agency challenged. In explaining or consoling, narrating or exorcising, praying or raging, we reassert human agency in the face of the apparent malevolence or indifference of the cosmos – or our human fellows. A religious studies approach to the "problem of evil" does not prejudge what responses to evils should look like, or what should count as an adequate response.

A Religious Studies Approach

Some theorists of religion have used the language of evil and theodicy (the justification of God's wisdom and justice in the face of evils) to denote a general religious problem, or a general existential problem which has been an important factor in the development of religious ideas. For Mircea Eliade, religion concerns the maintenance of sacred centers, rhythms, and symbols in collective or – in our "desacralized" age – individual lives. According to Eliade, the passage of time drains the world of our experience of sacred reality. Time itself is thus experienced as suffering by human beings thirsty for "being"; only religious ritual restores the original sacred state, "abolishing time."[1] Recent, more nuanced views of the dynamics of ritual like those of Catherine Bell underscore ritual's power as a way of responding to experiences of personal, social, cosmic disruption.[2] It would be naive to think that ritual – including even the ritual of discussing "perennial" problems like the problem of evil! – does not still do much of the work of helping people cope with evil.

Eliade's argument resonates with the approaches of other important theorists of religion. Clifford Geertz has suggested that despite their differences, the problems of suffering and evil, as threats to our confidence in order, are both aspects of the "Problem of Meaning." Peter Berger has intimated that chaos will engulf us if theodicies fail to buttress a society's "nomos."[3] Both build on the ideas of the great sociologist Max Weber (1864–1920). Weber argued that intellectuals in all cultures have an "inner compulsion to understand the world as a meaningful cosmos and to take up a position toward it."[4] Through the work of religious intellectuals, "the experience of the irrationality of the world" has been "the driving force of all religious evolution."[5]

---

1   See Mircea Eliade, *The Myth of the Eternal Return, or Cosmos and History*, trans. Willard R. Trask (Princeton: Princeton University Press, 1954); at least for most people in most historical periods, "'suffering' is equivalent to 'history'" (97n).
2   See Catherine Bell, *Ritual: Perspectives and Dimensions* (New York & Oxford: Oxford University Press, 1997).
3   Clifford Geertz, "Religion as a Cultural System," *The Interpretation of Cultures* (New York: Basic Books, 1973), 87–125, esp. 103–9; Peter Berger, *The Sacred Canopy: Elements of a Sociological Theory of Religion* (New York: Anchor, 1990), 55.
4   Max Weber, "The Sociology of Religion," trans. Ephraim Fischoff, in *Economy and Society: An Outline of Interpretive Sociology*, eds. Guenther Roth and Claus Wittich (Berkeley: University of California Press, 1978), 499.
5   Weber, "Politics as a Vocation," in *From Max Weber: Essays in Sociology*, eds. H. H. Gerth and C. Wright Mills (New York: Oxford University Press, 1946), 123.

While he never drew them together into a single discussion, Weber's observations on the role of theodicy in the development of religious practices, institutions, and ideas are an excellent foundation for a broader view of the ways people to respond to evils. Weber reminds us, for instance, that the common complaint about the suffering of the just and the prosperity of the wicked records social and political, not just existential realities. Those who suffer, suffer *more* for knowing that others – apparently not more deserving than they – do not suffer. The fortunate, too, seem to be troubled by the apparent arbitrariness of the distribution of fortune.

> The fortunate is seldom satisfied with the fact of being fortunate. Beyond this he needs to know that he has a *right* to his good fortune. He wants to be convinced that he 'deserves' it, and above all, that he deserves it in comparison with others. He wishes to be allowed the belief that the less fortunate also merely experience his due.[6]

This crucial distinction between the "theodicy of suffering" and the "theodicy of good fortune" probably has its roots in Karl Marx's (1818–83) definition of religion as "the general theory of this world . . . its general basis of consolation and justification,"[7] although Weber adds a far more complex view of what it takes for the same set of religious narratives, practices, and explanations to satisfy such different needs. Weber's view helps us recognize the diversity of experiences from which people articulate views of the origin, nature, and effects of evils. We should expect central religious stories and symbols to be multivalent. We should expect cultures to include a variety of sub- and counter-traditions. And we should not be surprised to find that theodicies have political implications.

Weber thought that there had been in history only three "rationally satisfying theodicies" (the "Indian doctrine of Kharma, Zoroastrian dualism, and the predestination decree of the *deus absconditus*," the "hidden God" of Calvinism), but these appear "in pure form" only as exceptions.[8] Rational closure is a sufficient criterion for theodicy choice among religious intellectuals, perhaps, but most people most of the time need religious nar-

---

6   Weber, "The Social Psychology of the World Religions," in ibid., 271.
7   Karl Marx, "Introduction to *Contribution to the Critique of Hegel's Philosophy of Right*," *The Marx–Engels Reader*, ed. Robert Tucker (New York: W. W. Norton, 1978), 53–4. Because of his half-digestion of the anthropology of Nietzsche's *Genealogy of Morality*, Weber is inconsistent on whether the fortunate need theodicy or not.
8   Weber, "Social Psychology of the World Religions," 275. Berger exploits a tension between this discussion and that in Weber's "Sociology of Religion" (519ff) to add a fourth, the "messianic-millenarian complex" of Jewish faith in a turning of the tables in the course of history (*The Sacred Canopy*, 193n2).

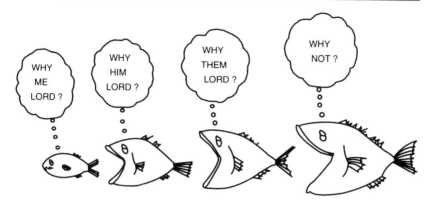

ratives and practices to be satisfying in other ways – practical, and emotional.[9]

The perspectives of these theorists suggest that evils are a problem for people in all traditions, not just monotheistic ones. But it is problematic simply to read the problem of evil into all traditions.[10] Paul Ricoeur has described the importance for "the traditions of the West" of the "presentiment that sin, suffering, and death express in different ways the human condition in its deepest unity."[11] It is not *obvious* that these phenomena belong together. As practical systems for making sense of the world, religions in fact invest less in lumping "evils" together than in distinguishing among them – between merited and unmerited suffering, between evils which are sent by good or by bad agencies, between those which must be borne and those which must be struggled against. The basic distinctions between real and merely apparent, and between remediable and irremediable evils are for all practical purposes more important to responding to evil than theoretical categories like "moral" and "natural" evil.[12]

9   For the argument that in the face of the "inherently contradictory" nature of the theodicy problem, myths – and the more of them the better – best answer "emotional" needs, see Wendy Doniger O'Flaherty, *The Origins of Evil in Hindu Mythology* (Berkeley: University of California Press, 1976). Weber actually thought the world so "ethically irrational" that rationally closed theodicies simply made things worse, driving religious thinkers into the world-rejecting mysticism of early Buddhism or the "innerworldly asceticism" of Calvinism.
10   See the essays collected in *The Anthropology of Evil*, ed. David Parkin (Oxford: Blackwell, 1985).
11   Paul Ricoeur, "Evil: A Challenge to Philosophy and Theology," *Journal of the American Academy of Religion*, 53, no. 3 (1985), 635–48, 636.
12   One largely overlooked implication of the long-standard view that every "evil" is really the privation of a good (*privatio boni*) is that evils need to be approached one by one. Such

While experiences of pain, guilt, loss, disappointment, disharmony, and senselessness are surely among those experiences all religions help people face, seeing these as constituting a single "problem of evil" is the historical exception. Even in the west, engagement with a single "problem of evil" is intermittent at best. Understanding the "problem of evil" as primarily philosophical – a problem for *thought* – is rarer yet. The very term "theodicy" is barely three centuries old: Gottfried Wilhelm Leibniz (1646–1716) coined it in the 1690s. Even in our times, the confusion and despair arising from the fact of evils, no less than the evils themselves, are objects of *practical* concern – ritual, ethical, communal, political. We will learn more if we pose the answerable question of why evil was constructed as a philosophical problem when and in the ways it was, rather than pursuing the unanswerable question of why evils were not aggregated into a single "problem" when they weren't.

The Trilemma

What exactly is the problem? *Unde malum?* (whence evil?) was a common refrain in classical writings, but evils only become a *problem* – give rise to an *argument* – when there are beliefs about the world with which they seem to conflict.[13] The existence of a benevolent, omniscient (all-knowing) and omnipotent (all-powerful) God is one such belief. The quantity and kinds of evils – perhaps the very existence of evils at all – seem to fly in the face of the central claims of theism.

One way of presenting the problem is mentioned in Boethius' (ca. 480 to 525/6) *Consolation of Philosophy*: "If . . . there be a God, from whence proceed so many evils? And if there be no God, from whence cometh any good?"[14] This is a powerful formulation, acknowledging at once the scandal of evil and the mysteriousness of good, but it has not been the

---

an understanding of evils is resolutely practical: it gets us thinking about how the "evil" came about, how to remedy it (or how to respond if it is beyond remedy), and if it is possible to prevent the recurrence of like problems.

13   Daniel Howard-Snyder persuasively argues for "argument from" rather than "problem of evil" in the preface to his collection *The Evidential Argument from Evil* (Bloomington: Indiana University Press, 1996). For reasons I suggest below, a conflict of belief, while necessary, is not a sufficient condition for the actual arising of arguments from evil.

14   *Si quidem deus est, unde mala? Bona uero unde, si non est?* (*The Consolation of Philosophy*, trans. "I. T." (1609) and revised by H. F. Stewart in Boethius, *The Theological Tractates; The Consolation of Philosophy* (London: Heinemann/Cambridge, Mass.: Harvard University Press, 1918), 150–1).

subject of recent discussions.[15] This neglect is unfortunate. The "problem of evil" and the "problem of good" may only *seem* to be parallel, but articulating why can be extremely illuminating. It is certainly very odd that the nature of the good — problematic or no — so rarely finds its way into discussions of the "problem of evil."

The problem with evils is more commonly treated as a *trilemma*, the apparently inconsistent set of propositions which asserts (a) God's goodness, (b) God's omnipotence, and (c) the existence of evil. (Omniscience is usually mentioned too, but rarely finds its way into the discussion, either fading into omnipotence or fading away altogether.) Marilyn McCord Adams and Robert Merrihew Adams have argued that an apparently inconsistent set of philosophical propositions need not be interpreted "atheistically." It can also be approached "*aporetically*, as generating a puzzle" which must — and can — be faced by Christian believers in a way both theologically and philosophically sound, though not perhaps without neglected theological resources.[16] Taken in this way, "such arguments present a constructive challenge to probe more deeply into the logical relations among these propositions, to offer more rigorous and subtle analyses of the divine perfections."[17]

There are yet other ways to respond to the trilemma than the atheistic and the "aporetic." This becomes clear if we ask who first articulated the "problem of evil" in this form — and why. There are three candidates. Considering the different ends these uses of the same argument serve is a good way to start thinking historically about the problem of evil.

It is customary to trace the trilemma to the Greek philosopher Epicurus (341–270 BCE). As the skeptical character Philo says in a much-quoted passage from David Hume's (1711–76) *Dialogues Concerning Natural Religion*,

Epicurus' old questions are yet unanswered.

Is he [God] willing to prevent evil, but not able? then is he impotent. Is he able, but not willing? then is he malevolent. Is he both able and willing? whence then is evil?[18]

15 This may be because good, more than evil, exposes what Marilyn McCord Adams has deemed the "myth of shared values" — the idea of "a religion-neutral value theory that is common to a theologian and believer." (Marilyn McCord Adams, *Horrendous Evils and the Goodness of God* (Ithaca: Cornell University Press, 1999), 11–12). Adams helpfully traces this "myth" to the foundational assumptions of ordinary language philosophy.

16 Adams, *Horrendous Evils*, 7. Marilyn Adams has done more than anyone else to retrieve the Christian tradition's wealth of ways of making religious sense of evils for the philosophy of religion.

17 Marilyn McCord Adams and Robert Merrihew Adams, introduction to *The Problem of Evil*, eds. Adams and Adams (Oxford: Oxford University Press, 1990), 2–3.

18 David Hume, *Dialogues Concerning Natural Religion*, ed. Richard H. Popkin (Indianapolis: Hackett, 1980), 63. (See p. 220 below.)

The source for "Epicurus' old questions" is the early Christian theologian Lactantius' (240 to ca. 320) *The Wrath of God*, written around 313.[19] From Lactantius' perspective, Epicurus was an atheist (and so he has been understood by Christians for centuries), but the Epicurean use of the trilemma is intended not to deny that there are gods, nor even that there is a god who is omnipotent and benevolent. It is a lesson about how to respond to evils. Epicurus clearly believed there were gods whose natures we could know. They are in fact neither willing nor able to prevent evil, but this is not because they are malevolent. It is because they (wisely) know better than to become involved with things. The Epicurean argument therefore doesn't stop at the difficulties with the Stoic (and later Christian) idea of a provident God, but goes on to articulate a view of the attitude of the gods to evils which we should emulate. The problem is not that the gods are not upset by evils, but that we *are*.

Was Epicurus in fact the originator of the questions? Lactantius wrote half a millennium after Epicurus, and the trilemma appears in no other fragments or discussions of Epicurus – and the other two sources predate Lactantius. One reason to doubt whether the trilemma was actually formulated or used by Epicurus (although it may well have been used by later Epicureans) is that for the purpose just described, a trilemma is not an optimal means. A well-constructed trilemma doesn't conclusively show anything; it induces paralysis. Each one of its three intuitively credible statements is compatible with the others taken singly – but not together – so it cannot tell you which one(s) to give up. The form of the trilemma makes it more likely that the question was of ancient skeptic provenance, perhaps the work of Carneades (214–129 BCE).[20] The trilemma was a form of argument perfected by the ancient skeptics.

It is in fact in Sextus Empiricus' manual of skepticism, the *Outlines of Pyrrhonism* (ca. 200 CE) that the oldest extant version of the trilemma appears (see p. 37 below). Sextus Empiricus' conclusion is that since "whether god exists is not apprehensible,"

those who firmly maintain that god exists will be forced into impiety; for if they say that he takes care of everything, they will be saying that god is the cause of evils, while if they say that he takes care of some things only or even of nothing,

---

19 For Lactantius, see p. 50 below. Hume probably encountered the argument in the article "Paulicians" in Pierre Bayle's *Historical and Critical Dictionary*. See Bayle, *Historical and Critical Dictionary: Selections*, trans. Richard H. Popkin (Indianapolis: Bobbs-Merrill, 1965), 169.

20 See Reinhold Glei, "Et invidis et imbecillus. Das angebliche Epikurfragment bei Laktanz, De ira Dei 13, 20–21," *Vigiliae Christianae*, 42 (1988), 47–58.

they will be forced to say that he is either malevolent or weak, and manifestly these are impious conclusions.[21]

The goal of ancient skepticism is *ataraxia*, "an untroubled or tranquil condition of the soul."[22] For the skeptic, the point of the trilemma is not that god is one way or the other – or not at all – but that in religious matters as in all others, it is best to avoid firmly maintaining anything.[23]

The third ancient version of the argument is roughly contemporaneous with the *Outlines of Pyrrhonism*. It is the only version to make explicit reference to Christian beliefs.

> If God is good . . . and has knowledge of the future, and also has power to avert evil, why did he suffer the man, deceived by the devil, to fall away from obedience to the law, and so to die? For the man was the image and likeness of God, or even God's substance, since from it the man's soul took its origin. So if, being good, he had wished a thing not to happen, and if, having foreknowledge, he had been aware that it would happen, and if he had had power and strength to prevent it from happening, that thing never would have happened which under these three conditions of divine majesty it was impossible should happen. But . . . as that did happen, the very opposite is proved, that God must be assumed to be neither good nor prescient nor omnipotent: because inasmuch as nothing of that sort could have happened if God had possessed these attributes of goodness and prescience and omnipotence, it follows that it did happen because God is devoid of these qualities.[24]

This argument was apparently made by Marcion, a leading second-century Gnostic. Marcion was one of the many Gnostics (the main rivals of Christianity at this time) who were *dualists*.[25] Gnostic dualists asserted the world to be the work of an inferior deity (the God of the Hebrew scriptures) rather than the God revealed in Jesus Christ.

It is clear why this argument would appeal to Marcion. Examining this world honestly for information about its maker, he argues, we won't arrive at an image of a God who is perfectly good, powerful or wise. (It is of

---

21   *The Sceptic Way: Sextus Empiricus's Outlines of Pyrrhonism*, trans. Benson Mates (New York & Oxford: Oxford University Press, 1996), 175.

22   *The Sceptic Way*, 90.

23   Although Philo's arguments are in part quite Epicurean, Hume's point in the *Dialogues* – and his intention in making use of the trilemma – was arguably the skeptical one.

24   Tertullian, *Adversus Marcionem*, ed. and trans. Ernest Evans, 2 vols. (Oxford: Clarendon, 1972), i.97–9 (II.5). I am grateful to John G. Gager for this reference. See his "Marcion and Philosophy," *VigiliaeChristianae*, 26 (1972), 53–9.

25   "Dualism," a term invented in England in 1700 to describe the religion of the ancient Persians, refers to views of the cosmos as a battlefield between two coeternal powers, usually in terms of light and darkness, spirit and matter. The most important dualist movements

course not clear that the imperfections of the world prove that its maker is *neither* good *nor* powerful *nor* wise.) Yet the apparent evil and disorder of the world are not mobilized by Marcion to argue for atheism or *ataraxia*, serene indifference to the troubles of the world or theological depth, but to argue for *gnosis*, knowledge of spiritual mysteries. Have nothing to do with the flawed creator of this world! Reject him and his work, and turn instead to the redeemer!

Marcion's Old Questions

Seeing the trilemma as a question which skeptics, gnostic dualists, Epicureans, aporetically inclined theists and atheists might pose for their very different reasons is a good way of broadening our view of the problem of evil. Confronting what is apparently the same "problem" can lead to dramatically different responses to evils.

There are two reasons why it might be better to think of the trilemma as "Marcion's old questions" than as Epicurus'. First, since the problem Marcion presented is explicitly not a trilemma, but a *quadrilemma* – evil is a challenge to the concept of a God perfectly good, powerful, *and wise* – omniscience is less likely to get lost. Recent thinkers have provocatively challenged inherited understandings of omnipotence and benevolence, but we shouldn't assume from the outset that these are the only relevant attributes. Marcion's argument reminds us to think about omniscience, too, and so helps us appreciate the significance of arguments about omniscience in medieval Neoplatonists like the Jewish philosopher Maimonides (1135–1204) or the Christian theologian Nicholas of Cusa (1401–64), for whom God's perfection means that he *can't* know of suffering in the world of finite and changing things.

Nor should we stop with the three attributes of omnipotence, omniscience, and benevolence. John Calvin (1509–64) refutes the Manichees with reference to the attributes of *immensity* and *spirituality*.[26] The French philosopher Nicolas Malebranche (1638–1715) emphasized the attributes of God's *ways* (see pp. 181–3 below). In our time, the attribute of *impassability* (the idea that God cannot suffer) has been fundamentally rethought, with dramatic consequences for theodicy. We need also to take the implications of the alleged *infinity* of the divine attributes seriously as

---

were the Zoroastrians, Gnosticism, and the Manichees (followers of Mani, 216–76/77); "gnostic" and "manichaean" are often used as synonyms for dualist.
26 John Calvin, *Institutes of the Christian Religion*, xiii.1.

well, and what this entails about our capacity – or incapacity – to comprehend them.

A deeper reason to think of the problem of evil as Marcion's rather than Epicurus' or Carneades' challenge is because this suggests a more accurate picture of the history of western thought and practice. For the better part of western history, the threats and temptations of dualism – in Manichee, gnostic, and other forms – were more important than those of scepticism and atheism.[27] The important theodicies of Irenaeus (ca. 130 to ca. 200), Plotinus (205–70) and Augustine (354–430) – and also of Leibniz – were responses to dualisms. Indeed, as Paul Ricoeur has argued, the distinctive characteristics of western thought on evil are the result of the encounter with gnostic dualism:

> Thinking would not have moved on from wisdom to theodicy if gnosticism had not elevated speculation to the level of a gigantomachy, where the forces of good are engaged in a merciless struggle with the armies of evil. . . . Western thought is in debt to gnosticism, broadly conceived, for having conceived the problem of evil in terms of one all-encompassing problematic: *Unde malum?*[28]

Why was dualism so persistent a challenge? It may be that any monotheism inevitably generates dualistic thinking. It may be, as Ricoeur has argued, that any experience of evil-doing involves a feeling of passivity, of being part of a "history of evil," which makes dualism tempting. It may be that what Elaine Scarry has called the "unmaking of the world" effected by pain[29] – but also betrayal and loss – is best expressed dualistically; even in our own time, quasi-Manichaean or Gnostic views of evil strike many as the best ways to take evil seriously. It is easy to underestimate the extent to which the structures and textures of practice determine what ideas are in William James's term "living options" for us.[30] It may be the very pervasiveness and *normality* of evil that makes it seem as real as the good.[31] For all its monotheistic or trinitarian doctrines, Chris-

27 Marcion serves as the figurehead of the dualist challenge in Hans Blumenberg's important *The Legitimacy of the Modern Age*, trans. Robert M. Wallace (Cambridge, Mass.: MIT Press, 1985).

28 Ricoeur, "Evil: A Challenge," 639.

29 See Elaine Scarry, *The Body in Pain: The Making and Unmaking of the World* (New York: Oxford University Press, 1985).

30 William James, "The Will to Believe," in *The Will to Believe and Other Essays in Popular Philosophy* (New York: Dover, 1956), 3. This is what a Weberian science of "elective affinities" seeks to establish.

31 See Bayle's startling suggestion that the mixture of good and evil in human experience suggests a kind of Hobbesian social contract between evil and good principles, pp. 188–9 below.

tian life and thought were (and are) shot through with dualism, as feminist historians in particular have shown. The Christians of most ages lived, moved, and thought in a world charged – and made intelligible – by struggle between Christ and Satan, between flesh and spirit.

Skepticism and Atheism

It may be useful to remind ourselves that until the modern period, dualism was a living option and atheism was not. Skepticism was regarded as a condition of the diseased or reprobate soul, atheism as an act of the perverse will; neither was seen as a coherent philosophical position. Religion was full of mysteries and belief required effort and grace. But only the wicked and – with the devil's help – the foolish overlooked the evidences for God. John Milton's (1608–74) discussion of God in his *Christian Doctrine* assembles the key scriptural passages:

That there is a God, many deny: *for the fool says in his heart, There is no God*, Psal. xiv. 1. But he has left so many signs of himself in the human mind, so many traces of his presence through the whole of nature, that no sane person can fail to realise that he exists. Job xii. 9: *who does not know from all these things?*; Psal. xix. 2: *the heavens declare the glory of God*; Acts xiv. 17: *he did not allow himself to exist without evidence*, and xvii. 27, 28: *he is not far from every one of us*; Rom. i. 19, 20: *that which can be known about God is obvious*, and ii. 14, 15: *the Gentiles show the work of the law written in their hearts; their conscience is evidence of the same thing*; 1 Cor. i. 21: *because, in accordance with God's wisdom, the world failed to know God by its wisdom, it pleased God to save those who believe by the foolishness of preaching.*[32]

Doubt and despair were sinful conditions requiring therapy[33] – gentle or aggressive – *not* philosophical engagement. Robert Burton's (1577–1640) cure for religious melancholy – the "devil's bath," the main cause of doubt and atheism – had nothing to do with argumentation: "*Be not solitary, be not idle.*"[34]

The view that questions about God's justice in the face of evil should not be encouraged by being engaged is found already in Augustine, whom

32   *The Englishman John Milton's Two Books of Investigations into Christian Doctrine, drawn from the sacred scriptures alone*, I.ii; quoted in the Norton Critical Edition of *Paradise Lost*, ed. Scott Elledge, 2nd edn. (New York: W. W. Norton, 1993), 401.

33   Ludwig Wittgenstein's understanding of philosophy as therapy is in some ways a twentieth-century version of the way skepticism was treated before Descartes construed is as a method for arriving at truth.

34   Robert Burton, *The Anatomy of Melancholy*, eds. Thomas C. Faulkner, Nicolas K. Kiessling, and Rhonda L. Blair (Oxford: Clarendon, 1989–), iii.445.

John Hick has rightly called the "fountainhead" of Christian theodicy.[35] All of Augustine's pronouncements on evil, G. R. Evans has argued, "must be read in the light of one central principle: that the effect of evil upon the world is to make it impossible for the sinner to think clearly, and especially to understand higher, spiritual truths and ideas."[36] Kenneth Surin amplifies:

> Without conversion, the very *process* of seeking an answer to the question "whence is evil" will be undermined by the distorted thinking of a crippled intellect. For the perversion of the human will is complemented by a perversion of the memory and the intellect ("the eye of the mind"); and so evil, inevitably and paradoxically, comes to be yet more deeply entrenched in the unconverted person's attempts to find a solution to this "problem."[37]

Similar arguments have been made with more or less pathos and paradox throughout Christian history. In the twentieth century, Karl Barth darkly argued that when we make sense of evil, we "accept it, incorporate it into our philosophical outlook, validate and exculpate it, and thus, if we are consistent, finally justify it, not regarding and treating it as null, but as an essential and necessary part of existence."[38] Even to understand what evil *is*, Barth thought, we need to recognize its power over our world, and the necessary brokenness of all our efforts to understand or respond to it.

Whether or not we can ever understand the nature of evil, if we are to learn anything from the history of western *understandings* of evil, we need to appreciate the commitments and constraints of the thinkers in question without condescension and without romanticization. With the help of resources like Wilfred Cantwell Smith's histories of concepts of piety and belief, John Milbank's genealogy of "secular reason," and Michael Allen Gillespie's history of nihilism,[39] we can begin to appreciate a topography of thought and practice regarding evil where philosophy and revelation are not opposed. This topography is one where despair and curiosity are vices, as the tools for human understanding of the world and the self

---

35 John Hick, *Evil and the God of Love*, 2nd edn. (New York: HarperSan Francisco, 1977).

36 G. R. Evans, *Augustine on Evil* (Cambridge: Cambridge University Press, 1982), 29.

37 Kenneth Surin, *Theology and the Problem of Evil* (Oxford: Blackwell, 1986), 11.

38 Karl Barth, *Church Dogmatics*, III/3, trans. G. W. Bromily and R. J. Ehrlich (Edinburgh: T. & T. Clarke, 1960), 298 (sec. 50.2).

39 Wilfred Cantwell Smith, *The Meaning and End of Religion: A New Approach to the Religious Traditions of the World* (Minneapolis: Fortress Press, 1991), and *Faith and Belief* (Princeton: Princeton University Press, 1979); John Milbank, *Theology and Social Theory: Beyond Secular Reason* (Oxford & Cambridge, Mass.: Blackwell, 1991); Michael Allen Gillespie, *Nihilism before Nietzsche* (Chicago: University of Chicago Press, 1995).

are gifts of God – whose existence is qualitatively more certain than anything else.

In his classic *The Problem of Unbelief in the Sixteenth Century* (1942), the
historian Lucien Febvre argued that before we can determine whether it
was *easy* for someone to be an unbeliever, we need first to ascertain
whether it was *possible*. Febvre argues that as recently as the age of Rabelais,
it was not.

Today we make a choice to be Christian or not. There was no choice in the sixteenth century. One was a Christian in fact. One's thoughts could wander far from
Christ, but these were plays of fancy, without the living support of reality. One
could not even abstain from observance. Whether one wanted to or not, whether
one clearly understood or not, one found oneself immersed from birth in a bath
of Christianity from which one did not emerge even at death. Death was of necessity Christian, Christian in a social sense, because of rituals that no one could
escape, even if one rebelled before death, even if one mocked and scoffed in one's
last moments. From birth to death stretched a long chain of ceremonies, traditions, customs, and observances, all of them Christian or Christianized, and
they bound a man in spite of himself, held him captive even if he claimed to be
free . . .[40]

Febvre warned against seeking "precursors" in the sixteenth century for
twentieth-century ideas. What look to us like arguments or anticipations
of later atheistic positions were not and could not have been understood
that way, perhaps *even by those who expressed them*. Part of what makes something an "argument" is whether it is accepted as such by others, whether
it is seen as transcending individual caprice or temperament and arriving
at the status of a "reasonable" position, a position for which *reasons* can be
given. For much of the history of western thinking about evil, dualism
was a position anathematized but resonant with the rhythms of life, skepticism a sickly inability to take a position, and atheism no position at all.

The Historicity of Theodicy

If we are to understand why we see the problem of evil as we now do –
why, that is, we see the "problem of evil" – we need to know how we got
here. A good history of the way a culture's answers and questions have
changed makes the legitimate claims of the present day clearer. Our questions today are in important ways different from those of the sources of our

40   Lucien Febvre, *The Problem of Unbelief in the Sixteenth Century: The Religion of Rabelais*,
trans. Beatrice Gottlieb (Cambridge, Mass.: Harvard University Press, 1982), 336; see 335–53.

traditions. But seeing the ways modern concerns have built on, outgrown, rejected, or refined earlier ones can only enrich our sense of the fate and possibilities of our own theoretical and practical responses to evils.

The dominant history of theodicy in English-speaking lands is John Hick's 1966 *Evil and the God of Love*. Despite its vast erudition, however, Hick's history is in some ways very unhistorical. Hick's central contrast between impersonal "Augustinian theodicy," which tells of a perfect world ruined by the Fall, and "Irenaean theodicy," which sees history as a gradual process of "person-" or "soul-making" (see pp. 355–62 below), may have proven illuminating in other contexts,[41] but it imposes a false coherence on the Christian tradition. Irenaeus and Augustine *seem* to be "doing theodicy" as they wrestle with gnostic and Manichee dualisms, but arguably their statements were never intended to be taken out of polemical and catechetical contexts. Further, as Hick freely admits, there is no continuous "Irenaean" tradition; from the time of the Greek Fathers to Schleiermacher it is virtually without representatives. Without an Irenaean "minority view," however, it makes no sense to think of the rest of the western Christian tradition as constituting the "majority view." Rather than expect to find a monolithic and essentially unchanging mainstream, we should listen for the multiplicity of voices which make up all traditions, along with the sub- and counter-traditions which the variety of social and individual experiences should lead us to expect.

Because "Augustinian" and "Irenaean" are presented as substantially unchanging types, present from the time of the Church Fathers on, Hick's narrative prevents us from even asking about the historicity of theodicy. Is "Irenaean theodicy," at least in its nineteenth- and twentieth-century versions, not really a modern phenomenon? More fundamentally, isn't the whole of what Terrence Tilley calls the "discourse of theodicy"[42] modern? Odo Marquard's suggestively-argued claim that "theodicy is specifically modern: where there is theodicy, there is modernity, and where there is modernity, there is theodicy," along with the more theological arguments of Surin and Tilley, deserve careful study.[43] Let me briefly mention three historical shifts whose importance for the arising of modern theodicy may not be obvious.

41   See, for instance, the many contributions to *Evil and the Response of World Religion*, ed. William Cenkner (St. Paul, Minn.: Paragon House, 1997), which identify "Irenaean" aspects of various traditions.
42   Terrence W. Tilley, *The Evils of Theodicy* (Washington, DC: Georgetown University Press, 1991).
43   Odo Marquard, "Unburdenings: Theodicy Motives in Modern Philosophy," in *In Defense of the Accidental: Philosophical Studies*, trans. Robert M. Wallace (New York: Oxford

A first development involves the Renaissance's revaluation of values: earthly happiness became the standard. Medieval theologians saw this life as a testing ground, valuing suffering as a sign of divine concern (on the logic of "the Lord reproves the one he loves" (Prov. 3:12; cf. Heb. 12:7)) and distrusting happiness. As Gregory the Great (ca. 540 to 604) wrote in his influential commentary on Job, "holy people are more fearful of prosperity in this world than of adversity."[44] This changed with the Renaissance. For better or worse, most people today are unimpressed by the insignificance of this life in comparison with eternity. We expect this world to make sense in its own terms, and so it makes sense to us to judge God as the "sum of his acts"[45] in this world.

A second and related development concerns the eclipse of belief in original sin in the Enlightenment,[46] which weakened the explanatory force of traditional accounts of the literally earth-shattering consequences of the Fall. As long as the Fall and original sin framed human experience of the world, there could be, strictly speaking, no such thing as *innocent* suffering to wonder about. Nobody *deserved* happiness. Instead of complaint at injustice, response to suffering was more like the psalmist's cry of "How long, Lord?" – not a protest of innocence but prayer or lament. The focal point of reflection on evil was on sin – a subject sinful human beings could hardly trust themselves to treat disinterestedly. In contemporary discussions, by contrast, suffering – paradigmatically "undeserved" and soul-destroying suffering – has become the center of concern.

A third development involves the dramatic changes in the quality of life brought about by modern medicine. Before the great fall in infant mortality and the rise of modern medicine and hygiene, pain and loss were constants of human experience. We should not be surprised to find many writers reflected on how to come to terms with the death of a child at a time when as many as 40 percent of all children died before the age of fifteen.[47] Marquard has argued that only in the modern period was theodicy *possible*, and only in the modern period was it *necessary*.

University Press, 1991), 8–28, 11. Marquard's most extended discussion appeared in *Schwierigkeiten mit der Geschichtsphilosophie: Aufsätze* (Frankfurt am Main: Suhrkamp, 1973). Cf. Surin, *Theology and the Problem of Evil*; Tilley, *The Evils of Theodicy*.

44   Quoted in Eleonore Stump, "Aquinas on the Sufferings of Job," in *The Evidential Argument from Evil*, ed. Howard-Snyder, 49–68, 56.

45   See William R. Jones, *Is God a White Racist? A Preamble to Black Theology* (Boston: Beacon, 1998).

46   Ernst Cassirer argued that theodicy appeared just as belief in original sin waned. See *The Philosophy of the Enlightenment*, trans. Fritz C. A. Koelln and James P. Pettegrove (Princeton: Princeton University Press, 1951), 137–60.

47   Roy Porter, *The Greatest Benefit to Mankind: A Medical History of Humanity* (New York: W. W. Norton, 1997), 237.

Experience of life seems to me to show that when one is up against suffering, under its immediate pressure, the problem is never theodicy; for what is important then is simply the ability to hold up through one's suffering or one's sympathy. It is stamina in enduring, in helping, and in comforting. How can I reach the next year, the next day, the next hour? In the face of this question, theodicy is not an issue, because a mouthful of bread, a breathing space, a slight abbreviation, a moment of sleep are all more important in these circumstances than the accusation and the defence of God. Only when the direct pressure of suffering and compassion relents, under conditions of distance, do we arrive at theodicy . . . [T]he modern age is the age of distance: the first epoch in which impotence and suffering are not the taken-for-granted and normal state of affairs for human beings.[48]

The problem of evil became acute only once suffering no longer seemed a necessary part of life, but exceptional. One benefit of trying to understand responses to evil in times when dualism or the problem of good might have been more accessible formulations is the realization that those times have not ended for many.

What should count as "evil" is no more obvious than what divine attributes are relevant to understanding God's relation to evils. "Theodicists do not describe, but declare, what is evil," as Terrence Tilley has put it.[49] The perspective gained by studying the history of the changing experience of evils should help us move beyond the too-easy breakdown of evils into "moral" and "natural" (or "physical") evil. This distinction is at home in the Augustinian view of the world as "perverted" by the misuse of free will, but arguably breaks under the weight of what we now see as innocent and unintentionally caused suffering.[50] Modern insights into human fragility and finitude, as well as into the dangers of ideology, should inform our responses to evil – especially in the light of the fact that even today not everyone has the good fortune of being able to frame the problem of evil the way we now do.

Aims of this Reader

The readings in the present collection have not been selected in order to arbitrate between the various views of the historicity or eternity of the

---

48   Marquard, "Unburdenings," 11–12.
49   Tilley, Evils of Theodicy, 235.
50   See the incisive critiques of Nel Noddings, Women and Evil (Berkeley: University of California Press, 1989) and Terrence Tilley, Evils of Theodicy, 244. The suffering caused by "cultural" (Noddings) or "social" (Tilley) evils – the unintended consequences of unjust institutions and practices – is legitimated by categories which relegate everything not the result of individual human will to the category of the "natural."

problem of evil, although I have tried to include passages germane to –
and others inconvenient to – each position. We may not yet be in a position to tell the full story of evil in western thought, and even if we were,
a reader like this one would hardly be an opportune form for it. Each
text excerpted here demands and deserves to be read in its entirety, in the
context of contemporaneous debates and the other works and concerns
of its author (although we neither can nor should lose sight of our own
questions entirely).[51] This reading in turn will have to be informed by a
sensitive history of the *practices* of western life, religious and secular. A
reader, focusing as it does on what gets *written down*, is not an ideal medium
for this kind of work, either.

Yet there are contributions a reader like this can perhaps make more
effectively than the monographs which contextualist scholarship may one
day give us. While it lacks the unity which eternal questions or timeless
contrasts seem to offer, there is a *tradition* (or better, traditions) here. Each
author must be understood as trying to make sense of some particular set
of circumstances, in the context of particular debates and challenges. The
resources mobilized, however, are often the same. The Book of Job, for
instance, has always been a resource for working through the relationship
of God and human suffering – although in more and different ways than
modern readings suggest – as have the arguments of Stoics like Seneca
and Epictetus.

A history of present questions inevitably has the character of a retrospective family tree: we have countless ancestors in the past, but they
appear to have strangely few descendants in the present. In compiling this
reader, I have tried to pursue the fates of the other progeny of the ancestors of modern theodicy. The artificial clarity (and comfort) of a single
lineage is lost, but in exchange we find the philosophical discourse of
theodicy to be closely related to efforts in other genres. The philosophical project can in this way be seen for what it has always been – one of
the important ways, but not the only or often the most important way, in
which humanity has learned to recognize and respond to evils.

---

51   See *Philosophy in History: Essays in the Historiography of Philosophy*, ed. Richard Rorty,
J. B. Schneewind, and Quentin Skinner (Cambridge: Cambridge University Press, 1984) and
Meaning and Context: Quentin Skinner and His Critics, ed. James Tully (Princeton: Princeton
University Press, 1988).

How to Use This Book

The selections in this Reader span a variety of genres from metaphysics to narrative, critique to sermon, liturgy to poetry. They have been chosen for the way they fit together as much as for the way they cover traditions, or represent the larger projects of their authors. The prefaces to the selections are concerned as much to establish connections with other selections as with the biographies of their authors. The index has been assembled to serve as a clearing-house of these connections, so that even a reader new to these questions can get a sense of the ongoing western conversations about evil.

This book can be read in several ways. You can read it from start to finish. More likely, you will work with the Index, which is set up to facilitate tracing the sources and legacies of important figures, as well as issues and arguments. Following up the references listed under, say, "best of all possible worlds," "Job: interpretations of," "children: suffering of," "God: attributes: anger" or "evil: as privation" is a good way to start exploring this history. As you read, take the time to check the index for any figure or idea which seems important. In this way, you will soon acquire a rich sense of the kinds of connections which make a tradition – and the discerning of which is one of the chief joys of intellectual history.

The next step is to go beyond the Reader. Read the whole of a work I have excerpted, asking yourself whether I chose the right few pages. Read works and figures not included in the Reader. The more you read, the more you will agree that the selections are too short – few texts worth excerpting *can* be excerpted without loss – but also that there aren't enough of them. This Reader will have succeeded if readers are constructively dissatisfied with the selections: "Wish there'd been more of X," "Can't believe there's no Y . . ."

The greatest omission is the Bible, without which the problems being addressed by most of the selections cannot even be understood. I have tried to make all scriptural citations explicit, but their overall importance recommends a careful reading at least of the opening chapters of Genesis, the Book of Job, the Psalter, the beatitudes, and Paul's Epistle to the Romans (esp. 9:14–23) before proceeding.

As you read each selection, you might ask yourself questions like these:

- What questions is the author addressing? Who posed these questions? Does the author understand the point of the questions? Do the questions shape the form or the content of the response in ways the author doesn't intend?
- What are the author's assumptions? What definitions (e.g. of the kinds of evils) are assumed or argued in the text? Who or what are her or his sources? What issues and perspectives doesn't he or she consider? Why not?
- Who is the work's intended audience? How was it was received? How is it regarded today?
- How do the author's views fit into her or his practical projects like consolation, ritual, ethical exhortation, or political activism?

Different kinds of questions will help you consider the relevance of the selections to present concerns, and to arrive at a sense of the most important strands of argument.

- How have the author's views, or views like them, been used in other contexts?
- How would the author view the questions and assumptions of our time? How might her or his arguments be made to speak to us today? What changed experiences and assumptions make the contemporary reception of these ideas difficult?
- Are there underlying continuities of problem and approach over the course of the history surveyed by the readings? Are there dramatic shifts or discernible schools?

You might also want to ask:

- Is the author right? Could her or his argument be made more persuasively?
- What are the costs and benefits of thinking of the "problem of evil" as a universal problem, as a necessary problem for monotheism, or as an artifact of particular times?
- How should we understand and respond to "evil(s)" today?

Beginnings

1

Plato, *Timaeus*

Until the scientific revolution, the *Timaeus* was the most carefully studied of the dialogues of Plato (427–347 BCE). While it is unclear that the Pythagorean Timaeus' views were being endorsed by Plato, the *Timaeus* was long assumed to be Plato's cosmogony. It is a main source of key Platonist arguments like that only eternal being – not temporal becoming – can be the object of certain knowledge. The *Timaeus* was a major source of the Neoplatonic philosophy of Plotinus, in the Middle Ages was seen as the source of a philosophy of nature compatible with Christianity, and was decisive for Renaissance Neoplatonists like Marsilio Ficino. A number of important components of later ways of thinking about evil receive a first (or an early) mention in the *Timaeus*, including metempsychosis and the argument that this is the best of all possible worlds. Thinkers from Plotinus to Leibniz struggled to overcome the dualism in Timaeus' assertion (at 48a–b) that "the creation of this world is the combined work of necessity and mind. Mind, the ruling power, persuaded necessity to bring the greater part of created things to perfection, and thus . . . through necessity made subject to reason, this universe was created."

Plato, *Timaeus*, 27c–31b, 41a–42e, trans. Benjamin Jowett, in *The Collected Dialogues*, eds. Edith Hamilton and Huntington Cairns (Bollingen Series LXXI) (Princeton: Princeton University Press, 1961), 1161–3, 1170–1.

TIMAEUS: All men, Socrates, who have any degree of right feeling, at the beginning of every enterprise, whether small or great, always call upon God. And we, too, who are going to discourse of the nature of the universe, how created or how existing without creation, if we be not altogether out of our wits, must invoke the aid of gods and goddesses and pray that our words may be above all acceptable to them and in consequence to ourselves . . .

First then, in my judgment, we must make a distinction and ask, What is that which always is and has no becoming and what is that which is always becoming and never is? That which is apprehended by intelligence and reason is always in the same state, but that which is conceived by opinion with the help of sensation and without reason is always in a process of becoming and perishing and never really is. Now everything that becomes or is created must of necessity be created by some cause, for without a cause nothing can be created. The work of the creator, whenever he looks to the unchangeable and fashions the form and nature of his work after an unchangeable pattern, must necessarily be made fair and perfect, but when he looks to the created only and uses a created pattern, it is not fair or perfect. Was the heaven then or the world, whether called by this or by any other more appropriate name – assuming the name, I am asking a question which has to be asked at the beginning of an inquiry about anything – was the world, I say, always in existence and without beginning, or created, and had it a beginning? Created, I reply, being visible and tangible and having a body, and therefore sensible, and all sensible things are apprehended by opinion and sense, and are in a process of creation and created. Now that which is created must, as we affirm, of necessity be created by a cause. But the father and maker of all this universe is past finding out, and even if we found him, to tell of him to all men would be impossible. This question, however, we must ask about the world. Which of the patterns had the artificer in view when he made it – the pattern of the unchangeable or of that which is created? If the world be indeed fair and the artificer good, it is manifest that he must have looked to that which is eternal, but if what cannot be said without blasphemy is true, then to the created pattern. Everyone will see that he must have looked to the eternal, for the world is the fairest of creations and he is the best of causes. And having been created in this way, the world has been framed in the likeness of that which is apprehended by reason and mind and is unchangeable, and must therefore of necessity, if this is as admitted, be a copy of something. Now it is all-important that the beginning of everything should be according to nature. And in speaking of the copy and the original we may assume that words are akin to the matter which they describe; when they relate to the lasting and permanent and intelligible, they ought to be lasting and unalterable, and, as far as their nature allows, irrefutable and invincible – nothing less. But when they express only the copy or likeness and not the eternal things themselves, they need only be likely and analogous to the former words. As being is to becoming, so is truth to belief. If then, Socrates, amidst the many opinions about the gods and the generation of the universe, we are not able to give notions which are altogether and in every respect exact and consistent with one another, do not be surprised. Enough if we adduce probabilities as likely as any others, for we must remember that I who am the speaker and you who are the judges are only mortal men, and we ought to accept the tale which is probable and inquire no further.

SOCRATES: Excellent, Timaeus, and we will do precisely as you bid us. The prelude is charming and is already accepted by us – may we beg of you to proceed to the strain?

TIMAEUS: Let me tell you then why the creator made this world of generation. He was good, and the good can never have any jealousy of anything. And being free from jealousy, he desired that all things should be as like himself as they could be. This is in the truest sense the origin of creation and of the world, as we shall do well in believing on the testimony of wise men. God desired that all things should be good and nothing bad, so far as this was attainable. Wherefore also finding the whole visible sphere not at rest, but moving in an irregular and disorderly fashion, out of disorder he brought order, considering that this was in every way better than the other. Now the deeds of the best could never be or have been other than the fairest, and the creator, reflecting on the things which are by nature visible, found that no unintelligent creature taken as a whole could ever be fairer than the intelligent taken as a whole, and again that intelligence could not be present in anything which was devoid of soul. For which reason, when he was framing the universe, he put intelligence in soul, and soul in body, that he might be the creator of a work which was by nature fairest and best. On this wise, using the language of probability, we may say that the world came into being – a living creature truly endowed with soul and intelligence by the providence of God.

This being supposed, let us proceed to the next stage. In the likeness of what animal did the creator make the world? It would be an unworthy thing to liken it to any nature which exists as a part only, for nothing can be beautiful which is like any imperfect thing. But let us suppose the world to be the very image of that whole of which all other animals both individually and in their tribes are portions. For the original of the universe contains in itself all intelligible beings, just as this world comprehends us and all other visible creatures. For the deity, intending to make this world like the fairest and most perfect of intelligible beings, framed one visible animal comprehending within itself all other animals of a kindred nature. Are we right in saying that there is one world, or that they are many and infinite? There must be one only if the created copy is to accord with the original. For that which includes all other intelligible creatures cannot have a second or companion; in that case there would

be need of another living being which would include both, and of which
they would be parts, and the likeness would be more truly said to resemble not them, but that other which included them. In order then that the
world might be solitary, like the perfect animal, the creator made not two
worlds or an infinite number of them, but there is and ever will be one
only-begotten and created heaven . . .

Now, when all of them, both those who visibly appear in their revolutions as well as those other gods who are of a more retiring nature, had
come into being, the creator of the universe addressed them in these
words. Gods, children of gods, who are my works and of whom I am the
artificer and father, my creations are indissoluble, if so I will. All that is
bound may be undone, but only an evil being would wish to undo that
which is harmonious and happy. Wherefore, since ye are but creatures, ye
are not altogether immortal and indissoluble, but ye shall certainly not be
dissolved, nor be liable to the fate of death, having in my will a greater
and mightier bond than those with which ye were bound at the time of
your birth. And now listen to my instructions. Three tribes of mortal
beings remain to be created – without them the universe will be incomplete, for it will not contain every kind of animal which it ought to
contain, if it is to be perfect. On the other hand, if they were created by
me and received life at my hands, they would be on an equality with the
gods. In order then that they may be mortal, and that this universe may
be truly universal, do ye, according to your natures, betake yourselves to
the formation of animals, imitating the power which was shown by me
in creating you. The part of them worthy of the name immortal, which
is called divine and is the guiding principle of those who are willing to
follow justice and you – of that divine part I will myself sow the seed,
and having made a beginning, I will hand the work over to you. And do
ye then interweave the mortal with the immortal and make and beget
living creatures, and give them food and make them to grow, and receive
them again in death.

Thus he spoke, and once more into the cup in which he had previously mingled the soul of the universe he poured the remains of the
elements, and mingled them in much the same manner; they were not,
however, pure as before, but diluted to the second and third degree. And
having made it he divided the whole mixture into souls equal in number
to the stars and assigned each soul to a star, and having there placed them
as in a chariot he showed them the nature of the universe and declared
to them the laws of destiny, according to which their first birth would be
one and the same for all – no one should suffer a disadvantage at his

hands. They were to be sown in the instruments of time severally adapted to them, and to come forth the most religious of animals, and as human nature was of two kinds, the superior race was of such and such a character, and would hereafter be called man. Now, when they should be implanted in bodies by necessity and be always gaining or losing some part of their bodily substance, then, in the first place, it would be necessary that they should all have in them one and the same faculty of sensation, arising out of irresistible impressions; in the second place, they must have love, in which pleasure and pain mingle – also fear and anger, and the feelings which are akin or opposite to them. If they conquered these they would live righteously, and if they were conquered by them, unrighteously. He who lived well during his appointed time was to return and dwell in his native star, and there he would have a blessed and congenial existence. But if he failed in attaining this, at the second birth he would pass into a woman, and if, when in that state of being, he did not desist from evil, he would continually be changed into some brute who resembled him in the evil nature which he had acquired, and would not cease from his toils and transformations until he helped the revolution of the same and the like within him to draw in its train the turbulent mob of later accretions made up of fire and air and water and earth, and by this victory of reason over the irrational returned to the form of his first and better state. Having given all these laws to his creatures, that he might be guiltless of future evil in any of them, the creator sowed some of them in the earth, and some in the moon, and some in the other instruments of time. And when he had sown them he committed to the younger gods the fashioning of their mortal bodies, and desired them to furnish what was still lacking to the human soul, and having made all the suitable additions, to rule over them, and to pilot the mortal animal in the best and wisest manner which they could and avert from him all but self-inflicted evils.

2

Lucretius, *On the Nature of the Universe*

The most eloquent expression of the philosophy of Epicurus (341–270 BCE) is *De rerum natura* (*On the Nature of the Universe* or *of Things*), one of the masterpieces of Latin poetry. Almost nothing is known about its author, Titus Lucretius Carus (ca. 94 to ca. 55 BCE). In conscious opposition to Stoic doctrines of providence, Lucretius uses poetry to explain Epicurus' view of a universe without design. "Even if I knew nothing of the atoms," he writes, "I would venture to assert on the evidence of the celestial phenomena themselves, supported by many other arguments, that the universe was certainly not created for us by divine power; it is so full of imperfections [*tanta stat praedita culpa*]." Random "swerves" lead atoms to unite temporarily to form worlds and beings, including gods. The gods neither can nor will help us. The ethical ideal of Epicureanism is not to worship the gods but to be as they are: unconcerned about the world, without fear or desire, accepting that all things are mortal. (One of the first uses of the word *religio* occurs as Lucretius condemns superstitions arising out of the fear of death, fanned by soothsayers and false philosophers.) The pessimistic Lucretius' hold on the ethical ideal of the serenely indifferent gods seems to have been less secure than that of his master, whom he praises in the passage below.

Lucretius, *On the Nature of the Universe*, VI.1–91, trans. R. E. Latham, revised by John Godwin (Harmondsworth: Penguin, 1994), 167–9.

In days of old it was from Athens of high renown that the knowledge of cereal crops was first disseminated among suffering mankind. It was Athens that built life on a new plan and promulgated laws. It was Athens no less that first gave to life a message of good cheer through the birth of that man, gifted with no ordinary mind, whose unerring lips gave utterance to the whole of truth. Even now, when he is no more, the widespread and long-established fame of his divine discoveries is exalted to the very skies.

He saw that, practically speaking, all that was wanted to meet men's vital needs was already at their disposal, and, so as could be managed, their livelihood was assured. He saw some men in the full enjoyment of riches and reputation, dignity and authority, and happy in the fair fame of the children. Yet, for all that, he found aching hearts in every home, racked incessantly by pangs the mind was powerless to assuage, forced to vent themselves in recalcitrant repining, concluded that the source of this illness was the container itself, which infected with its own malady everything that was collected outside and brought into it, however beneficial. He arrived at this conclusion partly because he perceived that the container was cracked and leaky, so that it could never by a possibility be filled: partly because he saw it taint whatever took in with the taste of its own foulness. Therefore he purged men's breasts with words of truth. He set bounds to desire and fear. He demonstrated what is the highest good, after which we all strive, and pointed the way by which we can achieve it, keeping straight ahead along a narrow track. He revealed the element of pain inherent in the life of mortals generally resulting whether casually or determinately from the operation of nature and prowling round in various forms. He showed what gate it is best to sally out against each one of these evils. And he made it clear that more often than not, it was quite needlessly that mankind stirred up stormy waves of disquietude within their breasts.

As children in blind darkness tremble and start at everything, so we in broad daylight are oppressed at times by fears as baseless as those horrors which children imagine coming upon them in the dark. This dread and darkness of the mind cannot be dispelled by the sunbeams, the shining shafts of day, but only by an understanding of the outward form and inner workings of nature. The more reason, then, why I should weave further the argument that I have started . . .

I have taught that the sky in all its zones is mortal and its substance was formed by a process of birth, and I have also elucidated most of the phenomena that occur in the heavens and that must inevitably occur. Listen now to what still remains to tell.

Since I have ventured to climb into the lofty chariot of the Muses, I will explain how the wrath of the winds is roused and how it is appeased and how all disturbances of nature are allayed when their fury is spent; also the other things on earth or in the heavens that frighten men, when the balance of their minds is upset by fear, and that abase their spirits with terror of the gods and crush them cringing on the ground, because ignorance of the causes of phenomena drives them to commit everything to the rule of the gods and to acknowledge their sovereignty. [They are in no way able to see what causes these things and they believe them to be done by the power of the gods.] For it may happen that men who have learnt the truth about the carefree existence of the gods fall to wondering by what power the universe is kept going, especially those movements that are seen overhead in the ethereal borderland. Then the poor creatures are plunged back into their old superstitions and saddle themselves with cruel masters whom they believe to be all-powerful. All this because they do not know what can be and what cannot – how the power of each thing is limited, and its boundary-stone sticks buried deep. Therefore they are the more prone to go astray, misled by blind reasoning. Unless you vomit such notions out of your mind and banish far away all thoughts unworthy of the gods and foreign to their tranquillity then the holy beings whom you thus diminish will often do you real harm. This is not because the supreme majesty of the gods can in fact be wronged, so as to be tempted in a fit of anger to wreak a savage revenge. No, the fault will be in you. Because you will picture the quiet ones in their untroubled peace as tossed on turbulent waves of anger, you will not approach their temples with a tranquil heart; you will not be able to admit into a breast at peace those images emanating from a holy body that bring to the minds of men their tidings of a form divine. From this you can gather what sort of life must ensue. If this is to be averted from us by true reason, there is still much to add in finely polished verse to the much that I have already delivered. I must grasp the system and phenomena of the heavens. I must sing of storms and the vivid lightning flash, their effects and the causes of their outbreak. Otherwise you may be so scared out of your wits as to map out different quarters of the sky and speculate from which one the darting fire has come or into which other it has passed: how it has entered a closed building, and how after taking possession of it has emerged victorious. [They are not in any way able to see the causes of these doings and they believe them to be done by the power of the gods.]

   For this task I invoke your aid, Calliope, most gifted of the Muses, repose of men and delight of gods.

3

Ovid, "Phaethon"

As modern thinkers from Hume to Weber have asserted, the moral chaos of human life makes polytheism intuitively plausible. Consider the limbo between myth and literature in which the gods of Greece and Rome lived on after the triumph of Christianity. Homer and the tragedies of Aeschylus and Sophocles continue to move us, but so do the less exalted myths retold by the Roman poet Publius Ovidius Naso (43 BCE to 17 CE) in his *Metamorphoses*. Perhaps because Ovid already wrote about the gods as quasi-literary characters, the *Metamorphoses* were one of the main points of entry for later ages into a world-view where every plant and animal has a story. These stories almost always involve undeserved human suffering (the story of "Phaethon," for instance, involves staggering collateral damage), but it is not their point. And yet, how sublimely moving these stories are! In the context of reflection on how people have lived with evil, it is worth savoring the cold comfort afforded by stories like these. As we enter the story, Phaethon, son by the Sun-god Phoebus of the human Clymene, has entered his father's palace for the first time, having been challenged by a friend to prove that he is, indeed, the son of a god.

Ovid, *Metamorphoses*, II, trans. A. D. Melville (Harmondsworth: Penguin, 1986), 25–36.

> . . . Phaethon, climbing the steep ascent,
> Entered his father's palace (fatherhood
> Uncertain still) and made his way direct
> Into the presence and there stood afar,
> Unable to approach the dazzling light.
> Enrobed in purple vestments Phoebus sat,

High on a throne of gleaming emeralds.
Attending him on either side stood Day
And Month and Year and Century, and Hours
Disposed at equal intervals between.
Young Spring was there, with coronet of flowers,
And naked Summer, garlanded with grain;
Autumn was there with trampled vintage stained,
And icy Winter, rime upon his locks.
    Enthroned amidst, the Sun who sees all things
Beheld the boy dismayed by sights so strange,
And said "What purpose brings, faring so far,
My son, a son no father would deny,
To this high citadel?" The boy replied
"O thou, Creation's universal light,
Phoebus, my father, if to use that name
Thou givest me leave, and Clymene spoke truth
And hides no guilt, give proof that all may know
I am thy son indeed, and end for ever
The doubt that grieves me." Then his father laid
Aside the dazzling beams that crowned his head
And bade him come and held him to his heart:
"Well you deserve to be my son", he said,
"Truly your mother named your lineage;
And to dispel all doubt, ask what you will
That I may satisfy your heart's desire; . . ."
He scarce had ended when the boy declared
His wish – his father's chariot for one day
With licence to control the soaring steeds.
    Grief and remorse flooded his father's soul,
And bitterly he shook his glorious head:
"Rash have your words proved mine! Would that I might
Retract my promise, Phaethon! This alone
I would indeed deny you. Yet at least
I may dissuade you. Dangerous is your choice;
You seek a privilege that ill befits
Your growing years and strength so boyish still.
Mortal your lot – not mortal your desire;
This, to which even the gods may not aspire,
In ignorance you claim. Though their own powers
May please the gods, not one can take his stand
Above my chariot's flaming axle-tree

Save I. Even he whose hand hurls thunderbolts,
Olympus' mighty lord, may never drive
My team — and who is mightier than Jove? . . .
   Steep is the way at first, which my steeds scarce
Can climb in morning freshness; in mid sky
The altitude is greatest and the sight
Of land and sea below has often struck
In my own heart an agony of fear.
The final part drops sheer; then above all
Control must be assured, and even she
Whose waters lie below to welcome me,
Tethys, waits fearful lest I headlong fall. . . .
Suppose my chariot yours: what then? Could you
Confront the spinning poles and not be swept
Away by the swift axis of the world?
Perhaps you fancy cities of gods are there
And groves and temples rich with offerings.
No! Wild beasts lie in wait and shapes of fear!
And though you keep your course and steer aright
Yet you shall meet the Bull, must brave his horns,
And face the Archer and the ravening Lion,
The long curved circuit of the Scorpion's claws,
The Crab whose claws in counter-menace wave.
My horses too, when fire within their breasts
Rages, from mouth and nostrils breathing flames,
Are hard to hold; even I can scarce restrain
Their ardent hearts, their necks that fight the rein.
But, O my son, amend, while time remains,
Your choice, so may my gift not be your doom.
Sure proof you seek of fatherhood; indeed
My dread sure proof affords: a father's fear
Proves me your father. Look into my eyes! . . ."
   So the Sun warned; but Phaethon would not yield
And held his purpose, burning with desire
To drive the chariot. Then his father, slow
And pausing as he might, led out the boy
To that high chariot, Vulcan's masterwork. . . .
   "If this advice at least you will obey,
Spare, child, the whip and rein them hard; they race
Unurged; the task's to hold them in their zeal.
Avoid the road direct through all five zones;

On a wide slanting curve the true course lies
Within the confines of three zones; beware
Alike the southern pole and northern Bear.
Keep to this route; my wheeltracks there show plain.
Press not too low nor strain your course too high;
Too high, you'll burn heaven's palaces; too low,
The earth; the safest course lies in between. . . .
    But Phaethon mounted, light and young and proud
And took the reins with joy, and looking down,
Thanked his reluctant father for the gift.
    Meanwhile the fourswift horses of the Sun,
Aethon, Eous, Pyrois and Phlegon,
Kick at the gates, neighing and snorting fire,
And Tethys then, her grandson's fate undreamt,
Draws back the bars and makes the horses free
Of all the boundless heavens. Forth they go,
Tearing away, and cleave with beating hooves
The clouds before them, and on wings outride
The winds that westwards from the morning blow.
But lightly weighs the yoke; the chariot moves
With ease unwonted, suspect buoyancy;
And like a ship at sea unballasted
That pitches in the waves for lack of weight,
The chariot, lacking now its usual load,
Bounced driverless, it seemed, in empty leaps.
The horses in alarm ran wild and left
The well-worn highway. Phaethon, dazed with fear,
Could neither use the reins nor find the road,
Nor were it found could make the team obey.
Then first the sunbeams warmed the freezing Bear,
Who sought vain refuge in forbidden seas;
The Snake that numb and harmless hitherto
Lay next the icy pole, roused by the heat
In newly kindled rage began to burn;
The Wagoner too, it's said, fled in dismay,
Though slow and hampered by his lumbering wain.
    And when poor hapless Phaethon from the height
Of highest heaven looked down and saw below,
Far, far below the continents outspread,
His face grew pale, his knees in sudden fear
Shook, and his eyes were blind with light so bright.

Would he had never touched his father's steeds,
Nor learnt his birth, nor won his heart's desire! . . .
  Then Phaethon saw the world on every side
Ablaze – heat more than he could bear. He breathed
Vapours that burned like furnace-blasts, and felt
The chariot glow white-hot beneath his feet.
Cinders and sparks past bearing shoot and swirl
And scorching smoke surrounds him; in the murk,
The midnight murk, he knows not where he is
Or goes; the horses whirl him where they will.
The Aethiops then turned black, so men believe,
As heat summoned their blood too near the skin.
Then was Sahara's dusty desert formed,
All water scorched away. . . .
Euphrates burned, river of Babylon,
Phasis, Danube and Ganges were on fire,
Orontes burned and racing Thermodon;
Alpheus boiled, fire scorched Spercheus' banks.
The gold that Tagus carries in his sands
Ran molten in the flames, and all the swans
That used to charm the Lydian banks with song
Huddled in mid Cayster sweltering.
The Nile in terror to the world's end fled
And hid his head, still hidden; his seven mouths
Gaped dusty, seven vales without a stream.
The same disaster dried the Thracian rivers,
Hebrus and Strymon, dried the lordly flow
Of western waters, Rhone and Rhine and Po,
And Tiber, promised empire of the world.
Earth everywhere splits deep and light strikes down
Into the Underworld and fills with fear
Hell's monarch and his consort; the wide seas
Shrink and where ocean lay a wilderness
Of dry sand spreads; new peaks and ranges rise,
Long covered by the deep, and multiply
The scattered islands of the Cyclades.
The fishes dive; the dolphins dare not leap
Their curving course through the familiar air,
And lifeless seals float supine on the waves; . . .
  But the Almighty Father, calling the gods
And him who gave the chariot to attest

Creation doomed were now his aid not given,
Mounted the highest citadel of heaven,
Whence he was wont to veil the lands with clouds
And roll his thunders and his lightnings hurl.
But then no clouds had he the lands to veil,
Nor rain to send from heaven to soothe their pain.
He thundered; and poising high his bolt to blast,
Struck Phaethon from the chariot and from life,
And fire extinguished fire and flame quenched flame.
The horses in wild panic leapt apart,
Burst from the traces and flung off the yoke.
There lie the reins, the sundered axle there,
Here the spokes dangle from a shattered wheel,
And far and wide the signs of wreckage fly.

And Phaethon, flames ravaging his auburn hair,
Falls headlong down, a streaming trail of light,
As sometimes through the cloudless vault of night
A star, though never falling, seems to fall.
His father, sick with grief, had hidden his face,
Shrouded in misery, and, if the tale
Is true, one day went by without the Sun.
The flaming fires gave light – some gain at least
In that disaster. Clymene, distraught
With sorrow, said whatever could be said
In woes so terrible and beat her breast,
And roamed the world to find his lifeless limbs
And then his bones, and found his bones at last
Buried beside a foreign river-bank.
And, prostrate there, she drenched in tears his name
Carved in the marble and hugged it to her breast.
His sisters too, the Sun's three daughters, wept
Sad tears, their futile tribute to the dead,
And long lay prostrate on their brother's tomb,
Bruising their breasts and calling day and night
Phaethon who never more would hear their moans.
Four times the waxing crescent of the moon
Had filled her orb, and, in their wonted way
(Wailing was now their wont) they made lament,
When Phaethusa, eldest of the three,
Meaning to kneel upon the ground, complained
Her feet were rigid. When Lampetie,

Her lovely sister, tried to come to her,
She found herself held fast by sudden roots;
The third, reaching to tear her hair, instead
Plucked leaves. One, in dismay, felt wood encase
Her shins and one her arms become long boughs.
And while they stood bewildered, bark embraced
Their loins and covered, inch by inch, their waists,
Breasts, shoulders, hands, till only lips were left,
Calling their mother. She, what can she do
But dart distractedly now here, now there,
And kiss them while she may. It's not enough.
She tries to tear the bark away and breaks
The tender boughs, but from them bloody drops
Ooze like a dripping wound. "Stop, mother, stop!"
Each injured girl protests; "I beg you, stop;
The tree you tear is me. And now, farewell!"
The bark lapped her last words. So their tears still
Flow on, and oozing from the new-made boughs,
Drip and are hardened in the sun to form
Amber and then the clear stream catches them
And carries them for Roman brides to wear. . . .

    The Sun meanwhile, dishevelled, his bright sheer
Subdued as in the gloom of an eclipse,
Loathing himself, loathing the light, the day,
Gives way to grief, and, grief rising to rage,
Denies his duty to the world. "Enough", He cries,
"Since time began my lot has brought
No rest, no respite. I resent this toil,
Unending toil, unhonoured drudgery.
Let someone else take out my chariot
That bears my sunbeams, or, if no one will,
And all the gods confess they can't, let Jove
Drive it, and, as he wrestles with the reins,
There'll be a while at least when he won't wield
His bolt to rob a father of his son;
And, when he's tried the fiery-footed team
And learnt their strength, he'll know no one should die
For failing to control them expertly."
    Then all the deities surround the Sun
And beg him and beseech him not to shroud
The world in darkness. Jove, indeed, defends

His fiery bolt and adds his royal threats.
So the Sun took in hand his maddened team,
Still terrified, and whipped them savagely,
Whipped them and cursed them for their guilt that they
Destroyed his son, their master, that dire day.

4

Seneca, "On Providence"

The statesman, tragedian and philosopher Lucius Annaeus Seneca (ca. 4 BCE to 65 CE) was the leading intellectual of mid first-century Rome, and the earliest Stoic whose writings have survived intact. Seneca was born in Cordoba (Spain); his eventful public career stretched from effectively governing Rome in the early years of the Emperor Nero to being compelled to commit suicide by the same Nero – something the philosopher did with an equanimity that added to his fame. The importance of Seneca for western thinking about providence and evil was immense. His philosophical works were read by Augustine and Jerome, consoled the imprisoned Boethius, inspired Dante, Petrarch, and Chaucer, were edited by Erasmus, studied by Calvin and Montaigne, inspired several operas, and shaped much of modern thought through thinkers like Rousseau and Kant.

Lucius Annaeus Seneca, "To Lucilius on Providence," in *Moral Essays*, trans. John W. Basore, 3 vols. (London: Heinemann/Cambridge, Mass.: Harvard University Press, 1970) (Loeb Classics), I.3, 7, 9, 11, 15, 25, 39–45.

Nature never permits good to be injured by good; between good men and the gods there exists a friendship brought about by virtue.

Friendship, do I say? Nay, rather there is a tie of relationship and a likeness, since, in truth, a good man differs from God in the element of time only; he is God's pupil, his imitator, and true offspring, whom his all-glorious parent, being no mild task-master of virtues, rears, as strict fathers do, with much severity. And so, when you see that men who are good and acceptable to the gods labour and sweat and have a difficult road to climb, that the wicked, on the other hand, make merry and abound in pleasures, reflect that our children please us by their modesty, while slave-boys by their forwardness; that we hold in check the former by sterner discipline, while we encourage the latter to be bold. Be assured that the same is true of God. He does not make a spoiled pet of a good man; he tests him, hardens him, and fits him for his own service.

You ask, "Why do many adversities come to good men?" No evil *can* befall a good man; opposites do not mingle. Just as the countless rivers, the vast fall of rain from the sky, and the huge volume of mineral springs do not change the taste of the sea, do not even modify it, so the assaults of adversity do not weaken the spirit of a brave man. It always maintains its poise, and it gives its own colour to everything that happens; for it is mightier than all external things . . .

Do you not see how fathers show their love in one way, and mothers in another? The father orders his children to be aroused from sleep in order that they may start early upon their pursuits, – even on holidays he does not permit them to be idle, and he draws from them sweat and sometimes tears. But the mother fondles them in her lap, wishes to keep them out of the sun, wishes them never to be unhappy, never to cry, never to toil. Toward good men God has the love of a father, he cherishes for them a manly love, and he says, "Let them be harassed by toil, by suffering, by losses, in order that they may gain true strength." . . .

. . . This much I now say, – that those things which you call hardships and accursed, are, in the first place, for the good of the persons themselves to whom they come; in the second place, that they are for the good of the whole human family, for which the gods have a greater concern than for single persons; again, I say that good men are willing that these things should happen and, if they are unwilling, that they deserve misfortune. I shall add, further, that these things befall good men by the same law which makes them good. I shall induce you, in fine, never to commiserate a good man. For he can be called miserable, but he cannot be so.

. . . [T]o be always happy and to pass through life without a mental pang is to be ignorant of one half of nature. You are a great man; but how do I know it if Fortune gives you no opportunity of showing your worth? You have entered as a contestant at the Olympic games, but none other besides you; you gain the crown, the victory you do not gain. . . . In like manner, also, I may say to a good man, if no harder circumstance has given him the opportunity whereby alone he might show the strength of mind, "I judge you unfortunate because you have never been unfortunate; you have passed through life without an antagonist; no one will know what you can do, – not even yourself." For if a man is to know himself, he must be tested; no one finds out what he can do except by trying . . .

What, then, is the part of a good man? To offer himself to Fate. It is a great consolation that it is together with the universe we are swept along;

whatever it is that has ordained us so to live, so to die, by the same necessity it binds also the gods. One unchangeable course bears along the affairs of men and gods alike. Although the great creator and ruler of the universe himself wrote the decrees of Fate, yet he follows them. He obeys forever, he decreed but once. "Why, however," do you ask, "was God so unjust in his allotment of destiny as to assign to good men poverty, wounds, and painful death?" It is impossible for the moulder to alter matter; to this law it has submitted. Certain qualities cannot be separated from certain others; they cling together, are indivisible. Natures that are listless, that are prone to sleep, or to a kind of wakefulness that closely resembles sleep, are composed of sluggish elements. It takes sterner stuff to make a man who deserves to be mentioned with consideration. His course will not be the level way; uphill and downhill must he go, be tossed about, and guide his bark through stormy waters; he must keep his course in spite of fortune. Much that is hard, much that is rough will befall him, but he himself will soften the one, and make the other smooth. Fire tests gold, misfortune brave men. See to what a height virtue must climb! you will find that it has no safe road to tread:

> The way is steep at first, and the coursers strain
> To climb it, fresh in the early morn. They gain
> The crest of heaven at noon; from here I gaze
> Adown on land and sea with dread amaze,
> And oft my heart will beat in panic fear.
> The roadway ends in sharp descent – keep here
> a sure control; 'twill happen even so
> That Tethys, stretching out her waves below,
> Will often, while she welcomes, be affright
> To see me speeding downward from the height.

Having heard the words, that noble youth [Phaethon; see p. 13 above] replied, "I like the road, I shall mount; even though I fall, it will be worth while to travel through such sights." But the other did not cease from trying to strike his bold heart with fear:

> And though you may not miss the beaten track,
> Nor, led to wander, leave the zodiac,
> Yet through the Bull's fierce horns, the Centaur's bow
> And raging Lion's jaws you still must go.

In reply to this he said, "Harness the chariot you offered; the very things that you think affright me urge me on. I long to stand aloft where even

the Sun-god quakes with fear." The groveller and the coward will follow
the safe path: virtue seeks the heights.

"But why," you ask, "does God sometimes allow evil to befall good
men?" Assuredly he does not. Evil of every sort he keeps far from them
– sin and crime, evil counsel and schemes for greed, blind lust and avarice
intent upon another's goods. The good man himself he protects and deliv-
ers: does any one require of God that he should also guard the good man's
luggage? Nay, the good man himself relieves God of this concern; he
despises externals. Democritus, considering riches to be a burden to the
virtuous mind, renounced them. Why, then, do you wonder if God suffers
that to be the good man's lot which the good man himself sometimes
chooses should be his lot? . . .

Think, then, of God as saying: "What possible reason have you to complain of me, you who have chosen righteousness? Others I have surrounded with unreal goods, and have mocked their empty minds, as it
were, with a long, deceptive dream. I have bedecked them with gold, and
silver, and ivory, but within them there is nothing good. . . . But to you
I have given the true and enduring goods, which are greater and better
the more anyone turns them over and views them from every side. I have
permitted you to scorn all that dismays and to disdain desires. Outwardly
you do not shine; your goods are directed inward. Even so the cosmos,
rejoicing in the spectacle of itself, scorns everything outside. Within I have
bestowed upon you every good; your good fortune is not to need good
fortune.

" 'Yet,' you say, 'many sorrows, things dreadful and hard to bear, do befall
us.' Yes, because I could not withdraw you from their path, I have armed
your minds to withstand them all; endure with fortitude. In this you may
outstrip God; he is exempt from enduring evil, while you are superior to
it. Scorn poverty; no one lives as poor as he was born. Scorn pain; it will
either be relieved or relieve you. Scorn Fortune; I have given her no
weapon with which she may strike your soul. Above all, I have taken pains
that nothing should keep you here against your will; the way out lies open.
If you do not choose to fight, you may run away. Therefore of all things
that I have deemed necessary for you, I have made nothing easier than
dying. . . .' "

5

Epictetus, *Encheiridion*

Epictetus (ca.50 to ca.120), the presumably Greek author of the *Encheirid-ion*, was born a slave (*epictētos* means "acquired") and exposed to the ideas of the Stoics while still a boy; crippled by his master and in poor health his whole life, Epictetus was living proof of the Stoic view that nothing that is beyond our control can truly harm us. In Rome, where he lectured on the thought of Chrysippus (ca. 280–207 BCE), he became a major spokesman for Roman Stoicism. Epictetus' thought is primarily concerned with prac-tical philosophy. All men are sons of God and in their minds kindred with the divinity; their natural self-interest is such that it can only be pursued by contributing to the common welfare. The will of God, which is the law of nature, can be discerned at work in human lives. "From everything that happens in the universe," Epictetus asserted, "it is easy for a man to find occasion to praise providence, if he has within himself these two qualities: the faculty of taking a comprehensive view of what has happened in each individual instance, and the sense of gratitude." Epictetus' most famous student was the emperor Marcus Aurelius (121–80). The repercussions of Epictetus' work, especially of the *Encheiridion* (handbook), resonate to our own time.

Gerard Boter, *The Encheiridion of Epictetus and Its Three Christian Adaptations: Transmission and Critical Editions* (Leiden, Boston, Köln: Brill, 1999), 276–310.

ch. 1 There are two classes of things: those that are under our control and those that are not. Under our control are our opinion, choice, desire, aversion and, in a word, everything that is our own doing; not under our control are our body, our possessions, our reputations, our offices and, in a word, everything that is not our own doing. The things that are under our control are by nature free, unhindered, unimpeded; the things that are not under our control are weak, slavish, hindered, up to others. Remember, therefore, that if you regard the things that are by nature slavish as free, and the things that are up to others as your own, you will be hampered, you will suffer, you will get upset, you will blame both gods and men; if, on the other hand, you regard as yours only what is in fact yours, and what is up to others – as it is – as up to others, nobody will ever compel you, nobody will hinder you, you will blame nobody, you will not reproach anyone, you will do nothing against your will, nobody will harm you, you will have no enemy, you will not suffer anything harmful. Thus, if you aim at such things, remember that you should not occupy yourself with them with modest effort, but that you must give up some things altogether, and postpone others for the present moment. If, however, you wish both to attain these things and to hold office and be rich, you risk failure even to obtain the latter, because you are also seeking the former; but you will inevitably fail to attain those things that alone procure freedom and happiness. Therefore you should do your best from the outset to say to every harsh impression, "You are an impression, and not at all what you seem to be"; then examine it and judge it by those standards that are at your disposal, in the first place and especially by this one, whether it belongs to the things that are under our control or to the things that are not under our control; and if it has to do with one of the things that are not under our control, bear in mind that it is nothing to you.

ch. 2 Remember that the promise of desire is to obtain what you desire, and the promise of aversion not to fall into what you avoid. And he who does not obtain what he desires is unfortunate, but he who falls into what is avoided suffers misfortune. If, then, you avoid only what is not in accordance with nature among the things that are under your control, you will not fall into any of the things you avoid; but if you avoid illness or death or poverty, you will suffer misfortune. Therefore take away aversion from all the things that are not under our control, and transfer it to the things that are unnatural among the things that are under our control. As to desire, refrain from it completely for the time being; for if you desire some of the things that are not under our control, you are sure to be unfortunate; and, on the other hand, none of the things that are under our control, which it would be good to desire, is as yet within your reach. Use only choice and refusal, lightly and with reservation and without straining . . .

ch. 5a People get upset not by what happens but by their opinions on what happens. For instance, death is nothing to be feared, because in that case it would have appeared so to Socrates as well; but the opinion about death, that it is to be feared, that is the thing to be feared. Therefore, whenever we are hampered or upset or grieved, let us never blame someone else, but ourselves, that is, our opinions.

ch. 5b An uneducated person accuses others for his failures; a person who has started his education accuses himself; an educated person accuses neither someone else nor himself . . .

ch. 7 Just as on a voyage, when the ship rides at anchor, if you should go ashore to get water, you will also collect a shell-fish or a bulb on your way, but you will have to keep watching the ship and continually look back in case the captain is calling, and if he should call, give up all these things, lest you should be thrown on board tied up like a sheep, so too *depends* in life, if instead of a shell-fish or a bulb you are given a wife or a child, *who the* there will be nothing against it; but if the captain calls, give up all these *is (?)* *captain* things and run to the ship, without so much as looking back; and if you are old, never move far away from the ship, lest you should be missing when he calls you.

ch. 8 Do not seek to have events happen as you wish, but wish them to happen as they do happen, and all will be well with you.

ch. 9 Illness is an impediment to the body, but not to choice, if it does not wish so itself. Lameness is an impediment to the leg, but not to choice. And tell yourself this about each of the things that happen to you; for you will find it to be an impediment to something else, but not to you.

ch. 10 At everything that happens to you remember to turn to yourself and find what capacity you have to deal with it. If you see a beautiful boy or girl, you will find self-control as the capacity to deal with it; if hard labour is imposed on you, you will find endurance; if abuse, you will find patience. And when you make a habit of this, the impressions will not carry you away.

ch. 11 Never say in the case of anything, "I have lost it"; but "I have *nice!* given it back." Your child has died? It has been given back. Your wife has died? She has been given back. Your land has been taken from you? That too has been given back. "But the one who took it from me is a wicked man." What concern is it of yours by whose intervention the giver asked it back from you? As long as these things are given to you, take care of them as things that belong to someone else, just as travellers mind the inn . . .

ch. 14a If you wish your children and your wife and your friends to live by all means, you are foolish; for you wish the things that are not under your control, and the things that belong to others to belong to you. In the same way, if you want your slave-boy to make no mistakes, you are stupid; for you wish badness not to be badness, but something else. But if you wish not to fail in what you desire, that is what you are able to achieve; therefore exercise yourself in those things that you are able to achieve.

ch. 14b Each man's master is the one who has the power to achieve or prevent what that man does or does not wish. Therefore everyone who wishes to be free should neither wish nor avoid any of the things that are under other people's control; if not so, it inevitably leads to slavery.

ch. 15 Remember to behave in life as if you were attending a banquet. Something is being carried around, and arrives at your place; reach out and take a modest share of it. It passes by: do not hold it back. It is not yet coming: do not stretch your desire towards it, but wait until it arrives at your place. In the same way towards your children, in the same way towards your wife, in the same way towards offices, in the same way towards wealth; and you will be worthy to share a banquet with the gods one day. If, however, you do not take these things even when they are put in front of you, but despise them, you will not only share a banquet with the gods, but also rule with them. For by acting in this way Diogenes and Heraclitus and men like them were deservedly gods and deservedly called so . . .

ch. 17 Remember that you are an actor in a play the character of which is determined by the playwright: a short play, if he wants it to be short; a long play, if he wants it to be long; if he wants you to play a beggar's role, remember to play this role properly too; and in the same way if he wants you to play a cripple, an official, a private person. For this is yours to do: to play well the role that is assigned to you; but picking it out is the task of someone else.

ch. 18 Whenever a crow croaks unfavourably, do not let yourself be carried away by the impression, but immediately draw a distinction in your mind and say, "None of these signs pertains to me, but they pertain to my body or my property or my reputation or my children or my wife. To me, however, all portents are favourable, if I wish them to be so; for whichsoever of these things may happen, it is under my control to benefit from them . . ."

ch. 26 The will of nature can be learnt from things in which we do not differ from each other. For instance, when someone else's slave breaks a cup, our immediate reaction is, "It is just one of those things that happen." Realize, then, that when your own cup is broken, you must react in the same way as when someone else's cup was broken. Transfer this to more important things as well. Someone else's child or wife has died? There is nobody who would not say, "That's life." But when someone's own child dies, he immediately goes, "Alas!" and "Poor me!" But we should remember how we feel when we hear such things about others.

ch. 27 Just as there is no target set up for misses, so there is no nature of evil in the universe either.

ch. 31 With regard to piety towards the gods you should know that the most important thing is to have the right opinions about them, namely that they exist and administer the universe well and justly, and to have set yourself to obey them and to submit to everything that happens to you, and to follow it voluntarily, because it is being brought about by the highest intelligence. For in this way you will never blame the gods nor reproach them for neglecting you. You can only realize this if you take away from good and evil the things that are not under our control, and place them exclusively in the things that are under our control . . .

6

Irenaeus of Lyons, *Against Heretics*

Historically revered by the Eastern church for his ideas of the perfectibility of human nature, by Roman Catholics for his arguments for authority, and by Protestants for his Biblicism, Irenaeus (ca. 130 to ca. 200) unfolded his theology in response to "heresies" he was combatting, the most important of which were the ideas of the Gnostics Valentinian and Marcion. (Until the discoveries at Nag Hammadi, *Against Heretics* was the major source of our knowledge of the varieties of Gnosticism.) Arguing for the canon of the Old Testament and (no more than) four gospels in the New, Irenaeus wrote of a kind of staggered revelation whose importance for theodicy has been asserted by John Hick. Hick sees in Irenaeus and other Greek Fathers of the church an alternative to the Augustinian "majority view" of western Christian history. Kenneth Surin and others have however questioned whether Irenaeus' views are intended for use beyond the context of catechizing Christian converts from Gnosticism. Do *all* Christians need answers to Gnostic questions?

Irenaeus, *Against Heretics*, IV: xxxvii–xix, in *The Ante-Nicene Christian Library, Vol. IX: Irenæus, Vol. II. – Hippolytus, Vol. II. – Fragments of Third Century*, eds. Rev. Alexander Roberts and James Donaldson (Edinburgh: T. & T. Clark, 1869), 36, 39–47.

Men are possessed of free will, and endowed with the faculty of making a choice. It is not true, therefore, that some are by nature good, and others bad

1. This expression [of our Lord], "How often would I have gathered thy children together, and thou wouldest not," [Mt. 23:37, Lk. 13:34] set forth

the ancient law of human liberty, because God made man a free [agent] from the beginning, possessing his own power, even as he does his own soul, to obey the behests of God voluntarily, and not by compulsion of God. For there is no coercion with God, but a good will [towards us] is present with Him continually. And therefore does He give good counsel to all. And in man, as well as in angels, He has placed the power of choice (for angels are rational beings), so that those who had yielded obedience might justly possess what is good, given indeed by God, but preserved by themselves. On the other hand, they who have not obeyed shall, with justice, be not found in possession of the good, and shall receive condign punishment: for God did kindly bestow on them what was good; but they themselves did not diligently keep it, nor deem it something precious, but poured contempt upon His super-eminent goodness . . .

5. And not merely in works, but also in faith, has God preserved the will of man free and under his own control, saying, "According to thy faith be it unto thee;" [Mt. 9:29] thus showing that there is a faith specially belonging to man, since he has an opinion specially his own. And again, "All things are possible to him that believeth;" [Mk. 9:23] and, "Go thy way; and as thou hast believed, so be it done unto thee." [Mt. 8:13] Now all such expressions demonstrate that man is in his own power with respect to faith. And for this reason, "he that believeth in Him has eternal life while he who believeth not the Son hath not eternal life, but the wrath of God shall remain upon him." [Jn. 3:36] In the same manner therefore the Lord, both showing His own goodness, and indicating that man is in his own free will and his own power, said to Jerusalem, "How often have I wished to gather thy children together, as a hen [gathereth] her chickens under her wings, and ye would not! Wherefore your house shall be left unto you desolate." [Mt. 23:37–8]

6. Those, again, who maintain the opposite to these [conclusions], do themselves present the Lord as destitute of power, as if, forsooth, He were unable to accomplish what He willed; or, on the other hand, as being ignorant that they were by nature "material," as these men express it, and such as cannot receive His immortality. "But He should not," say they, "have created angels of such a nature that they were capable of transgression, nor men who immediately proved ungrateful towards Him; for they were made rational beings, endowed with the power of examining and judging, and were not [formed] as things irrational or of a [merely] animal nature, which can do nothing of their own will, but are drawn by necessity and compulsion to what is good, in which things there is one mind and one usage, working mechanically in one groove, who are incapable of being anything else except just what they had been created." But upon

this supposition, neither would what is good be grateful to them, nor communion with God be precious, nor would the good be very much to be sought after, which would present itself without their own proper endeavour, care, or study, but would be implanted of its own accord and without their concern. Thus it would come to pass, that their being good would be of no consequence, because they were so by nature rather than by will, and are possessors of good spontaneously, not by choice; and for this reason they would not understand this fact, that good is a comely thing, nor would they take pleasure in it. For how can those who are ignorant of good enjoy it? Or what credit is it to those who have not aimed at it? And what crown is it to those who have not followed in pursuit of it, like those victorious in the contest?

7. . . . Moreover, the faculty of seeing would not appear to be so desirable, unless we had known what a loss it were to be devoid of sight; and health, too, is rendered all the more estimable by an acquaintance with disease; light, also, by contrasting it with darkness; and life with death. Just in the same way is the heavenly kingdom honourable to those who have known the earthly one. But in proportion as it is more honourable, so much the more do we prize it; and if we have prized it more, we shall be the more glorious in the presence of God. The Lord has therefore endured all these things on our behalf, in order that we, having been instructed by means of them all, may be in all respects circumspect for the time to come, and that, having been rationally taught to love God, we may continue in His perfect love: for God has displayed long-suffering in the case of man's apostasy; while man has been instructed by means of it, as also the prophet says, "Thine own apostasy shall heal thee;" [Jer. 2:19] God thus determining all things beforehand for the bringing of man to perfection, for his edification, and for the revelation of His dispensations, that goodness may both be made apparent, and righteousness perfected, and that the Church may be fashioned after the image of His Son, and that man may finally be brought to maturity at some future time, becoming ripe through such privileges to see and comprehend God.

Why man was not made perfect from the beginning

1. If, however, any one say, "What then? Could not God have exhibited man as perfect from the beginning?" let him know that, inasmuch as God is indeed always the same and unbegotten as respects Himself, all things are possible to Him. But created things must be inferior to Him who created them, from the very fact of their later origin; for it was not possible for things recently created to have been uncreated. But inasmuch as they are not uncreated, for this very reason do they come short of the

perfect. Because, as these things are of later date, so are they infantile; so are they unaccustomed to, and unexercised in, perfect discipline. For as it certainly is in the power of a mother to give strong food to her infant, [but she does not do so], as the child is not yet able to receive more substantial nourishment; so also it was possible for God Himself to have made man perfect from the first, but man could not receive this [perfection], being as yet an infant. And for this cause our Lord in these last times, when He had summed up all things into Himself, came to us, not as He might have come, but as we were capable of beholding Him. He might easily have come to us in His immortal glory, but in that case we could never have endured the greatness of the glory; and therefore it was that He, who was the perfect bread of the Father, offered Himself to us as milk, [because we were] as infants. He did this when He appeared as a man, that we, being nourished, as it were, from the breast of His flesh, and having, by such a course of milk nourishment, become accustomed to eat and drink the Word of God, may be able also to contain in ourselves the Bread of immortality, which is the Spirit of the Father.

2. And on this account does Paul declare to the Corinthians, "I have fed you with milk, not with meat, for hitherto ye were not able to bear it." [1 Cor. 3:2] That is, ye have indeed learned the advent of our Lord as a man; nevertheless, because of your infirmity, the Spirit of the Father has not as yet rested upon you. "For when envying and strife," he says, "and dissensions are among you, are ye not carnal, and walk as men?" [3:3] That is, that the Spirit of the Father was not yet with them, on account of their imperfection and shortcomings of their walk in life. As, therefore, the apostle had the power to give them strong meat – for those upon whom the apostles laid hands received the Holy Spirit, who is the food of life [eternal] – but they were not capable of receiving it, because they had the sentient faculties of the soul still feeble and undisciplined in the practice of things pertaining to God; so, in like manner, God had power at the beginning to grant perfection to man; but as the latter was only recently created, he could not possibly have received it, or even if he had received it, could he have contained it, or containing it, could he have retained it. It was for this reason that the Son of God, although He was perfect, passed through the state of infancy in common with the rest of mankind, partaking of it thus not for His own benefit, but for that of the infantile stage of man's existence, in order that man might be able to receive Him. There was nothing, therefore, impossible to and deficient in God, [implied in the fact] that man was not an uncreated being; but this merely applied to him who was lately created, [namely] man.

3. With God there are simultaneously exhibited power, wisdom, and goodness. His power and goodness [appear] in this, that of His own will

He called into being and fashioned things having no previous existence; His wisdom [is shown] in His having made created things parts of one harmonious and consistent whole; and those things which, through His super-eminent kindness, receive growth and a long period of existence, do reflect the glory of the uncreated One, of that God who bestows what is good ungrudgingly. For from the very fact of these things having been created, [it follows] that they are not uncreated; but by their continuing in being throughout a long course of ages, they shall receive a faculty of the Uncreated, through the gratuitous bestowal of eternal existence upon them by God. And thus in all things God has the pre-eminence, who alone is uncreated, the first of all things, and the primary cause of the existence of all, while all other things remain under God's subjection. But being in subjection to God is continuance in immortality, and immortality is the glory of the uncreated One. By this arrangement, therefore, and these harmonies, and a sequence of this nature, man, a created and organized being, is rendered after the image and likeness of the uncreated God, – the Father planning everything well and giving His commands, the Son carrying these into execution and performing the work of creating, and the Spirit nourishing and increasing [what is made], but man making progress day by day, and ascending towards the perfect, that is, approximating to the uncreated One. For the Uncreated is perfect, that is, God. Now it was necessary that man should in the first instance be created; and having been created, should receive growth; and having received growth, should be strengthened; and having been strengthened, should abound; and having abounded, should recover [from the disease of sin]; and having recovered, should be glorified; and being glorified, should see his Lord. For God is He who is yet to be seen, and the beholding of God is productive of immortality, but immortality renders one nigh unto God.

4. Irrational, therefore, in every respect, are they who await not the time of increase, but ascribe to God the infirmity of their nature. Such persons know neither God nor themselves, being insatiable and ungrateful, unwilling to be at the outset what they have also been created – men subject to passions; but go beyond the law of the human race, and before that they become men, they wish to be even now like God their Creator, and they who are more destitute of reason than dumb animals [insist] that there is no distinction between the uncreated God and man, a creature of to-day. For these, [the dumb animals], bring no charge against God for not having made them men; but each one, just as he has been created, gives thanks that he has been created. For we cast blame upon Him, because we have not been made gods from the beginning, but at first merely men, then at length gods; although God has adopted this course out of His pure

benevolence, that no one may impute to Him invidiousness or grudging-
ness. He declares, "I have said, Ye are gods; and ye are all sons of the
Highest." [Ps. 82:6] But since we could not sustain the power of divinity,
He adds, "But ye shall die like men," [82:7] setting forth both truths – the
kindness of His free gift, and our weakness, and also that we were possessed of power over ourselves. For after His great kindness He graciously
conferred good [upon us], and made men like to Himself, [that is] in their
own power; while at the same time by His prescience He knew the infirmity of human beings, and the consequences which would flow from it;
but through [His] love and [His] power, He shall overcome the substance
of created nature. For it was necessary, at first, that nature should be exhibited; then, after that, that what was mortal should be conquered and swallowed up by immortality, and the corruptible by incorruptibility, and that
man should be made after the image and likeness of God, having received
the knowledge of good and evil.

Man is endowed with the faculty of distinguishing good and evil;
so that, without compulsion, he has the power, by his own will and choice,
to perform God's commandments, by doing which he avoids the evils
prepared for the rebellious

1. Man has received the knowledge of good and evil. It is good to obey
God, and to believe in Him, and to keep His commandment, and this is
the life of man; as not to obey God is evil, and this is his death. Since
God, therefore, gave [to man] such mental power . . . man knew both the
good of obedience and the evil of disobedience, that the eye of the mind,
receiving experience of both, may with judgment make choice of the
better things; and that he may never become indolent or neglectful of
God's command; and learning by experience that it is an evil thing which
deprives him of life, that is, disobedience to God, may never attempt it at
all, but that, knowing that what preserves his life, namely, obedience to
God, is good, he may diligently keep it with all earnestness. Wherefore he
has also had a twofold experience, possessing knowledge of both kinds,
that with discipline he may make choice of the better things. But how, if
he had no knowledge of the contrary, could he have had instruction in
that which is good? For there is thus a surer and an undoubted comprehension of matters submitted to us than the mere surmise arising from an
opinion regarding them. For just as the tongue receives experience of
sweet and bitter by means of tasting, and the eye discriminates between
black and white by means of vision, and the ear recognises the distinctions of sounds by hearing; so also does the mind, receiving through the

experience of both the knowledge of what is good, become more tena-
cious of its preservation, by acting in obedience to God: in the first place,
casting away, by means of repentance, disobedience, as being something
disagreeable and nauseous; and afterwards coming to understand what it
really is, that it is contrary to goodness and sweetness, so that the mind
may never even attempt to taste disobedience to God. But if any one do
shun the knowledge of both these kinds of things, and the twofold perception of knowledge, he unawares divests himself of the character of a
human being.

2. How, then, shall he be a God, who has not as yet been made a man?
Or how can he be perfect who was but lately created? How, again, can
he be immortal, who in his mortal nature did not obey his Maker? For
it must be that thou, at the outset, shouldest hold the rank of a man, and
then afterwards partake of the glory of God. For thou dost not make God,
but God thee. If, then, thou art God's workmanship, await the hand of thy
Maker which creates everything in due time; in due time as far as thou
art concerned, whose creation is being carried out. Offer to Him thy heart
in a soft and tractable state, and preserve the form in which the Creator
has fashioned thee, having moisture in thyself, lest, by becoming hardened,
thou lose the impressions of His fingers. But by preserving the framework
thou shalt ascend to that which is perfect, for the moist clay which is in
thee is hidden [there] by the workmanship of God. His hand fashioned
thy substance; He will cover thee over [too] within and without with pure
gold and silver, and He will adorn thee to such a degree, that even "the
King Himself shall have pleasure in thy beauty." [Ps. 45:11] But if thou,
being obstinately hardened, dost reject the operation of His skill, and show
thyself ungrateful towards Him, because thou wert created a [mere] man,
by becoming thus ungrateful to God, thou hast at once lost both His
workmanship and life. For creation is an attribute of the goodness of God
but to be created is that of human nature. If then, thou shalt deliver up
to Him what is thine that is, faith towards Him and subjection, thou shalt
receive His handiwork, and shall be a perfect work of God.

7

Sextus Empiricus, "God"

Little is known about Sextus Empiricus, the compiler of the *Outlines of Pyrrhonism*, except that was a physician and headed a skeptical school around 200 CE. *Outlines* is not an original work, but preserves the fruits of Aenesidemus' and Agrippa's systematization of the skepticism of Pyrrho (ca. 360 to 275 BCE). The "skeptic way" Sextus describes involves juxtaposing inconsistent but equally credible ideas and experiences in order to produce first *epochē* (a state of mind where nothing is affirmed or denied) and then *ataraxia* (an untroubled tranquillity of soul). Arguments in the form of a trilemma ideally suit this purpose. The chapter on "God," below, contains the earliest surviving formulation of a trilemma counterposing divine attributes and the existence of evil in the world. Like much of classical thought, Sextus Empiricus' work was unknown in Europe for centuries; when it was republished in the 1560s, it had a major impact on early modern skeptics like Montaigne, Descartes, and Bayle.

Sextus Empiricus, *Outlines of Pyrrhonism*, III.3; in *The Skeptic Way: Sextus Empiricus's Outlines of Pyrrhonism*, trans. Benson Mates (New York: Oxford University Press, 1996), 173–5.

In view of the fact that the majority assert that god is a maximally productive cause, let us first give consideration to god, noting in advance that, on the one hand, we follow without doctrinal belief the common course of life and we say that there are gods, and we reverence gods and ascribe to them foreknowledge but, on the other hand, that we have the following points to make against the precipitancy of the Dogmatists.

When we conceive of objects or states of affairs, we are bound to conceive of their substances as well, for example, whether they are corporeal or incorporeal. And also of their forms; for nobody could conceive of a horse without first comprehending the form of the horse. Also, the object conceived of must be conceived of as being somewhere. Since, then, some of the Dogmatists say that god is corporeal and some that he is incorporeal, and some say that he is anthropomorphic and some that he is not, and some that he is located somewhere and others that he is not, while of those saying that he is located somewhere, some say that he is inside the cosmos and others that he is outside – how shall we be able to form a concept of god when we have no agreed-upon substance nor form of him, nor location where he is? Let the Dogmatists first agree and concur with one another that god is such and such and only then, when they have sketched this out for us, let them expect us to form a concept of god. But as long as they do not settle their disagreement we cannot tell what agreed-upon conception we are supposed to get from them

But, they say, when you have conceived of something immortal and blessed, consider that to be god. This, however, is silly, for just as whoever does not know Dion cannot conceive of accidents as belonging to Dion, so, since we do not know what god is, we are not able to learn about or even conceive of his accidents. And aside from these points, let the Dogmatists tell us what a "blessed" thing is, whether it is something that acts on its subordinates in accord with virtue and forethought, or it is something inactive, neither having any business of its own nor providing any for someone else; for, disagreeing without resolution about this, too, they have made the blessed, and consequently also god, inconceivable for us.

Furthermore, if we go by what the Dogmatists say, even if we form a conception of god it is necessary to suspend judgment concerning whether he exists or does not exist. For it is not pre-evident that god exists. If he affected us just of and by himself, the Dogmatists would agree about who, of what sort, and where he is; but their unresolved disagreement has made him seem non-evident to us and in need of proof. Now, anyone who proves that a god exists either does this by means of something pre-evident or by means of something non-evident. But certainly not by means of something pre-evident, for if what proves a god to exist were pre-evident, then in view of the fact that the thing proved is thought of relatively to what proves it and therefore is apprehended along with it, as we have established, the existence of a god will also be pre-evident, being apprehended along with the pre-evident fact that proves it. But it is not pre-evident, as we have shown. Therefore, it is not proved by means of something pre-evident. Nor is it proved by something non-evident. For if the non-evident proposition that is to prove that a god exists, and which itself needs proof, is said to be proved by means of something pre-evident, it will no longer be nonevident but rather pre-evident. But neither is it proved by means of something non-evident, for anyone who says that will fall into an infinite regress, since we shall always be asking for a proof of the non-evident proposition that is offered as proving the last one propounded. Therefore, that a god exists cannot be proved from any other proposition. And so, if it is not of itself pre-evident nor provable from something else, whether a god exists will not be apprehensible.

Further, this too should be said. Anyone who asserts that god exists either says that god takes care of the things in the cosmos or that he does not, and, if he does take care, that it is either of all things or of some. Now if he takes care of everything, there would be no particular evil thing and no evil in general in the cosmos; but the Dogmatists say that everything is full of evil; therefore god shall not be said to take care of everything. On the other hand, if he takes care of only some things, why does he take care of these and not of those? For either he wishes but is not able, or he is able but does not wish, or he neither wishes nor is able. If he both wished and was able, he would have taken care of everything; but, for the reasons stated above, he does not take care of everything; therefore, it is not the case that he both wishes and is able to take care of everything. But if he wishes and is not able, he is weaker than the cause on account of which he is not able to take care of the things of which he does not take care; but it is contrary to the concept of god that he should be weaker than anything. Again, if he is able to take care of everything but does not wish to do so, he will be considered malevolent, and if he neither wishes nor is able, he is both malevolent and weak; but to say that about god is impious. Therefore, god does not take care of the things in the cosmos.

Further, if god does not take care of anything and there is no work or product of his, nobody will be able to say from whence he apprehends that god exists, if indeed god neither appears of himself nor is apprehended through his products. And thus, whether god exists is not apprehensible. From these considerations we conclude that most likely those who firmly maintain that god exists will be forced into impiety; for if they say that he takes care of everything, they will be saying that god is the cause of evils, while if they say that he takes care of some things only or even of nothing, they will be force to say that he is either malevolent or weak, and manifestly these are impious conclusions.

8

Plotinus, "Providence: First Treatise"

Plotinus (ca. 205–70) was the founder of Neoplatonism in Rome. Very little is known of his life. He may have been Egyptian, and certainly studied philosophy in Alexandria before becaming a follower of the Platonist Ammonius "Saccus" (who may also have been the teacher of Origen). Plotinus' essays, written in Greek for his disciples and friends, were collected, chopped up, and collated by his student and biographer Porphyry in the *Enneads*. *Ennead* I.8 contains Plotinus' unhappy but influential attempt (motivated perhaps by his efforts to refute the Gnosticism of some members of his circle) to overcome Plato's dualism. The nature and source of evil is formless "Matter," which doesn't exist yet is discussed as if it were a positive force. As John Hick notes, Plotinus is the source for much of the "Augustinian tradition in theodicy," notably its "aesthetic" elements and the idea of the *plenum* – the idea that the world proceeds by emanation from God, generating the "great chain of being." The discussion of providence excerpted below shows marked Stoic influences.

Plotinus, *The Enneads*, III.2 ("Providence: First Treatise"), trans. Stephen MacKenna (Harmondsworth: Penguin, 1991), 135–41, 147–8, 150–4.

1. To make the existence and coherent structure of this Universe depend upon automatic activity and upon chance is against all good sense . . .

But there is still the question as to the process by which the individual things of this sphere have come into being, how they were made.

Some of them seem so undesirable as to cast doubts upon a Universal Providence; and we find, on the one hand, the denial of any controlling power, on the other the belief that the Cosmos is the work of an evil creator . . .

Of course the belief that after a certain lapse of time a Cosmos previously non-existent came into being would imply a foreseeing and a reasoned plan on the part of God providing for the production of the Universe and securing all possible perfection in it . . . But since we hold the eternal existence of the Universe, the utter absence of a beginning to it, we are forced, in sound and sequent reasoning, to explain the providence ruling in the Universe as a universal consonance with the divine Intelligence to which the Cosmos is subsequent not in time but in the fact of derivation, in the fact that the Divine Intelligence, preceding it in Kind, is its cause as being the Archetype and Model which it merely images, the primal by which, from all eternity, it has its existence and subsistence.

The relationship may be presented thus:

The authentic and primal Cosmos is the Being of the Intellectual Principle and of the Veritable Existent. This contains within itself no spatial distinction, and has none of the feebleness of division, and even its parts bring no incompleteness to it since here the individual is not severed from the entire. In this Nature inheres all life and all intellect, a life living and having intellection as one act within a unity: every part that it gives forth is a whole; all its content is its very own, for there is here no separation of thing from thing, no part standing in isolated existence estranged from the rest, and therefore nowhere is there any wronging of any other, any opposition. Everywhere one and complete, it is at rest throughout and shows difference at no point; it does not make over any of its content into any new form; there can be no reason for changing what is everywhere perfect. Why should Reason elaborate yet another Reason, or Intelligence another Intelligence? An indwelling power of making things is in the character of a being not at all points as it should be but making, moving, by reason of some failure in quality. Those whose nature is all blessedness have no more to do than to repose in themselves and be their being . . .

2. By derivation from that Authentic Cosmos, one within itself, there subsists this lower Cosmos, no longer a true unity. It is multiple, divided into various elements, thing standing apart from thing in a new estrangement. No longer is there concord unbroken; hostility, too, has entered as the result of difference and distance; imperfection has inevitably introduced discord; for a part is not self-sufficient, it must pursue something outside itself for its fulfillment, and so it becomes the enemy to what it needs . . .

The Intellectual Principle, then, in its unperturbed serenity has brought the universe into being, by communicating from its own store to Matter:

and this gift is the Reason-Form flowing from it. For the Emanation of the Intellectual Principle is Reason, an emanation unfailing as long as the Intellectual Principle continues to have place among beings.

The Reason-Principle within a seed contains all the parts and qualities concentrated in identity; there is no distinction, no jarring, no internal hindering; then there comes a pushing out into bulk, part rises in distinction with part, and at once the members of the organism stand in each other's way and begin to wear each other down . . .

Yet: Amid all that they effect and accept, the divine Realm imposes the one harmonious act; each utters its own voice, but all is brought into accord, into an ordered system, for the universal purpose, by the ruling Reason-Principle. This Universe is not Intelligence and Reason, like the Supernal, but participant in Intelligence and Reason: it stands in need of the harmonizing because it is the meeting ground of Necessity and divine Reason-Necessity pulling towards the lower, towards the unreason which is its own characteristic, while yet the Intellectual Principle remains sovereign over it. [cf. *Timaeus* 48ab]

The Intellectual Sphere [the Divine] alone is Reason, and there can never be another Sphere that is Reason and nothing else; so that, given some other system, it cannot be as noble as that first; it cannot be Reason: yet since such a system cannot be merely Matter, which is the utterly unordered, it must be a mixed thing. Its two extremes are Matter and the Divine Reason; its governing principle is Soul, presiding over the conjunction of the two, and to be thought of not as labouring in the task but as administering serenely by little more than an act of presence.

3. Nor would it be sound to condemn this Cosmos as less than beautiful, as less than the noblest possible in the corporeal; and neither can any charge be laid against its source.

The world, we must reflect, is a product of Necessity, not of deliberate purpose: it is due to a higher Kind engendering in its own likeness by a natural process. And none the less, a second consideration, if a considered plan brought it into being it would still be no disgrace to its maker – for it stands a stately whole, complete within itself, serving at once its own purpose and that of all its parts which, leading and lesser alike, are of such a nature as to further the interests of the total. It is, therefore, impossible to condemn the whole on the merits of the parts which, besides, must be judged only as they enter harmoniously or not into the whole, the main consideration, quite overpassing the members which thus cease to have importance . . .

There are, it would seem, degrees of participation: here no more than Existence, elsewhere Life; and, in Life, sometimes mainly that of Sensation, higher again that of Reason, finally Life in all its fullness. We have no right to demand equal powers in the unequal: the finger is not to be asked to see; there is the eye for that; a finger has its own business – to be finger and have finger power.

4. That water extinguishes fire and fire consumes other things should not astonish us. The thing destroyed derived its being from outside itself: this is no case of a self-originating substance being annihilated by an external; it rose on the ruin of something else, and thus in its own ruin it suffers nothing strange; and for every fire quenched, another is kindled . . .

This is not to accept the idea, sometimes urged, that order is an outcome of disorder and law of lawlessness, as if evil were a necessary preliminary to their existence or their manifestation: on the contrary order is the original and enters this sphere as imposed from without: it is because order, law and reason exist that there can be disorder; breach of law and unreason exist because Reason exists – not that these better things are directly the causes of the bad but simply that what ought to absorb the Best is prevented by its own nature, or by some accident, or by foreign interference. An entity which must look outside itself for a law, may be foiled of its purpose by either an internal or an external cause; there will be some flaw in its own nature, or it will be hurt by some alien influence, for often harm follows, unintended, upon the action of others in the pursuit of quite unrelated aims. Such living beings, on the other hand, as have freedom of motion under their own will sometimes take the right turn, sometimes the wrong.

Why the wrong course is followed is scarcely worth enquiring: a slight deviation at the beginning develops with every advance into a continuously wider and graver error – especially since there is the attached body with its inevitable concomitant of desire – and the first step, the hasty movement not previously considered and not immediately corrected, ends by establishing a set habit where there was at first only a fall.

Punishment naturally follows: there is no injustice in a man suffering what belongs to the condition in which he is; nor can we ask to be happy when our actions have not earned us happiness; the good, only, are happy; divine beings are happy only because they are good.

5. . . . One thing perishes, and the Cosmic Reason – whose control nothing anywhere eludes – employs that ending to the beginning of something new; and, so, when the body suffers and the Soul, under the afflic-

tion, loses power, all that has been bound under illness and evil is brought into a new set of relations, into another class or order. Some of these troubles are helpful to the very sufferers – poverty and sickness, for example – and as for vice, even this brings something to the general service: it acts as a lesson in right doing, and, in many ways even, produces good; thus, by setting men face to face with the ways and consequences of iniquity, it calls them from lethargy, stirs the deeper mind and sets the understanding to work; by the contrast of the evil under which wrong-doers labour it displays the worth of the right. Not that evil exists for this purpose; but, as we have indicated, once the wrong has come to be, the Reason of the Cosmos employs it to good ends; and, precisely, the proof of the mightiest power is to be able to use the ignoble nobly and, given formlessness, to make it the material of unknown forms . . .

11. Are we, then, to conclude that particular things are determined by Necessities rooted in Nature and by the sequence of causes, and that everything is as good as anything can be?

No: the Reason-Principle is the sovereign, making all: it wills things as they are and, in its reasonable act, it produces even what we know as evil: it cannot desire all to be good: an artist would not make an animal all eyes; and in the same way, the Reason-Principle would not make all divine; it makes Gods but also celestial spirits, the intermediate order, then men, then the animals; all is graded succession, and this in no spirit of grudging but in the expression of a Reason teeming with intellectual variety.

We are like people ignorant of painting who complain that the colours are not beautiful everywhere in the picture: but the Artist has laid on the appropriate tint to every spot. Or we are censuring a drama because the persons are not all heroes but include a servant and a rustic and some scurrilous clown; yet take away the low characters and the power of the drama is gone; these are part and parcel of it . . .

13. And we must not despise the familiar observation that there is something more to be considered than the present. There are the periods of the past and, again, those in the future; and these have everything to do with fixing worth of place . . .

It is not an accident that makes a man a slave; no one is a prisoner by chance; every bodily outrage has its due cause. The man once did what he now suffers. A man that murders his mother will become a woman and be murdered by a son; a man that wrongs a woman will become a woman, to be wronged . . .

15. These considerations apply very well to things considered as standing alone: but there is a stumbling-block, a new problem, when we think of all these forms, permanent and ceaselessly produced, in mutual relationship.

The animals devour each other: men attack each other: all is war without rest, without truce: this gives new force to the question how Reason can be author of the plan and how all can be declared well done . . .

This devouring of Kind by Kind is necessary as the means to the transmutation of living things which could not keep form for ever even though no other killed them: what grievance is it that when they must go their dispatch is so planned as to be serviceable to others?

Still more, what does it matter when they are devoured only to return in some new form? It comes to no more than the murder of one of the personages in a play; the actor alters his make-up and enters in a new role. The actor, of course, was not really killed; but if dying is but changing a body as the actor changes a costume, or even an exit from the body like the exit of the actor from the boards when he has no more to say or do, what is there so very dreadful in this transformation of living beings one into another? . . .

Murders, death in all its guises, the reduction and sacking of cities, all must be to us just such a spectacle as the changing scenes of a play; all is but the varied incident of a plot, costume on and off, acted grief and lament. For on earth, in all the succession of life, it is not the Soul within but the Shadow outside of the authentic man, that grieves and complains and acts out the plot on this world stage which men have dotted with stages of their own constructing . . .

16. . . . Now in the case of music, tones high and low are the product of Reason-Principles which, by the fact that they are Principles of harmony, meet in the unit of Harmony, the absolute Harmony, a more comprehensive Principle, greater than they and including them as its parts. Similarly in the Universe at large we find contraries – white and black, hot and cold, winged and wingless, footed and footless, reasoning and unreasoning – but all these elements are members of one living body, their sum-total; the Universe is a self-accordant entity, its members everywhere clashing but the total being the manifestation of a Reason-Principle. That one Reason-Principle, then, must be the unification of conflicting Reason-Principles whose very opposition is the support of its coherence and, almost, of its Being.

And indeed, if it were not multiple, it could not be a Universal Principle, it could not even be at all a Reason-Principle; in the fact of its being a Reason-Principle is contained the fact of interior difference. Now the maximum of difference is contrariety; admitting that this differentiation exists and creates, it will create difference in the greatest and not in the least degree; in other words, the Reason-Principle, bringing about differentiation to the uttermost degree, will of necessity create contrarieties: it will be complete only by producing itself not in merely diverse things but in contrary things.

17. . . . Thus, with the good we have the bad: we have the opposed movements of a dancer guided by one artistic plan; we recognize in his steps the good as against the bad, and see that in the opposition lies the merit of the design.

But, thus, the wicked disappear?

No: their wickedness remains; simply, their role is not of their own planning.

But, surely, this excuses them?

No; excuse lies with the Reason-Principle — and the Reason-Principle does not excuse them.

No doubt all are members of this Principle but one is a good man, another is bad — the larger class, this — and it goes as in a play; the poet while he gives each actor a part is also using them as they are in their own persons: he does not himself rank the men as leading actor, second, third; he simply gives suitable words to each, and by that assignment fixes each man's standing.

Thus, every man has his place, a place that fits the good man, a place that fits the bad: each within the two orders of them makes his way, naturally, reasonably, to the place, good or bad, that suits him, and takes the position he has made his own. There he talks and acts, in blasphemy and crime or in all goodness: for the actors bring to this play what they were before it was ever staged.

In the dramas of human art, the poet provides the words but the actors add their own quality, good or bad — for they have more to do than merely repeat the author's words — in the truer drama which dramatic genius imitates in its degree, the Soul displays itself in a part assigned by the creator of the piece.

As the actors of our stages get their masks and their costume, robes of state or rags, so a Soul is allotted its fortunes, and not at haphazard but always under a Reason: it adapts itself to the fortunes assigned to it, attunes itself, ranges itself rightly to the drama, to the whole Principle of the piece: then it speaks out its business, exhibiting at the same time all that a Soul can express of its own quality, as a singer in a song. A voice, a bearing, naturally fine or vulgar, may increase the charm of a piece; on the other hand, an actor with his ugly voice may make a sorry exhibition of himself, yet the drama stands as good a work as ever: the dramatist, taking the action which a sound criticism suggests, disgraces one, taking his part from him, with perfect justice: another man he promotes to more serious roles or to any more important play he may have, while the first is cast for whatever minor work there may be.

Just so the Soul, entering this drama of the Universe, making itself a part of the Play, bringing to its acting its personal excellence or defect, set in a definite place at the entry and accepting from the author its entire role – superimposed upon its own character and conduct – just so, it receives in the end its punishment and reward.

9

Lactantius, *The Wrath of God*

The *Divine Institutes* of the north African born Lucius Caecilius (or Caelius) Firmianus Lactantius (240 to ca. 320) was the first systematic account of Christian thought written for the cultivated classes of Rome. Relying more on classical authors than on scripture, Lactantius laid out Christian views by contrasting them with the dominant philosophies, Epicureanism and Stoicism. Lactantius' arguments for Christianity are not always persuasive, and his own ideas represent an uneasy synthesis of Judeo-Christian traditions with Pythagorean and Platonic dualism; he believed that God willed the existence of two opposing principles. (Jerome lamented: "If only Lactantius, almost a river of Ciceronian eloquence, had been able to uphold our cause with the same facility with which he overturns that of our adversaries!") *The Wrath of God* (313) is posterity's source for attributing the theodicy trilemma to Epicurus. Discussions of God and evil today rarely touch the divine attribute of anger which is Lactantius' theme – an indication of the Hellenistic pedigree of the "God of the philosophers."

Lactantius, "The Wrath of God (*De ira dei*)," in *The Minor Works*, trans. Sister Mary Frances McDonald, OP (The Fathers of the Church: A New Translation, vol. 54) (Washington, DC: Catholic University of America Press, 1965), 61–70, 89–93, 100–2, 106–7.

1. I HAVE OFTEN NOTICED, Donatus, that many people believe that which even some philosophers have held, namely, that God does not get angry. This is so either because the divine nature is only beneficent and it is not fitting to its most eminent and excellent power to harm anything, or because it has care for nothing at all, so that neither from its kindness should any good happen to us nor from its wickedness any evil. We must

refute their error, because it is a very great one, and because it tends to overthrow the foundation of human life, . . . Nor, however, are we so arrogant as to glory in the comprehension of the truth by our own ability, but we follow the doctrine of God who alone can know and reveal His secrets. The philosophers, having no part of this doctrine, have believed that the nature of things can be grasped by conjecture. Which is not at all possible, because the mind of man, walled in by the darksome dwelling-place of his body, is removed far from an accurate view of truth . . .

2. Although there are many steps by which an ascent is made to the dwelling of truth, it is not easy for anyone at all to be conducted to the summit. For when the eyes are blinded by the brilliance of the truth, those who cannot keep a firm hold are rolled back upon the level ground. The first step is to understand the false religions and to cast aside impious cults of things made by human hands. The next step, then, is to perceive with the mind that there is one supreme God whose power and providence brought about the world from the beginning and watches it in its continuance. The third step is to know His Minister and the Messenger whom He sent or delegated upon the earth, by whose teaching, being liberated from the error in which we are held and involved, and instructed in the worship of the true God, we might learn justice. From all of these steps, as I have said, there is a rapid and easy fall to ruin, unless the feet are fastened with unshakable stability. From the first step we see shaken off those who, although they understand the false things, yet do not find the true; and although they have despised the frail, earthly images, still the do not bring themselves to the worship of God, whom they know not, but marveling at the elements of the universe they venerate the sky, the land, the sea, the sun, and the other stars. But I have already demonstrated the stupidity of these in the second book of the *Divine Institutes*.

We say that those fall from the second step who, though they feel that there is one supreme God, yet at the same time are ensnared by the philosophers and, captivated by their false arguments, think about that only Majesty in a way other than that of strict truth. For they either say that God has no form, or they think that He is not moved by any affection because every affection is a mark of weakness, of which in God there is none at all.

But those fall headlong from the third step who, although they know the Ambassador of God, the very same Establisher of the divine and immortal temple, however, either do not receive Him or receive Him otherwise than faith demands . . .

Now, however, our discussion is against those who, having fallen from the second step, have wrong notions about the supreme God. For certain ones say that He neither is pleased nor angered with anything, but that, free from care and in repose, He enjoys the good of His own immortality. But others take away anger from God and leave kindness to Him, holding that a nature endowed with highest virtue, as it ought not to be hurtful, so ought to be kindly. Thus, all the philosophers agree in the matter of God's anger, but they differ about His kindness. But, in order that the discussion may proceed in order to the matter proposed, we must make an arrangement of this kind and follow it. Since anger and kindness are different and incompatible, either anger must be attributed to God and kindness withdrawn, or both must be equally withdrawn, or anger must be taken away and kindness attributed to Him, or both must be attributed to Him . . .

4. . . . [T]he school of Epicurus . . . teaches that just as there is no anger in God, so there is not even kindness. For since Epicurus thought that to do evil or do harm was foreign to God (an action which is generally sprung from the emotion of anger), he also took from Him beneficence because he saw it to be a consequence that, if God possessed anger, He would have kindness also. And so, lest he concede a vice to Him, he made Him deprived of a virtue also. "From this," he says, "He is blessed and incorrupt, because He cares for nothing, and He neither has any concern Himself, nor does He show it for another." . . .

5. The Stoics and some others are thought to have had a somewhat better notion about divinity, in holding that kindness resides in God but not anger. It is a very favorable and popular cant that this weakness of mind does not belong to God, that He who cannot be injured should believe that He has been injured by anyone; or that that serene and holy majesty should be aroused, disturbed, enraged, which is a mark of earthly frailty. For this opinion regards anger as an upsetting and disturbance of the mind, which is foreign to God . . .

They hold that so great, so pernicious an evil, however, ought to be absent from God. And if wrath and disturbance are absent from God because ugly and injurious, and if He does not do evil to anyone, there remains no other conclusion but that He is a gentle, tranquil, propitious, and kindly preserver. Thus, at length, He may be called both the common Father of all, and the best and greatest, which the divine and heavenly nature demands. For if among men it seems praiseworthy to help rather than to harm, to let live rather than to kill, to save rather than to destroy, and if not undeservedly innocence is counted among the virtues, and if he who does these things is loved, esteemed, adorned with all benedictions and honored with promises, and, in short, is judged because of his merits and benefits to be most like to God, how much more is it proper that God Himself, excelling in divinely perfect virtues and removed from every human failing, should act toward the whole race of men with heavenly kindness!

Things like that are said speciously and popularly, and they entice many to credence. Those who think these things approach, indeed, quite near to the truth, but they, in part, fall by considering the nature of the case only a little. For if God is not angry with the impious and the unjust, then, to be sure, neither does He love the pious and the just. So the error of those who take away both anger and kindness together is a more consistent one. For, in opposite things, it is necessary either to be moved toward each side or toward neither. Thus, he who loves the good also hates the evil, and he who does not hate the evil does not love the good, because, on one hand to love the good comes from hatred of evil, and to hate the evil rises from love of the good . . .

6. These are the opinions of the philosophers about God. No one of them has ever said anything else besides these things about God's anger. But if we have grasped that these things which were said were false, one last resort remains in which alone the truth can be found which has never been taken up nor at any time defended by the philosophers, namely that God's anger is a consequence of His kindness . . .

13. If one considers the entire administration of the world, he will certainly understand how true is the opinion of the Stoics who say that the world was arranged for our benefit. For all the things of which the world consists and which it generates from itself have been ordained to the usefulness of man. . . .

 . . . The Academics [skeptics], in arguing against the Stoics, usually ask why, if God made all things for the sake of men, many things contrary and harmful and injurious to us are also found both in the sea and on land. The Stoics refuted this, most foolishly not considering the truth. For they say that there are many things in the productions and numbers of animals, the utility of which still lies hidden, that will be discovered in the process of time, just as necessity and use have now discovered many things unknown to former ages. What utility, then, can be found in mice, in beetles, in serpents which are burdensome and harmful to man? . . .

They could have answered, however, rather briefly and very truly in this manner. When God made man as His image, the creation which was the summation of the divine workmanship, He breathed wisdom into him alone, so that he might subjugate all things to his power and sway and make use of all the advantages of the world. He put before him, however, both good things and evil, because He gave him wisdom, the whole reason of which rests in discerning good and evil. For no on can choose the better and know what is good unless he know at the same time, how to reject and avoid what things are evil. Both are mutually connected with each other, so that if one is removed, the other has to be taken away. Since good and evil things, therefore, have been set down, wisdom, at last, performs its work and, indeed, seeks the good for utility and rejects the evil for safety.

Therefore, as innumerable goods have been given which it might be able to enjoy, so also evils have been placed for it to avoid. For if there were no evil, no danger, nothing, in short, which could harm man, the whole matter of wisdom would be removed, nor would it even be necessary for man . . .

You see, then, that we need wisdom much more on account of evils. Unless these had been set before us, we would not be rational animals. And if this reasoning is true, which the Stoics could see in no way, that argument of Epicurus is dissolved also where he says: "God either wishes to take away evils and he cannot, or he can and does not wish to, or he neither wishes to nor is able, or he both wishes to and is able. If he wishes to and is not able, he is feeble, which does not fall in with the notion of god. If he is able to and does not wish to, he is envious, which is equally foreign to god. If he neither wishes to nor is able, he is both envious and feeble and therefore not god. If he both wishes to and is able, which alone is fitting to god, whence, therefore, are there evils, and why does he not remove them?" I know that quite a number of philosophers who defend the notion of providence are accustomed to be disturbed by this argument and, unwilling, they are almost forced to confess that God cares for nothing which Epicurus is especially aiming at. But when the reasoning has been examined, we easily bring this formidable argument to dissolution.

For God is able to do whatever He wishes, and there is no feebleness or envy in Him. He can, therefore, remove evils. But He may not wish to; nor is He, on that account, however, envious. This is the reason that He does not take them away since He granted wisdom at the same time, as I have explained, and there is more good and pleasure in wisdom than there is annoyance in evils. For wisdom brings it about that we know even

God and, through that knowledge, we seek immortality which is the highest good. And so, unless we first recognize the evil, we shall not be able to recognize the good. But Epicurus did not see this, nor anyone else, that if evils are taken away wisdom is equally removed; nor do any vestiges of virtue remain in man, the nature of which consists in sustaining and overcoming the bitterness of evils. So for the sake of the slight gain of having evils removed, we should be deprived of a very great good, a real good, and one proper to us. It stands therefore, that all things are proposed for man, evils and goods as well.

17. But the Stoics did not see that there is a difference between right and wrong, that wrath is just and also unjust, and because they did not find a cure of the thing, they wished to do away with it altogether. The Peripatetics, however, held that it should not be done away with but moderated; we have replied to them sufficiently in the sixth book of the *Institutes*. That the philosophers did not know what was the nature of anger is clear from their definitions which Seneca has enumerated in the books which he wrote *On Anger*. "Anger is," he says, "the desire of avenging an injury; or, as Posidonius says, the desire of punishing him by whom you think you have been hurt unfairly. Some define it thus: anger is the incitement of the mind to injure him who has either done an injury or wished to injure. Aristotle's definition is not much different from our own, for he says that anger is the desire of paying back pain." This is the unjust anger of which we spoke above, which resides even in the dumb beasts, and truly this should be restrained in man, lest through rage he should rush forth to exceedingly great evil. This cannot exist in God because He cannot be harmed, but it is found in man because he is frail. For injury inflames pain and pain causes a desire for revenge.

Where, then, is that just anger which causes reaction against offenders? This is surely not the desire for revenge since injury does not precede it. I do not speak of those who sin against the laws; for, although a judge can be angry with them without blame, still let us pretend that he ought to be of a calm mind when he inflicts punishment on the guilty, since he is a minister of the laws, not of his own mind or power, but thus they claim who try to root out anger. But I speak most of all about those who are within our power, for example, our slaves, children, wives, pupils. When we see these offend, we are aroused to reprove them. For it is necessary that things which are bad should displease one who is good and just, and he to whom evil is displeasing is moved when he sees it done. Therefore, we rise to punishment, not because we have been injured, but in order that discipline be preserved, morals corrected, and license suppressed. This is just anger. And just as it is necessary in man for the correction of evil, so certainly is it in God from whom example comes to man. As we ought to restrain those who are subject to our power, so also ought God to restrain the sins of all. And in order that He do this, He has to get angry, since it is natural for a good person to be moved and aroused at the sin of another. Therefore, they ought to make a definition thus: Anger is a movement of a mind arising to the restraint of offenses . . .

10

Augustine, *City of God*

John Hick calls Augustine of Hippo (354–430) the "fountainhead" of Christian theodicy. Like Lactantius a rhetor from Roman North Africa, Augustine was raised by a Christian mother but was briefly a Manichee before converting to Christianity. He is the most important source for subsequent Christian tradition of key arguments concerning evil, including evil as the privation of good, evil as a necessary part of the beauty of creation, and evil as the consequence of freedom of the will. Augustine is the origin also of the proto-dualist doctrine of original sin, a doctrine Paul Ricoeur has called "anti-gnostic Gnosis": "the previous content of the gnosis [dualism] is denied but the form of the discourse is reconstituted." Augustine's several views on the origin and nature of evils, many of which derive from Plotinus and the Stoics, do not fit comfortably together. Augustine developed them in the context of polemics against Manichees, Donatists, Pelagians, and, in the *Civitas dei* (*City of God*, 413–26), those who interpreted the sack of Rome as proof that converting to Christianity had been a mistake. When not polemicizing – in his *Confessions* (400) or *Enchiridion* (421), for instance – Augustine dwells less on the subject of evil, arguing that its privative nature makes seeking its origins pointless, and dangerous for the soul.

St. Augustine, *Concerning the City of God, against the Pagans*, trans. Henry Bettenson (Harmondsworth: Penguin, 1984), 447–9, 453–4, 473, 477–81.

Book XI

16. The distinctions among created things; and their different ranking by the scales of utility and logic

Now among those things which exist in any mode of being, and are distinct from God who made them, living things are ranked above inanimate objects; those which have the power of reproduction, or even the urge towards it, are superior to those who lack that impulse. Among living things, the sentient rank above the insensitive, and animals above trees. Among the sentient, the intelligent take precedence over the unthinking – men over cattle. Among the intelligent, immortal beings are higher than mortals, angels being higher than men.

This is the scale according to the order of nature; but there is another gradation which employs utility as the criterion of value. On this other scale we would put some inanimate things above some creatures of sense – so much so that if we had the power, we should be ready to remove these creatures from the world of nature, whether in ignorance of the place they occupy in it, or, though knowing that, still subordinating them to our own convenience. For instance, would not anyone prefer to have food in his house, rather than mice, or money rather than fleas? There is nothing surprising in this; for we find the same criterion operating in the value we place on human beings, for all the undoubted worth of a human creature. A higher price is often paid for a horse than for a slave, for a jewel than for a maidservant.

Thus there is a very wide difference between a rational consideration, in its free judgement, and the constraint of need, or the attraction of desire. Rational consideration decides on the position of each thing in the scale of importance, on its own merits, whereas need only thinks of its own interests. Reason looks for the truth as it is revealed to enlightened intelligence; desire has an eye for what allures by the promise of sensual enjoyment.

Now in establishing the order of rational beings, such weight is attached to the qualities of freedom and love, that although angels are superior to men in the order of nature, good men rank above the evil angels according to the criterion of righteousness. . . .

18. The beauty of the universe, made richer by God's providence, through the opposition of contraries

For God would never have created a man, let alone an angel, in the foreknowledge of his future evil state, if he had not known at the same time how he would put such creatures to good use, and thus enrich the course of the world history by the kind of antithesis which gives beauty to a poem. "Antithesis" provides the most attractive figures in literary composition: the Latin equivalent is "opposition," or, more accurately, "contraposition." The Apostle Paul makes elegant use of antithesis in developing a passage in the Second Epistle to the Corinthians,

By means of the arms of righteousness on right hand and left; through glory and ignominy, through infamy and high renown; as deceivers and yet truthful; as unknown and well-known; as dying, and here we are, alive; as punished, and yet not put to death; as full of grief, but always joyful; as in poverty, and yet enriching many others; as having nothing, while possessing everything. [2 Cor. 6, 7ff]

The opposition of such contraries gives an added beauty to speech; and in the same way there is beauty in the composition of the world's history arising from the antithesis of contraries – a kind of eloquence in events, instead of in words. This point is made very clearly in the book Ecclesiasticus, "Good confronts evil, life confronts death: so the sinner confronts the devout. And in this way you should observe all the works of the Most High; two by two; one confronting the other." [Ecclus. 33, 14f] . . .

22. The apparent evil in the universe

Thus we find a valid and appropriate explanation of creation in the goodness of God leading to the creation of good. When carefully considered and devoutly meditated it is an explanation which gives a final answer to all queries about the origin of the world. And yet there are heretics who fail to see this, because there are so many things which do not suit the inadequacy and frailty of our mortal flesh, which has already come under deserved punishment, many things which cause distress, like fire, cold, wild animals, and so on. They do not observe the value of those things in their own sphere and in their own nature, their position in the splendour of the providential order and the contribution they make by their own special beauty to the whole material scheme, as to a universal commonwealth. They even fail to see how much those same things contribute to our benefit, if we make wise and appropriate use of them. Even poisons, which are disastrous when improperly used, are turned into wholesome medicines by their proper application. By contrast, things which give pleasure, like food and drink, and even light itself, are experienced as harmful when used without restraint and in improper ways.

Divine providence thus warns us not to indulge in silly complaints about the state of affairs, but to take pains to inquire what useful purposes are served by things. And when we fail to find the answer, either through deficiency of insight or of staying power, we should believe that the purpose is hidden from us, as it was in many cases where we had great difficulty in discovering it. There is a useful purpose in the obscurity of the purpose; it may serve to exercise our humility or to undermine our pride. There is no such entity in nature as "evil"; "evil" is merely a name for the privation of good. There is a scale of value stretching from earthly to heavenly realities, from the visible to the invisible; and the inequality between these goods makes possible the existence of them all.

Now God is the great artificer in the great things; but that does not mean that he is an inferior artist in the small. For those small things are not to be measured by their size, which is next to nothing, but by the wisdom of their artificer. Take the case of a man's visible appearance. An eyebrow is virtually nothing compared with the whole body; but shave it off and what an immense loss to his beauty! For beauty does not depend on mere size, but on the symmetry and proportion of the component parts.

It is surely little cause for wonder that those who imagine that there is some evil in nature, which is derived and produced from a supposed "adverse first cause" of its own, refuse to accept that the reason for the creation of the universe was God's good purpose to create good. They believe instead that God was compelled to the creation of the vast structure of this universe by the utter necessity of repelling the evil which fought against him, that he had to mingle the nature of his creating, which was good, with the evil, which is to be suppressed and overcome, and that this good nature was thus so foully polluted, so savagely taken captive and oppressed that it was only with the greatest toil that he can cleanse it and set it free. And even then he cannot rescue all of it, and the part which cannot be purified from that defilement is to serve as the prison to enclose the Enemy after his overthrow.

This was the silly talk, or rather the delirious raving, of the Manicheans. They would not have babbled like this if they had believed in the truth, that the nature of God is unchangeable and completely incorruptible, and that nothing can do it harm; and if they had held, according to sound Christian teaching, that the soul, which could change for the worse through free choice, and could be corrupted by sin, is not a part of God, nor of the same nature as God, but is created by him, and is far inferior to its creator.

Book XII

2. *No existence is contrary to God. Non-existence is contrary to him, who is supreme existence*

The reason for saying all this is to prevent anyone from thinking, when we are talking of the apostate angels, that they could have had another kind of nature derived from some other First Principle, and that God was not the author of their nature. The quickest and easiest way for anyone to divest himself of that erroneous and blasphemous notion is to understand clearly what God said by the mouth of his angel when sending Moses to the children of Israel: God said, "I am HE WHO IS." [Exod. 3:14] For God is existence in a supreme degree – he supremely is – and he is therefore immutable. Hence he gave existence to the creatures he made out of nothing; but it was not his own supreme existence. To some he gave existence in a higher degree, to some in a lower, and thus he arranged a scale of existences of various natures . . .

Thus to this highest existence, from which all things that are derive their existence, the only contrary nature is the non-existent. Non-existence is obviously contrary to the existent. It follows that no existence is contrary to God, that is to the supreme existence and the author of all existence whatsoever. . . .

6. *The cause of the bliss of the good angels and of the misery of the bad*

The true cause . . . of the bliss of the good angels is their adherence to him who supremely is. When we ask the cause of the evil angels' misery, we find that it is the just result of their turning away from him who supremely is, and their turning towards themselves, who do not exist in that supreme degree. What other name is there for this fault than pride? "The beginning of all sin is pride." [Eccles. 10:13] Thus they refused to "keep watch for him who is their strength." [cf. Ps. 59:9] They would have existed in a higher degree, if they had adhered to him who exists in the highest degree; but in preferring themselves to him they chose a lower degree of existence.

This was the first defect, the first impoverishment, the first fault of that nature, which was so created that it did not exist in the supreme degree; yet it was capable of attaining blessedness in the enjoyment of him who supremely exists. Even when it turned away from him it did not become nothing; but it sank to a lower state of being, and therefore came to misery.

If you try to find the efficient cause of this evil choice, there is none to be found. For nothing causes an evil will, since it is the evil will itself which causes the evil act; and that means that the evil choice is the efficient cause of an evil act, whereas there is no efficient cause of an evil choice; since if anything exists, it either has, or has not, a will. If it has, that will is either good or bad; and if it is good, will anyone be fool enough to say that a good will causes an evil will? If it does, it follows that a good will is the cause of sin; and a more absurd conclusion cannot be imagined. Now if whatever is supposed to cause the evil will itself had an evil will, then I go on to ask what caused that evil will, and thus, to set a limit to these questions, I look for the cause of the first evil will. An evil will which is caused by an evil will is not the first; the first is that which has no cause, since cause precedes effect.

If it is replied that it had no cause, and therefore always existed, I ask whether it existed in any nature. If it was not in any nature, then it did not exist at all. If it existed in some nature, it vitiated that nature and corrupted it; it was harmful to it and therefore deprived it of good. Therefore a bad will cannot exist in a bad nature, but in a good but mutable nature, which this fault could harm. For if it did no harm, it obviously was not a fault, and if not a fault it could not rightly be called an evil will. And if it did harm, it must have done harm by destroying or diminishing good. Therefore an evil will could not be eternal in anything. For there would have to be a preceding goodness of nature for the evil will to harm and destroy. Then if that evil will was not eternally there, who created it?

The only possible answer is: Something which had no will. Was this, then, superior, inferior, or equal to it? If superior, it must be better. How then could it have no will? Must it not have a good will? The same applies if it is equal. When two things are equally good in will, the one cannot cause an evil will in the other. It remains that an inferior thing, without will, caused an evil will in the angelic nature, which first sinned.

But any existing thing which is inferior, even to the lowest depth of earth, is a nature and an existence, and therefore it is undoubtedly good, having its own mode and form in its own kind and order. How then can a good thing be the efficient cause of evil choice? How, I repeat, can good be the cause of evil? For when the will leaves the higher and turns to the lower, it becomes bad not because the thing to which it turns is bad, but because the turning is itself perverse. It follows that it is not the inferior thing which causes the evil choice; it is the will itself, because it is created, that desires the inferior thing in a perverted and inordinate manner.

Suppose that two men, of precisely similar disposition in mind and body, see the beauty of the same woman's body, and the sight stirs one of them to enjoy her unlawfully, while the other continues unmoved in his decision of chastity. What do we suppose to be the cause of an evil choice in the one and not in the other? What produced that evil will? It was not the beauty of the woman; for it did not have that effect in both of them, although both had precisely the same view of her. Was it the flesh of the beholder? Then why did it affect one and not the other? The mind? Why not the mind of both? For we assumed them to be alike in both mind and body. Are we to day that one of them was tempted by an unseen suggestion from a malignant spirit which would imply that he did not of his own will fall in with the suggestion, or whatever sort of persuasion it was?

It is just this consent, this evil choice which responded to the evil suggestion for which we are trying to find the efficient cause. Now if both experienced the same temptation, and one succumbed and consented to it, while the other remained unmoved, the only way to solve the difficulty is evidently to say that one refused and the other agreed to lose his chastity. What other reason could there be than this personal decision, given that their dispositions were precisely the same, in body and mind? The woman's beauty was seen by the eyes of both of them, the same beauty, in the same way. The unseen temptation was equally present in both of them. And so, if anyone tries to discover a cause which produced the evil choice in one of the pair, if he scrutinizes the situation carefully, no cause suggests itself.

Suppose we say that the man himself caused it? But before that evil choice he was simply a good nature, created by God, who is the immutable Good. Now we have assumed that these two men both had the same chance of seeing the beautiful body, and both were alike in mind and body, before the sight of the woman brought temptation; yet the one yielded to the persuasion of the Tempter to enjoy her unlawfully; the other resisted it. And so if anyone asserts that the man himself caused the evil choice, though before that evil choice he was undoubtedly good, he must go on to ask why he caused it. Was it because he is a natural being, or because his natural being is created from nothing? It will then be found that the evil choice takes its origin not from the fact that the man is a natural being, but from the fact that his natural being is created from nothing. For if nature is the cause of the evil will, can we help saying that evil is derived from good, and that good is the cause of evil? This must be so, if the evil will derives from a nature which is good. But how can this be? How can a nature which is good, however changeable, before it has an evil will, be the cause of any evil, the cause, that is, of that evil will itself?

7. We must not look for any efficient cause of the evil act of will

The truth is that one should not try to find an efficient cause for a wrong choice. It is not a matter of efficiency, but of deficiency; the evil will itself is not effective but defective. For to defect from him who is the Supreme Existence, to something of less reality, this is to begin to have an evil will. To try to discover the causes of such defection – deficient, not efficient causes – is like trying to see darkness or to hear silence. Yet we are familiar with darkness and silence, and we can only be aware of them by means of eyes and ears, but this is not by perception but by absence of perception.

No one therefore must try to get to know from me what I know that I do not know, unless, it may be, in order to learn not to know what must be known to be incapable of being known! For of course when we know things not by perception but by its absence, we know them, in a sense, but not-knowing, so that they are not-known by being known – if that is a possible or intelligible statement! For when with our bodily eyes, our glance travels over material forms, as they are presented to perception, we never see darkness except when we stop seeing. And we can only perceive silence by means of our ears, and through no other sense, and yet silence can only be perceived by not hearing. In the same way, the "ideas" presented to the intellect are observed by our mind in understanding them. And yet when these "ideas" are absent, the mind acquires knowledge by not-knowing. For "who can observe things that are lacking?" [cf. Ps. 19:12]

8. The perverse affection whereby the will defects from the immutable to the mutable good

This I do know; that the nature of God cannot be deficient, at any time, anywhere, in any respect, while things which were made from nothing are capable of deficiency. And such things have efficient causes, the higher their degree of reality, the greater their activity in good, for it is then that they are really active; but in so far as they fail, and consequently act wrongly, their activity must be futile, and they have deficient causes. I likewise know that when an evil choice happens in any being, then what happens is dependent on the will of that being; the failure is voluntary, not necessary, and the punishment that follows is just. For this failure does not consist in defection to things which are evil in themselves; it is the defection in itself that is evil. That is, it is not a falling away to evil natures; the defection is evil in itself, as a defection from him who supremely exists to something of a lower degree of reality; and this is contrary to the order of nature.

Greed, for example, is not something wrong with gold; the fault is in a man who perversely loves gold and for its sake abandons justice, which ought to be put beyond comparison above gold. Lust is not something wrong in a beautiful and attractive body; the fault is a soul which perversely delights in sensual pleasures, to the neglect of that self-control by which we are made fit for spiritual realities far more beautiful, with a loveliness which cannot fade. Boasting is not something wrong with the praise of men; the fault is in a soul which perversely loves the praise of others and cares nothing for the "witness of conscience." [2 Cor. 1:12] Pride is not something wrong in the one who love power, or in the power itself; the fault is in the soul which perversely loves its own power, and has no thought for the justice of the Omnipotent. By the same token, anyone who perversely loves the goodness of any nature whatsoever, even if he obtains the enjoyment of it, becomes evil in the enjoyment of the good, and wretched in being deprived of a higher good.

11

Pseudo-Dionysius,
On the Divine Names and
Mystical Theology

Although the majority of medieval theologians thought he was the Areopagite Dionysius mentioned in Acts 17:34 whose name he took, the thinker now known as "Pseudo-Dionysius" was probably a Syrian monk who lived in Athens around 500. Pseudo-Dionysius' theology united the Neoplatonism of Proclus (410–85) with patristic theology in views of the radical transcendence of God and the privative nature of evil which have been important for the Christian mystical tradition ever since. Acquaintance with the "negative theology" of which Pseudo-Dionysius was the father is important for understanding why the philosophical problem of evil was dismissed (or not noticed) by many medieval thinkers. Negative theology deconstructs the divine attributes, while "evil" is dissolved by the doctrine of privation.

Pseudo-Dionysius Areopagite, *On the Divine Names*, IV. 18, 19, 28, 30–3; *Mystical Theology*, 3–5; in *The Divine Names and Mystical Theology*, trans. John D. Jones (Milwaukee: Marquette University Press, 1980), 148–9, 157–61; 217–22.

On the Divine Names

IV. Concerning the Good, Light, Beauty, Love, Ecstasis and Zeal.
That Evil is Neither Be-ing, Nor From Be-ing, Nor in Beings

18. . . . [S]omeone will say, if the beautiful and good is loved, desired, and beloved by all, why do the many demons not desire the beautiful and good but, being inclined toward matter, fall from their angelic identities in their desire for the good and come to be the cause of all evils both to themselves and to all others which are said to be evil? Why in general do the tribe of demons not have a good form since they are brought forward

out of the good? How does a good which comes to be from the good come to be changed? What made them evil?

In general, what is evil? From what source does it subsist? In which beings is it? How did the good will to produce it? How was such a will possible? If evil is from another cause than the good, what cause is there for beings beside the good? How is there evil if there is providence? How does evil come to be at all? Why is it not destroyed? Finally, how does any being desire it instead of the good?

19. Such questions as these will perhaps be raised in a perplexed discourse. But we demand that one look away from such a discourse into the truth of the matter. Thus we shall at first say this freely and boldly. Evil is not from the good; if something is from the good, it is not evil. As what is cold does not bring forth fire, what is not good does not bring forth what is good. Now it is the nature of the good to produce and to conserve while that of evil is to destroy and to ruin. Thus if all beings are from the good, no being is from evil. Indeed, evil itself will not be, for it would be evil to itself.

If this is not so, evil will not be wholly evil but will have some aspect of the good according to which it is able to be at all. Further, if all beings desire the good and beautiful, if all these produce whatever they produce through producing what appears good, and if the intention of beings has the good as its source and end – for no being focuses on the nature of evil to produce what it produces – how will evil be in beings or be produced from such a good desire? Now if all beings are from the good and the good is beyond all beings, then that which is not is in the good. Thus, evil is neither be-ing (if not, [evil is] not wholly evil) nor not be-ing (for, nothing will be wholly non be-ing unless it is said to be in the good according to what is beyond being). The good lies beyond and is much prior to what simply is and what is not. Evil is neither in what is nor in what is not. Rather, it has a greater absence and estrangement from the good than what is not; it is more greatly without being than what is not.

28. We are not to accept the frequently asserted statement that evil is in matter as matter. For even matter has a share in the world, in beauty, and in form. But if matter is without these, without quality and formless, how can matter, which does not have the power in itself to be affected, produce anything? Otherwise, how is matter evil? For if it in no manner whatever is, it is neither good nor evil. But if it is somehow be-ing and all beings are from the good, then even matter is from the good. But then either the good is productive of evil and evil, which would be from the good

is good or evil is productive of good, which would then be from evil, and the good is evil. Or, again, these two sources are derived from some one higher source.

If someone says that matter is necessary for the completion of this world how is matter evil? For evil is one thing and what is necessary is another. How does the good bring forth something out of evil towards genesis? How is evil good if it flees from the nature of the good? How does matter generate and nurture nature if it is evil? For evil as evil is generative, nutritive. productive, and conservative of nothing at all. How will it be true to say that matter does not produce evil souls but draws the soul down to it? For many souls look to the good, but how would this come to be if the souls are entirely drawn down by matter into evil? In souls evil does not consist [in a freedom] from matter but in a disorderly and discordant motion. Moreover, if one says that these souls invariably follow matter, then unstable matter is necessary to those which are incapable of being established with respect to themselves. But how is evil what is necessary, or what is necessary, evil?

30. To speak in a summary fashion: the good is from one whole cause; evil is from many partial defects. God knows evil as good and with God the causes of evils are good-producing powers. But if evil is everlasting, creates, has power, is, and acts, whence does it obtain these? For either they are from the good or the good is from evil or they are both from other causes.

All that is in conformity with nature comes to be from defined causes. But if nature is without cause and undefined, it is not by nature. For that contrary to nature [does not come to be] by nature any more than what is contrary to art [comes to be] by art. But is not the soul the cause of evils, just as fire is the cause of what is hot, so that whatever comes in contact with it is full of evils? Is the nature of the soul good but does it not sometimes act in one manner and sometimes in another? But if the being and nature of the soul are evil, whence does it obtain these except from the good creative cause of the totality of what is? But if the soul is from this how is it evil in being? For all that is good is descended from the good creative cause. But if it is evil in its activities, this is not unchangeable. For if not, from whence does it obtain its virtues unless it itself has come to be good formed? Thus it remains that evil is a weakness and lack of the good.

31. The cause of all that is good is one. Hence if evil is opposed to the good, the causes of evil are many. But, clearly, those which are productive of evil are not logoi, powers, but weaknesses, impotencies, and a non-

symmetrical mixing of what is dissimilar. Now evils are neither unmoved nor do they always remain the same; rather, they are unlimited, undefined, and they move in others and are themselves unlimited. However, the source and goal of evils is the good. For all beings – both those which are good and those which are opposed to the good – are for the sake of the good. Even we do all that we do by desiring the good; for nothing focuses on evil to produce whatever it produces. Hence evil does not have subsistence but it is contrary to subsistence. Evil comes to be for the sake of the good and not for the safe of itself.

32. Evil is to be posited as accidental being. It emerges through another and not from its own proper source. Thus that which comes to be seems to be right because it comes to be for the sake of the good; yet in be-ing it is not right because what is not good is taken to be good. It is manifest that what is desired is other than that which comes to be. Hence evil is contrary to intention, contrary to the path, contrary to nature, contrary to cause, contrary to source, contrary to end, contrary to definition, contrary to wish, contrary to subsistence. Thus, evil is a privation, lack, weakness, non-symmetrical, failure, non-intention, non-beauty, non-life, non-logos, non-intellect, non-complete, unfounded, non-cause, undefined, unborn, inactive, weakness, dissimilar, unlimited, obscure, non-being, and itself be-ing in no manner whatever at all.

But then how is it possible for what is evil to be mixed with what is good? For that wholly apart from the good neither is nor is empowered. But if the good is be-ing, is willed, empowering, and active, how is it possible that something opposed to the good lacks being, desire, power, activity? Not all beings are evil to all others nor are the same things evil in every respect. For demons, evil is being contrary to a good formed intellect; for the soul, evil is being contrary to reason; for a body, evil is being contrary to nature.

33. How in general can there be evils if there is providence? Now evil as evil is neither be-ing nor in beings, and there is no being which is apart from providence. For, if constituted unmixed with the good, evil is not be-ing. If no being is without participation in the good, if evil is a lack of the good, and if no being lacks the beautiful and good, then the divine providence is in all beings and no being is without providence. For providence uses, in a good manner, even those which come to be evil with a view to the individual and the common benefit both of themselves and of others. Hence it properly provides for each being.

We do not accept the purposeless discourse of the many who say that providence should lead us unwillingly to virtue. For providence is not a destroyer of nature. Thus providence provides for the nature of each; it provides for the self-moving as self-moving. It provides for the whole and for individuals in a manner that is proper to the whole and to individuals insofar as the nature of those provided for receives the providential goodness which is given out by the universal and manifold goodness according to the analogy of each being.

Mystical Theology

III. The affirmative and negative theologies

In our *Outlines of Theology* we have treated what is of greatest importance in affirmative theology. That is, how the divine and good nature is called both one and three, what fatherhood and sonhood are in it, and what the theology of the spirit is. We have celebrated how the lights which remain in the heart of goodness have flowed forth from the immaterial and invisible good and, in so shooting up, have without wandering remained abiding and co-eternal in the good, in themselves, and in one another.

Further we have celebrated how Jesus, beyond being, took on being among human beings. We have celebrated whatever else is manifested in the writings in our *Outlines of Theology*. In the *Divine Names* we have celebrated how God is called good, be-ing, life, wisdom, power, and whatever else pertains to the intelligible divine names.

In our *Symbolic Theology* we have discussed the names which are transferred from sensibles to what is divine. Thus we have determined what are the divine forms, figures, parts, organs, places, worlds, curses, pains, sadnesses, indignations, drunks, hangovers, oaths, periods of ill sleep, periods of wakefulness, and whatever other sacredly molded forms which symbolize the divine form.

You will have noticed how much more extensive are the last than the former. Necessarily the *Outlines of Theology* and the unfolding of the *Divine Names* are more briefly spoken than the *Symbolic Theology*; for the higher we ascend the more our language becomes restricted by the more synoptic view of what is intelligible. Now, however, that we are to enter the darkness beyond intellect, you will not find a brief discourse but a complete absence of discourse and intelligibility. In affirmative theology the logos descends from what is above down to the last, and increases according to the measure of the descent towards an analogical multitude. But here, as we ascend from the highest to what lies beyond, the logos is drawn inward according to the measure of the ascent. After all ascent it will be wholly without sound and wholly united to the unspeakable.

But why, you will ask, do we begin the divine denial from the last of beings when we positioned the divine positions from the first beings? The reason is this: to position that beyond all position it is necessary to position the hypothetical affirmations from those which are more akin to it; in denying that beyond all denial, it is necessary to deny from those which are farthest away from it. For is it not life and goodness more than air and stones? And is it not drunkenness or not anger more than not spoken or not thought?

*IV. In preeminence, the cause of all that is sensible is
not anything sensible*

We say this of the cause of all be-ing beyond all:
It is
    not being-less,
  not lifeless,
  not without reason, not without intellect.
  Not body,
  not figure, not form,
  not what has quality, quantity, or mass,
    not in space,
  not visible,
  not what has sensible contact,
  not what has sensation or what is sensed,
  not what has disorder and confusion,
  not what is troubled by material passions,
  not powerless,
  not subjected to what happens to sensibles,
  not light in what lacks,
  not, and has not, alteration, destruction,
    privation, diminution, or anything else
    which pertains to what is sensed.

*V. In preeminence, the cause of all that is intelligible is
not anything intelligible*

Ascending higher we say:
It is
  not soul, not intellect,
  not imagination, opinion, reason and not
    understanding,
  not logos, not intellection,

not spoken, not thought,
not number, not order,
not greatness, not smallness
not equality, not inequality,
not likeness, not unlikeness,
not having stood, not moved, not at rest,
not powerful, not power,
not light,
not living, not life,
not being,
not eternity, not time,
not intellectual contact with it,
not knowledge, not truth,
not king, not wisdom,
not one, not unity,
not divinity,
not goodness,
not spirit (as we know spirit),
not sonhood, not fatherhood,
not something other [than that] which is known
  by us or some other beings,
not something among what is not,
not something among what is,
not known as it is by beings,
not a knower of beings as they are:
There is neither logos, name, or knowledge
  of it.
It is not dark nor light,
  not error, and not truth.
There is universally
  neither position nor denial of it.
While there are produced positions and denials of those
  after it,
we neither position nor deny it.

Since,
  beyond all position is
    the all-complete and single cause of all;
  beyond all negation:
    the preeminence of that
    absolutely absolved from all
    and beyond the whole.

12

Boethius, *The Consolation of Philosophy*

The Consolation of Philosophy was one of the most widely-read books of the middle ages. It was composed as its author, the Roman statesman and philosopher Anicius Manlius Severinus Boethius (ca. 480 to 525/6), awaited execution in prison on false charges of witchcraft and treason against his erstwhile employer, the Ostrogoth king Theodoric. *Consolation* describes the transformative conversation between a man (Boethius) resentful at the cruelty of fortune and Philosophy, who appears to him as a woman. By the end, Lady Philosophy's mostly Neoplatonic and Stoic arguments have helped Boethius transcend the point of view of human suffering; as Terrence Tilley has shown, Boethius' philosophical drama is a "script for reinscribing a self." While Boethius' translations of Aristotle's *Categories* and *On Interpretation* (he had hoped to translate all of Plato and Aristotle into Latin) became the basis of medieval scholasticism, *The Consolation of Philosophy* – rediscovered in the ninth century by Alcuin – was beloved especially by educated laypeople. Among its translators into English were Chaucer and Elizabeth I.

Boethius, *The Consolation of Philosophy*, IV.2–6; trans. V. E. Watts (Harmondsworth: Penguin, 1969), 116–46.

2. "Now, there are two things on which all the performance of human activity depends, will and power. If either of them is lacking, there is no activity that can be performed. In the absence of the will, a man is unwilling to do something and therefore does not undertake it; and in the absence of the power to do it, the will is useless. So that if you see someone who wants to get something which he cannot get, you can be sure that what he has been lacking is the power to get what he wanted."

"It is obvious," I said, "and cannot be denied."

"And if you see a man who has done what he wanted, you will hardly doubt that he had the power to do it, will you?"

"No."

"Therefore, men's power or ability is to be judged by what they can do, and their weakness by what they can't do."

"I agree."

"Do you, then, remember how earlier in the argument we reached the conclusion that the instinctive direction of the human will, manifested through a variety of pursuits, was entirely towards happiness?"

"I remember that this was proved as well."

"And you recall that happiness is the good itself and similarly that since they seek happiness, all men desire the good?"

"Not so much recall it, as hold it fixed in my mind."

"So that without any difference of instinct all men, good and bad alike, strive to reach the good."

"Yes, that follows."

"But surely men become good by acquiring goodness?"

"Yes."

"So that good men obtain what they are looking for?"

"It seems so."

"But if the wicked obtained what they want – that is goodness – they could not be wicked?"

"No."

"Since, then, both groups want goodness, and one obtains it and the other doesn't, surely there can be no doubt of the power of the good and the weakness of the bad?"

"Anyone who does doubt it is no judge either of reality or the logic of argument."

"Again," she said, "suppose there were two men who are set the same natural task, and one of them performs and completes it by natural action, while the other cannot manage the natural action, but uses another method contrary to nature, and does not actually complete the task but approximates to someone completing it; which would you say had the more power?"

"I can guess what you mean," I said, "but I would like to have it more clearly put."

"You will not deny that the action of walking is natural and human, will you?"

"No."

"And presumably you have no doubt that it is the natural function of the feet?"

"No, indeed."

"If, then, one man is able to proceed on foot and goes walking, and another lacks the natural function of the feet and tries to walk on his hands, which may properly be considered the more able or powerful?"

"Ask me another! No one could doubt that the man who can do the natural action is more able than the one who can't."

"Well, the supreme good is the goal of good men and bad alike, and the good seek it by means of a natural activity – the exercise of their virtues – while the bad strive to acquire the very same thing by means of their various desires, which isn't a natural method of obtaining the good. Or don't you agree?"

"Yes, for what follows is also obvious; from what I have already admitted it follows that the good are powerful and the bad weak." . . .

". . . I ask you, what is the cause of this flight from virtue to vice? If you say it is because they do not know what is good, I shall ask what greater weakness is there than the blindness of ignorance. And if you say that they know what they ought to seek for, but pleasure sends them chasing off the wrong way, this way too, they are weak through lack of self control because they cannot resist vice. And if you say they abandon goodness and turn to vice knowingly and willingly, this way they not only cease to be powerful, but cease to be at all. Men who give up the common goal of all things that exist, thereby cease to exist themselves. Some may perhaps think it strange that we say that wicked men, who form the majority of men, do not exist; but that is how it is. I am not trying to deny the wickedness of the wicked; what I do deny is that their existence is absolute and complete existence. Just as you might call a corpse a dead man, but couldn't simply call it a man, so I would agree that the wicked are wicked, but could not agree that they have unqualified existence. A thing exists when it keeps its proper place and preserves its own nature. Anything which departs from this ceases to exist, because its existence depends on the preservation of its nature.

"To the objection that evil men do have power, I would say that this power of theirs comes from weakness rather than strength. For they would not have the power to do the evil they can if they could have retained the power of doing good. This power only makes it more clear that they can do nothing, for if, as we concluded a short time ago [III.12], evil is nothing, it is clear that since they can only do evil, the wicked can do nothing."

3. ". . . It is clear that good deeds never lack reward, or crimes their appropriate punishment. The proper way of looking at it is to regard the goal of every action as its reward, just as the prize for running in the stadium is the wreath of laurels for which the race is run. Now, we have shown

that happiness is the very same good which motivates all activity; so that goodness itself is set as a kind of common reward of human activity. But goodness cannot be removed from those who are good; therefore, goodness never fails to receive its appropriate reward. So despite all the raging of the wicked, the wise man's crown of laurels will never fall from him or wither away. The wickedness of others can never wrest their individual glory from the good. If it was a borrowed glory that we prided ourselves upon, other people including the very one who conferred it on us could take it away; but since the glory is conferred on each one by his own goodness he will only lose his reward when he stops being good . . ."

". . . A short while ago you learned that all that exists is in a state of unity and that goodness itself is unity [III.11]; from which it follows that we must see everything that exists as good. This means that anything which turns away from goodness ceases to exist, and thus that the wicked cease to be what they once were. That they used to be human is shown by the human appearance of their body which still remains. So it was by falling into wickedness that they also lost their human nature. Now, since only goodness can raise a man above the level of human kind, it follows that it is proper that wickedness thrusts down to a level below mankind those whom it has dethroned from the condition of being human."

4. Then I said, "I agree, and I see the justice of saying that though they retain the outward appearance of the human body, wicked people change into animals with regard to their state of mind. But I could have wished that no freedom was allowed to the fury of cruel and wicked-minded men to bring destruction on the good."

"It's not a question of freedom," she said, "as I will show at the appropriate point. But supposing the freedom they are believed to enjoy were removed, it would to a large extent mean relieving criminals of their punishment. It may seem incredible to some, but it must be the case that the wicked are less happy if they achieve their desires than if they are unable to do what they want. For, if desiring something wicked brings misery, greater misery is brought by having had the power to do it, without which the unhappy desire would go unfulfilled. So, since each stage has its own degree of misery, if you see people with the desire to do something wicked, the power to do it and the achievement, they must necessarily suffer a triple degree of misfortune. . . ."

Then I said, "When I consider your arguments, I think nothing more true could be spoken. But when I turn to the opinions of ordinary men, few would even grant you a hearing, let alone believe you."

"It is true," she said. "Their eyes are used to the dark and they cannot raise them to the shining light of truth. They are like birds whose sight is sharpened by night and blinded by day. So long as they look only at their own desires and not the order of creation, they think of freedom to commit crimes and the absence of punishment as happy things. . . ."

5. Then I said, "Yes, I can see there is a kind of happiness and misery which are inseparable from the very actions of good and bad men. But I believe that there is both good and bad in the actual fortune of ordinary people. No wise man prefers being in exile, being poor and disgraced to being rich, respected, and powerful, and to remaining at home and flourishing in his own city. . . . I would be less surprised if I could believe that the confusion of things is due to the fortuitous operations of chance. But my wonder is only increased by the knowledge that the ruling power of the universe is God. Sometimes He is pleasant to the good and unpleasant to the bad, and other times He grants the bad their wishes and denies the good. But since He often varies between these two alternatives, what grounds are there for distinguishing between God and the haphazards of chance?"

"It is not surprising," she said, "if ignorance of the principle of its order makes people think a thing is unplanned and chaotic. But even if you don't know the reason behind the great plan of the universe, there is no need for you to doubt that a good power rules the world and that everything happens aright.

6. "No doubt your objection will be that it is impossible for there to be a more unjust confusion than when the fortune of good men and bad alike continually vary between adversity and prosperity. And I shall ask you if men have such soundness of mind as to be infallible in their judgement of who is good and who is bad. No, human judgements clash in this matter and some people think the same men deserve reward as other think worthy of punishment.

"Supposing, however, we grant that someone may be able to judge between good and bad, it will hardly enable him to see the inner hidden temperament, to borrow a term from physics, of men's minds. Indeed, your surprise is like that of a man who does not know why in the case of healthy bodies sweet things agree with some and bitter things with others, or why some sick people are helped by gentle remedies, others by sharp ones. But it is no surprise to the doctor who knows the difference between the manner and temper of health and of sickness. Now, we know that in the case of the mind health means goodness and sickness means wickedness. And that the protector of the good and scourge of the wicked is none other than God, the mind's guide and physician. He looks out from the watch-tower of Providence, sees what suits each person, and applies to him whatever He knows is suitable. . . . ;

". . . Some people are excessively afraid of suffering for which they actually have the endurance; others are full of scorn for suffering they cannot in fact bear. Both kinds she brings to self discovery through hardship. Some men at the price of a glorious death have won a fame that generations will venerate; some indomitable in the face of punishment have given others an example that evil cannot defeat virtue. There is no doubt that it is right that these things happen, that they are planned and that they are suited to those to whom they actually happen.

"The fact, too, that the wicked have their ups and downs of fortune is due to the same causes. When they suffer, no one is surprised, because everyone considers they deserve ill; and their punishments both deter others from crime and correct those on whom they are inflicted. And when they prosper, it is a powerful argument to good men about the kind of judgement they should make of such happiness as they often see wait upon the wicked. . . .

"And so a sovereign Providence has often produced a remarkable effect – evil men making other evil men good. For some, when they think they suffer injustice at the hands of the worst of men, burn with hatred for evil men, and being eager to be different from those they hate, have reformed and become virtuous. It is only the power of God to which evils may also be good, when by their proper use He elicits some good result. For a certain order embraces all things, and anything which departs from the order planned and assigned to it, only falls back into order, albeit a different order, so as not to allow anything to chance in the realm of Providence.

"But as the *Iliad* puts it,

'Tis hard for me to speak as though a God.

And it is not allowed to man to comprehend in thought all the ways of the divine work or expound them in speech. Let it be enough that we have seen that God, the author of all natures, orders all things and directs them towards goodness. He is quick to hold all that He has created in His own image, and by means of the chain of necessity presided over by Fate banishes all evil from the bounds of His commonwealth. Evil is thought to abound on earth. But if you would see the plan of Providence, you would not think there was evil anywhere . . ."

Before Theodicy

13

Anselm of Canterbury, *On the Fall of the Devil*

Anselm (1033–1109), the "Father of Scholasticism," argued that almost all revealed truths could be rationally demonstrated: "What we hold by faith regarding the divine nature and its persons – excluding the topics of incarnation – can be proven by compelling reasons apart from appeal to authority." Before he (evidently unwillingly) was made Archbishop of Canterbury, he spent many years at the monastery of Bec (France). *De casu diaboli* (*On the Fall of the Devil*) and the *Proslogion* were written at Bec at about the same time. The *Proslogion* famously argues from the "consideration" of "something than which nothing greater can be thought" to a God who must of necessity exist, be omnipotent, wise, merciful yet impassable, etc. In Anselm's clarification and enrichment of the logic of evil as privation, which was definitive for later scholasticism, Augustinian theological commitments are tempered by the attention to common parlance characteristic of Aristotle.

Anselm of Canterbury, "On the Fall of the Devil", in *The Major Works*, eds. Brian Davies and G. R. Evans (Oxford: Oxford University Press, 1998), 206–10, 230–2.

10. How evil seems to be something

Student. When you say that evil is the privation of the good, I agree, but none the less I see that good is a privation of evil. And just as I perceive in the privation of evil something else comes to be that we call good, so I note that in the privation of the good something comes to be that we call evil. Wherefore although evil can be shown by some arguments to be nothing, since evil is only vice or corruption, which are only in some

essence, and the more they are there, the more toward nothingness they
turn it, and if the same essence came wholly to nothing, vice and corruption would be found to be nothing; although, I say, in these and other
ways evil can be proved to be nothing, my mind cannot agree except on
the basis of faith alone, unless we can eliminate the difficulties that prove
to me on the contrary the reality of evil.

For when the word "evil" is heard, our hearts irrationally tremble at
what they understand in the meaning of this word, if it means only
nothing. Again, if this word "evil" is a noun, it is significant. But if it is
significant, it signifies. But it can only signify something. How then can
evil be nothing if its name signifies something? Finally since there seems
to be such tranquillity and repose while justice remains, in many instances
justice seems nothing more than the quieting of evil, as with charity and
patience, whereas when justice goes, such diverse and onerous and multiple feelings occupy the mind which like a cruel master forces this poor
homunculus to be concerned with so many laborious and base actions
and to take on the grave burden of these actions: if it is thus, it will seem
strange that nothing gives rise to all these.

11. That evil and nothing cannot be shown from their names to be something but only a quasi-something

Teacher: I do not think it is absurd for you to say that nothing is something, since no one can deny that "nothing" is a noun. If it cannot be
shown that nothing is real just because there is the word "nothing", how
would one think to prove that evil is real just because there is the word
"evil"? . . .

It is clear that the word "nothing" in no way differs in meaning from
the expression "not something". Moreover it is evident that "not something" indicates that every thing, whatever expresses any reality, should be
excluded from the mind nor anything whatsoever of its meaning be
retained. But since the negation of a thing must necessarily include in its
meaning the thing negated – no one could understand what is meant by
non-man unless he understands what man is – this term not-something,
by negating what is, signifies something. Since then taking away everything that is something signifies nothing, it makes up the essence that must
be retained in the mind of the listener: therefore "not-something" signifies no thing or reality.

The expression "non-being" then, according to these diverse considerations, in a way signifies reality and being and yet in no way signifies

reality and being, for it signifies them by way of denial and not positively. Thus the word "nothing" which does away with everything that is something and by so doing does not signify nothing but something, does not do so positively. So it is not necessary that nothing be something just because its name in a certain way signifies something; rather, it is necessary that nothing be nothing, because its name signifies something in this way. Similarly, there is nothing against the word "evil" being meaningful if it thus signifies something by excluding it and positively signifies nothing.

S. I cannot deny that, following your argument, the word "nothing" in some way signifies something, but it must be understood that the something which in this way is signified is not called "nothing," nor when we hear the word do we take it for the reality that is signified in this way. So I ask why this name is spoken, and what do we understand when we hear it: what I want to ask is, what is it? This is what the word properly signifies and since a word is because it signifies it, not because in the way stated above it signifies by denying something. Indeed it is accounted a name of its signification, which is called "nothing." I ask how that can be something if it is properly called "nothing," or how it is nothing if its name signifies something, or how something and nothing can be the same. That is what I am asking about "evil" and of what it means and what "evil" is the name of.

T. And you rightly pose this problem because although by the foregoing argument both "nothing" and "evil" signify something, evil and nothing are not what they signify. But there is another argument according to which they signify something and that something is signified, but not a true but a quasi-something.

There are many cases where the grammatical form does not correspond with the reality signified. For example, "to fear" is an active verb, grammatically speaking, but in reality to fear is passive. So too "blindness" grammatically indicates some thing, but in reality it is nothing positive. Just as we say that someone has sight and that sight is in him, so we say that he has blindness and that blindness is in him, although blindness is not something real but the lack of it, and to have blindness does not mean to say one has something but rather is deprived of it. In fact blindness is nothing other than non-sight or the absence of sight where it ought to be found. But non-sight or the absence of sight is certainly no more real where it ought to be found than where it ought not to be found. Many other things are expressed as reality from the point of view of the form of discourse, because we speak of them as if they existed, when no positive reality is involved.

It is in this way that "evil" and "nothing" signify things, that is, what is signified is not something in reality but only in grammatical form. "Nothing" signifies simply non-being or the lack of all that is real. And evil is only non-good or the absence of good where good ought to be found. But that which is only an absence of reality is certainly not real. Hence evil in truth is nothing and nothing is not real, and yet in a way evil and nothing are something because we speak of them as if they were real, as when we say, "He did nothing" and "He did evil," that is, that what he did was nothing or evil – in the same way, that we say "I did something and I did a good thing." So we deny that, what someone says is in any way something: "What you say is nothing." For "what" or "this" which are properly said only of realities, here are not said of realities but of quasi-realities. . . .

26. What horrifies about the word "evil" and the works that injustice is said to do if both are nothing

S. Although you have responded to all my questions, I still wait for you to explain what horrifies us when we hear the word "evil" and what causes the actions of injustice such as in theft, and lust – if evil is nothing.

T. I will reply briefly. That evil which is vice is always nothing; the evil that is suffering is sometimes without doubt nothing, as with blindness, and sometimes real, like sadness and sorrow, and we always detest the suffering that is something real. When then we hear the word "evil" we do not fear the evil that is nothing, but that which is something real and follows the lack of the good. Many sufferings follow on injustice and blindness and those in fact are nothing, but these sufferings are evil and are something real and it is these we fear when we hear the word "evil."

When we say that injustice causes theft or that blindness causes a man to fall in a ditch, we do not intend to say that injustice and blindness cause something real, but that if justice were in the will and sight in the eye, theft would not come about and one would not fall in the ditch. It is as when we say that the absence of the pilot causes the ship to go aground, or the absence of a bridle makes the horse run off, which are equivalent to: if the pilot and bridle had been present the wind would not have taken the ship nor the horse run off. For as the ship is governed by the pilot, so is the horse by the bridle; so too a man's will is governed by justice and his feet by sight.

S. You have satisfied me with respect to the evil that is injustice, such that all that this question raised in my mind has been clarified. The question concerning this evil seems to arise from the fact that, if it were some essence, it would be caused by God, from whom it is necessary that every thing that is comes, and from whom it is impossible that injustice and sin come. But the evil that in some way is something seems to cause difficulties for the true faith.

27. How evil came to an angel when he was good

S. . . . So I ask you whence comes for the first time that evil which is called injustice or sin in the angel who was created just.

T. Tell me whence comes the non-being in something real.

S. That which is nothing neither comes nor goes.

T. Then why do you ask where the evil that is injustice comes from?

S. Because when justice departs from where it was, we say that injustice has come.

T. Speak more clearly and properly, and ask me about the departure of justice. A well-formed question is easier to answer, whereas the ill-formed one makes it more difficult.

S. Why does justice depart from the just angel?

T. Speaking properly, it does not depart from him, but he abandons it by willing what he ought not.

S. Why does he abandon it?

T. When I say that by willing what he ought not he abandons it, I show openly why and how he abandons it. He abandons it because he wills what he ought not to will, and in this way it is by willing what he ought not that he abandons it.

S. Why does he will what he ought not?

T. No cause precedes this will except that he can will.

S. And he wills because he can?

T. No. Because the good angel could will similarly yet does not. No one wills what he can will because he can, without some other cause, although if he is unable to will he never does.

S. Why then does he will?

T. Only because he wills. For this will has no other cause by which it is forced or attracted, but it was its own efficient cause, so to speak, as well as its own effect.

14

Hildegard of Bingen, to the congregation of nuns

Hildegard (1098–1179), Benedictine abbess of the convent at Bingen in Germany (which she helped found), was perhaps the most influential woman of her time. Famous as a physician and healer and in our own time celebrated as a composer, Hildegard was a visionary. The *Scivias* (1141–52) described 26 prophetic and in part apocalyptic visions Hildegard had had since childhood, visions which, she claimed, were not the result of ecstasy. She promoted her causes in misogynist times by insisting that, weak woman that she was, all her writings were dictated by the Holy Spirit. The letter below (from before 1153), to the nuns in her charge, presents the drama of fall and redemption as a story about the purity and danger of woman – giving a cosmic significance to the nuns' lives. (Parts of the letter were presumably intended to be sung by the community.)

The Letters of Hildegard of Bingen, letter no. 192; trans. Joseph L. Baird and Radd K. Ehrman (New York: Oxford University Press, 1998), 159–63.

The Lord says to His daughters: In ancient times the Holy Spirit inspired certain persons from a certain nation that had not yet become deceitful. Oh, Oh, Oh! Afterwards, God placed Wisdom in the dawn.

Ach, Ach, Ach! And He created in Himself a means to serve His purpose: a lofty mountain of justice. Woe, Woe, Woe! Now the justice of that mountain has become like a shadow because of the gluttony of those going astray. But you, O strength of the mountain, you will not crumble completely, but will rise up into the high window where many eagles will look upon you.

O how great that entity, which did not lie hidden in any thing, so that, neither made nor created by anyone, it remains forever in itself alone. O life, you arose in the dawn when the great King mercifully revealed Wisdom, which in ancient days was with the Wise Man – mercifully, because woman entered death through the hole that the ancient traitor opened up. O grief, O sorrow, O woe for those who were formed in the woman!

O dawn, in the form of the first rib, you washed these things away. O feminine form, sister of Wisdom, how glorious you are, for mighty life arose in you, and death will never choke it off. Wisdom lifted you up so that all creatures were adorned by you and brought into a better part than they had received in the beginning. Wherefore:

> Hail, O greenest bough,
> You who came forth in the mighty wind
> of the saints, searching.
>
> When the time came
> that you flourished in your branches,
> you were greeted with "Ave, ave,"
> for the heat of the sun brought forth from you
> a fragrance like the aroma of balsam.
>
> In you the lovely flower blossomed
> and sent forth a fragrance
> to all the dried-up spices.
> And they all burst forth
> in full viridity.
>
> Then the heavens poured dew upon the grass
> and all the earth rejoiced,
> because her womb produced grain,
> and the birds of the air
> made their nests on that bough.
>
> Then food was produced for mankind,
> and those who feasted rejoiced with great joy.
> O sweet Virgin,
> joy is ever found in you.
>
> But Eve scorned all these things.
>
> Now, however, give praise to the Most High.
>
> Alleluia!
> O branch that intercedes for us,
> your holy womb

conquered death
and illumined all creation
with the beautiful flower
that arose from the sweet chastity
of your unsullied modesty.

What does all this mean?

O how great a miracle it is
that the King entered
into a submissive feminine form.
God acted thus
because humility is supreme over all things.
How great the felicity is
in that sex
because that malice –
which had flowed from woman –
was, later, wiped away by woman,
and she brought forth
the sweetest fragrance of the virtues,
and adorned heaven
more than woman had ever troubled earth.

O radiant Virgin Mary,
illumined
by divine radiance,
infused with the Word of God:
your womb flowered forth
at the entry of the Spirit of God,
Who breathed upon you
and sucked out of you
that which Eve contracted
when she cut herself off from chastity,
infected with contagion
at the devil's deception.

You miraculously concealed in yourself
unsullied flesh
in accordance with God's plan
when the Son of God
flourished in your womb.
Holy divinity brought Him forth

contrary to the law of the flesh
which Eve had established.
He was joined to wholeness
in the holiness of the womb.

Listen then, O human being, to this miracle:

Hail, Mary,
Author of life
by reestablishing salvation,
you who overthrew death
and crushed the serpent under your heel.
Eve raised herself before the serpent,
stiff-necked
and full of pride.
But you crushed the serpent
when you bore the Son of God,
come down from Heaven.

The Spirit of God
breathed Him forth.

O sweet, loving mother, hail.
You brought forth into the world
your Son sent from Heaven.

What does this mean?

O refulgent mother
of sacred healing,
through your holy Son
you have poured unguents
into the weeping wounds of death
that Eve wrought
as torments for our souls.
You destroyed death
and raised up life.

Pray for us
to your Son,
O star of the sea,
Mary.
O source of life,

gladsome ornament,
sweetness of all delights,
which will never fail in you!

Today has the closed portal
opened unto us,
the gate which the serpent had choked off through woman.
Therefore, the flower born of the Virgin Mary
radiates in the dawn.

Because a woman brought death into the world,
the radiant Virgin laid death low.
Therefore, supreme blessing is found
in the feminine form
beyond all creation,
for God became man
in that sweet, blessed Virgin.

O how precious is the virginity
of this Virgin,
who kept her gate closed,
and whose womb
was so infused with the heat
of holy divinity
that a flower burgeoned in her.

And the Son of God
came forth, like the dawn,
from her secret place.

Thus the sweet seed,
her Son,
opened Paradise
through her closed womb.

Let the earth hear, let the elements tremble. Why? Because all creation
joyfully received the One born of the Virgin, so that the heavens glowed
like the dawn at the sudden appearance of the virtues and at the radiant
strength that flashed in those virtues. For the Sun of truth breathed forth
the complete sanctification of souls through that Virgin.

Therefore, O my daughters, hear Me, the living fountain, speaking to
you: Be filled with holy and elect viridity, not with the power of the devil
that, sorely wounded, abandoned God. The good eye sees these words, the

good ear hears them, but a mind of stone does not perceive them, for it abandons God and embraces the devil, thereby raising a lofty tower in hell. O wholesome and upright desires, how resplendent you are when your sweet fragrance rises to God! But how hard it is for the human race to cast off the lust for worldly things.

Therefore, let my daughters hear these words: Primordial sin rashly and deceitfully choked off human work through a woman – woman, that turreted mountain in which the proper forms of upright feelings should have appeared, but which was instead cast out into lamentation. For the malevolent thief and great deceiver came and wrapped those feelings in the blackness of swift-moving sin and the stench of pollution, so that they could not be pure. Alas, alas, alas, for creation! Woe, woe, woe, for the world! Alas, alas, alas, for that perverse desire that inclined to death when it was cut off from heaven and set in hell, where the devil vomited it forth when he choked off innocence.

But the Son of God left this darkened desire behind, and it could not pass through the light. He came by another way where there was no guileful nature, and so through Him innocence rose again. And so He brought out the sons of Adam, born of perverted desire, drawing them to Himself by the wounds caused by the nails of the cross driven into His flesh. Thus He broke the bonds that bound them in the chain of the taste for wicked works, the teat of iniquity, and the delight of sin.

Therefore, O my daughters, remembering My Son, you ought always to crucify yourselves to your own concerns, so that you do not falter because of the deceitful tyrant. And, lest you fall from Me, do not let the poison of bitter wrath grow among you, nor a mind ablaze with pride, nor the vanity that rends asunder the glory of sanctification. Rather, let your joy be complete in Me [cf. John 16:24], and let your reward be the kingdom of heaven, and let holy peace be among you.

O daughters of Jerusalem [cf. Cant. 1:4], the Great Physician wants you to reach up to the highest desire for good, and no one can separate you from Him. And so through the holy gift of God "increase and multiply" [Gen. 1:22] over the mountains and hills of sanctification. Thus, may the earth cover with blessing whoever wishes to bless you, but whoever wishes to curse you will be cursed by the mighty Judge. For you are My mirror.

But what are you thinking in your hearts? [cf. Mark 2:8] You will find in Me that which I wish to perfect in you. What is this? It is justice. May you be steeped in the gift of God's grace so that you will not be overcome by the enemy. Therefore, do not abandon Me.

15

Moses Maimonides, *Guide of the Perplexed*

Moses Maimonides (1135–1204), the greatest medieval Jewish philosopher,
started his life in Cordoba and ended in Egypt. After writing important com-
mentaries (including the *Mish Torah*), Maimonides composed the *Guide of
the Perplexed* (1176–91), arguing for a more rational form of Judaism. The
Guide presents itself as ministering to a perplexed youth, reassuring him that
his *halakhic* way of living is worth continuing. Its argument seems to be that
while neither Biblical creationism nor Aristotelian eternalism can be proved,
the former is for various reasons preferable. Building on the work of Muslim
scholars, Maimonides articulated an uncompromising negative theology and
a profound critique of idolatry. His interpretation of the Book of Job shows
the cosmopolitan context of his thought (the Mu'tazila and Ash'ariyya mentioned below were important schools of Muslim thought), as well as his intel-
lectualism – his view that knowledge of truth (not just of goodness) is the
way to the divine.

Moses Maimonides, *The Guide of the Perplexed*, iii.22–3, trans. Schlomo Pines
(Chicago: University of Chicago Press, 1963), II: 486–97.

The story of *Job*, which is extraordinary and marvellous, . . . is a parable
intended to set forth the opinions of people concerning providence . . . I
refer to the assertion that a righteous and perfect man, who was just in
his actions and is most careful to avoid sins, was stricken – without his
having committed a sin entailing this – by great and consecutive calamities with respect to his fortune, his children, and his body . . . [T]he pro-
logue – I mean the discourse of *Satan*, that of God addressed to *Satan*,
and the giving over [of Job to Satan] – is indubitably, in the view of everyone endowed with intellect, a parable. However, it is not a parable like all

others, but one to which extraordinary notions *and things that are the mystery of the universe* are attached. Through it great enigmas are solved, and truths than which none is higher become clear . . .

[I]t mentions that this righteous and perfect man was delivered into the hands of this *Satan* and that all the calamities that befell him with respect to his fortune, his children, and his body, were caused by *Satan*. After having made this supposition it begins to set down speeches of people engaged in speculation with regard to this occurrence. Thus it mentions a certain opinion and ascribes it to *Job*, and ascribes other opinions to his friends. I shall make them clearly known to you; I am referring to those opinions about which there has been a conflict of thoughts and that are concerned with a story the cause of the whole of which was *Satan*; though all of them, *Job* and his friends, thought that God had done it Himself and not through the intermediary of *Satan*. The most marvellous and extraordinary thing about this story is the fact that knowledge is not attributed in it to *Job*. He is not said to be a *wise* or a *comprehending* or an *intelligent man*. Only moral virtue and righteousness in action are ascribed to him. For if he had been *wise*, his situation would not have been obscure for him, as will become clear . . .

The dictum [of Scripture] referring to *the sons of God* says in the two passages: *To present themselves before the Lord* [1:6, 2.1]. *Satan*, however, though he came among their crowd and multitude a first and a second time, is not said in the first passage *to present himself*. In the second passage, however, it says: *And Satan came also among them to present himself before the Lord* [2:1] . . . [T]he meaning of the words, *to present themselves before the Lord*, is that they exist as subject to His order in what He wills . . . It is consequently manifest that the status of *the sons of God* and that of *Satan* in what exists are not identical. For *the sons of God* are more permanent and lasting, while [Satan] also has a certain portion, below them in what exists.

Furthermore one of the marvels of this parable consists in the fact that when it mentions that *Satan* roams especially over the earth and accomplishes certain actions, it also makes clear that he is forbidden to gain dominion over the soul, that he has been given dominion over all terrestrial things, but that he is kept away by a barrier from the soul. This is the meaning of its saying: *Only spare his soul* [2:6]. I have already explained to you that in our language the term *soul* is equivocal and that it is applied to the thing that remains of man after death; this is the thing over which *Satan* has no dominion . . .

If it is supposed that the story of *Job* happened, the first thing that occurred was a matter on which there was general agreement between the five,

I mean *Job* and his friends, namely, that everything that had befallen *Job* was known to Him, may He be exalted, and that God had caused these misfortunes to befall him. All of them were also agreed that injustice was not permitted to Him and wrongdoing not to be ascribed to Him. You will find these notions frequently also in the discourse of *Job*. If now you consider the discourse of the five in the course of their conversation, you may almost think that whatever one of them says is said also by all the others, so that the same notions are repeated and overlap . . . All his friends are also agreed that everyone who does good obtains a reward and that everyone who does evil is punished; . . . This, however, is not the purpose of this story as a whole; for this purpose is rather to show the peculiarity of each of them and to make known each one's opinion concerning this story: namely, that the greatest and heaviest misfortunes befall the most perfect individual, who was the most unblemished of them in righteousness. *Job's* opinion on this is that this happening proves that the righteous man and the wicked are regarded as equal by Him, may He be exalted, because of His contempt for the human species and abandonment of it. This is what he says in all his speeches: *It is all one – therefore I say: He destroyeth the innocent and the wicked. If the flood slay suddenly, He will mock at the calamity of the guiltless* [9:22–3] . . . He also begins to cite as proof the good fortune and prosperity of the wicked, treating at great length of this subject . . . You know the dictum of the *Sages* that this opinion of *Job's* is most unsound. They say: *May there be dust upon Job's mouth.* And they say: *Job wanted to upset the plate.* And they say: *Job denied the resurrection of the dead.* They also say of him: *He began to blaspheme.* With regard to His saying, may He be exalted, to *Eliphaz: For ye have not spoken of Me the thing that is right, as My servant Job hath* [42:7] – the *Sages*, in order to find an excuse for it, say, *A man is not to be blamed for [what he does when] suffering*, meaning that he was excused because of his great sufferings. However, this kind of speech does not accord with the parable . . . [Job] said all that he did say as long as he had no true knowledge and knew the deity only because of his acceptance of authority, just as the multitude adhering to a Law know it. But when he knew God with a certain knowledge, he admitted that true happiness, which is the knowledge of the deity, is guaranteed to all who know Him and that a human being cannot be troubled in it by any of all the misfortunes in question. While he had known God only through the traditional stories and not by the way of speculation, *Job* had imagined that the things thought to be happiness, such as health, wealth, and children, are the ultimate goal. For this reason he fell into such perplexity and said such things as he did. This is the meaning of his dictum: *I had heard of Thee by the hearing of the ear; but now mine eye seeth Thee; wherefore I abhor myself and repent of dust and ashes* [42:5–6].This dictum may be supposed to mean, *Wherefore I abhor all that I used to desire and repent of my being in dust and ashes* – this being the position that he was supposed to be in: *And he sat among the ashes* [2:8]. It is because of this final discourse indicative of correct apprehension that it is said of him after this: *For ye have not spoken of Me the thing that is right, as My servant Job hath* [42:7].

The opinion of *Eliphaz* concerning this event is also one of the opinions professed concerning providence. For he says that everything that befell *Job* was deserved by him, for he had committed sins because of which he served, these misfortunes . . . [H]e believes that everything that befalls a man is deserved, but that the deficiencies for which we deserve punishment and the way in which we deserve to be punished because of them are hidden from our perception.

The opinion of *Bildad the Shuhite* on this question consists in the belief in compensation. For he says to *Job*: If you are innocent and have not sinned, the reason for these great events is to make great your reward. You will receive the finest of compensations. All this is good for you, so that the good that you will obtain in the end be increased. This is what he says to *Job*: *If thou art pure and upright, surely now He will awake for thee, and make the habitation of thy righteousness prosperous. And though thy beginning was small, yet thy end should greatly increase* [8:6–7] . . .

The opinion of *Zophar the Naamathite* is the one that considers that everything follows from the will alone; no reason whatever should be sought for His actions, and the question should not be posed: Why did He do this and why did He not do that? For this reason the point of view of justice or a requirement of wisdom should not be sought in whatever the deity does, for His greatness and true reality entail His doing what He wills. But we are incapable of penetrating the secrets of His wisdom, which necessitates His doing what He wills without there being another reason. This is what he says to *Job*: *That God would speak, and open His lips against thee; and that He would tell thee the secrets of wisdom, that they may teach thee doubly. Canst thou by searching find out God? Canst thou find out the Almighty unto perfection?* [11:6–7]

. . . The opinion attributed to *Job* is in keeping with the opinion of Aristotle; the opinion of *Eliphaz* is in keeping with the opinion of our Law; the opinion of *Bildad* is in keeping with the doctrine of the Mu'tazila; the opinion of *Zophar* is in keeping with the doctrine of the Ash'ariyya. These were the ancient opinions concerning providence.

Thereupon another opinion supervenes, namely, the one attributed to *Elihu*. Hence he is considered by them as superior. For it is mentioned that he was the youngest among them in point of age and the most perfect among them in knowledge. He started to reprove *Job* and to tax him with ignorance because of his having manifested his self-esteem and because of his not being able to understand how misfortunes could have befallen him though he performed good deeds. For he had expatiated at length on the goodness of his actions. He also described the opinions of [Job's] three friends on providence as senile drivel; and made extraordinary speeches that are full of enigmas, in such a way that if someone considers his discourse, he wonders and thinks that he does not in any respect make an addition to what was said by *Eliphaz, Bildad*, and *Zophar*, but merely repeats in different terms and with amplifications the notions contained in their speeches. For he does not go beyond blaming *Job*, ascribing the attribute of justice to God, describing His wonders in the universe, and stating that He, may He be exalted, does not care either for the obedience of those who obey or for the disobedience of those who disobey. Now all these notions had been expressed by his companions. However, when you consider the matter, the additional notion that he introduced will become clear to you; this notion is the one that is intended; it had not occurred before to one of the others. Together with that notion, however, he says all they have said, just as each of all the others – namely, *Job and his three friends* – repeats, as I have mentioned to you, the notion expressed by another among them. This is done in order to hide the notion that is peculiar to the opinion of each individual, so that at first it occurs to the multitude that all the interlocutors are agreed upon the selfsame opinion; however, this is not so. The notion added by *Elihu* and not mentioned by one of them is that which he expresses parabolically when he speaks of the intercession of an angel. For he says that it is an attested and well-known thing that when a man is ill to the point of death and when he is despaired of, if an angel intercedes for him – regardless of what angel – his intercession is accepted and he is raised from his fall. This invalid is accordingly saved and restored to the best of states. However, this does not continue always, there being no continuous intercession going on forever, for it only takes place two or three times. He says: *If there be for him an angel, an intercessor* [33:23], and so on. And, having described the various states of the convalescent and his joy at returning to the perfection of health, he says: *Lo, all these things doth God work, twice, yea thrice, with a man* [33:29]. This notion is made clear by *Elihu* alone. He also makes an addition – prior to speaking of this notion – by beginning to describe the how of prophecy in his dictum: *For God speaketh once, yea twice, yet [man] perceiveth it not. In a dream, in a vision of the night, when deep sleep falleth upon men.* [33:14–15] . . .

Similarly you will find that in the prophetic revelation that came to Job and through which his error in everything that he had imagined became

clear to him, there is no going beyond the description of natural matters
– namely, description of the elements or description of the meteorologi-
cal phenomena or description of the natures of the various species of
animals, but of nothing else. For what is mentioned therein in the way of
a description of the *firmaments* and the *heavens* and *Orion* and the *Pleiades*
[cf. 38:37, 31] occur because of their influence upon the atmosphere; for
He draws his attention only to what is beneath the sphere of the moon.
Elihu too derives his warnings from various species of animals. For he says:
*He teacheth us from the beasts of the earth, and maketh us wise from the fowls
of heaven* [35:11]. In this speech He dwells at the greatest length on a
description of *Leviathan*, who is a combination of corporeal properties
divided between the animals that walk, swim, and fly. The purpose of all
these things is to show that our intellects do not reach the point of appre-
hending how these natural things that exist in the world of generation
and corruption are produced in time and of conceiving how the existence
of the natural force within them has originated them. They are not things
that resemble what we make. How then can we wish that His governance
of, and providence for, them, may He be exalted, should resemble our governance of, and providence for, the things we do govern and provide for?
Rather is it obligatory to stop at this point and to believe that nothing is
hidden from Him, may He be exalted. As *Elihu* here says: *For His eyes are
upon the ways of man, and He seeth all his goings. There is no darkness, nor
shadow of death, where the workers of iniquity may hide themselves* [34:21–2].
But the notion of His providence is not the same as the notion of our
providence; nor is the notion of His governance of the things created by
Him the same as the notion of our governance of that which we govern.
The two notions are not comprised in one definition, contrary to what
is thought by all those who are confused, and there is nothing in common
between the two except the name alone. In the same way, our act does
not resemble His act; and the two are not comprised in one and the same
definition. Just as natural acts differ from those of craftsmanship, so do the
divine governance of, the divine providence for, and the divine purpose
with regard to, those natural matters differ from our human governance
of, providence for, and purpose with regard to, the things we govern, we
provide for, and we purpose. This is the object of the *Book of Job* as a
whole; I refer to the establishing of this foundation for the belief and the
drawing attention to the inference to be drawn from natural matters, so
that you should not fall into error and seek to affirm in your imagination
that His knowledge is like our knowledge or that His purpose and His
providence and His governance are like our purpose and our providence
and our governance. If man knows this, every misfortune will be borne

lightly by him. And misfortunes will not add to his doubts regarding the deity and whether He does or does not know and whether He exercises providence or manifests neglect, but will, on the contrary, add to his love, as is said in the conclusion of the prophetic revelation in question: *Wherefore I abhor myself, and repent of dust and ashes* [42:6]. As [the Sages], *may their memory be blessed*, have said: *Those who do out of love and are joyful in sufferings*.

16

Thomas Aquinas, *Summa Theologica*

The Italian Dominican Thomas Aquinas (ca. 1225 to 1274) was the great-est Scholastic philosopher. (His "five ways" of proving the existence of God are so well known that I omit them below.) Following the examples of the Islamic philosopher Avicenna, Maimonides, and his own teacher Albertus Magnus, Aquinas worked out a synthesis of theology with the thought of Aristotle, which had only recently resurfaced in the west. His views on evil are broadly Augustinian. Being as such is good, and evil is just the privation of good. "Boethius," he writes in the *Summa Contra Gentiles* (1258–64), "introduces a certain philosopher who asks: 'If God exists, whence comes evil?' But it could be argued to the contrary: 'If evil exists, God exists.' For, there would be no evil if the order of good were taken away, since its privation is evil. But this order would not exist if there were no God." Aquinas notes that God permits evils into his good creation for the usual reasons – it's better that there be many grades of good, some evils are necessary for some goods – but the discussions of good in Aquinas' work vastly outnumber the discussions of evil. In human experience, *culpa* (fault) is primary, and all human beings – even Job – need *poena* (pain, pun-ishment) in order to be cured of what Eleonore Stump, vividly updating Aquinas' view that "pains are a sort of medicine," has called the "spiritual cancer" of sin: like chemotherapy, pain is toxic, but it is the only hope for a cure.

St. Thomas Aquinas, *Summa Theologica*, Ia: Q.2, A.3; Q.48, AA.2,3; Q.49, A.3, in *Summa Theologica: Complete English Edition in Five Volumes*, trans. Fathers of the English Dominican Province (Allen, Tex.: Christian Classics, 1981 [1948]), I.13–14, 249–53, 255–6.

Q.2, A.3: Whether God Exists?

Objection 1. It seems that God does not exist; because if one of two contraries be infinite, the other would be altogether destroyed. But the word "God" means that He is infinite goodness. If, therefore, God existed, there would be no evil discoverable; but there is evil in the world. Therefore God does not exist.

Obj. 2. Further, it is superfluous to suppose that what can be accounted for by a few principles has been produced by many. But it seems that everything we see in the world can be accounted for by other principles, supposing God did not exist. For all natural things can be reduced to one principle, which is nature; and all voluntary things can be reduced to one principle, which is human reason, or will. Therefore there is no need to suppose God's existence.

On the contrary, It is said in the person of God: *I am Who am* (Exod. iii.14).

I answer that, The existence of God can be proved in five ways . . .

Reply Obj. 1. As Augustine says (*Enchir.* xi): *Since God is the highest good, He would not allow any evil to exist in His works, unless His omnipotence and goodness were such as to bring good even out of evil.* This is part of the infinite goodness of God, that He should allow evil to exist, and out of it produce good.

Reply Obj. 2. Since nature works for a determinate end under the direction of a higher agent, whatever is done by nature must needs be traced back to God, as to its first cause. So also whatever is done voluntarily must also be traced back to some higher cause other than human reason or will, since these can change and fail; for all things that are changeable and capable of defect must be traced back to an immovable and self-necessary first principle . . .

Q.48, A.2: Whether Evil Is Found in Things?

Objection 1. It would seem that evil is not found in things. For whatever is found in things, is either something, or a privation of something, that is a *not-being*. But [Pseudo-] Dionysius says (*Div. Nom.* iv) that *evil is distant from existence, and even more distant from nonexistence.* Therefore evil is not at all found in things.

Obj. 2. Further, *being* and *thing* are convertible. If, therefore, evil is a being in things, it follows that evil is a thing, which is contrary to what has been said ([Q.48,] A.1).

Obj. 3. Further, *the white unmixed with black is the most white*, as the Philosopher [Aristotle] says (*Topic.* iii.4). Therefore also the good unmixed with evil is the greater good. But God makes always what is best, much more than nature does. Therefore in things made by God there is no evil.

On the contrary, On the above assumptions, all prohibitions and penalties would cease, for they exist only for evils.

I answer that, As was said above (Q.47, AA.1,2), the perfection of the universe requires that there should be inequality in things, so that every grade of goodness may be realized. Now, one grade of goodness is that of the good which cannot fail. Another grade of goodness is that of the good which can fail in goodness, and this grade is to be found in existence itself; for some things there are which cannot lose their existence as incorruptible things, while some there are which can lose it, as things corruptible.

As, therefore, the perfection of the universe requires that there should be not only beings incorruptible, but also corruptible beings; so the perfection of the universe requires that there should be some which can fail in goodness, and thence it follows that sometimes they do fail. Now it is in this that evil consists, namely, in the fact that a thing fails in goodness. Hence it is clear that evil is found in things, as corruption also is found; for corruption is itself an evil.

Reply Obj. 1. Evil is distant both from simple being and from simple not-being, because it is neither a habit nor a pure negation, but a privation.

Reply Obj. 2. As the Philosopher says (*Metaph.* v., text. 14), being is twofold. In one way it is considered as signifying the entity of a thing, as divisible by the ten *predicaments*; and in that sense it is convertible with thing, and thus no privation is a being, and neither therefore is evil a being. In another sense being conveys the truth of a proposition which unites together subject and attribute by a copula, notified by this word *is*; and in this sense being is what answers to the question, *Does it exist?* and thus we speak of blindness as being in the eye; or of any other privation. In this way even evil can be called a being. Through ignorance of this distinction some, considering that things may be evil, or that evil is said to be in things, believed that evil was a positive thing in itself.

Reply Obj. 3. God and nature and any other agent make what is best in the whole, but not what is best in every single part, except in order to the whole, as was said above (Q.47, A.2). And the whole itself, which is the universe of creatures, is all the better and more perfect if some things in it can fail in goodness, and do sometimes fail, God not preventing this. This happens, firstly, because *it belongs to Providence not to destroy, but to save nature*, as Dionysius says (*Div. Nom.* iv); but it belongs to nature that what may fail should sometimes fail; secondly, because, as Augustine says (*Enchir.* 11), *God is so powerful that He can even make good out of evil.* Hence many good things would be taken away if God permitted no evil to exist; for fire would not be generated if air was not corrupted, nor would the life of a lion be preserved unless the ass were killed. Neither would avenging justice nor the patience of a sufferer be praised if there were no injustice.

Q.48, A.3: Whether Evil is in Good As in Its Subject?

Objection 1. It would seem that evil is not in good as its subject. For good is something that exists. But Dionysius says (*Div. Nom.* iv.4) that *evil does not exist, nor is it in that which exists.* Therefore, evil is not in good as its subject.

Obj. 2. Further evil is not a being; whereas good is a being. But *not-being* does not require being as its subject. Therefore, neither does evil require good as its subject.

Obj. 3. Further, one contrary is not the subject of another. But good and evil are contraries. Therefore, evil is not in good as in its subject.

Obj. 4. Further, the subject of whiteness is called white. Therefore, also, the subject of evil is evil. If, therefore, evil is in good as in its subject, it follows that good is evil against what is said (Isa. v.20): *Woe to you who call evil good, end good evil!*

On the contrary, Augustine says (*Enchir.* 14) that *evil exists only in good.*

I answer that, As was said above ([Q.48,] A.1), evil imports the absence of good. But not every absence of good is evil. For absence of good can be taken in a privative and in a negative sense. Absence of good, taken negatively, is not evil; otherwise, it would follow that what does not exist is evil, and also that everything would be evil, through not having the good belonging to something else; for instance, man would be evil who had not the swiftness of the roe, or the strength of a lion. But the absence of good, taken in a privative sense is an evil; as, for instance, the privation of sight is called blindness.

Now, the subject of privation and of form is one and the same – viz., being in potentiality whether it be being in absolute potentiality as primary matter, which is the subject of the substantial form, and of privation of the opposite form; or whether it be being in relative potentiality, and absolute actuality, as in the case of a transparent body, which is the subject both of darkness and light. It is, however, manifest that the form which makes a thing actual is a perfection and a good; and thus every actual being is a good; and likewise every potential being, as

such, is a good, as having a relation to good. For as it has being in potentiality, so has it goodness in potentiality. Therefore, the subject of evil is
good.

Reply Obj. 1. Dionysius means that evil is not in existing things as a
part, or as a natural property of any existing thing.

Reply Obj. 2. *Not-being,* understood negatively, does not require a
subject; but privation is negation in a subject, as the Philosopher says
(*Metaph.* iv., text. 4), and such *not-being* is an evil.

Reply Obj. 3. Evil is not in the good opposed to it as in its subject, but
in some other good, for the subject of blindness is not *sight* but *animal.*
Yet, it appears, as Augustine says (*Enchir.* 13), that the rule of dialectics here
fails, where it is laid down that contraries cannot exist together. But this
is to be taken as referring to good and evil in general, but not in reference to any particular good and evil. For white and black, sweet and bitter,
and the like contraries, are only considered as contraries in a special sense,
because they exist in some determinate genus; whereas good enters into
every genus. Hence one good can coexist with the privation of another
good.

Reply Obj. 4. The prophet invokes woe to those who say that good as
such is evil. But this does not follow from what is said above, as is clear
from the explanation given.

Q.48, A.5: Whether Evil is Adequately Divided Into Pain and Fault?

Objection 1. It would seem that evil is not adequately divided into pain
and fault. For every defect is a kind of evil. But in all creatures there is
the defect of not being able to preserve their own existence, which nevertheless is neither a pain nor a fault. Therefore evil is inadequately divided
into pain and fault.

Obj. 2. Further, in irrational creatures there is neither fault nor pain;
but, nevertheless, they have corruption and defect, which are evils. Therefore not every evil is a pain or a fault.

Obj. 3. Further, temptation is an evil, but it is not a fault; for *temptation which involves no consent, is not a sin, but an occasion for the exercise of
virtue,* as is said in a gloss on 2 Cor. xii.; nor is it a pain; because temptation precedes the fault, and the pain follows afterwards. Therefore, evil is
not sufficiently divided into pain and fault.

Obj. 4. *On the contrary,* It would seem that this division is superfluous:
for, as Augustine says (*Enchir.* 12), a thing is evil *because it hurts.* But whatever hurts is penal. Therefore every evil comes under pain.

I answer that, Evil, as was said above ([Q.48,] A.3) is the privation of good, which chiefly and of itself consists in perfection and act. Act, however, is twofold, first, and second. The first act is the form and integrity of a thing; the second act is its operation. Therefore evil also is twofold. In one way it occurs by the subtraction of the form, or of any part required for the integrity of the thing, as blindness is an evil, as also it is an evil to be wanting in any member of the body. In another way evil exists by the withdrawal of the due operation, either because it does not exist, or because it has not its due mode and order. But because good in itself is the object of the will, evil, which is the privation of good, is found in a special way in rational creatures which have a will. Therefore the evil which comes from the withdrawal of the form and integrity of the thing, has the nature of a pain; and especially so on the supposition that all things are subject to divine providence and justice, as was shown above (Q.22, A.2); for it is of the very nature of a pain to be against the will But the evil which consists in the subtraction of the due operation in voluntary things has the nature of a fault; for this is imputed to anyone as a fault to fail as regards perfect action, of which he is master by the will. Therefore every evil in voluntary things is to be looked upon as a pain or a fault.

Reply Obj. 1. Because evil is the privation of good, and not a mere negation, as was said above ([Q.48,] A.3), therefore not every defect of good is an evil, but the defect of the good which is naturally due. For the want of sight is not an evil in a stone, but it is an evil in an animal; since it is against the nature of a stone to see. So, likewise, it is against the nature of a creature to be preserved in existence by itself, because existence and conservation come from one and the same source. Hence this kind of defect is not an evil as regards a creature.

Reply Obj. 2. Pain and fault do not divide evil absolutely considered, but evil that is found in voluntary things.

Reply Obj. 3. Temptation, as importing provocation to evil, is always an evil of fault in the tempter; but in the one tempted it is not, properly speaking, a fault; unless through the temptation some change is wrought in the one who is tempted; for thus is the action of the agent in the patient. And if the tempted is changed to evil by the tempter he falls into fault.

Reply Obj. 4. In answer to the opposite argument, it must be said that the very nature of pain includes the idea of injury to the agent in himself, whereas the idea of fault includes the idea of injury to the agent in his operation; and thus both are contained in evil, as including the idea of injury.

Q.49, A.3: Whether There Be One Supreme Evil
Which Is the Cause of Every Evil?

Objection 1. It would seem that there is one supreme evil which is the cause of every evil. For contrary effects have contrary causes. But contrariety is found in things, according to Ecclus. xxxiii. 15: *Good is set against evil, end life against death; so also is the sinner against a just man.* Therefore there are many contrary principles, one of good, the other of evil.

Obj. 2. Further, if one contrary is in nature, so is the other. But the supreme good is in nature, and is the cause of every good, as was shown above (Q.2, A.3; Q.6, AA.2,4). Therefore, also, there is a supreme evil opposed to it as the cause of every evil.

Obj. 3. Further, as we find good and better things, so we find evil and worse. But good and better are so considered in relation to what is best. Therefore evil and worse are so considered in relation to some supreme evil . . .

On the contrary, The supreme good is the cause of every being, as was shown above (Q.2, A.3; Q.6, A.4). Therefore there can not be any principle opposed to it as the cause of evils.

I answer that, It appears from what precedes that there is no one first principle of evil, as there is one first principle of good.

First, indeed, because the first principle of good is essentially good, as was shown above (Q.6, AA.3,4). But nothing can be essentially bad. For it was shown above that every being, as such, is good (Q.5, A.3); and that evil can exist only in good as in its subject (Q.48, A.3).

Secondly, because the first principle of good is the highest and perfect good which pre-contains in itself all goodness, as shown above (Q.6, A.2). But there cannot be a supreme evil; because, as was shown above (Q.48, A.4), although evil always lessens good, yet it never wholly consumes it; and thus, while good ever remains, nothing can be wholly and perfectly bad. Therefore, the Philosopher says (*Ethic.* iv.5) that *if the wholly evil could be, it would destroy itself;* because all good being destroyed (which it need be for something to be wholly evil), evil itself would be taken away, since its subject is good.

Thirdly, because the very nature of evil is against the idea of a first principle; both because every evil is caused by good, as was shown above ([Q.49,] A.1), and because evil can be only an accidental cause, and thus it cannot be the first cause, for the accidental cause is subsequent to the direct cause.

Those, however, who upheld two first principles, one good and the other evil, fell into this error from the same cause, whence also arose other strange notions of the ancients; namely, because they failed to consider the universal cause of all being, and considered only the particular causes of particular effects. For on that account, if they found a thing hurtful to something by the power of its own nature, they thought that the very nature of that thing was evil; as, for instance, if one should say that the nature of fire was evil because it burnt the house of a poor man. The judgment, however, of the goodness of anything does not depend upon its order to any particular thing, but rather upon what it is in itself, and on its order to the whole universe, wherein every part has its own perfectly ordered place, as was said above (Q.47, A.2 *ad* 1).

Likewise, because they found two contrary particular causes of two contrary particular effects, they did not know how to reduce these contrary particular causes to the universal common cause; and therefore they extended the contrariety of causes even to the first principles. But since all contraries agree in something common, it is necessary to search for one common cause for them above their own contrary proper causes; as above the contrary qualities of the elements exists the power of a heavenly body; and above all things that exist, no matter how, there exists one first principle of being, as was shown above (Q.2, A.3).

Reply Obj. 1. Contraries agree in one genus, and they also agree in the nature of being; and therefore, although they have contrary particular causes, nevertheless we must come at last to one first common cause.

Reply Obj. 2. Privation and habit belong naturally to the same subject. Now the subject of privation is a being in potentiality, as was said above (Q.48, A.3). Hence, since evil is privation of good, as appears from what was said above (ibid., AA.1,2,3), it is opposed to that good which has some potentiality, but not to the supreme good, who is pure act.

Reply Obj. 3. Increase in intensity is in proportion to the nature of a thing. And as the form is a perfection, so privation removes a perfection. Hence every form, perfection, and good is intensified by approach to the perfect term; but privation and evil by receding from that term. Hence a thing is not said to be evil and worse, by reason of access to the supreme evil, in the same way as it is said to be good and better, by reason of access to the supreme good.

17

Three liturgies: *Stabat mater,*
a fifteenth-century Sarum,
and *Dies irae*

It would be highly misleading to survey religious understandings of evil
without considering the way the very experience of suffering is structured
by narratives and rituals. Religious practices can take the sufferer beyond her
own particular suffering, at once transcending her experience of guilt or
powerlessness, pain, rage, or grief, and validating it by placing it in a meaningful context. Suffering can be religiously significant, one of the individual's strongest ties to the earthly community, the community of saints, or to
God.

The *Stabat mater* attests to the abiding power and comfort of such religious practice. It is not known who wrote it – often attributed to Francis-
can Jacopone da Todi (ca. 1230–1306), it was more likely the work of
Innocent III (1161–1216) – but it spread throughout western Christendom
by the end of the fourteenth century. The *Stabat mater* was a vital part of the
Marian devotion which became an important focal point of Christian life
from the twelfth century on. Combining the desire to suffer with Mary and
the hope that she will help the human sufferer, the *Stabat mater* shows the
mutuality which makes experiences of religious identification so powerfully
consoling.

A different kind of identification is afforded by the use of the story of Job
in funerary offices. Medieval theology's Job is the "patient" Job of James 5:10,
not the protesting figure at the center of modern interpretation. Yet this does
not mean that Job's voice went unheard. Job's complaint was heard as an
almost involuntary expression of grief and pain, not as an argument. (Aquinas
praised Job: not to grieve at the loss of one's children as the Stoics recommended would be wrong.) The way religion recognizes and legitimates (and
perhaps co-opts) the expressions of grief is exemplified by the early fifteenth-
century Sarum below. (The Sarum Use was a rite centered at the Cathedral
of Salisbury, which is also known as Sarum. Abolished in 1547, it was among

those things the Oxford Movement sought to revive in 1833.) Through the Sarum, the grieving Job will have been among the few characters of the Bible whose *words* lay-Christians encountered regularly.

In the context of this reader, the Requiem's chant *Dies irae* serves as a reminder of the importance of the Last Judgment to medieval Christian life. Combining the hope of justice – the vindication of the innocent and the punishment of the guilty – with the fear of hell, anticipation of divine judgment not only structured the experience of death, but made the trials of life easier to bear. The *Dies irae*, based on the decription of the day of judgment in Zephaniah 1:15, is ascribed to Thomas of Celano (ca. 1190 to 1260), friend and biographer of Francis of Assisi. Hector Berlioz's use of the plainchant melody of the *Dies irae* in the "Witches' Sabbath" which ends his Symphonie Fantastique is testimony to the obsolescence of divine wrath in modern culture.

Rev. F. X. Lasance and Rev. Francis Augustine Walsh, OSB, *The New Roman Missal, In Latin and English* (New York: Benziger Brothers, 1937), 569–71 and 1503–5; *The Prymer or Lay Folks' Prayer Book*, ed. Henry Littlehales, 2 vols. (Early English Text Society, original series 105) (London: Kegan Paul, 1895), 52–78; quoted in Lawrence L. Besserman, *The Legend of Job in the Middle Ages* (Cambridge, Mass.: Harvard University Press, 1979), 59–62.

Stabat mater

Stabat Mater dolorosa	Next the cross in tears unceasing,
Juxta crucem lacrymosa,	Worn by sorrow aye increasing,
Dum pendebat Filius.	Stood the Mother 'neath her Son.
Cujus animam gementem,	Through her soul already risen,
Contristatam et dolentem,	Simeon's sword divinely driven,
Pertransivit gladius.	Edged with anguish, lo! hath run.
O quam tristis et afflicta	Sad, afflicted as no other,
Fuit illa benedicta	Was that chosen blessed Mother,
Mater Unigeniti!	Having none but Christ begot.
Quae maerebat, et dolebat,	Faithful Mother! upward gazing,
Pia Mater, dum videbat	Heart and hands to Son upraising,
Nati poenas inclyti.	Mourns and grieves His cruel lot.

Quis est homo, qui non fieret,
Matrem Christi si videret
In tanto supplicio?

Hard the man his tears refraining,
Watching Mary uncomplaining,
Bear a sorrow like to none.

Quis non posset contristari,
Christi Matrem contemplari
Dolentem cum Filio?

Hard the man that shares no sorrow,
With a Mother fain to borrow
Every pang that writhes her Son.

Pro peccatis suae gentis
Vidit Jesum in tormentis,
Et flagellis subditum.

Tortured, scourged in expiation
Of the sins that marred His Nation,
Mary watched His every pang.

Vidit suum dulcem natum
Moriendo desolatum,
Dum emisit spiritum.

She beheld her dear Begotten,
Stretched in death by all forgotten,
As on hoisted rood He hang.

Eia Mater, fons amoris,
Me sentire, vim doloris
Fac ut tecum lugeam.

Mother, fount of love, the purest,
Floods of sorrow thou endurest,
Turn them toward this heart of mine,

Fac, ut ardeat cor meum,
In amando Christum Deum,
Ut sibi complaceam.

With these waters purge its guileness,
Burn with love its innate vileness,
With the flames of love divine.

Sancta Mater, istud agas
Crucifixi fige plagas

Hallowed Mother, do this favor,
Those five wounds that gored my Saviour

Cordi meo valide.

Deeply on my heart engrave.

Tui nati vulnerati,
Tam dignati pro me pati,
Poenas mecum divide.

Pains thou gladly with Him sharest,
Anguish that thou bravely bearest,
Fully share with me, I crave.

Fac me tecum pie flere,
Crucifixo condolere,
Donec ego vixero.

Blend thy tears with mine in wailing,
Sorrow for my sins prevailing,
Till the break of endless dawn.

Juxta Crucem tecum stare
Et me tibi sociare
In planctu desidero.

Next the cross to take my station,
By thy side in desolation,
Thus, I long with thee to mourn.

Virgo virginum praeclara,	Maiden of all maidens fairest,
Mihi jam non sis amara:	Sate me with the grief thou bearest:
Fac me tecum plangere.	Spurn me not, but be thou kind.
Fac, ut portem Christi mortem,	Mine it be Christ's throes in sharing,
Passionis fac consortem,	Mine it be His anguish bearing,
Et plagas recolere.	These His wounds to keep in mind
Fac me plagis vulnerari,	May His scars my body carry.
Fac me Cruce inebriari,	May His cross and blood not tarry
Et cruore Filii.	Soul of mine to satiate!
Flammis ne urar succensus,	Thus inflamed with love consuming,
Per te, Virgo, sim defensus	Shall I not thy aid presuming
In die judicii.	Safe the reck'ning day await?
Christe, cum sit hinc exire,	When in death my eyes are closing,
Da per Matrem me venire	Opethem, Lord, to see reposing
Ad palmam victorieae.	Victory's crown in Mary's hand.
Quando corpus morietur,	When my frame by death is broken,
Fac, ut animae donetur	And my doom by Thee is spoken,
Paradisi gloria.	Be it, Lord, the better land.
Amen.	Amen.

A Sarum Use

Psalms 5–7

leccio iᵃ: Parce michi domine! (Job 7:16–21)

leccio iiᵃ: Tedet animam. (Job 10:1–7)

leccio iijᵃ: Manus tue. (Job 19:8–12)

Psalms 22, 24, 27

leccio iiijᵃ: Quantas habeo. (Job 13:23–8)

leccio vᵃ: Homo natus de muliere. (Job 14:1–6)

leccio vjᵃ: [Quis michi hoc tribuat]. (Job 14:13–16)

Psalms 39–41

leccio vij²: Spiritus meus. (Job 17:1–3, 11–15)

leccio viij²: pelli mee. (Job 19:20–7)

leccio ix²: Quare de vulua, & cetera. (Job 10:18–22)

Dies irae

Dies irae, dies illa,	Dreaded day, that day of ire,
Solvet saeclum in favilla,	When the world shall melt in fire,
Teste David cum Sibylla.	Told by Sibyl and David's lyre.
Quantus tremor est futurus,	Fright mens hearts shall rudely shift,
Quando judex est venturus,	As the Judge through gleaming rift
Cuncta stricte discussurus!	Comes each soul to closely sift.
Tuba mirum spargens sonum	Then, the trumpet's shrill refrain,
Per sepulchra regionum,	Piercing tombs by hill and plain,
Coget omnes ante thronum.	Souls to judgment shall arraign.
Mors stupebit et natura,	Death and nature stand aghast,
Cum resurget creatura,	As the bodies rising fast,
Judicanti responsura.	Hie to hear the sentence passed.
Liber scriptus proferetur,	Then, before Him shall be placed,
In quo totum continetur,	That whereon the verdict's based,
Unde mundus judicetur.	Book wherein each deed is traced.
Judex ergo cum sedebit,	When the Judge His seat shall gain,
Quidquid latet, apparebit:	All that's hidden shall be plain,
Nil inultum remanebit.	Nothing shall unjudged remain.
Quid sum miser tunc dicturus?	Wretched man, what can I plead?
Quem patronum rogaturus?	Whom to ask to intercede,
Cum vix justus sit securus.	When the just much mercy need?
Rex tremendae majestatis,	Thou, O awe-inspiring Lord,
Qui salvandos salvas gratis,	Saving e'en when unimplored,
Salva me fons pietatis.	Save me, mercy's fount adored.

Recordare, Jesu pie,
Quod sum causa tuae viae,
Ne me perdas illa die.

Quaerens me, sedisti lassus:
Redemisti crucem passus:
Tantus labor non sit cassus.

Juste judex ultionis,
Donum fac remissionis,
Ante diem rationis.

Ingemisco tamquam reus:
Culpa rubet vultus meus:
Supplicanti parce Deus.

Qui Mariam absolvisti,
Et latronem exaudisti,
Mihi quoque spem dedisti.

Preces meae non sunt dignae
Sed tu bonus fac benigne,
Ne perenni cremer igne.

Inter oves locum praesta,
It ab haedis me sequestra,
Statuens in parte dextra.

Confutatis maledictis,
Flammis acribus addictis,
Voca me cum benedictis.

Oro supplex et acclinis,
Cor contritum quasi cinis:
Gere curam mei finis.

Lacrymosa dies illa,
Qua resurget ex favilla
Judicandus homo reus.

Ah! Sweet Jesus, mindful be,
That Thou cam'st on earth for me:
Cast me not this day from Thee.

Seeking me Thy strength was spent
Ransoming Thy limbs were rent:
Is this toil to no intent?

Thou, awarding pains condign,
Mercy's ear to me incline,
Ere the reckoning Thou assign.

I, felon-like, my lot bewail,
Suffused cheeks my shame unveil:
God! O let my prayer prevail.

Mary's soul Thou madest white,
Didst to heaven the thief invite;
Hope in me these now excite.

Prayers of mine in vain ascend:
Thou art good and wilt forefend,
In quenchless fire my life to end.

When the cursed by shame opprest,
Enter names at Thy behest,
Call me then to join the blest.

Place amid Thy sheep accord,
Keep me from the tainted horde,
Set me in Thy sight, O Lord.

Prostrate, suppliant, now no more,
Unrepenting, as of yore,
Save me dying, I implore.

Mournful day that day of sighs,
When from dust shall man arise,
Stained with guilt his doom to know,

Huic ergo parce Deus: Mercy, Lord, on him bestow.
Pie Jesu Domine,   Jesus, kind! Thy souls release,
Dona eis requiem. Amen.   Lead them thence to realms of peace.

Amen.   Amen.

18

Meister Eckhart, "Blessed are the poor in spirit"

We have seen in Pseudo-Dionysius the way mystical theology dissolves the very words which could form questions about God and evil. This process is made explicit in the thought of the Dominican theologian and mystic Meister Eckhart (ca. 1260 to 1327/8). Although he was declared a heretic (he died while appealing the decision) and 28 statements from his work were condemned by Pope John XXII, Eckhart's thought was less scandalous than his later detractors – or fans – tend to think; it was certainly more ortho-dox than the dualistic mysticism of Jakob Böhme (1575–1624). Latin works like the sermon below show the better-known German works to be solidly grounded in Christian Neoplatonism and the theology of Eckhart's near contemporary and fellow Dominican, Thomas Aquinas.

Meister Eckhart, Sermons & Treatises, trans. M. O'C. Walshe, 3 vols. (Longmead, Shaftesbury, Dorset: Element Books, 1989), II.269–76.

Beati pauperes spiritu quia ipsorum est regnum caelorum (Matt. 5:3)

Beatitude itself opened its mouth of wisdom and said: "Blessed are the poor in spirit, for theirs is the kingdom of heaven." All angels, all saints, and everything that was ever born must keep silent when the wisdom of the Father speaks: for all the wisdom of angels and all creatures is pure folly before the unfathomable wisdom of God. This wisdom has declared that the poor are blessed.

Now there are two kinds of poverty. The one is external poverty, and this is good and much to be commended in the man who practises it voluntarily for the love of our Lord Jesus Christ, for he himself possessed this on earth. About this poverty I shall say no more now. But there is another poverty, an interior poverty, to which this word of our Lord applies when he says: "Blessed are the poor in spirit."

Now I beg you to be like this in order that you may understand this sermon for by the eternal truth I tell you that unless you are like this truth we are about to speak of, it is not possible for you to follow me.

Some people have asked me what poverty is in itself, and what a poor man is. This is how we shall answer.

Bishop Albert says a poor man is one who finds no satisfaction in all things God ever created, and this is well said. But we shall speak better, taking poverty in a higher sense: a poor man is one who wants nothing, knows nothing and has nothing. We shall now speak of these three points, and I beg you for the love of God to understand this wisdom if you can; but if you can't understand it, don't worry, because I am going to speak of such truth that few good people can understand.

Firstly, we say that a poor man is one who *wants* nothing. There are some who do not properly understand the meaning of this: these are the people who cling with attachment to penances and outward practices, making much of these. May God have mercy on such folk for understanding so little of divine truth! These people are called holy from their outward appearances, but inwardly they are asses, for they are ignorant of the actual nature of divine truth. These people say that a poor man is one who wants nothing and they explain it this way: A man should so live that he never does his own will in anything, but should strive to do the dearest will of God. It is well with these people because their intention is right, and we commend them for it. May God in His mercy grant them the kingdom of heaven! But by God's wisdom I declare that these folk are not poor men or similar to poor men. They are much admired by those who know no better, but I say that they are asses with no understanding of God's truth. Perhaps they will gain heaven for their good intentions, but of the poverty we shall now speak of they have no idea.

If, then, I were asked what *is* a poor man who wants nothing, I should reply as follows. As long as a man is so disposed that it is his *will* with which he would do the most beloved will of God, that man has not the poverty we are speaking about: for that man has a *will* to serve God's will – and that is not true poverty! For a man to possess true poverty he must be as free of his created will as he was when he was not. For I declare by the eternal truth, as long as you have the *will* to do the will of God, and longing for eternity and God, you are not poor: for a poor man is one who wills nothing and desires nothing.

While I yet stood in my first cause, I *had* no God and was my own cause: then I wanted nothing and desired nothing, for I was bare being and the knower of myself in the enjoyment of truth. Then I wanted myself and wanted no other thing: what I wanted I was and what I was I wanted, and thus I was free of God and all things. Bu when I left my free will behind and received my created being, *then* I had a God. For before there were creatures God was not "God": He was That which He was. But when creatures came into existence and received their *created* being, then God was not "God" in Himself – He was "God" in creatures.

Now we say that God, inasmuch as He is "God," is not the supreme goal of creatures, for the same lofty status is possessed by the least of creatures in God. And if it were the case that a fly had reason and could intellectually plumb the eternal abysm of God's being out of which it came, we would have to say that God with all that makes Him "God" would be unable to fulfil and satisfy that fly! Therefore let us pray to God that we may be free of God that we may gain the truth and enjoy it eternally, there where the highest angel, the fly and the soul are equal, there where I stood and wanted what I was and was what I wanted. We conclude, then: if a man is to be poor of will, he must will and desire as little as he willed and desired when he was not. And this is the way for a man to be poor by not wanting.

Secondly, he is a poor man who *knows* nothing. We have sometimes said that a man should live as if he did not live either for himself, or for truth, or for God. But now we will speak differently and go further, and say: For a man to possess *this* poverty he must live so that he is *unaware* that he does not live for himself, or for truth, or for God. He must be so lacking in all knowledge that he neither knows nor recognises nor feels that God lives in him: more still, he must be free of all the understanding that lives in him. For when that man stood in the eternal being of God, nothing *else* lived in him: what lived there was himself. Therefore we declare that a man should be as free from his own knowledge as he was when he was not. That man should let God work as He will, and himself stand idle.

For all that ever came out of God, a pure activity is appointed. The proper work of man is to love and to know. Now the question is Wherein does blessedness lie most of all? Some masters have said it lies in knowing, some say that it lies in loving: others say it lies in knowing and loving, and they say better. But we say it lies neither in knowing nor in loving: for there is something in the soul from which both knowledge and love flow: but it does not itself know or love in the way the powers of the soul do. Whoever knows this, knows the seat of blessedness. This has neither before nor after, nor is it expecting anything to come, for it can neither gain nor lose. And so it is deprived of the knowledge that God is at work in it: rather, it just is itself, enjoying itself God-fashion. It is in this manner, I declare, that a man should be so acquitted and free that he neither knows nor realises that God is at work in him: in that way can a man possess poverty.

The masters say God is a being, an intellectual being that knows all things. But we say God is not a being and not intellectual and does not know this or that. Thus God is free of all things, and so He is all things. To be poor in spirit, a man must be poor of all his own knowledge: not knowing any *thing*, not God, nor creature nor himself. For this it is needful that a man should desire to know and understand nothing of the works of God. In this way a man can be poor of his own knowledge.

Thirdly, he is a poor man who *has* nothing. Many people have said that perfection is attained when one has none of the material things of the earth, and this is true in one sense – when it is voluntary. But this is not the sense in which I mean it. I have said before, the poor man is not he who wants to fulfil the will of God but he who lives in such a way as to be free of his own will and of God's will, as he was when he was not. Of this poverty we declare that it is the *highest* poverty. Secondly, we have said he is a poor man who does not know of the working of God within him. He who stands as free of knowledge and understanding as God stands of all things, has the *purest* poverty. But the third is the *straitest* poverty, of which we shall now speak: that is when a man *has* nothing.

Now pay earnest attention to this! I have often said, and eminent authorities say it too, that a man should be so free of all things and all works, both inward and outward, that he may be a proper abode for God where God can work. Now we shall say something else. If it is the case that a man is free of all creatures, of God and of self, and if it is still the case that God finds a place *in him* to work, then we declare that as long as this is *in* that man, he is not poor with the strictest poverty. For it is not God's intention in His works that a man should have a place within himself for God to work in for poverty of spirit means being so free of God and all His works, that God, if He wishes to work in the soul, is Himself the place where He works – and this He gladly does. For, if he finds a man *so* poor, then God performs His own work, and the man is passive to God within him, and God is His own place of work, being a worker in Himself. It is just here, in *this* poverty, that man enters into that eternal essence that once he was, that he is now and evermore shall remain.

This is the word of St Paul. He says: "All that I am, I am by the grace of God" (1 Cor. 15:10). Now this sermon seems to rise above grace and being and understanding and will and all desire – so how can St Paul's words be true? The answer is that St Paul's words *are* true: it was needful for the grace of God to be in him, for the grace of God effected in him that the accidental in him was perfected as essence. When grace had ended and finished its work, Paul remained that which he *was*.

So we say that a man should be so poor that he neither is nor has any place for God to work in. To preserve a place is to preserve distinction. Therefore I pray to God to make me free of God, for my essential being is above God, taking God as the origin of creatures. For in that essence of God in which God is above being and distinction, there I was myself and knew myself so as to make this man. Therefore I am my own cause according to my essence, which is eternal, and not according to my becoming, which is temporal. Therefore I am unborn, and according to my unborn mode I can never die. According to my unborn mode I have eternally been, am now and shall eternally remain. That which I am by virtue of birth must die and perish, for it is mortal, and so must perish with time. In my birth all things were born, and I was the cause of myself and all things: and if I had so willed it, I would not have been, and all things would not have been. If I were not, God would not be either. I am the cause of God's being God: if I were not, then God would not be God. But you do not need to know this.

A great master says that his breaking-through is nobler than his emanation, and this is true. When I flowed forth from God, all creatures declared: "There is a God"; but *this* cannot make me blessed, for with this I acknowledge myself as a creature. But in my breaking-through, where I stand free of my own will, of God's will, of all His works, and of God himself, *then* I am above all creatures and am neither God nor creature, but I am that which I was and shall remain for evermore. There I shall receive an imprint that will raise me above all the angels. By this imprint I shall gain such wealth that I shall not be content with God inasmuch as He is God, or with all His divine works for this breaking-through guarantees to me that I and God are one. *Then* I am what I was, then I neither wax nor wane, for then I am an unmoved cause that moves all things. Here, God finds no place *in* man, for man by his poverty wins for himself what he has eternally been and shall eternally remain. Here, God is one with the spirit, and that is the strictest poverty one can find.

If anyone cannot understand this sermon, he need not worry. For so long as a man is not equal to this truth, he *cannot* understand my words, for this is a naked truth which has come direct from the heart of God.

That we may so live as to experience it eternally, may God help us. Amen.

19

Geoffrey Chaucer, "Patient Griselda"

The last story of Boccaccio's *Decameron* was a tale of male cruelty and heroic female virtue. When Petrarch rendered the story in Latin, he gave it a pious gloss, likening the suffering heroine to Job. The English poet Geoffrey Chaucer (ca. 1343–1400) preserved both of these stories and added an ironic spin of his own in the "Clerks' (or Oxford Scholar's) Tale" of his *Canterbury Tales*. The story of "Patient Griselda" is thus an excellent site for reflecting on the gendered character of discourses of submission, as well as on the polyphony of voices which only narrative can capture. The story tells of a marquis (Walter), who marries a virtuous maiden of no station (Griselda), and tests her patience and obedience in truly inhuman fashion. Taking their newborn daughter from her arms on the pretext that his subjects objected to the thought of a royal heir with commoner's blood, Walter tells Griselda the child is to be killed – something she humbly accepts without protest. A few years later when Griselda bears a son, he repeats the ordeal. (In fact, however, he has sent the children to be raised in Bologna.) The selections below describe the final ordeal, a dozen years later.

Geoffrey Chaucer, "The Oxford Scholar's Tale" from *The Canterbury Tales*, trans. David Wright (Harmondsworth: Penguin, 1985), 300–12.

> Meanwhile, and with his usual ruthlessness,
> This marquis, to assay her even more,
> Set out to put his wife to the uttermost
> Proof of her spirit, to be wholly sure
> That she was still as steadfast as before;
> And, at a public audience one day,
> Roughly addressed these words to Griselda:

"Indeed, Griselda, it's been very pleasant
To have had you for wife – more for your goodness
Constancy, loyalty, and obedience
Than any ancestry of yours, or riches;
But I now realize how true it is
That – as reflection leads me to conclude –
A great position brings great servitude.

"I may not do as any ploughman may.
My people are compelling me to take
Another wife, and clamour day by day;
Also the Pope, their rancour to abate,
I do assure you, gives consent to it;
And to be frank with you, this much I'll say:
My new wife is already on her way.

"So brace yourself to quit at once her place.
As for the dowry that you brought to me,
I waive it as a favour; take it back.
Now go home to your father's house," said he,
"No one can always have prosperity.
Take my advice, and bear the blows of chance
Or Fortune with a steadfast countenance."

And yet she answered him with fortitude:
"I knew, and I have always known," said she,
"There can be no comparison, my lord,
Between your splendour and my poverty;
For these are things nobody can deny.
I never thought I merited at all
To be your wife; nor yet your servant-girl.

"And in this house, where you have made me lady,
I call on God in heaven to witness,
As I hope for Him to comfort me and aid me,
I never played the chatelaine or mistress,
But was a humble servant to your lordship,
And will be always, while I've life and breath,
More than to any other soul on earth.

"That in your kindness you should have so long
Held me in honour, and exalted me
Here, where I was not worthy to belong,
I thank both God and you; to Him I pray
May He reward you! There's no more to say,

And to my father gladly I'll return;
Until I come to die, I'll live with him.

. . . .

Naked out of my father's house", said she,
"I came, and naked there I must return . . . "

Thus with her father for a certain space
She lived, this paragon of wifely patience,
And neither by her words nor by her face
In public or in private, gave a hint
Of any wrong done to her, or offence;
Nor did she, judging from her countenance,
Ever recall her former high estate.

No wonder: while she was a marchioness
Her soul displayed complete humility,
No pleasure-loving heart, no delicate tastes,
No love of pomp or royal ceremony,
For she was full of patience and of kindness,
Discreet, without pretension, honourable,
And to her husband ever amenable.

Job is remembered for his patience mostly,
A thing the learned love to expatiate on,
Especially as found in men – but really,
Though scholars give but little praise to women,
As far as patience is concerned, there's no man
Can behave as well as women can, or be
One half so true – if so, it's news to me . . .

[Once the new "wife" and her young brother arrive, Walter turns to
Griselda:]

"Griselda," said he, in a joking way,
"How do you like my new wife and her beauty?"
"Very much indeed, my lord; for, truth to say,
I never saw a lovelier girl than she.
God grant all happiness to her, I pray,"
Said Griselda, "and I hope He allows
Delight enough to last you all your days.

"But one request I make – a warning too –
That you will never goad with tormenting
This gentle girl, as I have seen you do

With others; for I'd say in her upbringing
She's been more tenderly nursed; and to my thinking
Could not sustain the same adversity
As one both born and bred in poverty."

And now, when Walter saw her happy face,
Her patience, with no rancour there at all,
However often he had done her mischief,
She stood as firm and steadfast as a wall,
Continuing in innocence through all,
His obdurate heart inclined to take pity
Upon Griselda's wifely constancy.

"My own Griselda, this will do," said he,
"So be no more afraid, no more distressed;
Your kindness, goodness, and your constancy,
I have put as searchingly to the test
In wealth and want, as woman's ever was.
Dear wife, I'm sure now of your steadfastness."
With which, he took her in his arms to kiss.

And she, in pure surprise, took no notice;
She did not seem to hear what Walter said,
Till out of her bewilderment she broke,
As if suddenly startled out of sleep.
"You are my wife," said he, by Christ Who died
For us! The only wife I have, or had,
Or ever mean to have, so help me God!

"This is your daughter, whom you had imagined
To be my wife; this boy will certainly
Become my heir, as I have always planned;
He is indeed the child of your body.
I kept them at Bologna secretly;
So take them back; for now you cannot say
Your children have been lost or put away.

"And as for those who've spoken against me,
Let them take note that I have done this deed
Neither from malice nor from cruelty,
But to put to the proof your womanhood,
And not to kill my children – God forbid!
But keep them hid away in secret till
I knew your constancy and strength of will."

At hearing this, she falls down in a swoon,
Heart-broken in her joy; then, recovering,
She calls both her young children to her bosom
And in her arms, most pitifully weeping,
Enfolds the two of them; tenderly kissing
Like any mother; and, in her embraces,
Her salt tears falling bathe their hair and faces . . .

What a heart-breaking thing it was to see
Her faint away, and hear her humble voice!
"A thousand thanks to you, my lord," said she,
"For you have saved for me my children's lives!
Now I don't care if here and now I die;
Since I am loved by you and have your heart,
What matters death, or when my soul departs?

"O my dear children, O my tender young!
Your sorrowing mother always thought that surely
Some horrible animal or cruel hound
Had eaten you; but God in His mercy
And your kind father, have so tenderly
Kept you both safe" – and at that moment she
All suddenly slid senseless to the ground.

And as she fainted she held on so tightly
To the two children still in her embrace,
That it was only with great difficulty
And skill that they at length could extricate
The children. Tears on many a pitying face
Ran down; and the bystanders who were there
Could scarcely bring themselves to stay with her.

Walter comforts her, and her grief abates,
And she gets up, half shamefaced, from her trance;
They all make much of her, until at last
She has regained her poise and countenance.
And Walter tries with so much diligence
To please her, you'd delight to see the pleasure
Between the two, now that they were together . . .

For many a year, in great prosperity,
These two lived on in harmony and peace,
Having seen their daughter marry splendidly
With a rich lord, one of the worthiest

In all of Italy; and Walter kept
Griselda's father with them at his court
In ease and quiet, till his soul departed.

His son succeeded to his heritage
In tranquil peace, after his father's day;
And he was lucky too in his marriage,
Although it's true he did not seek to try
His wife so hard; the world, one can't deny,
Is not so tough now as it used to be;
So listen to what Petrarch has to say:

"This tale has not been told so that wives should
Imitate Griselda in humility
They'd find it intolerable if they did!
But that everyone, whatever his degree,
Should be as steadfast in adversity
As Griselda." That's why Petrarch tells
This tale, and in the loftiest of styles.

For if a woman was so patient
To a mere mortal, how much more ought we
Accept what God sends us without complaint,
For it is reasonable, sirs, that He
Should test what He has made; He will not tempt
Those whom He has redeemed, as St James says
In his epistle; never fear, He tries

His people all the time; and He allows
The biting lashes of adversity
To scourge us for our good, in various ways,
Not just to test the will, for surely He
From the beginning knew our frailty;
Then let us, since His rule is for our good,
Live in virtue and in patient fortitude.

Just one word, gentlemen, before I go:
It would be pretty hard to find, these days,
In any town three Griseldas, or two;
Because, should they be put to such assays,
Their gold's so poor now, made with such alloys
That, though the coin looks good enough to you,
Instead of bending, it will break in two.

So for the sake of the good wife from Bath –
Whose great authority may the Lord maintain
And that of all her sex; too bad if not!
I'll cheer you up by singing you a song,
For I feel fresh, and in excellent form;
We've had enough of being serious.
Now listen to my song; it goes like this:

Chaucer's Epilogue

Griselda's dead, so is her patience,
And both are deader than a coffin nail;
I warn all husbands in the audience
Not to be too precipitate to assail
The patience of their wives, in hope to find
Griselda's; it is certain they will fail.

You high-born wives, so famous for prudence,
Should you permit humility to nail
Your tongues, or give the scholars evidence
For an even more unimaginable tale
Than Griselda's, so patient and so kind,
Beware lest Chichevache devour you all!

Take after Echo; she keeps in silence,
Her disposition is antiphonal;
Don't be made fools of by your innocence,
Be on your toes instead, and take control,
And fix this lesson firmly in your mind;
The general good of all shall then prevail.

Superwives, stand up in your own defence!
Each is as huge and strong as a camel.
Then why permit a man to give offence?
You smaller wives, though feeble in battle,
Be fiercer than a tiger or a fiend,
Clack on and on like windmills, I counsel.

Why should you fear, or pay them reverence?
For if your husband armed himself in mail
The cutting arrows of your eloquence
Would pierce his breastplate and his tough ventail.

Take my tip too, and see you make him blind
With jealousy – he'll cower like a quail!

If you be fair, when others are present
Show off your beauty and your apparel!
If you be ugly, use extravagance,
For this will win you friends so you prevail.
Be light and gay as a leaf in the wind,
Leave him to weep and worry, whine and wail!

20

Julian of Norwich, *Showings*

Not even the name is known of the author of the *Revelations of Divine Love*. The anchoress who lived in a cell attached to the church of St. Julian in the English city of Norwich (ca. 1342 to ca. 1415) had had 16 "showings" in a near-death experience in 1373, which she expounded with great theological originality in both a shorter and a longer text several decades later. Writing of God as mother as well as father, Julian is a trinitarian mystic. She develops an understanding of the divine–human relationship as a relation of care which transcends blame. Both Marilyn McCord Adams and John Hick have found in her thinking resources for a religiously transformative understanding of the suffering of individuals.

Julian of Norwich, *Showings*, Long Text; in *Revelations of Divine Love*, trans. Elisabeth Spearing (Harmondsworth: Penguin, 1998), 79–80, 85–6, 112–13, 146–7, 178.

27

After this, our Lord reminded me of the longing I had for him; and I saw that nothing kept me from him but sin, and I saw that this is so with all of us. And I thought that if sin had never existed, we should all have been pure and like himself, as God made us; and so I had often wondered before now in my folly why, in his great foreseeing wisdom, God had not prevented the beginning of sin; for then, I thought, all would have been well. I ought certainly to have abandoned these thoughts, but nevertheless I grieved and sorrowed over the question with no reason or judgement. But Jesus, who in this vision informed me of all that I needed to know, answered with this assurance: "Sin is befitting, but all shall be well, and all shall be well, and all manner of things shall be well."

With this bare word "sin" our Lord brought to my mind the whole extent of all that is not good, and the shameful scorn and the utter humiliation that he bore for us in this life, and his dying, and all the pains and sufferings of all his creatures, both in body and spirit – for we are all to some extent brought to nothing and shall be brought to nothing as our master Jesus was, until we are fully purged: that is to say until our mortal flesh is brought completely to nothing, and all those of our inward feelings which are not truly good. He gave me insight into all these things, along with all pains that ever were and ever shall be; and compared with these I realize that Christ's Passion was the greatest pain and went beyond them all. And all this was shown in a flash, and quickly changed into comfort; for our good Lord did not want the soul to be afraid of this ugly sight.

But I did not see sin; for I believe it has no sort of substance nor portion of being, nor could it be recognized were it not for the suffering it causes. And this suffering seems to me to be something transient, for it purges us and makes us know ourselves and pray for mercy; for the Passion of our Lord supports us against all this, and that is his blessed will. And because of the tender love which our good Lord feels for all who shall be saved, he supports us willingly and sweetly, meaning this: "It is true that sin is the cause of all manner of suffering, but all shall be well, and all shall be well, and all manner of things shall be well." These words were said very tenderly, with no suggestion that I or anyone who will be saved was being blamed. It would therefore be very strange to blame or wonder at God because of my sin, since he does not blame be for sinning.

And in these same words I saw a marvellous great mystery hidden in God, a mystery which we will make openly known to us in heaven; in which knowledge he shall truly see the reason why he allowed sin to exist; and seeing this we shall rejoice eternally in our Lord God.

32

At one time our good Lord said: "All manner of things shall be well"; and at another time he said, "You shall see for yourself that all manner of things shall be well"; and the soul understood these two sayings differently. On the one hand he wants us to know that he does not only concern himself with great and noble things, but also with small, humble and simple things, with both one and the other; and this is what he means when he says, "All manner of things shall be well"; for he wants us to know that the smallest thing shall not be forgotten. But another thing understood is this: deeds are done which appear so evil to us and people suffer such terrible evils that it does not seem as though any good will ever come of them; and we consider this, sorrowing and grieving over it so that we cannot find peace in the blessed contemplation of God as we should do; and this is why: our reasoning powers are so blind now, so humble and so simple, that we cannot know the high, marvellous wisdom, the might and the goodness of the Holy Trinity. And this is what he means when he says, "You shall see for yourself that all manner of things shall be well," as if he said, "Pay attention to this now, faithfully and confidently, and at the end of time you will truly see it in the fullness of joy." . . .

It appears to me that there is a deed which the Holy Trinity shall do on the last day, and when that deed shall be done and how it shall be done is unknown to all creatures under Christ, and shall be until it has been done. And he wants us to know this because he wants us to feel more ease in our souls and more at peace in love, rejoicing in him and no longer considering all the tumults which might keep us from the truth. This is the great deed ordained by our Lord God from eternity, treasured up and hidden in his blessed breast, only known to himself, and by this deed he shall make all things well; for just as the Holy Trinity made all things from nothing, so the Holy Trinity shall make all well that is not well.

And I wondered greatly at this revelation, and considered our faith, wondering as follows: our faith is grounded in God's word, and it is part of our faith that we should believe that God's word will be kept in all things; and one point of our faith is that many shall be damned – like the angels who fell out of heaven from pride, who are now fiends, and men on earth who die outside the faith of Holy Church, that is, those who are heathens, and also any man who has received Christianity and lives an unChristian life and so dies excluded from the love of God. Holy Church teaches me to believe that all these shall be condemned everlastingly to hell. And given all this, I thought it impossible that all manner of things should be well, as our Lord revealed at this time. And I received no other answer in showing from our Lord God but this: "What is impossible to you is not impossible to me. I shall keep my word in all things and I shall make all things well." . . .

49

Now this was a great marvel to the soul, continually shown in everything and considered with great attentiveness: that in regard to himself our Lord God cannot forgive, for he cannot be angry – it would be an impossibility. For this is what was shown: that our life is all grounded and rooted in love, and without love we cannot live; and therefore to the soul through which God's special grace sees so much of his great and marvellous goodness, and sees that we are joined to him in love forever, it is the greatest impossibility conceivable that God should be angry, for anger and friendship are two contraries. It must needs be that he who wears away and extinguishes our anger and makes us gentle and kind is himself always consistently loving, gentle and kind, which is the contrary of anger; for I saw quite clearly that where our Lord appears, everything is peaceful and there is no place for anger; for I saw no kind of anger in God, neither for a short time nor for a long one; indeed, it seems to me that if God could be even slightly angry we could never have any life or place or being; for as truly as we have our being from the eternal strength of God and from the eternal wisdom and from the eternal goodness, though we feel vengeful, quarrelsome and contentious, yet we are all mercifully enclosed in the kindness of God and in his gentleness, in his generosity and in his indulgence; for I saw quite certainly that our eternal support, our dwelling, our life and our being are all in God; for as his endless goodness protects us when we sin so that we do not perish, the same endless goodness continually negotiates a peace in us in place of our anger and our contentious falling, and makes us see that what is needed is that with true fear we should heartily beseech God for forgiveness with a gracious longing for our salvation; for we cannot be blessedly saved until we are truly in a state of peace and love, for that is what our salvation means . . .

63

Here we can see that to hate sin comes to us truly by nature and to hate sin comes to us truly by grace; for nature is all good and fair of itself and grace was sent out to save nature and destroy sin and bring fair kind nature back to the blessed point from which it came, that is God, and with greater nobility and glory through the virtuous work of grace; for it shall be seen before God by all his holy ones in eternal joy that nature has been tried in the fire of tribulation and no lack or fault has been found there. So nature and grace are in harmony, for grace is God as nature is God. He is double in his way of working and single in love, and neither of them works without the other, nor can they be separated. And when through God's mercy and with his help we put ourselves into harmony with nature and grace, we shall truly see that sin is much more vile and painful than hell, without comparison, for it is contrary to our fair nature; for as truly as sin is unclean, so is it truly unnatural, and therefore appears a horrible thing to the loved soul that wants to be all fair and shining in the eyes of God as nature and grace teach us.

But let us not be afraid of this except in so far as fear can help us, but let us humbly lament to our dearest Mother, and he will sprinkle us all over with his precious blood and make our soul very soft and tender, and in the course of time he will heal us completely, just as is most honourable for him and most joyful for us eternally. And he will never pause nor cease in this good, tender work until all his dearest children have been born and delivered. And he showed this where he showed how spiritual thirst was to be understood, that is the love-longing which will last until Judgement Day.

So our life is grounded in our true mother, Jesus, in his own foreseeing wisdom since before time began, with the great power of the Father, and the great and supreme goodness of the Holy Ghost. And in taking on our human nature he gave us life, in his blessed death on the cross he gave us birth into life everlasting; and from that time, and now, and for ever until Judgement Day, he feeds and fosters us, just as the great and supreme kind nature of motherhood and the natural need of childhood demands. To the eyes of our soul, our heavenly Mother is good and tender; to the eyes of our heavenly Mother the children of grace are precious and lovely, with humility and gentleness and all the fair virtues which belong to children by nature; for naturally the child does not despair of the mother's love; naturally the child does not set itself up presumptuously; naturally the child loves the mother and each one loves the other; these are the fair virtues, with all others that are like them, with which our heavenly Mother is honoured and pleased. And I understood that in this life no one grows beyond childhood, in feebleness and inadequacy of body and mind, until the time when our gracious Mother has brought us up into our Father's bliss. And when we shall really understand what he means in these sweet words where he says, "All shall be well, and you shall see for yourself that all manner of things shall be well." And then the bliss of our motherhood in Christ will begin again in the joys of our God; a new beginning which will last without end, always beginning again.

So I understood that all his blessed children who come from him by nature shall be bought back into him by grace.

85

And I marvelled greatly at this sight; for in spite of our ignorant way of life and our blindness here, our kind Lord everlastingly watches our behaviour and rejoices. And of all things we can please him best by wisely and truly believing this and rejoicing with him and in him; for as surely as we shall be in God's bliss everlastingly, praising and thanking him, so, through God's providence, have we been known and loved in his everlasting purpose since before time began; and in this love without beginning he protects us and never allows us to be so harmed that our bliss would be less. And therefore when the judgement is given, and we are all brought up above, we shall clearly see in God the mysteries which are now hidden from us. Then none of us shall be moved to say in any way, "Lord, it would have been very good if it had been like this," but we shall all affirm silently, "Lord, may you be blessed! For it is thus and it is good. And now we truly see that all is done as it was ordained before anything was made."

21

Thomas à Kempis, *The Imitation of Christ*

The *Imitation of Christ* is one of the most popular of Christian spiritual works. It may have been written by a German Augustinian active in Holland known as Thomas à Kempis (1379/80–1471), although evidence is scanty. It is a devotional manual unaffected by contemporary theological developments, and uninterested in life outside the monastery; it ends with an extended meditation on the sacrament of the eucharist – indispensable on the author's account to a life following the example of Christ. *Imitation's* emphasis on personal experience rather than active engagement with the world made it especially beloved among Protestant pietists. Among the many thinkers influenced by the book were Alexander Pope (who claims to have written a paraphrase of it at the age of 12), Samuel Johnson, and John Wesley.

Thomas à Kempis, *The Imitation of Christ*, II.9, III.13, IV.13 (New York: Dutton/Everyman's Library, 1960), 63–5, 105–6, 226–7.

Of the Want of all Consolation

It is not hard to despise all human consolation when we have divine.

But it is much, and very much, to be able to forgo all comfort, both human and divine, and to be willing to bear this interior banishment for God's honour, and to seek oneself in nothing, nor to think of one's own merit.

What so great thing is it, if thou be cheerful and devout when grace comes? This hour is desirable to all.

He rides pleasantly enough who is carried by the grace of God.

And what wonder if he feel no weight, who is borne up by the Almighty, and led on by the Sovereign Guide.

2. We love to have something to comfort us, and it is with difficulty that a man can put off himself.

The holy Martyr Lawrence, with his priest, overcame the world, because he despised whatever seemed delightful in this world; and for the love of Christ, he suffered the High Priest of God, Sixtus, whom he exceedingly loved, to be taken away from Him.

He overcame, therefore, the love of man by the love of the Creator; and instead of the consolation he had in man, he made choice rather of God's good pleasure.

So, do thou also learn to part with an intimate and beloved friend for the love of God.

And take it not to heart when thou art forsaken by a friend, knowing that at last we must all be separated one from another.

3. A man must have a great and a long conflict within himself, before he can learn fully to overcome himself, and to direct his whole affection towards God.

When a man stands upon himself, he easily inclines after human consolations.

But a true lover of Christ, and a diligent pursuer of virtue does not fall back upon comforts, nor seek such sensible delights but rather prefers hard exercises, and to sustain severe labour for Christ.

4. Therefore, when God gives spiritual consolation, receive it with thanksgiving; but know that it is God's free gift, and no merit of thine.

Be not lifted up, be not overjoyed, nor vainly presume, but rather be the more humble for this gift, more cautious, too, and fearful in all thy actions; for that hour will pass away, and temptation follow.

When consolation shall be taken away from thee, do not presently despair, but with humility and patience await the heavenly visitation, since God is able to restore to thee more abundant consolation.

This is no new nor strange occurrence to those who have known the way of God; for among the great Saints and ancient Prophets there has often been this kind of vicissitude.

5. Hence there was one who, when grace was with him, exclaimed: "I said in my abundance, I shall not be moved for ever."

But when grace was withdrawn, he tells what he experienced in himself, saying: "Thou hast turned away Thy face from me, and I became troubled."

Yet even then he despaireth not, but more earnestly prayeth to the Lord, and saith: "Unto Thee, O Lord, will I cry; and to my God will I make supplication."

At length he receiveth the fruit of his prayer, and witnesseth that he was heard, saying: "The Lord hath heard, and hath had mercy on me: the Lord hath become my helper."

But in what way? "Thou hast turned," he saith, "my mourning into joy, and Thou hast encompassed me with gladness." [Ps. 30:6–8, 10–11]

If it hath been thus with great Saints, we that are weak and poor must not be discouraged if we are sometimes fervent, sometimes cold, because the Spirit cometh and goeth according to his own good pleasure.

Wherefore holy Job saith: "Thou visitest him early in the morning, and on a sudden Thou triest him." [7:18]

6. Wherein then, can I hope, or in what must I put my trust, but in God's great mercy alone, and in the hope of heavenly grace?

For whether I have with me good men, or devout brethren, or faithful friends, or holy books, or beautiful treatises, or sweet canticles and hymns, all these help but little, give me but little relish, when I am forsaken by grace and left in my own poverty.

At such a time there is no better remedy than patience, and denying of myself according to the will of God.

7. I never found anyone so religious and devout as not sometimes to experience a withdrawal of grace, or feel a diminution of fervour.

No Saint was ever so sublimely rapt and illuminated as not to be tempted sooner or later.

For he is not worthy the sublime contemplation of God, who has not, for God's sake, been exercised with some tribulation.

For preceding temptation is usually a sign of ensuing consolation.

For heavenly comfort is promised to such as have been proved by temptation.

"To him that shall overcome," saith the Lord, "I will give to eat of the tree of life." [Rev. 2:7]

8. Now divine consolation is given that a man may the better be able to support adversities.

And temptation followeth, that he may not be elated by the good.

The devil sleepeth not, neither is the flesh yet dead; therefore thou must not cease to prepare thyself for the battle; for on the right hand and on the left are enemies that never rest.

That Temporal Miseries are to be Borne with Equanimity after the Example of Christ

Son, I came down from heaven for thy salvation; I took upon Me thy miseries, not of necessity, but moved thereto by charity, that thou mightest learn patience and bear without repining temporal miseries.

For from the hour of my birth until I expired upon the Cross I was not without the endurance of grief; moreover, I suffered great want of all earthly things.

I frequently heard many complaints against Me; I meekly bore disgrace and reproaches; for benefits I received ingratitude; for miracles, blasphemies; for heavenly doctrine, reproofs.

2. Lord, because Thou wast patient in Thy lifetime, herein especially fulfilling the commandment of Thy Father, it is fitting that I, a wretched sinner, should, according to Thy will, bear myself patiently and, as long as Thou pleasest, support the burden of this corruptible life, in order to my salvation.

For though this present life is felt to be burdensome, yet it is now rendered, through Thy grace, very meritorious; and by Thy example and the footsteps of Thy Saints, more bright and supportable to the weak.

It is also much more full of consolation than it was formerly under the law, when the gate of heaven remained shut; and even the way to heaven seemed more obscure, when so few concerned themselves to seek the kingdom of heaven.

Moreover, too, they who were then just, and to be saved, could not enter into Thy heavenly kingdom before Thy Passion and the payment of our debt by Thy sacred death.

3. Oh, what great thanks am I bound to render unto Thee, for having vouchsafed to show me and all the faithful a right and good way to Thine everlasting kingdom!

For Thy life is our way; and by holy patience we walk on to Thee, who art our crown.

If Thou hadst not gone before and instructed us, who would have cared to follow?

Alas, how many would have stayed afar off and a great way behind, had they not before their eyes Thy glorious example!

Behold, we are still tepid, notwithstanding all Thy miracles: and instructions which we have heard; what, then, would it be if we had not so great light to follow Thee?

That Man should not be a Curious Searcher into this Sacrament, but a Humble Follower of Christ, Submitting his Sense to Holy Faith

THE VOICE OF THE BELOVED

Thou must beware of curious and useless scrutiny into this most profound Sacrament, if thou wouldst not sink into the depth of doubt.

He that is a searcher of majesty, shall be overwhelmed by glory.

God is able to effect more than man is able to understand.

A pious and humble inquiry after truth is permitted, as it is always prepared to be instructed, and studieth to walk in sound doctrine of the Fathers.

2. Blessed is that simplicity, which leaveth the difficult paths of questionings, and goeth on in the plain and sure path of God's commandments.

Many have lost devotion, whilst they would search into matters.

It is faith and an upright life that are required of thee; not the loftiness of intellect, nor diving deep into the Mysteries of God.

If thou dost neither understand nor comprehend those things which are beneath thee, how mayest thou comprehend such as are above thee?

Submit thyself to God, and humble thy sense to faith, and the light of knowledge shall be given thee, according as shall be advantageous and necessary for thee.

3. Some are grievously tempted concerning faith and the Sacrament; but this is not to be imputed to them, but rather to the enemy.

Be not thou anxious, nor stop to dispute with thy thoughts, nor answer doubts which the Devil suggests; but believe the words of God, believe His Saints and Prophets, and the wicked enemy will fly from thee.

It is often very profitable that the servant of God should suffer such things.

For the Devil tempteth not unbelievers and sinners, whom he already surely possesseth; but the faithful and devout he tempteth and molesteth in many ways.

4. Go forward, therefore, with a simple and undoubting faith, and with lowly reverence approach the Sacrament; and whatsoever thou art not able to understand, securely commit to God, the omnipotent.

God doth not deceive thee; but he is deceived, who trusteth too much to himself.

God walketh with the simple, revealeth Himself to the humble, and giveth understanding to little ones; He discloseth His meaning to pure minds, and hideth His grace from the curious and proud.

Human reason is weak, and may be deceiving; but true faith cannot be deceived.

5. All reason and natural investigation ought to follow, and not precede or infringe upon it.

For faith and love are here most especially predominant, and operate by occult ways in the most holy and super-excelling Sacrament.

God, the eternal and immense, and of power infinite, doth things great and inscrutable in heaven and in earth; and there is no searching out His wonderful works.

If the works of God were such that they could easily be comprehended by human reason, they could neither be called wonderful or unspeakable.

22

Martin Luther, Prefaces to Job, Ecclesiastes, and the Psalter

---

The views on evil of the German reformer Martin Luther (1483–1546) were largely consistent with his Augustinian background. Human life is a battlefield: "Christians know that there are two kingdoms in the world, which are bitterly opposed to each other. In one of them Satan reigns, who is therefore called by Christ 'the ruler of this world' [John 12:31] and by Paul 'the god of this world' [2 Cor. 4:4]. He holds captive to his will all who are not snatched away from him by the Spirit of Christ . . . In the other kingdom, Christ reigns, and his kingdom ceaselessly resists and makes war on the kingdom of Satan. Into this Kingdom we are transferred, not by our own power but by the grace of God." Powerless before Satan without the help of Christ and the angels, Christians must be ever prayerful and vigilant. Part of this vigilance is to reject questions about the justice of God. "Whoso, without the word of grace and prayer, disputes with the devil will lose," not only because Satan has had thousands of years of practice, but because our guilty consciences undermine us. In this struggle, every Christian not only has a right to direct access to Scripture, but *needs* it. As Luther's prefaces to his translations of the Books of the Bible movingly explain, only in the Bible can the believer find a language in which to make sense of the trials and joys of life without falling into despair and sin.

Martin Luther, "Prefaces to the Books of the Bible," trans. C. M. Jacobs, in *Works of Martin Luther*, vol. VI (Philadelphia: A. J. Holman & The Castle Press, 1932), 383–8.

Preface to the Book of Job (1524)

The book of Job deals with the question, whether misfortune can come to the righteous from God. Job stands fast, and holds that God chastises even the righteous without reason, to His praise, as Christ also says, in John [9:3], of the man who was born blind.

His friends take the other side and make a great, long talk, defending God's justice, and saying that He punishes no righteous man; if He punishes, then the man who is punished must have sinned. They have a worldly and human idea of God and His righteousness, as though He were like a man and His law were like the world's law.

Job, to be sure, when he is in danger of death, talks, in his human weakness, too much against God, and thus sins amidst his sufferings; nevertheless, he insists that he has not deserved this suffering more than others have; and that is true. But at last God decides that Job, by speaking against Him, has spoken wrongly, in his suffering; but that he spoke the truth in what he said, replying to his friends, about his innocence before the suffering came.

Thus this book leads the history up to this point, – God alone is righteous, and yet one man is more righteous than another, even before God. It is written for our comfort, in order that we may know that God allows even His great saints to stumble, especially in adversity. Before Job comes into fear of death, he praises God at the theft of his goods and the death of his children; but when death is in prospect and God withdraws Himself, his words show what kind of ideas a man, however holy he may be, has against God, when he gets the notion that God is not God, but only a judge and wrathful tyrant, who applies force and cares nothing about a good life. This is the finest part of this book. It is understood only by those who also experience and feel what it is to suffer the wrath and judgment of God, and to have His grace hidden . . .

Preface to the Preacher of Solomon (1524)

[T]his book ought really have the title, "Against the Free Will"; for all of it tends to show that all men's counsels, proposals, and undertakings are vain and fruitless and always have a different end from that which we want and expect. Thus he would teach us to be passive and let God alone do everything, above and against and without our knowledge and counsel. Therefore you must not understand this book to be abusing God's creatures when it says, "All is vanity and misery"; for God's creatures are all good (Genesis i [1:31] and II Timothy iv [4:4]), and this book itself says that one shall be happy with one's wife and enjoy life, etc. It teaches, rather, that the proposals and purposes of men for dealing with creatures all go wrong and are all in vain, if one is not satisfied with what is ready to hand, but wants to be master and ruler of things that are yet to come. In that case, everything goes backwards, and a man has had only his trouble for his pains, and things turn out, anyhow, as God wills and purposes, not as man wills and purposes. To put it briefly, Christ says, in Matthew vi [6:34], "Be not anxious about the morrow, for the morrow will have its own anxiety; it is enough that every day has its own evil." That saying is a gloss and table of contents for this book. Anxiety for us is God's affair; our anxiety goes wrong anyhow, and is only lost trouble.

Preface to the Psalter (1531)

Many of the holy fathers praised and loved the Psalter above all other books of Scripture; and although the work itself gives praise enough to its master, nevertheless we must give evidence of our own praise and thanks.

In past years very many books have been peddled around, legends of the saints and passionals, books of examples and stories, and the world has been filled with them, so that the Psalter lay, meanwhile, under the bench and in such darkness that not one Psalm was rightly understood; and yet it gave off such a fine and precious fragrance that all pious hearts felt the devotion and power in the unknown words, and loved the book for them.

I hold, however, that no book of examples or legends of the saints finer than the Psalter has ever come, or can come, to the earth. If one were to wish that, from all the examples, legends and histories, the best should be selected and brought together and put in the best form, the result would have to be the present Psalter. For here we find not only what one or two saints have done, but what He has done who is the head of all saints, and what the saints still do – the attitude they take toward God, toward friends and enemies, the way they conduct themselves in all dangers and sufferings; all this, beside the divine and wholesome and commandments of every kind that are contained there.

The Psalter ought to be a dear and beloved book, if only because it promises Christ's death and resurrection so clearly, and so typifies His kingdom and the condition and nature of all Christendom that it might well be called a little Bible. It puts everything that is in all the Bible most beautifully and briefly, and is made an *Enchiridion*, or handbook, so that I have a notion that the Holy Ghost wanted to take the trouble to compile a short Bible and example-book of all Christendom, or of all saints. Thus, whoever could not read the whole Bible would here have almost an entire summary of it, comprised in one little book.

But above all this, the Psalter has this fine virtue and quality: – other books make great ado over the works of the saints, but say very little about their words; but the Psalter is a pattern; it gives forth so sweet a fragrance, when one reads it, because it tells not only the works of the saints, but also their words, how they spoke with God and prayed, and still speak and pray. The other legends and examples, when compared to the Psalter, present to us only dumb saints; but the Psalter pictures really bold, living saints.

Compared with a speaking man, a dumb man is to be thought a half-dead man; and there is no mightier or nobler work of man than speech, since it is by speech, more than by his shape or by any other work, that man is most distinguished from other animals. By the carver's art a block of wood can be given the shape of a man, and a beast, as well as a man, can see, hear, smell, sing, walk, stand, eat, drink, fast, thirst, and suffer from hunger, frost, and a hard bed.

Moreover, the Psalter does still more than this. It presents to us not the simple, common speech of the saints, but the best of their language, that which they used when they talked with God Himself, with great earnest-ness, on the most important matters. Thus it lays before us, not only their words, rather than their works, but their very hearts and the innermost treasure of their souls, so that we can look down to the foundation and source of their words and works, that is, into their hearts, and see there what kind of thoughts they had, and how their hearts were set and how they acted in all kinds of cases, in danger and in need. The legends, or examples, which speak only of the works and miracles of the saints, do not and cannot do this; for I cannot know how a man's heart is, even though I see or hear of many great works that he does. And just as I would rather hear what a saint says than see the works he does, so I would far rather see his heart, and the treasure in his soul, than hear his words. And that is the richest thing about the saints that the Psalter gives us, – we can be certain of how their hearts were toward God, and what words they used to God and every man.

A human heart is like a ship on a wild sea, driven by the storm-winds from the four quarters of the world. Here it is struck with fear, and worry about coming disaster; there comes grief and sadness because of present evil. Here breathes a breeze of hope and of expectation of happiness to come; there blows security and joy in present blessings. These storm-winds teach us to speak with earnestness, and open the heart, and pour out what lies at the bottom of it: He who sticks in fear and need speaks of misfortune very differently from him who floats on joy; and he who floats on joy speaks and sings of joy quite differently from him who sticks in fear. It is not from the heart, men say, when a sad man laughs or a glad man weeps; that is, the depths of his heart are not open, and what is in them does not come out.

What is the greatest thing in the Psalter but this earnest speaking amid these storm-winds of every kind? Where does one find such words of joy as in the psalms of praise and thanksgiving? There you look into the hearts of all the saints, as into fair and pleasant gardens, nay, as into heaven, and see what fine and pleasant flowers of the heart spring up from fair and happy thoughts of every kind toward God, because of His benefits. On the other hand, where do you find deeper, more sorrowful, more pitiful words of sadness than in the psalms of lamentation? There again you look into the hearts of all the saints, as into death, nay, as into hell. How gloomy and dark it is there, with all kinds of troubled outlooks on the wrath of God! So, too, when they speak of fear and hope, they use such words that no painter could so depict fear or hope, and no Cicero, or orator, so portray them.

And, as was said, it is the best thing of all that they speak these words to God and with God. This gives the words double earnestness and life, for when men speak with men about these matters, what they say does not come so strongly from the heart, and burn and live and press so greatly. Hence it comes that the Psalter is the book of all saints, and everyone, in whatever case he is, finds in it psalms and words that fit his case and suit him exactly, as though they were put thus for his sake only, so that he could not put it better himself, or find better words, or wish for better. And this, too, is good; for when these words please a man and suit him, he becomes sure that he is in the communion of saints, and that it has gone with all the saints as it goes with him, since they all sing one song with him. It is especially so, if he can speak to God as they have done, which must be done in faith, for their words have no flavor to a godless man.

Finally, there is in the Psalter security and a well-tried escort, so that one can follow all saints in it without peril. The other examples and the legends of the dumb saints bring forward many works that one cannot imitate; but they also bring forward many more works which it is dangerous to imitate, and which commonly start sects and disturbances, and lead away from the communion of saints, and tear it apart. But the Psalter holds you to the communion of saints and away from sects for it teaches you to be of like mind in joy, fear, hope, sorrow, and to think and speak as all the saints have thought and spoken.

In a word, would you see the holy Christian Church painted in living color and form and put in one little picture? Then take up the Psalter and you have a fine, bright, pure mirror that will show you what the Church is; nay, you will find yourself also in it and the true *gnothi seauton* [know thyself], and God Himself, besides, and all creatures . . .

23

John Calvin, *The Institutes of the Christian Religion*

Like Augustine, the French reformer Jean Calvin (1509–64) argued that a misuse of freedom "perverted the whole order of nature in heaven and on earth"; even animals suffer only as "part of the punishment deserved by man." Calvin thought that it was mere wordplay to deny that "God not only foresaw the fall of the first man; but also at his own pleasure arranged it." His uncompromising doctrine of *double* predestination makes the justice of God's decision to bestow mercy on some and reprobate others the focal point of reflection on evil – or would, did he not condemn all speculation: "His [God's] immensity surely ought to deter us from measuring him by our sense, while his spiritual nature forbids us to indulge in carnal or earthly speculation concerning him." The Christian life is one of charity and self-sacrifice, a self-sacrifice attended by an almost Stoic "tranquillity and endurance." Without this resignation, "the many accidents to which we are liable" make people "curse their life, detest the day of their birth, execrate the light of heaven, even censure God, and (as they are eloquent with blasphemy) charge him with cruelty and injustice."

John Calvin, *Institutes of the Christian Religion*, XXIII.2–5; ed. John T. Mitchell and trans. Ford Lewis Battles (Library of Christian Classics, vol. XXI) (Philadelphia: Westminster, 1960), 949–53.

God's will is the rule of righteousness

To the pious and moderate and those who are mindful that they are men, these statements should be quite sufficient. Yet because these venomous dogs spew out more than one kind of venom against God, we shall answer each individually, as the matter requires.

Foolish men contend with God in many ways, as though they held him liable to their accusations. They first ask, therefore, by what right the Lord becomes angry at his creatures who have not provoked him by any previous offense; for to devote to destruction whomever he pleases is more like the caprice of a tyrant than the lawful sentence of a judge. It therefore seems to them that men have reason to expostulate with God if they are predestined to eternal death solely by his decision, apart from their own merit. If thoughts of this sort ever occur to pious men, they will be sufficiently armed to break their force even by the one consideration that it is very wicked merely to investigate the causes of God's will. For his will is, and rightly ought to be, the cause of all things that are. For if it has any cause, something must precede it, to which it is, as it were, bound; this is unlawful to imagine. For God's will is so much the highest rule of righteousness that whatever he wills, by the very fact that he wills it, must be considered righteous. When, therefore, one asks why God has so done, we must reply: because he has willed it. [So frequently Augustine; e.g., *On Genesis, Against the Manichees* I.ii.4 (MPL 34.175).] But if you proceed further to ask why he so willed, you are seeking something greater and higher than God's will, which cannot be found. Let men's rashness, then, restrain itself, and not seek what does not exist, lest perhaps it fail to find what does exist. This bridle, I say, will effectively restrain anyone who wants to ponder in reverence the secrets of his God. Against the boldness of the wicked who are not afraid to curse God openly, the Lord himself will sufficiently defend himself by his righteousness, without our help, when, by depriving their consciences of all evasion, he will convict them and condemn them.

And we do not advocate the fiction of "absolute might"; because this is profane, it ought rightly to be hateful to us. We fancy no lawless god who is a law unto himself. For, as Plato says, men who are troubled with lusts are in need of law; but the will of God is not only free of all fault but is the highest rule of perfection, and even the law of all laws. But we deny that he is liable to render an account; we also deny that we are competent judges to pronounce judgment in this cause according to our own understanding. Accordingly, if we attempt more than is permitted, let that threat of the psalm strike us with fear: God will be the victor whenever he is judged by mortal man [Ps. 51:4; cf. 50:6, Vg.].

God is just toward the reprobate

So keeping silence, God can restrain his enemies. But lest we allow them to mock his holy name with impunity, out of his Word he supplies us with weapons against them. Accordingly, if anyone approaches us with such expressions as: "Why from the beginning did God predestine some to death who, since they did not yet exist, could not yet have deserved the judgment of death?" [Augustine, *Unfinished Treatise Against Julian* I.xlviii; II.viii (MPL 45.1069 f., 1145).] let us, in lieu of reply, ask them, in turn, what they think God owes to man if He would judge him according to His own nature. As all of us are vitiated by sin, we can only be odious to God, and that not from tyrannical cruelty but by the fairest reckoning of justice. But if all whom the Lord predestines to death are by condition of nature subject to the judgment of death, of what injustice toward themselves may they complain?

Let all the sons of Adam come forward; let them quarrel and argue with their Creator that they were by his eternal providence bound over before their begetting to everlasting calamity. What clamor can they raise against this defense when God, on the contrary, will call them to their account before him? If all are drawn from a corrupt mass, no wonder they are subject to condemnation! Let them not accuse God of injustice if they are destined by his eternal judgment to death, to which they feel – whether they will or not – that they are led by their own nature of itself. How perverse is their disposition to protest is apparent from the fact that they deliberately suppress the cause of condemnation, which they are compelled to recognize in themselves, in order to free themselves by blaming God. But though I should confess a hundred times that God is the author of it – which is very true – yet they do not promptly cleanse away the guilt that, engraved upon their consciences, repeatedly meets their eyes.

God's decree is also hidden in his justice

Again they object: were they not previously predestined by God's ordinance to that corruption which is now claimed as the cause of condemnation? When, therefore, they perish in their corruption, they but pay the penalties of that misery in which Adam fell by predestination of God, and dragged his posterity headlong after him. Is he not, then, unjust who so cruelly deludes his creatures? [Erasmus, *De libero arbitrio*, ed. von Walter, p. 80.] Of course, I admit that in this miserable condition wherein men are now bound, all of Adam's children have fallen by God's will. And this is what I said to begin with, that we must always at last return to the sole decision of God's will, the cause of which is hidden in him. But it does not directly follow that God is subject to this reproach. For with Paul we shall answer in this way: "Who are you, O man, to argue with God? Does the molded object say to its molder, 'Why have you fashioned me thus?' Or does the potter have no capacity to make from the same lump one vessel for honor, another for dishonor?" [Rom. 9:20–1].

They will say that God's righteousness is not truly defended thus but that we are attempting a subterfuge such as those who lack a just excuse are wont to have. For what else seems to be said here than that God has a power that cannot be prevented from doing whatever it pleases him to do? But it is far otherwise. For what stronger reason can be adduced than when we are bidden to ponder who God is? For how could he who is the Judge of the earth allow any iniquity [cf. Gen. 18:25]? If the execution of Judgment properly belongs to God's nature, then by nature he loves righteousness and abhors unrighteousness Accordingly, the apostle did not look for loopholes of escape as if he were embarrassed in his argument but showed that the reason of divine righteousness is higher than man's standard can measure, or than man's slender wit can comprehend. The apostle even admits that such depth underlies God's judgments [Rom. 11:33] that all men's minds would be swallowed up if they tried to penetrate it. But he also teaches how unworthy it is to reduce God's works to such a law that the moment we fail to understand their reason, we dare to condemn them. That saying of Solomon's is well known, although few properly understand it: "The great Creator of all things pays the fool his wages, and the transgressors theirs" [Prov. 26:10, cf. Geneva Bible]. For he is exclaiming about the greatness of God, in whose decision is the punishment of fools and transgressors, although he does not bestow on them his Spirit. Monstrous indeed is the madness of men, who desire thus to subject the immeasurable to the puny measure of their own reason! Paul calls the angels who stood in their uprightness "elect" [I Tim. 5:21]; if their steadfastness was grounded in God's good pleasure, the rebellion of the others proves the latter were forsaken. No other cause of this fact can be adduced but reprobation, which is hidden in God's secret plan.

God's hidden decree is not to be searched out but obediently marveled at

Come now, suppose some follower of Mani or Coelestius, a slanderer of divine providence, is present. I say with Paul that we ought not to seek

any reason for it because in its greatness it far surpasses our understanding [cf. Rom. 9:19–23]. What marvel, this, or what absurdity? Would
he wish God's might so limited as to be unable to accomplish any more
than his mind can conceive? With Augustine I say: the Lord has created
those whom he unquestionably foreknew would go to destruction. This
has happened because he has so willed it. But why he so willed, it is not
for our reason to inquire, for we cannot comprehend it. [Augustine, *Letters*,
clxxxvi.7.23 (MPL 33.824; tr. FC 30.207).] And it is not fitting that God's
will should be dragged down into controversy among us, for whenever
mention is made of it, under its name is designated the supreme rule
of righteousness. Why raise any question of unrighteousness where righteousness clearly appears? And let us not be ashamed, following Paul's
example, to stop the mouths of the wicked, and whenever they dare
to rail, repeat the same thing: "Who are you, miserable men, to make
accusation against God?" [Rom. 9:20 p.]. Why do you, then, accuse
him because he does not temper the greatness of his works to your
ignorance? As if these things were wicked because they are hidden from
flesh! It is known to you by clear evidence that the judgments of God
are beyond measure. You know that they are called a "great deep" [Ps.
36:6]. Now consider the narrowness of your mind, whether it can grasp
what God has decreed with himself. What good will it do you in your
mad search to plunge into the "deep," which your own reason tells you
will be your destruction? Why does not some fear at least restrain you
because the history of Job as well as the prophetic books proclaim God's
incomprehensible wisdom and dreadful might? If your mind is troubled,
do not be ashamed to embrace Augustine's advice: "You, a man, expect
an answer from me; I too am a man. Therefore, let both of us hear one
who says, 'O man, who are you?' [Rom. 9:20]. Ignorance that believes is
better than rash knowledge. Seek merits; you will find only punishment.
'O depth!' [Rom. 11:33]. Peter denies; the thief believes. 'O depth!'
Thou seekest reason? I tremble at the depth. Reason, thou; I will marvel.
Dispute, thou; I will believe. I see the depth; I do not reach the bottom.
Paul rested, for he found wonder. He calls God's judgments 'unsearchable,'
and thou settest out to search them? He speaks of his ways as 'inscrutable'
[Rom. 11:33], and thou dost track them down?" [Augustine, *Sermons*,
xxvii.3.4; 6.6; 7.7 (MPL 38.179–82).] It will do us no good to proceed
farther, for neither will it satisfy their petulance nor does the Lord need
any other defense than what he used through his Spirit, who spoke
through Paul's mouth; and we forget to speak well when we cease to speak
with God.

24

John Donne, "Batter my heart, three-personed God"

The "Holy Sonnets" of John Donne (1572–1631), the leading poet of the Metaphysical School of English poetry, well express the increasingly paradoxical feel of traditional Christian understandings of suffering in a changing Europe.

"Holy Sonnet" no. 14, *The Norton Anthology of English Literature*, gen. ed. M. H. Abrams, 6th edn. (New York: W. W. Norton, 1993), I.1117.

> Batter my heart, three-personed God; for you
> As yet but knock, breathe, shine, and seek to mend;
> That I may rise and stand, o'erthrow me, and bend
> Your force to break, blow, burn, and make me new.
> I, like an usurped town, to another due,
> Labor to admit you, but O, to no end;
> Reason, your viceroy in me, me should defend,
> But is captived, and proves weak or untrue.
> Yet dearly I love you, and would be loved fain,
> But am betrothed unto your enemy.
> Divorce me, untie or break that knot again;
> Take me to you, imprison me, for I,
> Except you enthrall me, never shall be free,
> Nor ever chaste, except you ravish me.

The Rise of Theodicy

25

Thomas Hobbes, *Leviathan*

The *Leviathan* of Thomas Hobbes (1588–1679), composed in Paris in 1651 as England was convulsed with religious and political struggle, is perhaps the greatest work of political philosophy in the English language. A skeptic and materialist, Hobbes argued that human vulnerability and the uncertainty of all human knowledge make necessary the establishment of states whose sovereigns have virtually unlimited power to set the terms for the lives of their citizens. The most scandalous aspect of *Leviathan* to Hobbes' contemporaries was its argument for the sovereign's right to insist even on religious uniformity (though Hobbes also allowed for religious pluralism when this was more likely to conduce to social peace), an argument built on the foundation of an exalted theology of an inconceivable God. As the famous chapter on the "Kingdome of God by Nature" below shows, Hobbes thought the human relationship to God is from the outset established by his sheer power over us; the form public worship should take, however, is to be decided by the political sovereign. The omnipotence-centered theology of Hobbes, and the political absolutism which seemed to follow from it, were among the main targets of Leibniz's antivoluntarism in politics, ethics, and philosophical theology.

Thomas Hobbes, *Leviathan*, ch. 31; ed. Richard Tuck (Cambridge: Cambridge University Press, 1991), 245–53.

That the condition of meer Nature, that is to say, of absolute Liberty such as is theirs, that neither are Soveraigns, nor Subjects, is Anarchy, and the condition of Warre: That the Praecepts, by which men are guided to avoyd that condition, are the Lawes of Nature: That a Common-wealth, without Soveraign Power, is but a word without substance, and cannot stand: That

Subjects owe to Soveraigns, simple Obedience, in all things, wherein their
obedience is not repugnant to the Lawes of God, I have sufficiently proved,
in that which I have already written. There wants onely, for the entire
knowledge of Civill duty, to know what are those Lawes of God. For
without that, a man knows not, when he is commanded any thing by the
Civill Power, whether it be contrary to the Law of God, or not: and so,
either by too much civill obedience, offends the Divine Majesty, or
through feare of offending God, transgresses the commandements of the
Common-wealth. To avoyd both these Rocks, it is necessary to know what
are the Lawes Divine. And seeing the knowledge of all Law, dependeth on
the knowledge of the Soveraign Power; I shall say something in that which
followeth, of the KINGDOME OF GOD . . .

The Right of Nature, whereby God reigneth over men, and punisheth
those that break his Lawes, is to be derived, not from his Creating them
as if he required obedience, as of Gratitude for his benefits; but from his
Irresistible Power. I have formerly shewn, how the Soveraign Right ariseth
from Pact: To shew how the same Right may arise from Nature, requires
no more, but to shew in what case it is never taken away. Seeing all men
by Nature had Right to All things, they had Right every one to reigne
over all the rest. But because this Right could not be obtained by force,
it concerned the safety of every one, laying by that Right, to set up men
(with Soveraign Authority) by common consent, to rule and defend them:
whereas if there had been any man of Power Irresistible; there had been
no reason, why he should not by that Power have ruled, and defended
both himselfe, and them, according to his own discretion. To those therefore whose Power is irresistible, the dominion of all men adhaereth naturally by their excellence of Power; and consequently it is from that Power,
that the Kingdome over men, and the Right of Afflicting men at his pleasure, belongeth Naturally to God Almighty; not as Creator, and Gracious;
but as Omnipotent. And though Punishment be due for Sinne onely,
because by that word is understood Affliction for Sinne; yet the Right of
Afflicting, is not alwayes derived from mens Sinne, but from Gods Power.

This question, *Why Evill men often Prosper, and Good men suffer Adversity*,
has been much disputed by the Antient, and is the same with this of ours,
by what Right God dispenseth the Prosperities and Adversities of this life; and is
of that difficulty, as it hath shaken the faith, not onely of the Vulgar, but
of Philosophers, and which is more, of the Saints, concerning the Divine
Providence. *How Good* (saith David) *is the God of Israel to those that are
Upright in Heart; and yet my feet were almost gone, my treadings had well-nigh
slipt; for I was grieved at the Wicked, when I saw the Ungodly in such Prosperity* [Ps. 72:1-3]. And *Job*, how earnestly does he expostulate with God, for

the many Afflictions he suffered, notwithstanding his Righteousnesse? This question in the case of *Job*, is decided by God himselfe, not by arguments derived from *Job's* Sinne, but his own Power. For whereas the friends of *Job* drew their arguments from his Affliction to his Sinne, and he defended himselfe by the conscience of his Innocence, God himselfe taketh up the matter, and having justified the Affliction by arguments drawn from his Power, such as this, *Where wast thou when I layd the foundations of the earth* [Job 38:4], and the like, both approved *Job's* Innocence, and reproved the Erroneous doctrine of his friends. Conformable to this doctrine is the sentence of our Saviour, concerning the man that was born Blind, in these words, *Neither hath this man sinned, nor his fathers; but that the works of God might be made manifest in him* [Jn. 9:3]. And though it be said, *That Death entred into the world by sinne* [Rom. 5:12] (by which is meant that if Adam had never sinned, he had never dyed, that is, never suffered any separation of his soule from his body,) it follows not thence, that God could not justly have Afflicted him, though he had not Sinned, as well as he afflicteth other living creatures, that cannot sinne.

Having spoken of the Right of Gods Soveraignty, as grounded onely on Nature; we are to consider next, what are the Divine Lawes, or Dictates of Naturall Reason; which Lawes concern either the naturall Duties of one man to another, or the Honour naturally due to our Divine Soveraign. The first are the same Lawes of Nature, of which I have spoken already in the 14. and 15. Chapters of this Treatise; namely, Equity, Justice, Mercy, Humility, and the rest of the Morall Vertues. It remaineth therefore that we consider, what Praecepts are dictated to men, by their Naturall Reason onely, without other word of God, touching the Honour and Worship of the Divine Majesty.

Honour consisteth in the inward thought, and opinion of the Power, and Goodnesse of another: and therefore to Honour God, is to think as Highly of his Power and Goodnesse, as is possible. And of that opinion, the externall signes appearing in the Words, and Actions of men, are called *Worship*; which is one part of that which the Latines understand by the word *Cultus*: For *Cultus* signifieth properly, and constantly, that labour which a man bestowes on any thing, with a purpose to make benefit by it. Now those things whereof we make benefit, are either subject to us, and the profit they yeeld, followeth the labour we bestow upon them, as a naturall effect; or they are not subject to us, but answer our labour, according to their own Wills. In the first sense the labour bestowed on the Earth, is called *Culture*; and the education of Children a *Culture* of their mindes. In the second sense, where mens wills are to be wrought to our purpose, not by Force, but by Compleasance, it signifieth as much as

Courting, that is, a winning of favour by good offices; as by praises, by acknowledging their Power, and by whatsoever is pleasing to them from whom we look for any benefit. And this is properly *Worship*: . . .

The End of Worship amongst men, is Power. For where a man seeth another worshipped, he supposeth him powerfull, and is the readier to obey him; which makes his Power greater. But God has no Ends: the worship we do him, proceeds from our duty, and is directed according to our capacity, by those rules of Honour, that Reason dictateth to be done by the weak to the more potent men, in hope of benefit, for fear of dammage, or in thankfulnesse for good already received from them.

That we may know what worship of God is taught us by the light of Nature, I will begin with his Attributes. Where, First, it is manifest, we ought to attribute to him *Existence*: For no man can have the will to honour that, which he thinks not to have any Beeing.

Secondly, that those Philosophers, who sayd the World, or the Soule of the World was God, spake unworthily of him; and denyed his Existence: For by God, is understood the cause of the World; and to say the World is God, is to say there is no cause of it, that is, no God.

Thirdly, to say the World was not Created, but Eternall, (seeing that which is Eternall has no cause,) is to deny there is a God.

Fourthly, that they [Epicureans] who attributing (as they think) Ease to God, take from him the care of Man-kind; take from him his Honour: for it takes away mens love, and fear of him; which is the root of Honour.

Fifthly, in those things that signifie Greatnesse, and Power; to say he is *Finite*, is not to Honour him: For it is not a signe of the Will to Honour God, to attribute to him lesse than we can; and Finite, is lesse than we can; because to Finite, it is easie to adde more.

Therefore to attribute *Figure* to him, is not Honour; for all Figure is Finite:

Nor to say we conceive, and imagine, or have an Idea of him, in our mind: for whatsoever we conceive is Finite:

Nor to attribute to him *Parts*, or *Totality*; which are the Attributes onely of things Finite:

Nor to say he is in this, or that *Place*: for whatsoever is in Place, is bounded, and Finite:

Nor that he is *Moved*, or *Resteth*: for both these Attributes ascribe to him Place:

Nor that there be more Gods than one; because it implies them all Finite: for there cannot be more than one Infinite.

Nor to ascribe to him (unlesse Metaphorically, meaning not the Passion, but the Effect) Passions that partake of Griefe; as *Repentance, Anger, Mercy*:

or of Want; as *Appetite, Hope, Desire*; or of any Passive faculty: For Passion, is Power limited by somewhat else.

And therefore when we ascribe to God a *Will*, it is not to be understood, as that of Man, for a *Rationall Appetite*; but as the Power, by which he effecteth every thing.

Likewise when we attribute to him *Sight*, and other acts of Sense; as also *Knowledge*, and *Understanding*, which in us is nothing else, but a tumult of the mind, raised by externall things that presse the organicall parts of mans body: For there is no such thing in God; and being things that depend on naturall causes, cannot be attributed to him.

Hee that will attribute to God, nothing but what is warranted by naturall Reason, must either use such Negative Attributes, as *Infinite, Eternall, Incomprehensible*, or Superlatives, as *Most High, most Great*, and the like; or Indefinite, as *Good, Just, Holy, Creator*, and in such sense, as if he meant not to declare what he is, (for that were to circumscribe him within the limits of our Fancy,) but how much wee admire him, and how ready we would be to obey him; which is a signe of Humility, and of a Will to honour him as much as we can: For there is but one Name to signifie our Conception of his Nature, and that is, I AM [cf. Exod. 3:14]: and but one Name of his Relation to us, and that is *God*; in which is contained Father, King, and Lord . . .

[I]t is a part of Rationall Worship, to speak Considerately of God; for it argues a Fear of him, and Fear, is a confession of his Power. Hence followeth, . . . that disputing of Gods nature is contrary to his Honour: For it is supposed, that in this naturall Kingdome of God, there is no other way to know any thing, but by naturall Reason; that is, from the Principles of naturall Science; which are so farre from teaching us any thing of Gods nature, as they cannot teach us our own nature, nor the nature of the smallest creature living. And therefore, when men out of the Principles of naturall Reason, dispute of the Attributes of God, they but dishonour him: For in the Attributes which we give to God, we are not to consider the signification of Philosophicall Truth; but the signification of Pious Intention, to do him the greatest Honour we are able . . .

Lastly, Obedience to his Lawes (that is, in this case to the Lawes of Nature,) is the greatest worship of all. For as Obedience is more acceptable to God than Sacrifice; so also to set light by his Commandements, is the greatest of all contumelies. And these are the Lawes of that Divine Worship, which naturall Reason dictateth to private men.

But seeing a Common-wealth is but one Person, it ought also to exhibite to God but one Worship; which then it doth, when it commandeth it to be exhibited by Private men, Publiquely. And this is Publique

Worship; the property whereof, is to be *Uniforme*: For those actions that are done differently, by different men, cannot be said to be a Publique Worship. And therefore, where many sorts of Worship be allowed, proceeding from the different Religions of Private men, it cannot be said there is any Publique Worship, nor that the Common-wealth is of any Religion at all.

And because words (and consequently the Attributes of God) have their signification by agreement, and constitution of men; those Attributes are to be held significative of Honour, that men intend shall so be; and whatsoever may be done by the wills of particular men, where there is no Law but Reason, may be done by the will of the Common-wealth, by Lawes Civill. And because a Common-wealth hath no Will, nor makes no Lawes, but those that are made by the Will of him, or them that have the Soveraign Power; it followeth that those Attributes which the Soveraign ordaineth, in the Worship of God, for signes of Honour, ought to be taken and used for such, by private men in their publique Worship . . .

26

John Milton, *Paradise Lost*

The English poet, historian, and pamphleteer John Milton (1608–74) wrote the Christian epic *Paradise Lost* in 1667 (and amplified it in 1674). He declares his intentions:

> Of Man's first disobedience, and the fruit
> Of that forbidden tree whose mortal taste
> Brought death into the World, and all our woe,
> With loss of Eden, till one greater Man
> Restore us, and regain the blissful seat,
> Sing, Heav'nly Muse, that, on the secret top
> Of Oreb, or of Sinai, didst inspire
> That shepherd who first taught the chosen seed
> In the beginning how the heav'ns and earth
> Rose out of Chaos: or, if Sion hill
> Delight thee more, and Siloa's brook that flowed
> Fast by the oracle of God, I thence
> Invoke thy aid to my advent'rous song,
> That with no middle flight intends to soar
> Above th' Aonian mount, while it pursues
> Things unattempted yet in prose or rhyme.
> And chiefly thou, O Spirit, that dost prefer
> Before all temples th' upright heart and pure,
> Instruct me, for thou know'st; thou from the first
> Wast present, and, with mighty wings outspread,
> Dove-like sat'st brooding on the vast Abyss,
> And mad'st it pregnant: what in me is dark
> Illumine, what is low raise and support;
> That, to the height of this great argument,

> I may assert Eternal Providence,
> And justify the ways of God to men.
>
> Yet Milton's greatest accomplishment seems to have been his compelling literary characterization of Satan. William Blake famously wrote that Milton was "a true Poet, and of the Devil's party without knowing it," and Percy Bysshe Shelley argued that Satan was the true hero of the epic, its God either dull or wicked. Milton does seem to have been some kind of dualist; his treatise of *Christian Doctrine* (printed in 1825) denied the creation *ex nihilo*. Yet the intention of *Paradise Lost* was surely not to undermine but to vindicate the justice and wisdom of God. Bypassing Satan entirely, the selection below presents the beginning and end of "Adam's Dream," the conclusion of the poem. Here the Archangel Michael shows Adam the consequences of his Fall while Eve sleeps, even before the expulsion from the Garden.

John Milton, *Paradise* Lost, I.1–19, XI.423–554, XII.375–435, 466–78, 553–87; *Paradise Lost: Norton Critical Edition*, 2nd edn., ed. Scott Elledge (New York: W. W. Norton, 1993), 7–9, 271–4, 293–6, 298–9.

"Adam, now ope thine eyes; and first behold
Th' effects, which thy original crime hath wrought
In some to spring from thee; who never touched
Th' excepted tree; nor with the snake conspired;
Nor sinned thy sin; yet from that sin derive
Corruption, to bring forth more violent deeds."
    His eyes he opened, and beheld a field,
Part arable and tilth, whereon were sheaves
New reaped; the other part sheep-walks and folds;
I' th' midst an altar as the land-mark stood,
Rustick, of grassy sord; thither anon
A sweaty reaper from his tillage brought
First fruits, the green ear, and the yellow sheaf,
Unculled, as came to hand; a shepherd next,
More meek, came with the firstlings of his flock,
Choicest and best; then, sacrificing, laid
The inwards and their fat, with incense strowed,
On the cleft wood, and all due rights performed:
His offering soon propitious fire from Heaven

Consumed with nimble glance, and grateful steam;
The other's not, for his was not sincere;
Whereat he inly raged, and, as they talked,
Smote him into the midriff with a stone
That beat out life; he fell; and, deadly pale,
Groaned out his soul with gushing blood effused.
Much at that sight was Adam in his heart
Dismayed, and thus in haste to the Angel cried.
   "O Teacher, some great mischief hath befall'n
To that meek man, who well had sacrificed;
Is piety thus and pure devotion paid?"
   T' whom Michael thus, he also moved, replied.
"These two are brethren, Adam, and to come
Out of thy loins; the unjust the just hath slain,
For envy that his brother's offering found
From Heaven acceptance; but the bloody fact
Will be avenged; and th' other's faith, approved,
Lose no reward; though here thou see him die,
Rolling in dust and gore." To which our sire.
   "Alas! both for the deed, and for the cause!
But have I now seen Death? Is this the way
I must return to native dust? O sight
Of terrour, foul and ugly to behold,
Horrid to think, how horrible to feel!"
   To whom thus Michaël. "Death thou hast seen
In his first shape on Man; but many shapes
Of Death, and many are the ways that lead
To his grim cave, all dismal; yet to sense
More terrible at th' entrance, than within.
Some, as thou saw'st, by violent stroke shall die;
By fire, flood, famine, by intemperance more
In meats and drinks, which on the earth shall bring
Diseases dire, of which a monstrous crew
Before thee shall appear; that thou may'st know
What misery th' inabstinence of Eve
Shall bring on Men." Immediately a place
Before his eyes appeared, sad, noisome, dark;
A lazar-house it seemed; wherein were laid
Numbers of all diseased; all maladies
Of ghastly spasm, or racking torture, qualms
Of heart-sick agony, all feverous kinds,

Convulsions, epilepsies, fierce catarrhs,
Intestine stone and ulcer, colick-pangs,
Demoniack phrenzy, moaping melancholy,
And moon-struck madness, pining atrophy,
Marasmus, and wide-wasting pestilence,
Dropsies, and asthmas, and joint-racking rheums.
Dire was the tossing, deep the groans; Despair
Tended the sick busiest from couch to couch;
And over them triumphant Death his dart
Shook, but delayed to strike, though oft invoked
With vows, as their chief good, and final hope.
Sight so deform what heart of rock could long
Dry-eyed behold? Adam could not, but wept,
Though not of woman born; compassion quelled
His best of man, and gave him up to tears
A space, till firmer thoughts restrained excess;
And, scarce recovering words, his plaint renewed.
    "O miserable mankind, to what fall
Degraded, to what wretched state reserved!
Better end here unborn. Why is life giv'n
To be thus wrested from us? rather, why
Obtruded on us thus? who, if we knew
What we receive, would either not accept
Life offered, or soon beg to lay it down;
Glad to be so dismissed in peace. Can thus
Th' image of God in Man, created once
So goodly and erect, though faulty since,
To such unsightly sufferings be debased
Under inhuman pains? Why should not Man,
Retaining still divine similitude
In part, from such deformities be free,
And, for his Maker's image sake, exempt?"
    "Their Maker's image," answered Michael, "then
Forsook them, when themselves they vilified
To serve ungoverned Appetite; and took
His image whom they served, a brutish vice,
Inductive mainly to the sin of Eve.
Therefore so abject is their punishment,
Disfiguring not God's likeness, but their own;
Or if his likeness, by themselves defaced;
While they pervert pure Nature's healthful rules

To loathsome sickness; worthily, since they
God's image did not reverence in themselves."
    "I yield it just," said Adam, "and submit.
But is there yet no other way, besides
These painful passages, how we may come
To death, and mix with our connatural dust?"
    "There is," said Michael, "if thou well observe
The rule of Not too much; by temperance taught,
In what thou eat'st and drink'st; seeking from thence
Due nourishment, not gluttonous delight,
Till many years over thy head return:
So mayest thou live; till, like ripe fruit, thou drop
Into thy mother's lap; or be with ease
Gathered, nor harshly plucked; for death mature:
This is Old Age; but then, thou must outlive
Thy youth, thy strength, thy beauty; which will change
To withered, weak, and gray; thy senses then,
Obtuse, all taste of pleasure must forego,
To what thou hast; and, for the air of youth,
Hopeful and cheerful, in thy blood will reign
A melancholy damp of cold and dry
To weigh thy spirits down, and last consume
The balm of life." To whom our ancestor.
    "Henceforth I fly not death, nor would prolong
Life much; bent rather, how I may be quit,
Fairest and easiest, of this cumbrous charge;
Which I must keep till my appointed day
Of rendering up, and patiently attend
My dissolution." Michaël replied.
    "Nor love thy life, nor hate; but what thou livest
Live well; how long, or short, permit to Heav'n: . . . "

[After showing him other important episodes of the Old Testament,
Michael tells Adam that a virgin will bear a saviour, to which Adam
replies:]

    "O prophet of glad tidings, finisher
Of utmost hope! now clear I understand
What oft my steadiest thoughts have searched in vain;
Why our great Expectation should be called
The seed of Woman: Virgin Mother, hail,

High in the love of Heav'n; yet from my loins
Thou shalt proceed, and from thy womb the Son
Of God Most High: so God with Man unites!
Needs must the Serpent now his capital bruise
Expect with mortal pain: Say where and when
Their fight, what stroke shall bruise the victor's heel."
     To whom thus Michael. "Dream not of their fight,
As of a duel, or the local wounds
Of head or heel: Not therefore joins the Son
Manhood to Godhead, with more strength to foil
Thy enemy; nor so is overcome
Satan, whose fall from heav'n, a deadlier bruise,
Disabled, not to give thee thy death's wound:
Which he, who comes thy Saviour, shall recure,
Not by destroying Satan, but his works
In thee, and in thy seed: Nor can this be,
But by fulfilling that which thou didst want,
Obedience to the law of God, imposed
On penalty of death, and suffering death;
The penalty to thy transgression due,
And due to theirs which out of thine will grow:
So only can high Justice rest appaid.
The law of God exact he shall fulfil
Both by obedience and by love, though love
Alone fulfil the law; thy punishment
He shall endure, by coming in the flesh
To a reproachful life, and cursèd death;
Proclaiming life to all who shall believe
In his redemption; and that his obedience,
Imputed, becomes theirs by faith; his merits
To save them, not their own, though legal, works.
For this he shall live hated, be blasphemed,
Seized on by force, judged, and to death condemned
A shameful and accursed, nailed to the Cross
By his own nation; slain for bringing life:
But to the Cross he nails thy enemies,
The law that is against thee, and the sins
Of all mankind, with him there crucified,
Never to hurt them more who rightly trust
In this his satisfaction; so he dies,
But soon revives; Death over him no power

Shall long usurp; ere the third dawning light
Return, the stars of morn shall see him rise
Out of his grave, fresh as the dawning light,
Thy ransom paid, which Man from death redeems,
His death for Man, as many as offered life
Neglect not, and the benefit embrace
By faith not void of works: This God-like act
Annuls thy doom, the death thou shouldest have died,
In sin for ever lost from life; this act
Shall bruise the head of Satan, crush his strength,
Defeating Sin and Death, his two main arms;
And fix far deeper in his head their stings
Than temporal death shall bruise the Victor's heel,
Or theirs whom he redeems; a death, like sleep,
A gentle wafting to immortal life . . . "

So spake the Arch-Angel Michaël; then paused,
As at the world's great period; and our sire,
Replete with joy and wonder, thus replied.
   "O Goodness infinite, Goodness immense!
That all this good of evil shall produce,
And evil turn to good; more wonderful
Than that which by creation first brought forth
Light out of darkness! Full of doubt I stand,
Whether I should repent me now of sin
By me done, and occasioned; or rejoice
Much more, that much more good thereof shall spring;
To God more glory, more good-will to Men
From God, and over wrath grace shall abound. . . . "

"How soon hath thy prediction, Seer blest,
Measured this transient world, the race of time,
Till time stand fixed! Beyond is all abyss,
Eternity, whose end no eye can reach.
Greatly-instructed I shall hence depart;
Greatly in peace of thought; and have my fill
Of knowledge, what this vessel can contain;
Beyond which was my folly to aspire.
Henceforth I learn, that to obey is best,
And love with fear the only God; to walk
As in his presence; ever to observe
His providence; and on him sole depend,

Merciful over all his works, with good
Still overcoming evil, and by small
Accomplishing great things, by things deemed weak
Subverting worldly strong, and worldly wise
By simply meek: that suffering for truth's sake
Is fortitude to highest victory,
And, to the faithful, death the gate of life;
Taught this by his example, whom I now
Acknowledge my Redeemer ever blest."
  To whom thus also the Angel last replied.
"This having learned, thou hast attained the sum
Of wisdom; hope no higher, though all the stars
Thou knewest by name, and all th' ethereal powers,
All secrets of the deep, all nature's works,
Or works of God in heav'n, air, earth, or sea,
And all the riches of this world enjoy'dst,
And all the rule, one empire; only add
Deeds to thy knowledge answerable; add faith,
Add virtue, patience, temperance; add love,
By name to come called charity, the soul
Of all the rest: then wilt thou not be loth
To leave this Paradise, but shalt possess
A paradise within thee, happier far."

27

Baruch Spinoza, *Ethics*

Friedrich Nietzsche, the nineteenth century's greatest "revaluer of values" and prophet of *amor fati* (loving your fate), thought of the Dutch Jewish philosopher Baruch (Benedict de) Spinoza (1632–77) as a precursor. Spinoza's posthumously published *Ethics* argued that most human concepts – including concepts of human or divine freedom – rest on ignorance of the true necessity underlying things. God, as a perfect being, necessarily creates everything possible, so questions of God's wisdom or power in creating the world the way it is lose their meaning. The language of *goodness*, for its part, is exposed as a projection of human will which has no place in thinking about God: "we neither strive for, nor will, neither want, nor desire anything because we judge it to be good; on the contrary, we judge something to be good because we strive for it, will it, want it, and desire it." Spinoza's philosophy has many affinities with the thought of Stoics like Epictetus. Spinoza thinks genuine joy can be experienced in appreciating the necessity of things; indeed, in understanding this necessity we become one with the mind of God. While condemned for a century as atheist, Spinoza's philosophy profoundly influenced the Romantics, including Schleiermacher and his friend Novalis, who famously described Spinoza as a "God-intoxicated man."

Baruch Spinoza, *Ethics* I, Appendix, in *The Ethics and Selected Letters*, trans. Samuel Shirley (Indianapolis: Hackett, 1982), 57–62.

I have now explained the nature and properties of God: that he necessarily exists, that he is one alone, that he is and acts solely from the necessity of his own nature, that he is the free cause of all things and how so, that all things are in God and are so dependent on him that they can neither be nor be conceived without him, and lastly, that all things have been predetermined by God, not from his free will or absolute pleasure, but from the absolute nature of God, his infinite power. Furthermore, whenever the opportunity arose I have striven to remove prejudices that might hinder the apprehension of my proofs. But since there still remain a considerable number of prejudices, which have been, and still are, an obstacle – indeed, a very great obstacle – to the acceptance of the concatenation of things in the manner which I have expounded, I have thought it proper at this point to bring these prejudices before the bar of reason.

Now all the prejudices which I intend to mention here turn on this one point, the widespread belief among men that all things in Nature are like themselves in acting with an end in view. Indeed, they hold it as certain that God himself directs everything to a fixed end; for they say that God has made everything for man's sake and has made man so that he should worship God. So this is the first point I shall consider, seeking the reason why most people are victims of this prejudice and why all are so naturally disposed to accept it. Secondly, I shall demonstrate its falsity and lastly I shall show how it has been the source of misconceptions about good and bad, right and wrong, praise and blame, order and confusion, beauty and ugliness, and the like.

However, it is not appropriate here to demonstrate the origin of these misconceptions from the nature of the human mind. It will suffice at this point if I take as my basis what must be universally admitted, that all men are born ignorant of the causes of things, that they all have a desire to seek their own advantage, a desire of which they are conscious. From this it follows, firstly, that men believe that they are free, precisely because they are conscious of their volitions and desires; yet concerning the causes that have determined them to desire and will they do not think, not even dream about, because they are ignorant of them. Secondly, men act always with an end in view, to wit, the advantage that they seek. Hence it happens that they are always looking only for the final causes of things done, and are satisfied when they find them having, of course, no reason for further doubt. But if they fail to discover them from some external source, they have no recourse but to turn to themselves, and to reflect on what ends would normally determine them to similar actions, and so they necessarily judge other minds by their own. Further, since they find within themselves and outside themselves a considerable number of means very convenient for the pursuit of their own advantage – as, for instance, eyes for seeing, teeth for chewing, cereals and living creatures for food, the sun for giving light, the sea for breeding fish – the result is that they look on all the things of Nature as means to their own advantage. And realising that these were found, not produced by them, they come to believe that there is someone else who produced these means for their use. For looking on things as means, they could not believe them to be self-created, but on the analogy of the means which they are accustomed to produce for themselves, they were bound to conclude that there was some governor or governors of Nature, endowed with human freedom, who have attended to all their needs and made everything for their use. And having no information on the subject, they also had to estimate the character of these rulers by their own and so they asserted that the gods direct everything for man's use so that they may bind men to them and be held in the highest honour by them. So it came about that every individual devised different methods of worshipping God as he thought fit in order that God should love him beyond others and direct the whole of Nature so as to serve his blind cupidity and insatiable greed. Thus it was that this misconception developed into superstition and became deep-rooted in the minds of men, and it was for this reason that every man strove most earnestly to understand and to explain the final causes of all things. But in seeking to show that Nature does nothing in vain – that is, nothing that is not to man's advantage – they seem to have shown only this, that Nature and the gods are as crazy as mankind.

Consider, I pray, what has been the upshot. Among so many of Nature's blessings they were bound to discover quite a number of disasters, such as storms, earthquakes, diseases and so forth, and they maintained that these occurred because the gods were angry at the wrong done to them by men, or the faults committed in the course of their worship. And although daily experience cried out against this and showed by any number of examples that blessings and disasters befall the godly and the ungodly alike without discrimination, they did not on that account abandon their ingrained prejudice. For they found it easier to regard this fact as one among other mysteries they could not understand and thus maintain their innate condition of ignorance rather than to demolish in its entirety the theory they had constructed and devise a new one. Hence they made it axiomatic that the judgment of the gods is far beyond man's understanding. Indeed, it is for this reason, and this reason only, that truth might have evaded mankind forever had not Mathematics, which is concerned not with ends but only with the essences and properties of figures, revealed to men a different standard of truth. And there are other causes too – there is no need to mention them here – which could have made men aware of these widespread misconceptions and brought them to a true knowledge of things.

. . . There is no need to spend time in going on to show that Nature has no fixed goal and that all final causes are but figments of the human imagination . . . Again, this doctrine negates God's perfection; for if God acts with an end in view, he must necessarily be seeking something that he lacks . . .

I must not fail to mention here that the advocates of this doctrine, eager to display their talent in assigning purpose to things, have introduced a new style of argument to prove their doctrine, i.e. a reduction, not to the impossible, but to ignorance, thus revealing the lack of any other argument in its favour. For example, if a stone falls from the roof on somebody's head and kills him, by this method of arguing they will prove that the stone fell in order to kill the man; for if it had not fallen for this purpose by the will of God, how could so many circumstances (and there are often many coinciding circumstances) have chanced to concur? Perhaps you will reply that the event occurred because the wind was blowing and the man was walking that way. But they will persist in asking why the wind blew at that time and why the man was walking that way at that very time. If you again reply that the wind sprang up at that time because on the previous day the sea had begun to toss after a period of calm and that the man had been invited by a friend, they will again persist – for there is no end to questions – "But why did the sea toss, and why was the man invited for that time?" And so they will go on and on asking the causes of causes, until you take refuge in the will of God – that is, the sanctuary of ignorance. Similarly, when they consider the structure of the human body, they are astonished, and being ignorant of the causes of such skilful work they conclude that it is fashioned not by mechanical art but by divine or supernatural art, and is so arranged that no one part shall injure another.

As a result, he who seeks the true causes of miracles and is eager to understand the works of Nature as a scholar, and not just to gape at them like a fool, is universally considered an impious heretic and denounced by those to whom the common people bow down as interpreters of Nature and the gods. For these people know that the dispelling of ignorance would entail the disappearance of that astonishment, which is the one and only support for their argument and for the safeguarding their authority . . .

When men become convinced that everything that is created is created on their behalf, they were bound to consider as the most important quality in every individual thing that which was most useful to them, and to regard as of the highest excellence all those things by which they were most benefited. Hence they came to form these abstract notions to explain the natures of things: – Good, Bad, Order, Confusion, Hot, Cold, Beauty, Ugliness; and since they believed that they are free, the following abstract notions came into being: – Praise, Blame, Right, Wrong. The latter I shall deal with later on after I have treated of human nature; at this point I shall briefly explain the former.

All that conduces to well-being and to the worship of God they call Good, and the contrary, Bad. And since those who do not understand the nature of things, but only imagine things, make no affirmative judgments about things themselves and mistake their imagination for intellect, they are firmly convinced that there is order in things, ignorant as they are of things and of their own nature. For when things are in such arrangement that, being presented to us through our senses, we can readily picture them and thus readily remember them, we say that they are well arranged; if the contrary, we say that they are ill-arranged, or confused. And since those things we can readily picture we find pleasing compared with other things, men prefer order to confusion, as though order were something in Nature other than what is relative to our imagination. And they say that God has created all things in an orderly way, without realising that they are thus attributing human imagination to God – unless perchance they mean that God, out of consideration for the human imagination, arranged all things in the way that men could most easily imagine. And perhaps they will find no obstacle in the fact that there are any number of things that far surpass our imagination, and a considerable number that confuse the imagination because of its weakness.

But I have devoted enough time to this. Other notions, too, are nothing but modes of imagining whereby the imagination is affected in various ways, and yet the ignorant consider them as important attributes of things because they believe – as I have said – that all things were made on their behalf, and they call a thing's nature good or bad, healthy or rotten and corrupt, according to its effect on them. For instance, if the motion communicated to our nervous system by objects presented through our eyes is conducive to our feeling of well-being, the objects which are its cause are said to be beautiful, while the objects which provoke a contrary motion are called ugly. Those things that we sense through the nose are called fragrant or fetid, through the tongue sweet or bitter, tasty or tasteless, those that we sense by touch are called hard or soft, rough or smooth, and so on. Finally, those that we sense through our ears are said to give forth noise, sound, or harmony, the last of which has driven men to such madness that they used to believe that even God delights in harmony. There are philosophers who have convinced themselves that the motions of the heavens give rise to harmony. All this goes to show that everyone's judgment is a function of the disposition of his brain, or rather, that he mistakes for reality the way his imagination is affected. Hence it is no wonder – as we should note in passing – that we find so many controversies arising among men, resulting finally in scepticism. For although human bodies agree in many respects, there are very many differences, and so one man thinks good what another thinks bad; what to one man is well-ordered, to another is confused; what to one is pleasing, to another is displeasing, and so forth. I say no more here because this is not the place to treat at length of this subject, and also because all are well acquainted with it from experience. Everybody knows those sayings: – "So many heads, so many opinions," "everyone is wise in his own sight," "brains differ as much as palates," all of which show clearly that men's judgment is a function of the disposition of the brain, and they are guided by imagination rather than intellect. For if men understood things, all that I have put forward would be found, if not attractive, at any rate convincing, as Mathematics attests.

We see therefore that all the notions whereby the common people are wont to explain Nature are merely modes of imagining, and denote not the nature of any thing but only the constitution of the imagination. And because these notions have names as if they were the names of entities existing independently of the imagination I call them "entities of imagination" (*entia imaginationis*) rather than "entities of reason" (*entia rationis*). So all arguments drawn from such notions against me can be easily refuted. For many are wont to argue on the following lines: if everything has followed from the necessity of God's most perfect nature, why does Nature display so many imperfections, such as rottenness to the point of putridity, nauseating ugliness, confusion, evil, sin, and so on? But, as I have just pointed out, they are easily refuted. For the perfection of things should be measured solely from their own nature and power; nor are things more or less perfect to the extent that they please or offend human senses, serve or oppose human interests. As to those who ask why God did not create men in such a way that they should be governed solely by reason, I make only this reply, that he lacked not material for creating all things from the highest to the lowest degree of perfection; or, to speak more accurately, the laws of his nature were so comprehensive as to suffice for the production of everything that can be conceived by an infinite intellect . . .

28

Ralph Cudworth, *The True Intellectual System of the Universe*

Ralph Cudworth (1617–88), the leading systematic expositor of the seventeenth-century philosophical school known as Cambridge Platonism, was raised a Puritan, but found himself unable to accept the doctrines of predestination and total depravity, and moved into what was to become the Latitudinarian wing of the Anglican church. His *True Intellectual System of the Universe* (1678) is presented as a refutation of the arguments of ancient "atheists" like Epicurus and Lucretius. Cudworth's true targets are made clear by his likening the ancient atheists to the Puritans, Descartes, and Hobbes. In his attack on these voluntarists, he assembles the traditional Neoplatonic and Stoic arguments commonly associated nowadays with the name of Leibniz. *The True Intellectual System* was widely read, but many (like the poet Dryden) thought it presented the problems to theism more powerfully than it answered them.

Ralph Cudworth, *The True Intellectual System of the Universe*, 4 vols. (London: Richard Priestley, 1820), IV.159–67.

Having quite routed and vanquished the Atheists' main body, we shall now blow away the remainder of their weaker and scattered forces, viz. Their objections against Providence, their queries, and their arguments from interest, with a breath or two. Their first objection is against Providence, as to the fabric of the world, from the faultiness of the mundane system, intellectually considered, and in order to ends; "Quia tanta stat praedita culpa" [Lucretius]; That because it is so ill-made, – therefore it could not be made by a God. Where the Atheist takes it for granted, that whosoever asserts a God, or a perfect mind, to be the original of all things, does therefore *ipso facto* suppose all things to be well made, and as they should be. And this doubtless was the case of all the ancient Theologers, however some modern Theists deviate therefore; these concluding the perfection of the Deity not at all to consist in goodness, but in power and arbitrary will only. As if to have a will determined by a rule or reason of good, were the virtue of weak, impotent, and obnoxious beings only, or of such as have a superior over them to give law to them, that is, of creatures; but the prerogative of a being irresistibly powerful, to have a will absolutely indifferent to all things, and undetermined by any thing but itself, or to will nothing because it is good, but to make its own arbitrary or contingent and fortuitous determination the sole reason of all its actions, nay, the very rule or measure of goodness, justice, and wisdom itself. And this is supposed by them to be the liberty, sovereignty and dominion of the Deity. Wherefore such Theists as these would think themselves altogether unconcerned in these atheistic objections against Providence, or in defending the fabric of the world, as faultless, they being as ready as the Atheists themselves, to acknowledge, that the world might really have been much better made than it now is; only that it must be said to be well, because so made, but pretending nevertheless, that this is no impeachment at all of the existence of a God, "Quia Deus non tenetur ad optimum," because God is no way bound or obliged to the best; – he being indeed, according to them, nothing but arbitrary will omnipotent. But what do these Theists else, than whilst they deny the fortuitous motion of senseless matter to be the first original of all things, themselves in the mean time enthrone fortuitousness and contingency in the will of an omnipotent Being, and there give it an absolute sovereignty and dominion over all? So that the controversy betwixt the Atheists and these Theists seems to be no other than this, whether senseless matter fortuitously moved, or a fortuitous will omnipotent, such as is altogether undetermined by goodness, justice, and wisdom, to be the sovereign Numen, and original of all things. Certainly we mortals could have little better ground for our faith and hope, in such an omnipotent arbitrary will as this, than we could have in the motions of senseless atoms furiously agitated, or of a rapid whirlwind. Nay, one would think, that of the two it should be more desirable to be under the empire of senseless atoms, fortuitously moved, than of a will altogether undetermined by goodness, justice, and wisdom, armed with omnipotence; because the former could harbor no hurtful or mischievous designs against any, as the latter might. But this irrational will, altogether undetermined by goodness, justice, and wisdom, is so far from being the highest liberty, sovereignty, and dominion, the greatest perfection, and the divinest thing of all, that it is indeed nothing else but weakness and impotency itself, or brutish folly and madness. And therefore those ancients, who affirmed, that Mind was Lord over all, and the supreme King of heaven and earth, held at the same time, that God was the sovereign monarch of the universe, Good reigning in Mind, and together with it, because Mind is that, which orders all things for the sake of the Good; and whatsoever doth otherwise, was, according to them, . . . not Mens but Dementia, and consequently no god. . . . [As Origen says,] We Christians (who hold the resurrection) say as well as you, that God can do nothing, which is in itself evil, inept, or absurd; no more than he is able not to be God. For if God do any evil, he is no God. – And again, . . . "God willeth nothing unbecoming himself, or what is truly indecorous; forasmuch as this is inconsistent with his Godship." – And to the same purpose Plotinus, . . . "The Deity acteth according to its own nature and essence; and its nature and essence displayeth goodness and justice: for if these things be not there, where should they else be found?" [*Ennead* III.2.13] – And again, elsewhere, . . . "God is essentially that, which ought to be; and therefore he did not happen to be such as he is: and this first *ought to be* is the principle of all things whatsoever, that ought to be." [*Ennead* VI.8.9] – Wherefore the Deity is not to be conceived, as mere arbitrariness, humour, or irrational will and appetite omnipotent (which would indeed be but omnipotent chance), but as an overflowing fountain of love and goodness, justice, and wisdom; or decorousness, fitness, and ought itself, willing; so that . . . that, which is absolutely the best, is . . . an indispensable law to it, because its very essence. – God is . . . an impartial balance, – lying even, equal and indifferent to all things, and weighing out heaven and earth, and all the things herein, in the most just and exact proportions, and not a grain too much or too little of any thing. Nor is the Deity therefore bound or obliged to do the best, in any way of servility (as men fondly imagine this to be contrary to his liberty), much less by the law and command of any superiour (which is a contradiction), but only by the perfection of its own nature, which it cannot possibly deviate from, no more than ungod itself. In conclusion, therefore, we acknowledge the Atheist's argument to be thus far good; that if there be a God, then of necessity must all things be well made, and as they should be; *et vice versa*. But no Atheist will ever be able to prove, that either the whole system of the world could have been better made, or that so much as any one thing therein is made ineptly.

There are indeed many things in the frame of nature, which we cannot reach to the reasons of, they being made by a knowledge far superiour and transcendent to that of ours, and our experience and ratiocination but slowly discovering the intrigues and connivances of Providence therein; witness the circulation of the blood, the milky and lymphatic vessels, and other things (without which the mechanical structure of the bodies of

animals cannot be understood), all but so lately brought to light; wherefore we must not conclude, that whatsoever we cannot find out the reason
of, or the use, that it serveth to, is therefore ineptly made. . . .

In the next place, the Atheist supposes, that, according to the general
persuasion of Theists, the world and all things therein were created only
for the sake of man, he thinking to make some advantage for his cause
from hence. But this seemeth, at first, to have been an opinion only of
some straight-laced Stoics, though afterward indeed recommended to
others also, by their own self-love, their over-weaning and puffy conceit
of themselves. And so fleas and lice, had they understanding, might conclude the bodies of other greater animals, and men also, to have been made
only for them. But the whole was not properly made for any part, but
the parts for the whole, and the whole for the Maker thereof. And yet
may the things of this lower world be well said to have been made principally (though not only) for man. For we ought not to monopolize the
Divine goodness to ourselves, there being other animals superiour to us,
that are not altogether unconcerned neither in this visible creation; and
it being reasonable to think, that even the lower animals likewise, and
whatsoever hath conscious life, was made partly also, to enjoy itself. But
Atheists can be no fit judges of worlds being made well or ill, either in
general, or respectively to mankind, they having no standing measure for
well and ill, without a God and morality, nor any true knowledge of themselves, and what their own good or evil consisteth in. That was at first but
a froward speech of some sullen discontented persons, when things falling
not out agreeably to their own private, selfish, and partial appetites, they
would revenge themselves, by railing upon nature (that is, Providence), and
calling her a stepmother only to mankind, whilst she was a fond, partial,
and indulgent mother to other animals; and though this be elegantly set
off by Lucretius [de rerum natura V.223], yet there is nothing but poetic
flourish in it all, without any philosophical truth; the advantages of
mankind being so notoriously conspicuous above those of brutes.

But as for evils in general, from whence the Atheist would conclude
the God of the Theist to be either impotent or envious; it hath been
already declared, that the true original of them is from the necessity of
imperfect beings, and the incompossibility of things; but that the Divine
art and skill most of all appeareth in bonifying these evils, and making
them, like discords in music, to contribute to the harmony of the whole,
and the good of particular persons.

Moreover, a great part of those evils, which men are afflicted with, is
not from the reality of things, but only from their own fancy and opinions, according to that of the moralist . . . "It is not things themselves, that

disturb men, but only their own opinions concerning things." [*Epictetus, Encheiridion* 5] – And therefore it being much in our power to be freed from these, Providence is not to be blamed upon the account of them. . . .

29

Anne Conway, *The Principles of the Most Ancient and Modern Philosophy*

Anne Finch Conway (1631–79), a student and friend of Cambridge Platonist Henry More, developed a Neoplatonic philosophy influenced by the Jewish mystical tradition of Kabbalah. Conway encountered Kabbalah (which Christian fans like Conway erroneously believed the "most ancient" philosophy) from her friend Francis Mercury van Helmont. Van Helmont was one of the compilers of the *Cabbala denudata*, a Christian Platonist appropriation of the system of Isaac Luria (1534–72). Ecumenical and optimistic, Conway believed that all creation would eventually achieve salvation, and that suffering was God's educative punishment; to the horror of her friends, she became a Quaker. In her *Principles*, written in the 1670s and published posthumously in 1690, Conway tried to demonstrate the goodness of God in the face of human suffering by arguing that God created a world in which every thing achieves salvation through its own efforts over many incarnations. It has been argued that the historical optimism of century thought has a root in the radical optimism of the Lurianic Kabbalah through von Helmont, Conway, and Leibniz, who was familiar with their work.

Anne Conway, *The Principles of the Most Ancient and Modern Philosophy*, III.1–4, VI.5, 7–9, VII.1, trans. Allison P. Coudert and Taylor Corse (Cambridge: Cambridge Univeristy Press, 1996), 15–16, 31–2, 35–7, 42–3.

Chapter III

S. 1. [I]f the . . . attributes of God are duly considered, and especially these two, namely his wisdom and goodness, then it is possible utterly to refute and eliminate that indifference of the will which the Scholastics and those falsely called Philosophers believe to be in God and which they incorrectly call free will. For although the will of God is most free so that whatever he does in regard to his creatures is done without any external force or compulsion or without any cause coming from the creatures (since he is free and acts spontaneously in whatever he does), nevertheless, that indifference of acting or not acting can in no way be said to be in God, for this would be an imperfection and would make God like his corruptible creatures. For this indifference of will is the basis for all mutability and corruptibility in creatures, so that there would be no evil in creatures if they were not mutable. If the same indifference of will were predicated of God, he would be assumed to be mutable and consequently would become like corruptible man, who often acts from pure will but without any true and solid reason or the guidance of wisdom. Thus, he would be like those cruel tyrants in the world who do most things from their own pure will, relying on their power, so that they are unable to give any explanation for their actions other than their own pure will. Yet, since any good man is able to give a suitable explanation for what he does or will do because he understands that true goodness and wisdom require that he do so, he therefore wishes to act as he does because it is right and knows that if he does not, he will neglect his duty.

S. 2. Therefore true justice or goodness has no latitude or indifference in itself but is like a straight line drawn from one point to another, where it is impossible to have two or more equally straight lines between two points, because only one line can be straight and all others must be more or less curved to the extent that they depart from that straight line . . . For this reason God is both a most free agent and a most necessary one, so that he must do whatever he does to and for his creatures since his infinite wisdom, goodness, and justice are a law to him which cannot be superseded.

S. 3. Therefore it clearly follows that God was not indifferent about whether or not to give being to creatures, but he made them from an inner impulse of his divine goodness and wisdom. And so he created worlds and creatures as quickly as he could, for it is the nature of a necessary agent to do as much as he can. Since he could have created worlds or creatures from time immemorial, before the year six thousand or sixty thousand or six hundred thousand, it follows that he has done this . . .

S. 4. When these divine attributes have been duly considered, it also follows that an infinity of worlds or creatures was made by God. For since God is infinitely powerful, there can be no number of creatures to which he could not always add more. And, as has now been proven, he does as much as he can. Certainly his will, goodness, and kindness are as full and far-reaching as his power. Thus it clearly follows that his creatures are infinite and created in an infinity of ways, so that they cannot be bounded or limited by number or measure . . .

Chapter VI

S. 5. there are those who maintain that all things are one substance, of which they are the real and proper parts. These confuse God and his creatures, as if these two notions were only one essential thing, so that sin and the devils would be nothing but parts or the slightest modification of this divine being. From this come dangerous consequences. Although I would not want this to be taken badly by all those who have fallen into this opinion by mistake, I should warn my readers where such principles lead so that they might consider them better and avoid their absurdity. Second, there are others who maintain that there are two kinds of substance, God, that supreme and utterly immutable being, and creatures, the lowest and altogether mutable beings. These, moreover, do not sufficiently consider that excellent order, described above, which appears in all things. Since they might perhaps have observed elsewhere that in addition to the two extremes there is also a certain mediator which partakes of both, and this is Jesus Christ, whom the wiser among the Jews recognize, no less than some among the so-called Gentiles, maintaining that there is such a mediator which they call by different names such as Logos, Son of God, first-born Son of God, Mind, Wisdom, the Celestial Adam, etc. . . . those who acknowledge such a mediator and believe in him can be said truly to believe in Jesus Christ, even though they do not yet know it and are not convinced that he has already come in the flesh . . .

There are others, moreover, who multiply specific entities into their own distinct essences and attributes almost to infinity. This altogether upsets that exceptional order of things and quite obscures the glory of the divine attributes so that it cannot shine with its due splendor in creatures. For if a creature were entirely limited by its own individuality and totally constrained and confined within the very narrow boundaries of its own species to the point that there was no mediator through which one creature could change into another, then no creature could attain further perfection and greater participation in divine goodness, nor could creatures act and react upon each other in different ways . . .

S. 7. . . . there is a certain justice in all these things, so that in the very transmutation from one species to another, either by ascending from a lower to a higher or by descending in the opposite way, the same justice appears. For example, is it not just that if a man lives a pure and holy life on this earth, like the heavenly angels, that he is elevated to the rank of angels after he dies and becomes like them, since the angels also rejoice over him? However, a man who lives such an impious and perverse life that he is more like the devil raised from hell than like any other creature, then, if he dies in such a state without repenting, does not the same justice hurl him down to hell, and does he not justly become like the devils, just as those who live an angelic life become equal to angels? But if someone lives neither an angelic nor a diabolical life but rather a brutish or animal life, so that his spirit is more like the spirit of beasts than any other creature, does the same justice not act most justly, so that just as he became a brute in spirit and allowed his brutal part and spirit to have dominion over his more excellent part, he also (at least as regards his external shape) changes his corporeal shape into that species of beast to which he is most similar in terms of the qualities and conditions of his mind? . . .

S. 8. . . . all degrees and kinds of sin have their appropriate punishments, and all these punishments tend toward the good of creatures, so that the grace of God will prevail over judgment and judgment turn into victory for the salvation and restoration of creatures. Since the grace of God stretches over all his work, why do we think that God is more severe and more rigorous a punisher of his creatures than he truly is? . . .

S. 9. For the common notion of God's justice, namely, that whatever the sin, it is punished by hellfire and without end, has generated a horrible idea of God in men, as if he were a cruel tyrant rather than a benign father towards all his creatures. . . .

Chapter VII

S. 1. . . . any thing can approach or recede more or less from the condition of a body or spirit. Moreover, because spirit is the more excellent of the two in the true and natural order of things, the more spiritual a certain creature becomes (that is, if it does not degenerate in other ways), the closer it comes to God, who, as we all know, is the highest spirit. Thus, a body is always able to become more and more spiritual to infinity since God, who is the first and highest spirit, is infinite and does not and cannot partake of the least corporeality. Consequently, it is the nature of a creature, unless it degenerates, always to become more and more like the creator. But because there is no being which is in every way contrary to God (surely nothing exists which is infinitely and immutably bad, as God is infinitely and immutably good, and there is nothing which is infinitely dark as God is infinitely light, nor is anything infinitely a body having no spirit, as God is infinitely spirit having no body), it is therefore clear that no creature can become more and more a body to infinity, although it can become more and more a spirit to infinity . . . For this reason, nothing can be bad to infinity, although it can become better and better to infinity. Thus, in the very nature of things there are limits to evil, but none to goodness. In the same way, every degree of evil or sin has its own punishment, pain, and chastisement appropriate to the nature of the deed itself; by means of which evil turns back again to good. Although the creature does not immediately recognize it when it sins, the punishment or chastisement adheres in the sins which creatures commit in such a way that it appears at the appropriate time. At this time every sin will have its own punishment and every creature will feel pain and chastisement, which will return that creature to the pristine state of goodness in which it was created and from which it can never fall again because, through its great punishment, it has acquired a greater perfection and strength. Consequently, from that indifference of will which it once had for good or evil, it rises until it only wishes to be good and is incapable of wishing any evil.

Hence one can infer that all God's creatures, which have previously fallen and degenerated from their original goodness, must be changed and restored after a certain time to a condition which is not simply as good as that in which they were created, but better. The work of God cannot cease, and thus it is the nature of every creature to be always in motion and always changing from good to better and from good to evil or from evil back to good. And because it is not possible to proceed towards evil to infinity since there is no example of infinite evil, every creature must necessarily turn again towards good or fall into eternal silence, which is contrary to nature. But if anyone should say that it falls into eternal torment, I answer: if you understand by eternity an infinity of ages which will never end, this is impossible because all pain and torment stimulates the life or spirit existing in everything which suffers. As we see from constant experience and as reason teaches us, this must necessarily happen because through pain and suffering whatever grossness or crassness is contracted by the spirit or body is diminished; and so the spirit imprisoned in such grossness or crassness is set free and becomes more spiritual and, consequently, more active and effective through pain.

Thus, since a creature cannot proceed infinitely toward evil nor fall into inactivity or silence or utter eternal suffering, it irrefutably follows that it must return toward the good, and the greater its suffering, the sooner its return and restoration.

30

Nicolas Malebranche, *Dialogues on Metaphysics and on Religion*

The French Oratorian Nicolas Malebranche (1638–1715) was troubled by "monsters" (deformities in nature) and waste. Did not such disorder cast doubt on providence? Malebranche didn't deny the existence of dysteleo-logical events (the apparently irrational distribution of suffering among vir-tuous and vicious people is for Malebranche an instance of a more general problem), nor was he content with the old aesthetic argument that defor-mity in the part can contribute to beauty in the whole. Malebranche's claim that monsters and waste are foreseen but unintended consequences of the "general wills" by which God created and maintains the world influenced Pope, Rousseau, and Hume, and has become a standard feature of theod-icy in the age of science. The characters in the *Dialogues on Metaphysics and on Religion* (1688), the fullest and most convincing expression of his views, are the Malebranchian Theodore; Aristes, an empiricist intrigued but unper-suaded by Malebranche's philosophy; and the rather acerbic Theotimus, also a Malebranchian.

Nicolas Malebranche, *Dialogues on Metaphysics and on Religion*, IX, ed. Nicholas Jolley, trans. David Scott (Cambridge: Cambridge University Press, 1997), 160–4.

IX. THEODORE. Let us attempt to understand properly the most general principles, Aristes. For afterwards all the rest follows of itself, everything is unfolded to the mind with order and a wonderful clarity. Thus, let us again consider, in the notion of the infinitely perfect Being, what the plans of God can be. I am not claiming that we shall be able to discover their details, but perhaps we shall recognize what is most general in them, and in what follows you will see that the little we have discovered about them will be of great use to us. Thus, do you think that God wills to create the most beautiful and the most perfect work He can?

ARISTES. Yes, undoubtedly, for the more perfect His work, the more it will express the qualities and perfections in which God glories. That is evident by everything you have just told us.

THEODORE. Therefore, the universe is the most perfect God can create? What! So many monsters, so many disorders, the great number of impious people; does all this contribute to the perfection of the universe?

ARISTES. You confuse me, Theodore. God wills to make the most perfect possible work. For the more perfect it is, the more it will honor Him. That appears evident to me. But I clearly conceive that it would be more accomplished if it were free of the thousands and thousands of defects which disfigure it. That is a contradiction which stops me short. It seems that God has not executed His plan or has not adopted the plan most worthy of His attributes.

THEODORE. That is because you have still not properly understood the principles. You have not sufficiently meditated on the notion of the infinitely perfect Being which contains them. You still do not know how to make God act according to what He is.

THEOTIMUS. But, Aristes, might it not be that the irregularities of nature, monsters, and even the impious are like the shadows of a painting, which lend force to the work and relief to the figures?

ARISTES. That thought has an "I know not what" which pleases the imagination, but the mind is not satisfied by it. For I understand quite well that the universe would be more perfect if there were nothing irregular in any of the parts comprising it, and on the contrary there is almost no place where there is not some defect.

THEOTIMUS. Thus, it is because God did not will His work to be perfect.

ARISTES. That is not the reason either. For God cannot positively and directly will the irregularities which disfigure His work and which express none of the perfections He possesses and in which He is glorified. That appears evident to me. God permits disorder, but He does not create it, He does not will it.

THEOTIMUS. "God permits": I do not really understand this expression. Whom does God permit to freeze the vines and ruin the harvest He made grow? Why does He permit monsters in His work which He does not make and does not will? What then! Is the universe not such as God willed it?

ARISTES. No, for the universe is not such as God made it.

THEOTIMUS. That may be true in respect of the disorders which have crept into it through the poor use of freedom. For God did not make the impious. He permitted people to become that way. I do indeed understand that, although I do not know the reasons for it. But certainly it is only God who makes monsters.

ARISTES. What strange creatures these monsters are, if they do not do honor to Him who gives them being. Do you know, Theotimus, why God, who today covers the entire countryside with flowers and fruit, will tomorrow ravage it with frost or hail?

THEOTIMUS. That is because the countryside will be more beautiful in its sterility than in its fecundity, although that does not suit us. Often we judge the beauty of God's works by the utility we derive from them, and we deceive ourselves.

ARISTES. Still, it is better to judge them by their utility than by their inutility. What a beautiful thing, a country desolated by a tempest!

THEOTIMUS. Quite beautiful. A country inhabited by sinners should be in desolation.

ARISTES. If the tempest spared the lands of good people, perhaps you would be right. It would be even more appropriate to refuse rain to the field of a brute, than to make his wheat germinate and grow in order to cut it down by hail. That would surely be the shortest route. But it is often, however, the less culpable who are the more ill-treated. What seeming contradictions in the action of God! Theodore has already given me the principles which dispel these contradictions. But I understood them so poorly that I no longer remember them. If you do not wish, Theotimus, to set me on the correct path, let Theodore speak, for I see that you are entertained by the difficulty in which I find myself.

THEOTIMUS. That is fair.

X. THEODORE. You see, Aristes, that it is not enough to have glimpsed the principles; it is necessary to have understood them properly, in order that they be present to the mind when necessary. Listen, therefore, since Theotimus does not wish to tell you what he knows perfectly well.

You are not deceived in believing that the more perfect a work is, the more it expresses the perfections of the workman, and that it does him greater honor the more the perfections it expresses please him who possesses them, and that thus God wills to make His work the most perfect possible. But you grasp only half of the principle, and that is what leaves you perplexed. God wills that His work honors Him; you understand that well. Note, however, that God does not will that His ways dishonor Him. That is the other half of the principle. God wills that His action as well as His work bear the character of His attributes. Not content that the universe honors Him through its excellence and beauty, He wills that His ways glorify Him through their simplicity, their fecundity, their universality, through the characteristics which express the qualities He is glorified in possessing.

Thus, do not imagine that God willed absolutely to make the most perfect work possible, but only the most perfect in relation to the ways most worthy of Him. For what God wills uniquely, directly, absolutely in His plans is always to act as divinely as possible. It is to make His action as well as His work bear the character of His attributes; it is to act exactly according to what He is and according to all that He is. From all eternity God saw all possible works and all the possible ways of producing each of them, and as He acts only for His glory, only according to what He is, He determined to will that work which could be produced and conserved in those ways which, combined with that work, would honor Him more than any other work produced in any other way. He formed the plan which would better convey the character of His attributes, which would express more exactly the qualities He possesses and glories in possessing. Fully embrace this principle, Aristes, lest it escape you, for of all principles it is perhaps the most fertile.

Once again, do not imagine that God ever forms His plan blindly, I mean, without having compared it with the ways necessary for its implementation. That is how people act who often regret their decisions because of the difficulties in which they find themselves. Nothing is difficult to God. Note, however, that not everything is equally worthy of Him. His ways as well as His work must bear the character of His attributes. Thus, God must have regard for the ways as well as the work. It is not enough that His work honors Him through its excellence; His ways must further glorify Him through their divinity. And if a world more perfect than ours could be created and conserved only in ways which are correspondingly less perfect, in such a manner that the expression, as it were, which this new world and its new ways gave the divine qualities was less than their expression in our world, I am not afraid to say this to you: God is too wise, He loves His glory too much, He acts too exactly according to what He is, to prefer this new world to the universe He has created. For in His plans God is indifferent only when they are equally wise, equally divine, equally glorious for Him, equally worthy of His attributes, and only when the relation, composed of the beauty of the work and the simplicity of His ways, is exactly equal. When this relation is unequal, although God is able to do nothing since He is self-sufficient, He cannot choose and adopt the worse one. He is able not to act, but He cannot act in vain, nor can

He multiply His ways without proportionally augmenting the beauty of His work. His wisdom protects Him against adopting, from all possible plans, that which is not the wisest. The love He bears Himself does not allow Him to choose the plan which does not honor Him the most.

31

Pierre Bayle, "Manicheans"; Note D

The question Leibniz's *Theodicy* tried to answer was posed by the scholar and theorist of toleration Pierre Bayle (1647–1706) in the powerful discussions of dualism in his *Historical and Critical Dictionary* (1697). A French Protestant in exile in Holland, Bayle argued that dualism – while false – was the only rational conclusion to be drawn from the mixed character of human experience. Bayle's Calvinist background is clear when he asserts that "Evil is a problem that reduces all philosophy to helplessness," adding that the believer should admit that God permits evil for reasons "that are really worthy of his infinite wisdom, but which are incomprehensible to me," and not allow discussion with skeptics or heretics to go any further. Yet the skeptical passion with which Bayle defended heresies and challenged every orthodoxy (his *Dictionary* became the "arsenal of the enlightenment"), along with the way he hid his most controversial points in extended footnotes like the one below (or footnotes to footnotes!), made his intentions easy to misconstrue. The eighteenth-century *philosophes* thought he was merely pretending to be a fideist, but was really an atheist.

Pierre Bayle, *Historical and Critical Dictionary: Selections*, trans. Richard H. Popkin (Indianapolis: Bobbs-Merrill [The Library of Liberal Arts], 1965), 144–52.

Manicheans, heretics whose infamous sect, founded by a certain Manes, sprang up in the third century, and took root in several provinces, and lasted a long time. Nevertheless, they taught what should have struck everyone with the greatest horror. The weak side of their view did not consist, as it appeared at first, in the doctrine of the two principles, one good and the other wicked; but in the particular explanations they gave of this and in the practical consequences they drew from it. It must be admitted that this false doctrine, much older than Manes, and incapable of being maintained as soon as one accepts Scripture, in whole or part, would be rather difficult to refute if maintained by pagan philosophers skilled in disputing (*𝒟*). It was fortunate that St. Augustine, who was so well versed in all the arts of controversy, abandoned Manicheanism; for he had the capability of removing all the grossest errors from it and making of the rest of it a system, which in his hands would have perplexed the orthodox . . .

Note *𝒟*. (. . . *would be rather difficult to refute if maintained by pagan philoso-phers skilled in disputing.*) They would soon have been defeated by a priori arguments; their strength lay in a posteriori arguments. With these they could have fought a long time, and it would have been difficult to defeat them. My point will be better understood from the exposition that follows. The most certain and the clearest ideas of order teach us that a Being who exists by himself, who is necessary, who is eternal, must be one, infinite, all-powerful, and endowed with every kind of perfection. Thus, by consulting these ideas, one finds that there is nothing more absurd than the hypothesis of two principles, eternal and independent of each other, one of which has no goodness and can stop the plans of the other. These are what I call the a priori arguments. They lead us neces-sarily to reject this hypothesis and to admit only one principle in all things. If this were all that was necessary to determine the goodness of a theory, the trial would be over, to the confusion of Zoroaster and all his follow-ers. But every theory has need of two things in order to be considered a good one: first, its ideas must be distinct; and second, it must account for experience. It is necessary then to see if the phenomena of nature can be easily explained by the hypothesis of a single principle. When the Manicheans tell us that, since many things are observed in the world that are contrary to one another – cold and heat, white and black, light and darkness – therefore there necessarily are two principles, they argue piti-fully. The opposition that exists among these entities, fortified as much as one likes by what are called variations, disorders, irregularities of nature, cannot make half an objection against the unity, simplicity, and immutabil-ity of God. All these matters are explained either by the various faculties that God has given to bodies, or by the laws of motion he has established, or by the concourse of intelligent occasional causes by which he has been pleased to regulate himself . . . The heavens and the whole universe declare the glory, the power, and the unity of God. Man alone – this masterpiece of his Creation among the visible things – man alone, I say, furnishes some very great objections against the unity of God. Here is how:

Man is wicked and miserable. Everybody is aware of this from what goes on within himself, and from the commerce he is obliged to carry on with his neighbor. It suffices to have been alive for five or six* years to be completely convinced of these two truths. Those who live long and who are much involved in worldly affairs know this still more clearly. Travel gives continual lessons of this. Monuments to human misery and wickedness are found everywhere – prisons, hospitals, gallows, and beggars . . . Scholars who never leave their study acquire the most knowledge about these two matters because in reading history they make all the centuries and all the countries of the world pass in review before their eyes. Properly speaking, history is nothing but the crimes and misfortunes of the human race. But let us observe that these two evils, the one moral and the other physical, do not encompass all history or all private experience. Both moral good and physical good are found everywhere, some examples of virtue, some examples of happiness; and this is what causes the difficulty. For if all mankind were wicked and miserable, there would be no need to have recourse to the hypothesis of two principles. It is the mixture of happiness and virtue with misery and vice that requires this hypothesis. It is in this that the strength of the sect of Zoroaster lies. . . .

To make people see how difficult it would be to refute this false system, and to make them conclude that it is necessary to have recourse to the light of revelation in order to destroy it, let us suppose here a dispute between Melissus and Zoroaster. They were both pagans and great philosophers. Melissus, who acknowledged only one principle, would say at the outset that his theory agrees admirably with the ideas of order. The necessary Being has no limits. He is therefore infinite and all-powerful, and thus he is one. And it would be both monstrous and inconsistent if he did not have goodness and did have the greatest of all vices – an essential malice. "I confess to you," Zoroaster would answer, "that your ideas are well connected; and I shall willingly acknowledge that in this respect your hypothesis surpasses mine . . . I allow you the advantage of being more conformable to the notion of order than I am. But by your hypothesis explain a little to me how it happens that man is wicked and so subject to pain and grief. I defy you to find in your principles the explanation of this phenomenon, as I can find it in mine. I then regain the advantage.

* By this age one has done and suffered malicious acts, one has felt chagrin and pain, one has sulked many times, etc.

You surpass me in the beauty of ideas and in a priori reasons, and I surpass you in the explanation of phenomena and in a posteriori reasons. And since the chief characteristic of a good system is its being capable of accounting for experience, and since the mere incapacity of accounting for it is a proof that a hypothesis is not good, however fine it appears to be in other respects, you must grant that I hit the nail on the head by admitting two principles and that you miss it by admitting only one.

"If man is the work of a single supremely good, supremely holy, supremely powerful principle, is it possible that he can be exposed to illnesses, to cold, to heat, to hunger, to thirst, to pain, to vexation? Is it possible he should have so many bad inclinations and commit so many crimes? Is it possible that the supreme holiness would produce so criminal a creature? Is it possible that the supreme goodness would produce so unhappy a creature? Would not the supreme power joined to an infinite goodness pour down blessings upon its work and defend it from everything that might annoy or trouble it?" If Melissus consults the ideas of order, he will answer that man was not wicked when God created him. He will say that man received a happy state from God, but not having followed the lights of his conscience, which according to the intention of his author would have conducted him along the virtuous path, he became wicked, and he deserved that the supremely just and supremely good God made him feel the effects of His wrath. Then it is not God who is the cause of moral evil; but he is the cause of physical evil, that is to say, the punishment of moral evil – punishment which, far from being incompatible with the supremely good principle, necessarily flows from one of God's attributes, I mean that of justice, which is no less essential to man than God's goodness. This answer, the most reasonable that Melissus could make, is basically fine and sound. But it can be combatted by arguments which have something in them more specious and dazzling. For Zoroaster would not fail to set forth that, if man were the work of an infinitely good and holy principle, he would have been created not only with no actual evil but also without an inclination to evil, since that inclination is a defect that cannot have such a principle for a cause. It remains then to be said that, when man came from the hands of his creator, he had only the power of self determination to evil, and that since he determined himself in the way, he is the sole cause of the crime that he committed and the moral evil that was introduced into the universe. But, (1) we have no distinct idea that could make us comprehend how a being not self-existent should, however, be the master of its own actions. Then Zoroaster will say that the free will given to man is not capable of giving him an actual determination since its being is continuously and totally supported by the action of God. (2) He will pose the question, "Did God foresee that man would make bad use of free will?" If the answer is affirmative he will reply that it appears impossible to foresee what depends entirely on an undetermined cause. "But I will readily agree with you," he will say, "that God foresaw the sin of his creature; and I conclude from this that he would have prevented it; for the ideas of order will not allow that an infinitely good and holy cause that can prevent the introduction of moral evil does not stop it, especially when by permitting it he will find himself obliged to pour down pains and torments upon his own work. If God did not foresee the fall of man, he must at least have judged that it was possible; therefore, since he saw he would be obliged to abandon his parental goodness if the fall ever did occur, only to make his children miserable by exercising upon them the role of a severe judge, he would have determined man to moral good as he has determined him to physical good. He would not have left in man's soul any power for carrying himself toward sin, just as he did not leave any power for carrying himself toward misery in so far as it was misery. This is where we are led by the clear and distinct ideas of order when we follow, step by step, what an infinitely good principle ought to do. For, if a goodness as limited as that of a human father necessarily requires that he prevent as much as possible the bad use which his children might make of the goods he gives them, much more will an infinite and all-powerful goodness prevent the bad effects of its gifts. Instead of giving them free will, it will determine its creatures to good; or if it gives them free will, it will always efficiently watch over them to prevent their falling into sin." I very well believe that Melissus would not be silenced at this point, but whatever he might answer would be immediately combatted by reasons as plausible as his, and thus the dispute would never terminate.

If he had recourse to the method of retortion, he would perplex Zoroaster greatly; but in granting him for once his two principles, he would leave him a broad highway for reaching the discovery of the origin of evil. Zoroaster would go back to the time of chaos: this is a state with regard to his two principles much like what Thomas Hobbes calls the state of nature, which he supposes to have preceded the establishments of societies. In this state of nature man was a wolf to man; everything belonged to the first who had it; no one was the master of anything except by force. In order to get out of this abyss each agreed to give up his rights to the whole so that he would be given the ownership of some part. They entered into agreements; war ceased. The two principles, weary of the chaos in which each confounded and overthrew what the other wanted to do, mutually consented to agree. Each gave up something. Each had a share in the production of man and in forming the laws of the union of the soul. The good principle obtained those that give man thousands of pleasures, and consented to those which expose man to thousands of pains; and if the good principle consented that moral good in mankind should be infinitely small in proportion to moral evil, that principle made up for that loss in some other species of creatures in which the proportion of vice would be correspondingly smaller than that of virtue. If many men in this life have more misery than happiness, this is recompensed in another state; what they do not have under the human form, they will find under another form.* By this accord chaos was unraveled; chaos, I say, a passive principle that was the battlefield of the two active ones. The poets have represented this unraveling with the image of a quarrel being terminated. There is what Zoroaster could have claimed, priding himself that he did not make the good principle responsible for the intentional production of a work that would be so wicked and miserable except after it had found that it could not possibly do better nor more effectively oppose the horrible plans of the bad principle. To render his hypothesis less shocking he could deny that there had been a long way between these two principles, and he could toss out all those combat and prisoners that the Manicheans have spoken of. The whole business could be reduced to the certain knowledge that the two principles could have had, that the one could only obtain from the other such and such conditions. The accord could have been made on this basis for eternity.

A thousand great difficulties could be proposed to this philosopher; but as he would still find answers and after that demand that he be given a better hypothesis and claim that he had thoroughly refuted that of Melissus, he would never be led back to the truth. Human reason is too feeble for this. It is a principle of destruction and not of edification. It is only proper for raising doubts, and for turning things on all sides in order to make disputes endless; and I do not think I am mistaken if I say of natural revelation, that is to say, the light of reason, what the theologians say of the Mosaic Dispensation. They say that it was only fit for making man realize his own weakness and the necessity of a redeemer and a law of grace. It was a teacher – these are their terms – to lead us to Jesus Christ. Let us say almost the same thing about reason. It is only fit to make man aware of his own blindness and weakness, and the necessity for another revelation. That is the one of Scripture. It is there that we find the means to refute invincibly the hypothesis of the two principles and all the objec-

---

* Note that all those, or most of those who had admitted two principles, have held the doctrine of metempsychosis.

tions of Zoroaster. There we find the unity of God and his infinite perfections, the fall of the first man, and what follows from it. Let someone
tell us with a great apparatus of arguments that it is not possible that moral
evil should introduce itself into the world by the work of an infinitely
good and holy principle, we will answer that this however is in fact the
case, and therefore this is very possible . . . The Manicheans were aware
of what I have just pointed out. That is why they rejected the Old Testament. But what they retained of Scripture furnished enough strong arms
to the orthodox. Thus it was no difficult task to confound those heretics,
who, in addition, childishly embarrassed themselves when they entered
into details. Now since Scripture furnishes us with the best solutions, I
was not wrong in saying that a pagan philosopher would be very difficult
to defeat on this matter.

32

G. W. Leibniz, *Theodicy*

The German mathematician, diplomat, and philosopher Gottfried Wilhelm Leibniz (1646–1716) coined the term "theodicy" in the 1690s but never defined it. "Theodicy" – from the Greek *theos* (God) and *dikē* (justice) – has long been understood in Milton's terms as "*justifying* the ways of God to man," but Leibniz seems simply to have meant the "justice of God": Leibniz's *Theodicy* is an ethics. Bayle's arguments from evil are addressed because they threaten to undermine confidence that God's justice is comprehensible to men, or worthy of emulation. The voluntarist ideas of "liberty, necessity, and destiny" which Leibniz thought followed from Bayle's queries (and were expounded by Leibniz's real targets, Descartes and Hobbes) make God a tyrant we cannot love. Leibniz's use of the old Platonic argument that this is "the best of all possible worlds" needs to be understood as part of what he below calls "Fatum Christianum," a philosophically grounded faith that we "have to do with a good master." Unlike Voltaire's Pangloss, Leibniz thought theism could be demonstrated *a priori*, but not *a posteriori*: we cannot know enough to demonstrate why *any* evil (or good) is part of the best of all possible worlds – not even (as Malebranche had argued) the incarnation of Christ. Ironically, then, the original *Theodicy* is not what philosophers of religion now, following Alvin Plantinga, call a "theodicy" at all, but a "defense"!

G. W. Leibniz, *Theodicy: Essays on the Goodness of God, the Freedom of Man, and the Origin of Evil*, trans. E. M. Huggard (Chicago: Open Court, 1985), 53–9, 105–7, 126–9, 134–7.

Preface

There are two famous labyrinths where our reason very often goes astray: one concerns the great question of the Free and the Necessary, above all in the production and origin of Evil; the other consists in the discussion of continuity and of the indivisibles which appear to be the elements thereof, and where the consideration of the infinite must enter in. The first perplexes almost all the human race, the other exercises philosophers only . . . But if the knowledge of continuity is important for speculative enquiry, that of necessity is none the less so for practical application; and it, together with the questions therewith connected, to wit, the freedom of man and the justice of God, forms the object of this treatise.

Men have been perplexed in well-nigh every age by a sophism which the ancients called the "Lazy Reason," because it tended towards doing nothing, or at least towards being careful for nothing and only following inclination for the pleasure of the moment. For, they said, if the future is necessary, that which must happen will happen, whatever I may do. Now the future (so they said) is necessary, whether because the Divinity foresees everything, and even pre-establishes it by the control of all things in the universe; or because everything happens of necessity, through the concatenation of causes; or, finally, through the very nature of truth, which is determinate in the assertions that can be made on future events, as it is in all assertions, since the assertion must always be true or false in itself, although we know not always which it is . . .

The false conception of necessity, being applied in practice, has given rise to what I call *Fatum Mahometanum*, fate after the Turkish fashion, because it is said of the Turks that they do not shun danger or even abandon places infected with plague, owing to their use of such reasoning as that just recorded. For what is called *Fatum Stoicum* was not so black as it is painted: for it did not divert men from the care of their affairs, but it tended to give them tranquillity in regard to events, through the consideration of necessity, which renders our anxieties and our vexations needless. In which respect these philosophers were not far removed from the teaching of our Lord, who deprecates these anxieties in regard to the morrow, comparing them with the needless troubles he would give himself in labouring to increase his stature.

It is true that the teachings of the Stoics (and perhaps also of some famous philosophers of our time), confining themselves to this alleged necessity, can only impart a forced patience; whereas our Lord inspires thoughts more sublime, and even instructs us in the means of gaining contentment by assuring us that since God, being altogether good and wise, has care for everything, even so far as not to neglect a single hair of our head, our confidence in him ought to be entire. And thus we should see, if we were capable of understanding him, that it is not even possible to wish for anything better (as much in general as for ourselves) than what he does. It is as if one said to men: Do your duty and be content with that which shall come of it, not only because you cannot resist divine providence, or the nature of things (which may suffice for tranquillity, but not for contentment), but also because you have to do with a good master. And that is what may be called *Fatum Christianum.*

Nevertheless it happens that most men, and even Christians, introduce into their dealings some mixture of fate after the Turkish fashion, although they do not sufficiently acknowledge it. It is true that they are not inactive or negligent when obvious perils or great and manifest hopes present themselves; for they will not fail to abandon a house that is about to fall and to turn aside from a precipice they see in their path; and they will burrow in the earth to dig up a treasure half uncovered, without waiting for fate to finish dislodging it. But when the good or evil is remote or uncertain and the remedy painful or little to our taste, the lazy reason seems to us to be valid . . .

But it is taking an unfair advantage of this alleged necessity of fate to employ it in excuse for our vices and libertinism. I have often heard it said by smart young persons, who wished to play the freethinker, that it is useless to preach virtue, to censure vice, to create hopes of reward or fears of punishment, since it may be said of the book of destiny, that what is written is written, and that our behaviour can change nothing therein . . . It is untrue that the event happens whatever one may do: it will happen because one does what leads thereto; and if the event is written beforehand, the cause that will make it happen is written also. Thus the connexion of effects and causes, so far from establishing the doctrine of a necessity detrimental to conduct, serves to overthrow it . . .

Some go even further: not content with using the pretext of necessity to prove that virtue and vice to neither good nor ill, they have the hardihood to make the Divinity accessory to their licentious way of life, and they imitate the pagans of old, who ascribed to the gods the cause of their crimes, as if a divinity drove them to do evil. The philosophy of Christians, which recognizes better than that of the ancients the dependence of things upon the first Author and his co-operation with all the actions of creatures, appears to have increased this difficulty. Some able men in our own time have gone so far as to deny all action to creatures, and M. Bayle, who tended a little towards this extraordinary opinion, made use of it to restore the lapsed dogma of the two principles, or two gods, the one good,

the other evil, as if this dogma were a better solution to the difficulties
over the origin of evil . . .

Even though there were no co-operation by God in evil actions, one
could not help finding difficulty in the fact that he foresees them and that,
being able to prevent them through his omnipotence, he yet permits them.
This is why some philosophers and even some theologians have rather
chosen to deny to God any knowledge of the detail of things and, above
all, of future events, than to admit what they believed repellent to his
goodness . . .

They are doubtless much mistaken; but others are not less so who, convinced that nothing comes to pass save by the will and the power of God,
ascribe to him intentions and actions so unworthy of the greatest and the
best of all beings that one would say these authors have indeed renounced
the dogma which recognizes God's justice and goodness. They thought
that, being supreme Master of the universe, he could simply without any
detriment to his holiness cause sins to be committed, simply at his will
and pleasure, or in order that he might have the pleasure or punishing;
and even that he could take pleasure in eternally afflicting innocent people
without doing any injustice, because no one has the right or the power
to control his actions . . .

I believe that many people of otherwise good intentions are misled by
these ideas, because they have not sufficient knowledge of their consequences. They do not see that, properly speaking, God's justice is thus over-
thrown. For what idea shall we form of such a justice as has only will for
its rule, that is to say, where the will is not guided by the rules of good
and even tends directly towards evil? . . . But one will soon abandon
maxims so strange and so unfit to make men good and charitable through
the imitation of God. For one will reflect that a God who would take
pleasure in the misfortune of others cannot be distinguished from the evil
principle of the Manichaeans, assuming that this principle had become
sole master of the universe; and that in consequence one must attribute
to the true God sentiments that render him worthy to be called the good
principle . . .

Preliminary Discourse on the Conformity of
Faith with Reason

57. . . . M. Bayle is right in saying . . . that those who claim that the
behaviour of God with respect to sin and the consequences of sin contains nothing but what they can account for, deliver themselves up to the

mercy of their adversary. But he is not right in here combining two very different things, "to account for a thing," and "to uphold it against objections"; as he does when he presently adds: "They are obliged to follow him [their adversary] everywhere whither he shall wish to lead them, and it would be to retire ignominiously and ask for quarter, if they were to admit that our intelligence is too weak to remove completely all the objections advanced by a philosopher."

58. It seems here that, according to M. Bayle, "accounting for" comes short of "answering objections," since he threatens one who should undertake the first with the resulting obligation to pass on to the second. But it is quite the opposite: he who maintains a thesis (the *respondens*) is not bound to account for it, but he is bound to meet the objections of an opponent. A defendant in law is not bound (as a general rule) to prove his right or to produce his title to possession; but he is obliged to reply to the arguments of the plaintiff. I have marvelled many times that a writer so precise and so shrewd as M. Bayle so often here confuses things where so much difference exists as between these three acts of reason: to comprehend, to prove, and to answer objections; as if when it is a question of reason in theology one term were as good as another . . .

60. . . . [T]heologians usually distinguish between what is above reason and what is against reason. They place *above* reason that which one cannot comprehend and which one cannot account for. But *against* reason will be all opinion that is opposed by invincible reasons, or the contrary of which can be proved in a precise and sound manner. They avow, therefore, that the Mysteries are above reason, but they do not admit that they are contrary to it . . . M. Bayle . . . is not quite satisfied with the accepted distinction . . . [H]e distinguishes . . . between these two theses: the one, *all the dogmas of Christianity are in conformity with reason*; the other, *human reason knows that they are in conformity with reason*. He affirms the first and denies the second. I am of the same opinion, if in saying "that a dogma conforms to reason" one means that it is possible to account for it or to explain its *how* by reason; for God could doubtless do so, and we cannot. But I think that one must affirm both theses if by "knowing that a dogma conforms to reason" one means that we can demonstrate, if need be, that there is no contradiction between this dogma and reason, repudiating the objections of those who maintain that this dogma is an absurdity.

61. M. Bayle explains himself here in a manner not at all convincing. He acknowledges fully that our Mysteries are in accordance with the supreme and universal reason that is in the divine understanding, or with reason in general; yet he denies that they are in accordance with that part of reason which man employs to judge things. But this portion of reason

which we possess is a gift of God, and consists in the natural light that
has remained with us in the midst of corruption; thus it is in accordance
with the whole, and it differs from that which is in God only as a
drop of water differs from the ocean or rather as the finite from the infinite. Therefore Mysteries may transcend it, but they cannot be contrary to
it. One cannot be contrary to one part without being contrary to the
whole . . .

Essays on the Justice of God, the Freedom of Man and the Origin of Evil

6. . . . Our end is to banish from men the false ideas that represent God
to them as an absolute prince employing a despotic power, unfitted to be
loved and unworthy of being loved. These notions are the more evil in
relation to God inasmuch as the essence of piety is not only to fear him
but also to love him above all things: and that cannot come about unless
there be knowledge of his perfections capable of arousing the love which
he deserves, and which makes the felicity of those that love him. Feeling
ourselves animated by a zeal such as cannot fail to please him, we have
cause to hope that he will enlighten us, and that he will himself aid us in
the execution of a project undertaken for his glory and for the good of
men. A cause so good gives confidence: if there are plausible appearances
against us there are proofs on our side, and I would dare to say to an
adversary:

> *Aspice, quam mage sit nostrum penetrabile telum.*
> "See whether our weapon be not the more piercing!" –
> [Virgil, *Aeneid*, 10.481]

7. *God is the first reason of things*: for such things as are bounded, as all
that which we see and experience, are contingent and have nothing in
them to render their existence necessary, it being plain that time, space
and matter, united and uniform in themselves and indifferent to everything, might have received entirely other motions and shapes, and in
another order. Therefore one must seek the reason for the existence of the
world, which is the whole assemblage of *contingent* things, and seek it in
the substance which carries with it the reason for its existence, and which
in consequence is *necessary* and eternal. Moreover, this cause must be intelligent: for this existing world being contingent and an infinity of other
worlds being equally possible, and holding, so to say, equal claim to existence with it, the cause of the world must needs have had regard or ref-

erence to all these possible worlds in order to fix upon one of them. This regard or relation of an existent substance to simple possibilities can be nothing other than the *understanding* which has the ideas of them, while to fix upon one of them can be nothing other than the act of the *will* which chooses. It is the *power* of this substance that renders its will efficacious. Power relates to *being*, wisdom or understanding to *truth*, and will to *good*. And this intelligent cause ought to be infinite in all ways and absolutely perfect in *power*, in *wisdom* and in *goodness*, since it relates to all that which is possible. Furthermore, since all is connected together, there is no ground for admitting more than one. Its understanding is the source of *essences*, and its will is the origin of *existences*. There in few words is the proof of one only God with his perfections, and through him of the origin of things.

8. Now this supreme wisdom, united to a goodness that is no less infinite, cannot but have chosen the best. For as a lesser evil is a kind of good, even so a lesser good is a kind of evil if it stands in the way of a greater good; and there would be something to correct in the actions of God if it were possible to do better. As in mathematics, when there is no maximum nor minimum, in short nothing distinguished, everything is done equally, or when that is not possible nothing at all is done: so it may be said likewise in respect of perfect wisdom, which is no less orderly than mathematics, that if there were not the best (*optimum*) among all possible worlds, God would not have produced any. I call "World" the whole succession and the whole agglomeration of all existent things, lest it be said that several worlds could have existed in different times and different places. For they must needs be reckoned all together as one world or, if you will, as one Universe. And even though one should fill all times and all places, it still remains true that one might have filled them in innumerable ways, and that there is an infinitude of possible worlds among which God must needs have chosen the best, since he does nothing without acting in accordance with supreme reason.

9. Some adversary not being able to answer this argument will perchance answer the conclusion by a counter-argument, saying that the world could have been without sin and without sufferings; but I deny that then it would have been *better*. For it must be known that all things are *connected* in each one of the possible worlds: the universe, whatever it may be, is all of one piece, like an ocean: the least movement extends its effect there to any distance whatsoever, even though this effect become less perceptible in proportion to the distance. Therein God has ordered all things beforehand once for all, having foreseen prayers, good and bad actions, and all the rest; and each thing *as an idea* has contributed, before its existence, to the resolution that has been made upon the existence of all

things; so that nothing can be changed in the universe (any more than in a number) save its essence or if you will, save its *numerical individuality*. Thus, if the smallest evil that comes to pass in the world were missing in it, it would no longer be this world; which, with nothing omitted and all allowance made, was found the best by the Creator who chose it.

10. It is true that one may imagine possible worlds without sin and without unhappiness, and one could make some like Utopian or Sevarambian romances: but these same worlds again would be very inferior to ours in goodness. I cannot show you this in detail. For can I know and can I present infinities to you and compare them together? But you must judge with me *ab effectu*, since God has chosen this world as it is . . .

19. . . . The ancients had puny ideas of the works of God, and St. Augustine, for want of knowing modern discoveries, was at a loss when there was question of explaining the prevalence of evil. It seemed to the ancients that there was only one world inhabited, and even of that men held the antipodes in dread: the remainder of the world was, according to them, a few shining globes and a few crystalline spheres. To-day, whatever bounds are given or not given to the universe, it must be acknowledged that there is an infinite number of globes, as great as and greater than ours, which have as much right as it to hold rational inhabitants, though it follows not at all that they are human . . . What will become of the consideration of our globe and its inhabitants? Will it not be something incomparably less than a physical point, since our earth is as a physical point in comparison with the distance of some fixed stars? Thus since the proportion of that part of the universe of which we know is almost lost in nothingness compared to that which is unknown, and which we yet have cause to assume, and since all the evils that may be raised in objection before us are in this near nothingness, haply it may be that all evils are almost nothingness in comparison with the good things which are in the universe.

20. But it is necessary also to meet the more speculative and metaphysical difficulties which have been mentioned, and which concern the cause of evil. The question is asked first of all, whence does evil come? *Si Deus est, unde malum? Si non est, unde bonum?* The ancients attributed the cause of evil to *matter*, which they believed uncreate and independent of God: but we, who derive all being from God, where shall we find the source of evil? The answer is, that it must be sought in the ideal nature of the creature, in so far as this nature is contained in the eternal verities which are in the understanding of God, independently of his will. For we must consider that there is an *original imperfection in the creature* before sin, because the creatures is limited in its essence; whence ensues that it cannot

know all, and that it can deceive itself, and commit other errors. Plato said in *Timaeus* [48a–b] that the world originated in Understanding united to Necessity. Others have united God and Nature. This can be given a reasonable meaning. God will be the Understanding; and the Necessity, that is, the essential nature of things, will be the object of the understanding, in so far as this object consists in the eternal verities. But this object is inward and abides in the divine understanding. And therein is found not only the primitive form of good, but also the origin of evil: the Region of the Eternal Verities must be substituted for matter when we are concerned with seeking out the source of things.

This region is the ideal cause of evil (as it were) as well as of good: but, properly speaking, the formal character of evil has no *efficient* cause, for it consists in privation, as we shall see, namely, in that which the efficient cause does not bring about. That is why the Schoolmen are wont to call the cause of evil *deficient*.

21. Evil may be taken metaphysically, physically and morally. *Metaphysical evil* consists in mere imperfection, *physical evil* in suffering, and *moral evil* in sin. Now although physical evil and moral evil be not necessary, it is enough that by virtue of the eternal verities they be possible. And as this vast Region of Verities contains all possibilities, it is necessary that there be an infinitude of possible worlds, that evil enters into divers of them, and that even the best of all contain a measure thereof. Thus has God been induced to permit evil.

22. But someone will say to me: why speak you to us of "permitting"? Is it not God that doeth the evil and that willeth it? Here it will be necessary to explain what "permission" is, so that it may be seen how this term is not employed without reason. But before that one must explain the nature of will, which has its own degrees. Taking it in the general sense, one may say that *will* consists in the inclination to do something in proportion to the good that it contains. This will is called *antecedent* when it is detached and considers each good separately in the capacity of a good. In this sense it may be said that God tends to all good, as good, *ad perfectionem simpliciter simplicem*, to speak like the Schoolmen, and that by an antecedent will. He is earnestly disposed to sanctify and to save all men, to exclude sin, and to prevent damnation. It may even be said that this will is efficacious *of itself* (*per se*), that is, in such sort that the effect would ensue if there were not some stronger reason to prevent it: for this will does not pass into final exercise (*ad summum conatum*), else it would never fail to produce its full effect, God being the master of all things. Success entire and infallible belongs only to the *consequent will*, as it is called. This it is which is complete; and in regard to it this rule obtains, that one never

fails to do what one wills, when one has the power. Now this consequent will, final and decisive, results from the conflict of all the antecedent wills, of those which tend towards good, even as of those which repel evil; and from the concurrence of all these particular wills comes the total will. So in mechanics compound movement results from all the tendencies that concur in one and the same moving body, and satisfies each one equally, in so far as it is possible to do all at one time. It is as if the moving body took equal account of these tendencies . . . In this sense also it may be said that the antecedent will is efficacious in a sense and even effective with success.

23. Thence it follows that God wills *antecedently* the good and *consequently* the best. And as for evil, God wills moral evil not at all, and physical evil or suffering he does not will absolutely. Thus it is that there is no absolute predestination to damnation; and one may say of physical evil, that God wills it often as a penalty owing to guilt, and often also as a means to an end, that is, to prevent greater evils or to obtain greater good . . .

33

Alexander Pope, *An Essay on Man*

If the eighteenth century was the century of optimism, its bard was the Catholic poet and satirist Alexander Pope (1688–1744). Pope's *Essay on Man* (1733–4) was an international best-seller: within its first century, it appeared in over a hundred editions in eighteen languages, making Pope the first English poet to enjoy contemporary fame on the European continent. The philosophy of Pope's *Essay* was Stoic, Plotinian, and Augustinian boilerplate; the poem's appeal has as much to do with its sublime account of the grandeur of the universe, and the place of perplexed humanity within it. Pope, the author of the famous exhortation "Know then thyself, presume not God to scan, / The proper study of mankind is man," was Kant's favorite poet.

Alexander Pope, *An Essay on Man*, I.113–30, 139–46, 279–94; IV.49–52, 111–16, 131–46.

Epistle I

Go, wiser thou! and in thy scale of sense
Weigh thy Opinion against Providence;
Call Imperfection what thou fancy'st such,
Say, here he gives too little, there too much;
Destroy all creatures for thy sport or gust,
Yet cry, If Man's unhappy, God's unjust;
If Man alone ingross not Heav'n's high care,
Alone made perfect here, immortal there:
Snatch from his hand the balance and the rod,
Re-judge his justice, be the GOD of GOD!

In Pride, in reas'ning Pride, our error lies;
All quit their sphere, and rush into the skies.
Pride still is aiming at the blest abodes,
Men would be Angels, Angels would be Gods.
Aspiring to be Gods, if Angels fell,
Aspiring to be Angels, Men rebel;
And who but wishes to invert the laws
Of ORDER, sins against th' Eternal Cause.
    Ask for what end the heav'nly bodies shine,
Earth for whose use? Pride answers, "'Tis for mine: . . ."
. . . But errs not Nature from this gracious end,
From burning suns, when livid deaths descend,
When earthquakes swallow, or when tempests sweep
Towns to one grave, whole nations to the deep?
"No ('tis reply'd) the first Almighty Cause
"Acts not by partial, but by gen'ral laws . . .

    All are but parts of one stupendous whole,
Whose body Nature is, and God the soul;
That, chang'd thro' all, and yet in all the same,
Great in the earth, as in th'aethereal frame,
Warms in the sun, refreshes in the breeze,
Glows in the stars, and blossoms in the trees,
Lives thro' all life, extends thro' all extent,
Spreads undivided, operates unspent,
Breathes in our soul, informs our mortal part,
As full, as perfect, in a hair as heart;
As full, as perfect, in vile Man that mourns,
As the rapt Seraph that adores and burns;
To him no high, no low, no great, no small;
He fills, he bounds, connects, and equals all.
    Cease then, nor ORDER Imperfection name:
Our proper bliss depends on what we blame.
Know thy own point: This kind, this due degree
Of blindness, weakness, Heav'n bestows on thee.
Submit – In this, or any other sphere,
Secure to be as blest as thou canst bear:
Safe in the hand of one disposing Pow'r,
Or in the natal, or the mortal hour.
All Nature is but Art, unknown to thee;
All Chance, Direction, which thou canst not see;

All Discord, Harmony, not understood;
All partial Evil, universal Good:
And, spite of Pride and erring Reason's spite,
One truth is, "Whatever IS, is RIGHT."

Epistle IV

ORDER is Heav'n's first law; and this confest,
Some are, and must be, greater than the rest,
More rich, more wise; but who infers from hence
That such are happier, shocks all common sense . . .
What makes all physical or moral ill?
There deviates Nature, and here wanders Will.
God sends not ill; if rightly understood,
Or partial Ill is universal Good,
Or Change admits, or Nature lets it fall,
Short and but rare, 'till man improv'd it all
But still this world (so fitted for the knave)
Contents us not. A better shall we have?
A kingdom of the Just then let it be:
But first consider how those Just agree.
The good must merit God's peculiar care;
But who, but God, can tell us who they are?
One thinks on Calvin Heav'n's own spirit fell,
Another deems him instrument of hell;
If Calvin feel Heav'n's blessing, or its rod,
This cries there is, and that, there is no God.
What shocks one part will edify the rest,
Nor with one system can they all be blest.
The very best will variously incline,
And what rewards your Virtue, punish mine.
"Whatever IS, is RIGHT." – This world, 'tis true,
Was made for Caesar – but for Titus too: . . .

34

Voltaire, "The Lisbon Earthquake: An Inquiry into the Maxim, 'Whatever is, is right'"

The Lisbon earthquake of November 1755, in which some 60,000 people died, is often seen as a turning point in the history of ideas, but its significance seems to have been largely retrospective. It did, however, mark a turning point in the career of François-Marie Arouet, Voltaire (1694–1778), the most famous of the French *philosophes* and the author of probably the most famous book about the problem of evil, *Candide, or Optimism* (1759). The "Poem on the Earthquake of Lisbon" and *Candide* are passionate acts of self-purgation. Candide's fatuous teacher Pangloss is the source of most people's acquaintance with the claim that this is the "best of all possible worlds," but the word "optimism" (from *optimum*, the best) was in fact coined in 1737 not for Leibniz or his follower Christian Wolff (the model for Pangloss), but for Pope – and the eager Anglophile Voltaire! In consequence of a growing skepticism about philosophical systems, human freedom, and progress, Voltaire's optimism was shaky already by the time of his "Zadig" (1748), well before 1755. In his *Philosophical Dictionary* (1764), he would come close to Bayle's endorsement-by-default of dualism, but the pious-sounding claim "I prefer to worship a limited God than a wicked one" cloaks an atheist rather than a fideist skepticism.

Voltaire, "The Lisbon Earthquake: An Inquiry into the Maxim, 'Whatever is, is right,'" trans. Tobias Smollett and others, in *The Portable Voltaire*, ed. Ben Ray Redman (Harmondsworth: Penguin, 1949), 560–9: 560–2, 564–9.

Oh wretched man, earth-fated to be cursed;
Abyss of plagues, and miseries the worst!
Horrors on horrors, griefs on griefs must show,
That man's the victim of unceasing woe,
And lamentations which inspire my strain,
Prove that philosophy is false and vain.
Approach in crowds, and meditate awhile
Yon shattered walls, and view each ruined pile,
Women and children heaped up mountain high,
Limbs crushed which under ponderous marble lie;
Wretches unnumbered in the pangs of death,
Who mangled, torn, and panting for their breath,
Buried beneath their sinking roofs expire,
And end their wretched lives in torments dire.
Say, when you hear their piteous, half-formed cries,
Or from their ashes see the smoke arise,
Say, will you then eternal laws maintain,
Which God to cruelties like these constrain?
Whilst you these facts replete with horror view,
Will you maintain death to their crimes was due?
And can you then impute a sinful deed
To babes who on their mothers' bosoms bleed?
Was then more vice in fallen Lisbon found,
Than Paris, where voluptuous joys abound?
Was less debauchery to London known,
Where opulence luxurious holds her throne?
Earth Lisbon swallows; the light sons of France
Protract the feast, or lead the sprightly dance.
Spectators who undaunted courage show,
While you behold your dying brethren's woe;
With stoical tranquillity of mind
You seek the causes of these ills to find;
But when like us Fate's rigors you have felt,
Become humane, like us you'll learn to melt.
When the earth gapes my body to entomb,
I justly may complain of such a doom.
Hemmed round on every side by cruel fate,
The snares of death, the wicked's furious hate,
Preyed on by pain and by corroding grief
Suffer me from complaint to find relief.
'Tis pride, you cry, seditious pride that still

Asserts mankind should be exempt from ill.
The awful truth on Tagus' banks explore,
Rummage the ruins on that bloody shore,
Wretches interred alive in direful grave
Ask if pride cries, "Good Heaven, thy creatures save."
If 'tis presumption that makes mortals cry,
"Heav'n, on our sufferings cast a pitying eye."
All's right, you answer, the eternal cause
Rules not by partial, but by general laws.
Say what advantage can result to all,
From wretched Lisbon's lamentable fall?
Are you then sure, the power which could create
The universe and fix the laws of fate,
Could not have found for man a proper place,
But earthquakes must destroy the human race?
Will you thus limit the eternal mind?
Should not our God to mercy be inclined?
Cannot then God direct all nature's course?
Can power almighty be without resource?
Humbly the great Creator I entreat,
This gulf with sulphur and with fire replete,
Might on the deserts spend its raging flame,
God my respect, my love weak mortals claim;
When man groans under such a load of woe,
He is not proud, he only feels the blow.
Would words like these to peace of mind restore
The natives sad of that disastrous shore?
Grieve not, that others' bliss may overflow,
Your sumptuous palaces are laid thus low;
Your toppled towers shall other hands rebuild;
With multitudes your walls one day be filled;
Your ruin on the North shall wealth bestow,
For general good from partial ills must flow;
You seem as abject to the sovereign power,
As worms which shall your carcasses devour.
No comfort could such shocking words impart,
But deeper wound the sad, afflicted heart.
When I lament my present wretched state,
Allege not the unchanging laws of fate;
Urge not the links of the eternal chain,
'Tis false philosophy and wisdom vain . . .

This is the fatal knot you should untie,
Our evils do you cure when you deny?
Men ever strove into the source to pry,
Of evil, whose existence you deny.
If he whose hand the elements can wield,
To the winds' force makes rocky mountains yield;
If thunder lays oaks level with the plain,
From the bolts' strokes they never suffer pain.
But I can feel, my heart oppressed demands
Aid of that God who formed me with His hands.
Sons of the God supreme to suffer all
Fated alike; we on our Father call.
No vessel of the potter asks, we know,
Why it was made so brittle, vile, and low?
Vessels of speech as well as thought are void;
The urn this moment formed and that destroyed,
The potter never could with sense inspire,
Devoid of thought it nothing can desire.
The moralist still obstinate replies,
Others' enjoyments from your woes arise,
To numerous insects shall my corpse give birth,
When once it mixes with its mother earth:
Small comfort 'tis that when Death's ruthless power
Closes my life, worms shall my flesh devour . . .
Yet in this direful chaos you'd compose
A general bliss from individuals' woes?
Oh worthless bliss! in injured reason's sight,
With faltering voice you cry, "What is, is right"?
The universe confutes your boasting vain,
Your heart retracts the error you maintain.
Men, beasts, and elements know no repose
From dire contention; earth's the seat of woes:
We strive in vain its secret source to find.
Is ill the gift of our Creator kind?
Do then fell Typhon's cursed laws ordain
Our ill, or Arimanius doom to pain?
Shocked at such dire chimeras, I reject
Monsters which fear could into gods erect.
But how conceive a God, the source of love,
Who on man lavished blessings from above,
Then would the race with various plagues confound

Can mortals penetrate His views profound?
Ill could not from a perfect being spring,
Nor from another, since God's sovereign king;
And yet, sad truth! in this our world 'tis found,
What contradictions here my soul confound!
A God once dwelt on earth amongst mankind,
Yet vices still lay waste the human mind;
He could not do it, this proud sophist cries,
He could, but he declined it, that replies;
He surely will, ere these disputes have end,
Lisbon's foundations hidden thunders rend,
And thirty cities' shattered remnants fly,
With ruin and combustion through the sky,
From dismal Tagus' ensanguined shore,
To where of Cadiz' sea the billows roar.
Or man's a sinful creature from his birth,
And God to woe condemns the sons of earth;
Or else the God who being rules and space,
Untouched with pity for the human race,
Indifferent, both from love and anger free,
Still acts consistent to His first decree:
Or matter has defects which still oppose
God's will, and thence all human evil flows;
Or else this transient world by mortals trod,
Is but a passage that conducts to God.
Our transient sufferings here shall soon be o'er,
And death will land us on a happier shore.
But when we rise from this accursed abyss,
Who by his merit can lay claim to bliss?
Dangers and difficulties man surround,
Doubts and perplexities his mind confound.
To nature we apply for truth in vain,
God should His will to human kind explain.
He only can illume the human soul,
Instruct the wise man, and the weak console.
Without Him man of error still the sport,
Thinks from each broken reed to find support.
Leibnitz can't tell me from what secret cause
In a world governed by the wisest laws,
Lasting disorders, woes that never end
With our vain pleasures real sufferings blend;

Why ill the virtuous with the vicious shares?
Why neither good nor bad misfortunes spares?
I can't conceive that "what is, ought to be,"
In this each doctor knows as much as me . . .
If in a life midst sorrows past and fears,
With pleasure's hand we wipe away our tears,
Pleasure his light wings spreads, and quickly flies,
Losses on losses, griefs on griefs arise.
The mind from sad remembrance of the past.
Is with black melancholy overcast;
Sad is the present if no future state,
No blissful retribution mortals wait,
If fate's decrees the thinking being doom
To lose existence in the silent tomb.
All may be well; that hope can man sustain,
All now is well; 'tis an illusion vain.
The sages held me forth delusive light,
Divine instructions only can be right.
Humbly I sigh, submissive suffer pain,
Nor more the ways of Providence arraign.
In youthful prime I sung in strains more gay,
Soft pleasure's laws which lead mankind astray.
But times change manners; taught by age and care
Whilst I mistaken mortals' weakness share,
The light of truth I seek in this dark state,
And without murmuring submit to fate.
A caliph once when his last hour drew nigh,
Prayed in such terms as these to the most high:
"Being supreme, whose greatness knows no bound,
I bring thee all that can't in Thee be found;
Defects and sorrows, ignorance and woe."
Hope he omitted, man's sole bliss below.

35

Jean-Jacques Rousseau, "Letter from J.-J. Rousseau to Mr. de Voltaire, August 18, 1756"

The most influential statement on theodicy of the Genevan philosopher, novelist, and pedagogue Jean-Jacques Rousseau (1712–78) is delivered by the Savoyard Vicar in his novel *Émile* (1762): "Man, seek the author of evil no longer. It is yourself. No evil exists other than that which you do or suffer, and both come to you from yourself . . . Take away our fatal progress, take away our errors and our vices, take away the work of man, and everything is good." The Savoyard Vicar is usually taken to be articulating Rousseau's own view, but Rousseau's passional nature is better represented by the letter he wrote to Voltaire in response to his poem on the Lisbon earthquake. The letter employs mostly traditional Christian Stoic arguments, but its heart is an *ad hominem* attack on Voltaire. Revealingly, elements of the critique of progress Rousseau had just published in his *Discourses* are grafted onto traditional ways of dismissing the claims of those who question God's providence based on temperament and the absence of grace-infused faith.

Jean-Jacques Rousseau, *Discourse on the Origins of Inequality (Second Discourse), Polemics, and Political Economy* (*The Collected Writings of Rousseau*, vol. 3), ed. Roger D. Masters and Christopher Kelly, trans. Judith R. Bush, Roger D. Masters, Christopher Kelly, and Terence Marshall (Hanover: Dartmouth College/University Press of New England, 1992), 108–21.

. . . I expected from [your poem on the disaster of Lisbon] some results more worthy of the humanity which appears to have inspired you to write it. You reproach Pope and Leibniz for condemning our misfortunes, in maintaining that everything is good, and you so amplify the picture of our miseries that you aggravate the feeling of them: instead of the consolations for which I hoped, you only cause me to be afflicted. One might say that you fear that I do not see well enough how unfortunate I am; and it seems you expect to placate me a good deal by proving to me that everything is bad.

Do not deceive yourself on this, Sir; it happens entirely to the contrary of what you maintain. This optimism that you find so cruel, nevertheless consoles me in the very miseries that you depict to me as intolerable.

Pope's poem sweetens my troubles and leads me to patience; yours embitters my pains, invites me to grumbling, and depriving me of everything beyond a troubled hope, it reduces me to despair. . . . "Man, have patience," Pope and Leibniz tell me. "Your ills are a necessary consequence of your nature, and of the constitution of this universe. The eternal and beneficent Being who governs you would have liked to safeguard you from them. Of all the economies possible, he has chosen the one which combined the least bad with the most good, or (to say the same thing more bluntly, if it is necessary) if he has not done better, it is that he could not do better."

What does your poem now tell me? "Suffer forever, wretches. If there is a God who has created you, no doubt he is omnipotent; he could have prevented all your ills: do not hope then that they will ever end; for one would not know how to see why you exist, if it is not to suffer and die." I do not know what such a doctrine could possess that is more consoling than optimism and even fatalism. As for me, I acknowledge it appears to me even crueler than Manichaeism. If perplexity concerning the origin of evil forces you to alter one of the perfections of God, why do you wish to justify his power at the expense of his goodness? If it is necessary to choose between two errors, I like the first one even better.

You do not wish, Sir, that your work be regarded as a poem against Providence; and I shall indeed restrain myself from giving it this name, although you have characterized as a book against the human race a writing wherein I pleaded the cause of the human race against itself. I know the distinction that must be made between an author's intentions, and the consequences that can be drawn from his doctrine. The just defense of myself obliges me only to have you observe, that in depicting human miseries, my purpose was excusable, and even praiseworthy, as I believe, for I showed men how they caused their miseries themselves, and consequently how they might avoid them.

I do not see that one can seek the source of moral evil other than in man free, perfected, thereby corrupted; and as for physical ills, if sensitive and impassive matter is a contradiction, as it seems to me, they are inevitable in any system of which man is a part; and then the question is not at all why is man not perfectly happy, but why does he exist? More-over I believe I have shown that with the exception of death, which is an evil almost solely because of the preparations which one makes preceding it, most of our physical ills are still our own work. Without departing from your subject of Lisbon, admit, for example, that nature did not construct twenty thousand houses of six to seven stories there, and that if the inhab-itants of this great city had been more equally spread out and more lightly lodged, the damage would have been much less, and perhaps of no account. All of them would have fled at the first disturbance, and the next day they would have been seen twenty leagues from there, as gay as if nothing had happened; but it is necessary to remain, to be obstinate about some hovels, to expose oneself to new quakes, because what is left behind is worth more than what can be brought along. How many unfortunate people have perished in this disaster because of one wanting to take his clothes, another his papers, another his money? Is it not known that the person of each man has become the least part of himself, and that it is almost not worth the trouble of saving it when one has lost all the rest?

You would have wished (and who would not have wished the same) that the quake had occurred in the middle of a wilderness rather than in Lisbon . . . Should it be said then that the order of the world ought to change according to our whims, that nature ought to be subjugated to our laws, and that in order to interdict an earthquake in some place, we have only to build a City there? . . .

You think along with Erasmus that few people would want to be reborn in the same conditions in which they have lived; . . . whom should I believe that you have consulted on that? Some rich people, perhaps, sated by false pleasures, but ignorant of genuine ones, always bored with life and always trembling over losing it; perhaps some literary people, of all the orders of men the most sedentary, the most unhealthy, the most reflective, and consequently the most unhappy. Do you want to find some men of better composition, or at least commonly more sincere, and who, forming the greatest number, at least because of that ought to be heard by prefer-ence? Consult an honest *bourgeois* who will have spent an obscure and tranquil life without projects and without ambition; a good artisan, who lives commodiously by his trade; even a peasant, not from France, where it is claimed that it is necessary to cause them to die of misery, in order for them to enable us to live, but of the country, for example, where you are, and generally of any free country. . . .

On the good of the whole, preferable to that of its parts, you have man say: "I ought to be as dear to my master, I, a thinking and feeling being, as the planets which probably do not feel at all." Undoubtedly this material universe ought not to be dearer to its Author than a single thinking and feeling being. But the system of this universe which produces, conserves, and perpetuates all the thinking and feeling beings ought to be dearer to him than a single one of these beings; he can therefore, despite all his goodness, or rather through his very goodness, sacrifice something of the happiness of individuals to the conservation of the whole. I believe, I hope, I am worth more in the eyes of God than the land of a planet; but if the planets are inhabited, as is probable, why would I be worth more in his eyes than all the inhabitants of Saturn? These ideas have been nicely turned to ridicule. It is certain that all the analogies favor this population, and that it is only human pride that might be opposed. But this population being assumed, the conservation of the universe seems to have, for God himself, a morality which multiplies itself by the number of inhabited worlds . . .

To return, Sir, to the system that you attack, I believe that one cannot examine it suitably without distinguishing carefully particular evil, whose existence no Philosopher has ever denied, from the general evil that the optimist denies. It is not a question of knowing whether each one of us suffers or not; but whether it be good that the universe exists, and whether our ills be inevitable in the constitution of the universe. Thus . . . in place of *Everything is good*, it would be more worthwhile to say: *The whole is good*, or *Everything is good for the whole*. Then it is quite evident that no man would know how to give direct proof either for or against; for these proofs depend on a perfect knowledge of the constitution of the world and of the purpose of its Author, and this knowledge is incontestably above human intelligence. The true principles of optimism can be drawn neither from the properties of matter, nor from the mechanics of the universe, but only by inference from the perfections of God who presides over everything; so that one does not prove the existence of God by the system of Pope, but the system of Pope by the existence of God, and it is incontrovertible that from the question of Providence is derived that of the origin of evil. But if these two questions have not been better treated, the one before the other, it is because one has always reasoned so badly on Providence that the absurd things that have been spoken about it have gravely confused all the corollaries that could be drawn from this great and consoling dogma.

The first who spoiled the cause of God are the Priests and the Devout, who do not allow that anything occurs according to the established order, but always have Divine justice intervene in purely natural events, and in order to be sure of their occurrence, punish and chastise the wicked, put to the proof or requite the good indiscriminately with some benefits or misfortunes, according to the event. For myself, I do not know whether it is a good Theology; but I find it a bad manner of reasoning, to base the proofs of Providence indiscriminately on the pros and cons, and to attribute to it unselectively everything which would equally occur without it.

The Philosophers, in their turn, hardly seem to me to be more reasonable, when I see them blame Heaven that they are not insensitive, cry that all is lost when they have a tooth ache, or when they are poor, or when they have been robbed, and charge God, as Seneca says, to watch over their valise. [See p. 22 above.] If some tragic accident had caused Cartouche or Caesar to perish in their infancy one would have said: What crimes have they committed? These two brigands lived, and we say: Why were they permitted to live? In contrast the devout person will say in the first instance: God wanted to punish the father by taking his son from him; and in the second: God preserved the child for the chastisement of the people. Thus, whatever part nature might have taken, Providence is always right among the Devout and always wrong among the Philosophers. Perhaps in the order of things human it is neither wrong nor right, because everything keeps to the shared law, and because there is no exception for anyone. It is to be believed that particular events are nothing here below in the eyes of the Master of the universe, that his Providence is only universal, that he is content to preserve the genera and the species, and to preside over the whole without being disturbed by the manner in which each individual spends this brief life . . .

To think rightly in this respect, it seems that things ought to be considered relatively in the physical order, and absolutely in the moral order: with the result that the greatest idea that I can give myself of Providence is that each material being be disposed the best way possible in relation to the whole, and each intelligent and sensitive being the best way possible in relation to himself; which signifies in other terms that for whom ever feels his existence, it is worth more to exist than not to exist. But it is necessary to apply this rule to the total duration of each sensitive being, and not to several particular instances of its duration, such as human life; which shows how much the question of Providence depends on that of the immortality of the soul in which I have the good fortune to believe, without being unaware that reason can doubt it, and on that of the eternity of punishments which neither you nor I, nor ever a man thinking well of God, will ever believe.

If I restore these different questions to their common principle, it seems to me that they are all related to that of the existence of God. If God exists, he is perfect; if he is perfect, he is wise, powerful, and just; if he is wise and powerful, all is good; if he is just and powerful, my soul is immortal; if my soul is immortal, thirty years of life are nothing for me, and are perhaps necessary for the maintenance of the universe. If one grants me the first proposition, never will one shake those following; if one denies it, it is not necessary to dispute over its consequences . . .

As for me, I naively admit to you that neither the pro nor the con seems to me demonstrated on this point by the lights of reason, and that if the Theist bases his sentiments only on probabilities, the Atheist, even less precise, seems to me only to base his own on some contrary possibilities. Moreover, the objections, on both sides, are always insoluble because they take in some things of which men have no genuine idea at all. I agree to all that, and yet I believe in God quite as strongly as I believe in any other truth, because to believe and not to believe are the things which depend least on me, because the state of doubt is a state too violent for my soul, because when my reason wavers, my faith cannot for long remain in suspense, and is determined without it, that at least a thousand subjects of preference entice me from the most consoling side and join the weight of hope to the equilibrium of reason . . .

I cannot refrain, Sir, from noting in this connection a quite singular opposition between you and me over the subject of this letter. Surfeited with glory, and undeceived by vain grandeur, you live free in the bosom of abundance; quite sure of immortality, you philosophize peacefully on the nature of the soul; and if the body or the heart suffers, you have Tronchin for a doctor and for a friend: however, you find only evil on the Earth. And I, obscure, poor, and tormented by an incurable malady, I meditate with pleasure in my retreat, and find that all is good. From whence might these apparent contradictions come? You yourself have explained it: you enjoy, but I hope, and hope adorns everything.

I have as much difficulty in leaving this tiresome letter as you will have in finishing it. Pardon me, great man, for a zeal which is perhaps indiscreet, but which would not be vented on you, if I esteemed you less.

36

David Hume, *Dialogues concerning Natural Religion*

The modern source of the trilemma is *Dialogues concerning Natural Religion* by the Scottish critic, historian, and philosopher David Hume (1711–76). Hume arranged for the *Dialogues,* composed mostly in the 1750s, to be published after his death; they were the final component of his devastating critique of all forms of religion. Hume's arguments have long been celebrated by atheists, but Jennifer Herdt has recently shown that Hume attacked religion less because he thought it false than because he thought its "spirit of faction" the greatest obstacle to moral and social progress. Like its model, Cicero's *On the Nature of the Gods,* Hume's *Dialogues* uses the dialogue form to make a skeptical point. "Any question of philosophy," the work's young narrator Pamphilus explains, "which is so *obscure* and *uncertain,* that human reason can reach no fixed determination with regard to it; if it should be treated at all; seems to lead us naturally into the style of dialogue and conversation. Reasonable men may be allowed to differ, where no one can reasonably be positive." This point seems to be accepted in the dialogue by the melancholy skeptic Philo and his sanguine friend, the natural theologian Cleanthes, but not by the fideist Demea, who eventually leaves the conversation. Philo demolishes all the arguments of Demea and Cleanthes (in the process reinventing Epicurus' argument and anticipating the "evidential problem of evil") but the work ends in a sort of tie. Pamphilus concludes: "I cannot but think that Philo's principles are more probable than Demea's, but that those of Cleanthes approach still nearer to the truth."

David Hume, *Dialogues Concerning Natural Religion*, ed. Richard H. Popkin (Indianapolis: Hackett, 1980), 58–66, 74–6.

X

Demea: It is my opinion, I own, replied *Demea*, that each man feels, in a manner, the truth of religion within his own breast; and, from a consciousness of his imbecility and misery rather than from any reasoning, is led to seek protection from that Being on whom he and all nature are dependent. So anxious or so tedious are even the best scenes of life that futurity is still the object of all our hopes and fears. We incessantly look forward and endeavor, by prayers, adoration, and sacrifice, to appease those unknown powers whom we find, by experience, so able to afflict and oppress us. Wretched creatures that we are! What resource for us amidst the innumerable ills of life did not religion suggest some methods of atonement, and appease those terrors with which we are incessantly agitated and tormented?

Philo: I am indeed persuaded, said *Philo*, that the best and indeed the only method of bringing everyone to a due sense of religion is by just representations of the misery and wickedness of men. And for that purpose a talent of eloquence and strong imagery is more requisite than that of reasoning and argument. For is it necessary to prove what everyone feels within himself? It is only necessary to make us feel it, if possible, more intimately and sensibly.

Demea: The people, indeed, replied *Demea*, are sufficiently convinced of this great and melancholy truth. The miseries of life, the unhappiness of man, the general corruptions of our nature, the unsatisfactory enjoyment of pleasures, riches, honors; these phrases have become almost proverbial in all languages. And who can doubt of what all men declare from their own immediate feeling and experience?

Philo: In this point, said *Philo*, the learned are perfectly agreed with the vulgar; and in all letters, sacred and profane, the topic of human misery has been insisted on with the most pathetic eloquence that sorrow and melancholy could inspire. The poets, who speak from sentiment, without a system, and whose testimony has therefore the more authority, abound in images of this nature . . .

Demea: . . . Look round this library of *Cleanthes*. I shall venture to affirm that, except authors of particular sciences, such as chemistry or botany, who have no occasion to treat of human life, there is scarce one of those innumerable writers from whom the sense of human misery has not, in some passage or other, extorted a complaint and confession of it . . .

Philo: There you must excuse me, said *Philo*: *Leibniz* has denied it, and is perhaps the first who ventured upon so bold and paradoxical an opinion; at least, the first who made it essential to his philosophical system.

Demea: And by being the first, replied *Demea*, might he not have been sensible of his error? For is this a subject in which philosophers can propose to make discoveries especially in so late an age? And can any man hope by a simple denial (for the subject scarcely admits of reasoning) to bear down the united testimony of mankind, founded on sense and consciousness?

And why should man, added he, pretend to an exemption from the lot of all other animals? The whole earth, believe me, Philo, is cursed and polluted. A perpetual war is kindled amongst all living creatures. Necessity, hunger, want stimulate the strong and courageous: fear, anxiety, terror agitate the weak and infirm. The first entrance into life gives anguish to the new-born infant and to its wretched parent: weakness, impotence, distress attend each stage of that life, and it is, at last, finished in agony and horror.

Philo: Observe, too, says *Philo*, the curious artifices of nature in order to embitter the life of every living being. The stronger prey upon the weaker and keep them in perpetual terror and anxiety. The weaker, too, in their turn, often prey upon the stronger, and vex and molest them without relaxation . . .

Demea: Man alone, said *Demea*, seems to be, in part, an exception to this rule. For by combination in society he can easily master lions, tigers, and bears, whose greater strength and agility naturally enable them to prey upon him.

Philo: On the contrary, it is here chiefly, cried *Philo*, that the uniform and equal maxims of nature are most apparent. Man, it is true, can, by combination, surmount all his *real* enemies and become master of the whole animal creation: But does he not immediately raise up to himself *imaginary* enemies, the demons of his fancy, who haunt him with superstitious terrors and blast every enjoyment of life? His pleasure, as he imagines, becomes in their eyes a crime: His food and repose give them umbrage and offence; his very sleep and dreams furnish new materials to anxious fear: And even death, his refuge from every other ill, presents only the dread of endless and innumerable woes. Nor does the wolf molest more the timid flock than superstition does the anxious breast of wretched mortals.

Besides, consider, *Demea*: This very society by which we surmount those wild beasts, our natural enemies, what new enemies does it not raise to us? What woe and misery does it not occasion? Man is the greatest enemy of man. Oppression, injustice, contempt, contumely, violence, sedition, war, calumny, treachery, fraud; by these they mutually torment each other, and they would soon dissolve that society which they had formed were it not for the dread of still greater ills which must attend their separation.

Demea: But though these external insults, said *Demea*, from animals, from men, from all the elements, which assault us form a frightful catalogue of woes, they are nothing in comparison of those which arise within ourselves, from the distempered condition of our mind and body. How many lie under the lingering torment of diseases? Hear the pathetic enumeration of the great poet.

> Intestine stone and ulcer, colic-pangs,
> Demoniac frenzy, moping melancholy,
> And moon-struck madness, pining atrophy,
> Marasmus, and wide-wasting pestilence.
> Dire was the tossing, deep the groans: *Despair*
> Tended the sick, busiest from couch to couch.
> And over them triumphant *Death* his dart
> Shook: but delay'd to strike, though oft invok'd
> With vows, as their chief good and final hope.
>   [Milton, *Paradise Lost*, XI.484–93]

The disorders of the mind, continued *Demea*, though more secret, are not perhaps less dismal and vexatious. Remorse, shame, anguish, rage, disappointment, anxiety, fear, dejection, despair: who has ever passed through life without cruel inroads from these tormentors? How many have scarcely ever felt any better sensations? Labor and poverty, so abhorred by everyone, are the certain lot of the far greater number: And those few privileged persons who enjoy ease and opulence never reach contentment or true felicity. All the goods of life united would not make a very happy man: But all the ills united would make a wretch indeed; and any one of them almost (and who can be free from every one), nay, often the absence of one good (and who can possess all) is sufficient to render life ineligible . . .

Philo: . . . But if they were really as unhappy as they pretend, says my antagonist, why do they remain in life?

> Not satisfied with life, afraid of death.

This is the secret chain, say I, that holds us. We are terrified, not bribed to the continuance of our existence . . . And is it possible, *Cleanthes*, said *Philo*, that after all these reflections, and infinitely more which might be suggested, you can still persevere in your anthropomorphism, and assert the moral attributes of the Deity, his justice, benevolence, mercy, and rectitude, to be of the same nature with these virtues in human creatures? His power, we allow, is infinite; whatever he wills is executed: But neither man nor any other animal is happy; therefore, he does not will their happiness. His wisdom is infinite; He is never mistaken in choosing the means to any end; But the course of nature tends not to human or animal felicity: Therefore, it is not established for that purpose. Through the whole compass of human knowledge there are no inferences more certain and infallible than these. In what respect, then, do his benevolence and mercy resemble the benevolence and mercy of men?

Epicurus' old questions are yet unanswered.

Is he willing to prevent evil, but not able? then is he impotent. Is he able, but not willing? then is he malevolent. Is he both able and willing? whence then is evil?

You ascribe, Cleanthes (and I believe justly), a purpose and intention to nature. But what, I beseech you, is the object of that curious artifice and machinery which she had displayed in all animals? The preservation alone of individuals, and propagation of the species? It seems enough for her purpose, if such a rank be barely upheld in the universe, without any care or concern for the happiness of the members that compose it. No resource for this purpose: No machinery in order merely to give pleasure or ease: No fund of pure joy and contentment: No indulgence without some want or necessity accompanying it. At least, the few phenomena of this nature are overbalanced by opposite phenomena of still greater importance.

Our sense of music, harmony, and indeed beauty of all kinds, gives satisfaction, without being absolutely necessary to the preservation and propagation of the species. But what racking pains, on the other hand, arise from gouts, gravels, megrims, toothaches, rheumatisms, where the injury to the animal machinery is either small or incurable? Mirth, laughter, play, frolic seem gratuitous satisfactions which have no further tendency; spleen, melancholy, discontent, superstition are pains of the same nature. How then does the divine benevolence display itself, in the sense of you anthropomorphites? None but we mystics, as you were pleased to call us, can account for this strange mixture of phenomena, by deriving it from attributes infinitely perfect but incomprehensible.

Cleanthes: And have you, at last, said Cleanthes smiling, betrayed your intentions, Philo? Your long agreement with Demea did indeed a little surprise me, but I find you were all the while erecting a concealed battery against me. And I must confess that you have now fallen upon a subject worthy of your noble spirit of opposition and controversy. If you can make out the present point, and prove mankind to be unhappy or corrupted, there is an end at once of all religion. For to what purpose establish the natural attributes of the Deity, while the moral are still doubtful and uncertain?

Demea: You take umbrage very easily, replied *Demea*, at opinions the most innocent and the most generally received, even amongst the religious and devout themselves; and nothing can be more surprising than to find a topic like this – concerning the wickedness and misery of man – charged with no less than atheism and profaneness. Have not all pious divines and preachers who have indulged their rhetoric on so fertile a subject; have they not easily, I say, given a solution of any difficulties which may attend it? This world is but a point in comparison of the universe; this life but a moment in comparison of eternity. The present evil phenomena, therefore, are rectified in other regions, and in some future period of existence. And the eyes of men, being then opened to larger views of things, see the whole connection of general laws, and trace, with adoration, the benevolence and rectitude of the Diety through all the mazes and intricacies of his providence.

Cleanthes: No! replied *Cleanthes*, no! These arbitrary suppositions can never be admitted, contrary to matter of fact, visible and uncontroverted. Whence can any cause be known but from its known effects? Whence can any hypothesis be proved but from the apparent phenomena? To establish one hypothesis upon another is building entirely in the air; and the utmost we ever attain by these conjectures and fictions is to ascertain the bare possibility of our opinion, but never can we, upon such terms, establish its reality.

The only method of supporting divine benevolence (and it is what I willingly embrace) is to deny absolutely the misery and wickedness of man. Your representations are exaggerated; your melancholy views mostly fictitious; your inferences contrary to fact and experience. Health is more common than sickness: Pleasure than pain: Happiness than misery. And for one vexation which we meet with, we attain, upon computation, a hundred enjoyments.

Philo: Admitting your position, replied *Philo*, which yet is extremely doubtful, you must at the same time allow that, if pain be less frequent than pleasure, it is infinitely more violent and durable. One hour of it is often able to outweigh a day, a week, a month of our common insipid enjoyments; and how many days, weeks, and months are passed by several in the most acute torments? . . .

But I will be contented to retire still from this retrenchment, for I deny that you can ever force me in it. I will allow that pain or misery in man is *compatible* with infinite power and goodness in the Deity, even in your sense of these attributes: what are you advanced by all these concessions? A mere possible compatibility is not sufficient. You must *prove* these pure, unmixed and uncontrollable attributes from the present mixed and confused phenomena, and from these alone. A hopeful undertaking! Were the phenomena ever so pure and unmixed, yet, being finite, they would be insufficient for that purpose. How much more, where they are also so jarring and discordant! . . .

XI

[**Philo:**] . . . Look round this universe. What an immense profusion of beings, animated and organized, sensible and active! You admire this prodigious variety and fecundity. But inspect a little more narrowly these living existences, the only beings worth regarding. How hostile and destructive to each other! How insufficient all of them for their own happiness! How contemptible or odious to the spectator! The whole presents nothing but the idea of a blind nature, impregnated by a great vivifying principle, and pouring forth from her lap, without discernment or parental care, her maimed and abortive children!

Here the Manichaean system occurs as a proper hypothesis to solve the difficulty; and, no doubt, in some respects it is very specious and has more probability than the common hypothesis, by giving a plausible account of the strange mixture of good and ill which appears in life. But if we consider, on the other hand, the perfect uniformity and agreement of the parts of the universe, we shall not discover in it any marks of the combat of a malevolent with a benevolent being. There is indeed an opposition of pains and pleasures in the feelings of sensible creatures; But are not all the operations of nature carried on by an opposition of principles, of hot and cold, moist and dry, light and heavy? The true conclusion is that the original source of all things is entirely indifferent to all these principles, and has no more regard to good above ill than to heat above cold, or to drought above moisture, or to light above heavy.

There may *four* hypotheses be framed concerning the first causes of the universe: *that* they are endowed with perfect goodness; *that* they have perfect malice; *that* they are opposite and have both goodness and malice; *that* they have neither goodness nor malice. Mixed phenomena can never prove the two former unmixed principles; and the uniformity and steadiness of general laws seem to oppose the third. The fourth, therefore, seems by far the most probable.

What I have said concerning natural evil will apply to moral with little or no variation; and we have no more reason to infer that the rectitude of the Supreme Being resembles human rectitude than that his benevolence resembles the human. Nay, it will be thought that we have still greater cause to exclude from him moral sentiments, such as we feel them; since moral evil, in the opinion of many, is much more predominant above moral good than natural evil above natural good . . .

Demea: Hold! hold! cried *Demea*: Whither does your imagination hurry you? I joined in alliance with you in order to prove the incomprehensible nature of the Divine Being, and refute the principles of *Cleanthes*, who would measure everything by human rule and standard. But I now find you running into all the topics of the greatest libertines and infidels, and betraying that holy cause which you seemingly espoused. Are you secretly, then, a more dangerous enemy than *Cleanthes* himself?

Cleanthes: And are you so late in perceiving it? replied *Cleanthes*. Believe me, *Demea*, your friend *Philo*, from the beginning, has been amusing himself at both our expense; and it must be confessed that the injudicious reasoning of our vulgar theology has given him but too just a handle of ridicule. The total infirmity of human reason, the absolute incomprehensibility of the Divine Nature, the great and universal misery, and still greater wickedness of men; these are strange topics, surely, to be so fondly cherished by orthodox divines and doctors. In ages of stupidity and ignorance, indeed, these principles may safely be espoused; and perhaps no views of things are more proper to promote superstition than such as encourage the blind amazement, the diffidence, and melancholy of mankind. But at present . . .

37

Immanuel Kant, "On the miscarriage of all philosophical trials in theodicy"

The 1791 essay "On the miscarriage of all philosophical trials in theodicy" of German philosopher Immanuel Kant (1724–1804) is often seen as marking the end of theodicy, but the story is more complicated. While Kant, like Voltaire, left behind a youthful optimism, his mature position is more like Rousseau's – it doesn't so much declare theodicy defeated as dismiss complaint. Kant's *Critique of Pure Reason* (1781) rendered the world of "things in themselves" inaccessible to experience, and radically redefined the status of our knowledge of God. All *a priori* arguments for the existence of God were demolished, along with arguments from the seemingly purposive design of the world. In their place, Kant offered a religion of hope like Rousseau's, yet based not on "theoretical" but on "practical reason." It is the needs of our moral lives, especially when the moral arbitrariness of the world of our experience makes us wonder whether moral effort is meaningful, that permit us to believe there is a God to coordinate the moral and natural worlds. At the same time that it pulls the ground out from under complaints to God, therefore, Kant's religion actually gains its force from the experience of moral *disorder*.

Immanuel Kant, "On the miscarriage of all philosophical trials in theodicy," trans. George di Giovanni, in *Religion and Rational Theology*, trans. & ed. Allen W. Wood and George di Giovanni (Cambridge: Cambridge University Press, 1996), 19–37.

By "theodicy" we understand the defense of the highest wisdom of the creator against the charge which reason brings against it for whatever is counterpurposive in the world. – We call this "the defending of God's cause," even though the cause might be at bottom no more than that of our presumptuous reason failing to recognize its limitations. This is indeed not the best of causes, yet one that can be condoned insofar as (aside from that self-conceit) the human being is justified, as rational, in testing all claims, all doctrines which impose respect upon him, before he submits himself to them, so that this respect may be sincere and not feigned.

Now for this vindication it is required that the would-be advocate of God prove *either* that whatever in the world we judge counterpurposive is not so; *or*, if there is any such thing, that it must be judged not at all as an intended effect but as the unavoidable consequence of the nature of things; *or*, finally, that it must at least be considered not as an intended effect of the creator of all things but, rather, merely of those beings in the world to whom something can be imputed, i.e. of human beings (higher spiritual beings as well, good or evil, as the case may be).

The author of a theodicy agrees, therefore, that this juridical process be instituted before the tribunal of reason; he further consents to represent the accused side as advocate through the formal refutation of all the plaintiff's complaints; he is not therefore allowed to dismiss the latter in the course of the process of law through a decree of incompetency of the tribunal of human reason (*exceptio fori*), i.e. he cannot dismiss the complaints with a concession of the supreme wisdom of the author of the world, imposed upon the plaintiff, which would immediately explain away as groundless even without examination, all doubts that might be raised against it; he must rather attend to the objections, and make comprehensible how they in no way derogate from the concept of the highest wisdom by clarifying and removing them. – Yet there is one thing he need not attend to, namely a proof of God's wisdom from what the experience of this world teaches; for in this he would simply not succeed, since omniscience would be required to recognize in a given world (as gives itself to cognition in experience) that perfection of which we could say with certainty that absolutely none other is possible in creation and its government.

Now whatever is counterpurposive in the world, and may be opposed to the wisdom of its creator, is of a threefold kind:

I. The absolutely counterpurposive, or what cannot be condoned or desired either as end or means;
II. The conditionally counterpurposive, or what can indeed never co-exist with the wisdom of a will as end, yet can do so as means.

The *first* is the morally counterpurposive, evil proper (sin); the *second*, the physically counterpurposive, ill (pain). – But now, there still is a purposiveness in the proportion of ill to moral evil, if the latter is once there, and neither can nor should be prevented – namely in the conjunction of ills and pains, as penalties, with evil, as crime. It is of this purposiveness in the world that one asks whether, in this respect, everyone in the world gets his due. Consequently, yet a

IIIrd kind of counterpurposiveness must be thinkable in the world namely the disproportion between crimes and penalties in the world.

The attributes of the world-author's supreme wisdom against which these [three kinds of] counterpurposiveness stand out as objections are, therefore, likewise three:

First, the *holiness* of the author of the world, as *law*-giver (creator), in opposition to the moral evil in the world.
Second, his *goodness*, as *ruler* (preserver), in contrast with the countless ills and pains of the rational beings of the world.
Third, his *justice*, as *judge*, in comparison to the bad state which the disproportion between the impunity of the depraved and their crimes seems to indicate in the world.*

The case against those three charges must be presented, therefore, along the three above mentioned kinds [of counterpurposiveness], and must be tested against their validity.

I. Against the complaint over the holiness of the divine will for the moral evil which disfigures the world, God's work, the first vindication consists in this:

a) There is no such thing as an absolute counterpurposiveness which we take the trespassing of the pure laws of our reason to be, but there are violations only against human wisdom; divine wisdom judges these accord-

---

* These three attributes, none of which can in any way be reduced to the others – as, for instance, justice to goodness, and so the whole to a smaller number – together constitute the moral concept of God. Nor can their order be altered (as by making benevolence, for instance, the supreme condition of world creation to which the holiness of legislation is subordinated) without doing violence to religion, which has this very concept for foundation. Our own pure (hence practical) reason determines this order of rank, for if legislation accommodated itself to benevolence, its dignity would no longer be there, nor a firm concept of duties. Indeed the human being wishes to be happy first; but then he sees, and (though reluctantly) accepts, that the worthiness to be happy, i.e. the conformity of the employment of his freedom with the holy law, must in God's decision be the condition of his benevolence, and must, therefore, necessarily precede it . . . For under divine rule even the best of human beings cannot found his wish to fare well on divine justice but must found it on God's beneficence for one who only does what he owes can have no rightful claim on God's benevolence.

ing to totally different rules, incomprehensible to us, where, what we with right find reprehensible with reference to our practical reason and its determination might yet perhaps be in relation to the divine ends and the highest wisdom precisely the most fitting means to our particular welfare and the greatest good of the world as well; the ways of the most high are not our ways (*sunt supris sua iura* [those on high have their own laws]), and we err whenever we judge what is law only relatively to human beings in this life to be so absolutely, and thus hold what appears counterpurposive to our view of things from so lowly a standpoint to be such also when considered from the highest. – This apology, in which the vindication is worse than the complaint, needs no refutation; surely it can be freely given over to the detestation of every human being who has the least feeling for morality.

b) The second alleged vindication would indeed allow for the actuality of moral evil in the world, but it would excuse the author of the world on the ground that it could not be prevented, because founded upon the limitations of the nature of human beings, as finite. – However, the evil would thereby be justified, and, since it could not be attributed to human beings as something for which they are to be blamed, we would have to cease calling it "a moral evil."

c) The third rejoinder, that even conceding that it is really a matter of what we call moral evil, a guilt resting on the human being, yet no guilt may be ascribed to God, for God has merely tolerated it for just causes as a deed of human beings: in no way has he condoned it, willed or promoted it – this rejoinder incurs one and the same consequence as the previous apology (b) . . . : namely, since even for God it was impossible to prevent this evil without doing violence to higher and even moral ends elsewhere, the ground of this ill (for so we must now truly call it) must inevitably be sought in the essence of things, specifically in the necessary limitations of humanity as a finite nature; hence the latter can also not be held responsible for it.

II. With respect to the complaint brought against divine goodness for the ills, namely the pains, in this world, its vindication equally consists

a) in this: It is false to assume in human fates a preponderance of ill over the pleasant enjoyment of life, for however bad someone's lot, yet everyone would rather live than be dead, . . . But surely the reply to this sophistry may be left to the sentence of every human being of sound mind who has lived and pondered over the value of life long enough to pass judgment, when asked, on whether he had any inclination to play the game of life once more, I do not say in the same circumstances but in any other he pleases (provided they are not of a fairy world but of this earthly world of ours).

b) To the second vindication – namely, the preponderance of painful feelings over pleasant ones cannot be separated from the nature of an animal creature such as the human being . . . – the retort to this is that, if that is the way it is, then another question arises, namely why the creator of our existence called us into life when the latter, in our correct estimate, is not desirable to us . . .

c) The third way of untying the knot is supposed to be this: God has put us here on earth for the sake of a future happiness, hence out of his goodness; yet an arduous and sorrowful state in the present life must without exception precede that hoped-for superabundant blessedness – a state in which we are to become worthy of that future glory precisely through our struggle with adversities. – But, that before the highest wisdom this time of trial (to which most succumb, and in which even the best is not happy about his life) must without exception be the condition of the joy eventually to be savored by us, and that it was not possible to let the creature be satisfied with every stage of his life – this can indeed be pretended but in no way can there be insight into it; in this way one can indeed cut the knot loose through an appeal to the highest wisdom which willed it, but one cannot untie the knot, which is what theodicy claims to be capable of accomplishing.

III. To the last charge, namely against the justice of the world's judge,* is replied:

a) The pretension that the depraved go unpunished in the world is ungrounded, for by its nature every crime already carries with it its due punishment, inasmuch as the inner reproach of conscience torments the depraved even more harshly than the Furies. – But in this judgment there obviously lies a misunderstanding. For here the virtuous man lends to the depraved the characteristic of his own constitution, namely, a conscientiousness in all its severity which, the more virtuous a human being is, all the more harshly punishes him because of the slightest indiscretion frowned upon by the moral law in him . . . – If that charge shall be further

---

* It is remarkable that of all the difficulties in reconciling the course of world events with the divinity of their creator, none imposes itself on the mind as starkly as that of the semblance in them of a lack of *justice*. If it comes about (although it seldom happens) that an unjust, especially violent, villain does not escape unpunished from the world, then the impartial spectator rejoices, now reconciled with heaven. No purposiveness of nature will so excite him in admiration of it and, as it were, make him detect God's hand in it. Why? Because nature is here moral, solely of the kind we seldom can hope to perceive in the world.

b) refuted by this: It is indeed not to be denied that there is absolutely no relation according to justice between guilt and punishment in this world, and in the ways of this world one must often witness with indignation a life led with crying injustice and yet happy to the end; this is not, however, something inherent in nature and deliberately promoted, hence not a moral dissonance, for it is a property of virtue that it should wrestle with adversities (among which is the pain that the virtuous must suffer through comparison of his own unhappiness with the happiness of the depraved), and sufferings only serve to enhance the value of virtue; thus this dissonance of undeserved ills resolves itself before reason into a glorious moral melody – the objection to this solution is that, although these ills, when they *precede* virtue or accompany it as its whetting stone, can indeed be represented as in moral harmony with it if at least the end of life crowns virtue and punishes the depraved; yet, if even such an end (as experience thereof gives many examples) fails against sense to materialize, then the suffering seems to have occurred to the virtuous, not *so that* his virtue should be pure, but *because* it was pure (and accordingly contrary to the rules of prudent self-love); and this is the very opposite of the justice of which the human being can form a concept for himself. For as regards the possibility that the end of this terrestrial life might not perhaps be the end of all life, such a possibility cannot count as *vindication* of providence; rather, it is merely a decree of morally believing reason which directs the doubter to patience but does not satisfy him.

c) If, finally, an attempt is made at the third resolution to this disharmonious relation between the moral worth of human beings and the lot that befalls them, by saying: In this world we must judge all well-being and ill merely as the consequence of the use of the human faculties according to the laws of nature, in proportion to the skill and the prudence of their application, and also in proportion to the circumstances they accidentally come by, but not according to their agreement with supersensible ends; in a future world a different order of things will obtain instead, and each will receive that which his deeds here below are worthy of according to moral judgment – [if this is said,] then this assumption too is arbitrary. Rather, unless reason, as a faculty of moral legislation, is pronouncing a decree in accordance with this legislative interest, it must find it probable, according to the mere laws of theoretical cognition, that the way of the world determines our fates in the future just as it does here, according to the order of nature . . .

Now the outcome of this juridical process before the forum of philosophy is this: Every previous theodicy has not performed what it promised, namely the vindication of the moral wisdom of the world-government against the doubts raised against it on the basis of what the experience of this world teaches – although, to be sure, as objections, so far as our reason's inherent insight regarding them goes, neither can these doubts prove the contrary. But again, whether in time yet more solid grounds of vindication will perhaps be found for the indicted reason – for absolving it not (as hitherto) merely *ab instantia* – this still remains undecided; if we do not succeed in establishing with certainty that our reason is absolutely incapable of insight into *the relationship in which any world as we may ever become acquainted with through experience stands with respect to the highest wisdom*, then all further attempts by a putative human wisdom to gain insight into the ways of the divine wisdom are fully dismissed. Hence, in order to bring this trial to an end *once and for all*, it must yet be proven that at least a negative wisdom is within our reach – namely, insight into the necessary limitation of what we may presume with respect to that which is too high for us – and this may very well be done.

For in the arrangement of this world we have the concept of an *artistic wisdom* – a concept which, in order to attain to a physico-theology, is not wanting in objective reality for our speculative faculty of reason. And we also have in the moral idea of our own practical reason a concept of a *moral wisdom* which could have been implanted in a world in general by a most perfect creator. – But of the *unity in the agreement* in a sensible world between that artistic and moral wisdom we have no concept; nor can we ever hope to attain one. For to be a creature and, as a natural being, merely the result of the will of the creator; yet to be capable of responsibility as a freely acting being (one which has a will independent of external influence and possibly opposed to the latter in a variety of ways); but again, to consider one's own deed at the same time also as the effect of a higher being – this is a combination of concepts which we must indeed think together in the idea of a world and of a highest good, but which can be intuited only by one who penetrates to the cognition of the supersensible (intelligible) world and sees the manner in which this grounds the sensible world. The proof of the world-author's moral wisdom in the sensible world can be founded only on this insight – for the sensible world presents but the appearance of that other [intelligible] world – and that is an insight to which no mortal can attain.

All theodicy should truly be an *interpretation* of nature insofar as God announces his will through it. Now every interpretation of the declared will of a legislator is either *doctrinal or authentic*. The first is a rational inference of that will from the utterances of which the law-giver has made use, in conjunction with his otherwise recognized purposes; the second is made by the law-giver himself.

As a work of God, the world can also be considered by us as a divine publication of his will's *purposes*. However, in this respect the world is *often* a closed book for us, and it is so *every time* we look at it to extract from it God's *final aim* (which is always moral) even though it is an object of experience. Philosophical trials in this kind of interpretation are doctrinal; they constitute theodicy proper – which we can therefore call "doctrinal." – Yet we cannot deny the name of "theodicy" also to the mere dismissal of all objections against divine wisdom, if this dismissal is a *divine decree*, or (for in this case it amounts to the same thing) if it is a pronouncement of the same reason through which we form our concept of God – necessarily and prior to all experience – as a moral and wise being. For through our reason God then becomes himself the interpreter of his will as announced through creation; and we can call this interpretation an *authentic* theodicy . . . I find such an authentic interpretation expressed allegorically in an ancient holy book.

Job is portrayed as a man whose enjoyment of life included everything which anyone might possibly imagine as making it complete. He was healthy, well-to-do, free, master over others whom he can make happy, surrounded by a happy family, among beloved friends – and on top of all of this (what is most important) at peace with himself in a good conscience. A harsh fate imposed in order to test him suddenly snatched from him all these blessings, except the last. Stunned by this unexpected reversal, as he gradually regains his senses, he breaks out in lamentation over his unlucky star; whereupon a dispute soon develops between him and his friends – supposedly gathered to console him – in which the two sides expound their particular theodicy to give a moral explanation for that deplorable fate, each side according to its particular way of thinking (above all, however, according to its station). Job's friends declare themselves for that system which explains all ills in the world from God's *justice*, as so many punishments for crimes committed; and, although they could name none *for* which the unhappy man is guilty, yet they believed they could judge *a priori* that he must have some weighing upon him, for his misfortune would otherwise be impossible according to divine justice. Job – who indignantly protests that his conscience has nothing to reproach him for in his whole life; and, so far as human unavoidable mistakes are concerned, God himself knows that he has made him a fragile creature – Job declares himself for the system of *unconditional divine decision*. "He has decided," Job says, "He does as he wills." [Job 23:13]

There is little worthy of note in the subtle or hypersubtle reasonings of the two sides; but the spirit in which they carry them out merits all the more attention. Job speaks as he thinks, and with the courage which he, as well as every human being in his position, can well afford; his friends, on the contrary, speak as if they were being secretly listened to by the mighty one, over whose cause they are passing judgment, and as if gaining his favor through their judgment were closer to their heart than the truth. Their malice in pretending to assert things into which they yet must admit they have no insight, and in simulating a conviction which they in fact do not have, contrasts with Job's frankness – so far removed from false flattery as to border almost on impudence – much to his advantage. "Will you defend God unjustly" he asks. "Will you give his person [special] consideration? Will you plead for God? He shall punish you, if you secretly have consideration for persons! – There will be no hypocrite before him!" [Job 13:7–11,16]

The outcome of the story actually confirms this. For God deigned to lay before Job's eyes the wisdom of his creation, especially its inscrutability. He allowed him glimpses into the beautiful side of creation, where ends comprehensible to the human being bring the wisdom and the benevolent providence of the author of the world unambiguously to light; but also, by contrast, into the horrible side, by calling out to him the products of his might, among which also harmful and fearsome things, each of which appears indeed to be purposively arranged for its own sake and that of its species, yet, with respect to other things and to human beings themselves, as destructive, counterpurposive, and incompatible with a universal plan established with goodness and wisdom. And yet God thereby demonstrates an order and a maintenance of the whole which proclaim a wise creator, even though his ways, inscrutable to us, must at the same time remain hidden – indeed already in the physical order of things, and how much more in the connection of the latter with the moral order (which is all the more impenetrable to our reason). – The conclusion is this: Since Job admits having hastily spoken about things which are too high for him and which he does not understand – not *as if wantonly*, for he is conscious of his honesty, but only unwisely – God finds against his friends, for (as conscientiousness goes) they have not spoken as well of God as God's servant Job . . . [O]nly sincerity of heart and not distinction of insight; honesty in openly admitting one's doubts; repugnance to pretending conviction where one feels none, especially before God (where this trick is pointless enough) – these are the attributes which, in the person of Job, have decided the preeminence of the honest man over the religious flatterer in the divine verdict.

The faith, however, which sprang in him for such a vexing resolution of his doubts – namely merely from being convinced of ignorance – could only arise in the soul of a man who, in the midst of his strongest doubts, could yet say (Job 27:5–6): "Till I die I will not remove mine integrity from me, etc." For with this disposition he proved that he did not found his morality on faith, but his faith on morality: in such a case, however weak this faith might be, yet it alone is of a pure and true kind, i.e. the kind of faith that founds not a religion of supplication, but a religion of good life conduct.

Concluding Remark

. . . This leads to yet the following brief reflection on a big subject, namely sincerity, which is the principal requirement in matters of faith, as contrasted with the propensity to falsehood and impurity which is the principal affliction of human nature.

One cannot always stand by the *truth* of what one says to oneself or to another (for one can be mistaken); however, one can and must stand by the *truthfulness* of one's declaration or confession, because one has immediate consciousness of this. For in the first instance we compare what we say with the object in a logical judgment (through the understanding), whereas in the second instance, where we declare what we hold as true, we compare what we say with the subject (before conscience). Were we to make our declaration with respect to the former without being conscious of the latter, then we lie, since we pretend something else than what we are conscious of. – The observation that there is such an impurity in the human heart is not new (for Job already made it); yet one is tempted to believe that attention to it is new to the teachers of morality and religion, one so seldom finds them making a sufficient use of it despite the difficulty associated with a purification of the dispositions in human beings even when they *want* to act according to duty . . . [I]f someone says to himself (or – what is one and the same in religious professions – before God) that *he believes*, without perhaps casting even a single glimpse into himself – whether he is in fact conscious of thus holding a truth or at least of holding it to some degree – then such a person *lies*. And not only is his lie the most absurd (before a reader of hearts): it is also the most sinful, for it undermines the ground of every virtuous intention. It is not difficult to see how quickly these blind and external *professions* (which can very easily be reconciled with an internal profession just as false) can, if they yield *means of gain*, bring about a certain falsehood in a community's very way of thinking . . .

Beyond Optimism

38

Thomas Robert Malthus, *An Essay on the Principle of Population*

Is sex the root of all evil? In a way, this is the properly Victorian upshot of the work of the English geographer and economist Thomas Robert Malthus (1766–1834), who discovered that human populations grow geometrically in size, while their food sources grow only arithmetically. As this state of permanent struggle seemed hard to reconcile with a benevolent providence, the first edition (1798) of Malthus's *Essay on the Principle of Population* concluded with a full-fledged theodicy. "The impressions and excitements of this world are the instruments with which the supreme Being forms matter into mind," Malthus argues there, but this is a goal which can be accomplished only through struggle. "Evil exists in the world, not to create despair, but activity." While sublime, this was too abstract. Starting in the second edition Malthus argued, less sublimely but more practically, that human beings will need war, pestilence and starvation to limit their populations unless and until they learn to control the growth of population through "moral restraint."

Thomas Robert Malthus, *An Essay on the Principle of Population*, IV.2; in *An Essay on the Principle of Population: The sixth edition (1826) with variant readings from the second edition (1803)*, 2 vols., eds. E. A. Wrigley and David Souden (*The Works of Thomas Robert Malthus*, vols. 2–3) (London: William Pickering, 1986), III.474–81.

One of the principal reasons which have prevented an assent to the doctrine of the constant tendency of population to increase beyond the means of subsistence, is a great unwillingness to believe that the Deity would by the law of nature bring beings into existence, which by the laws of nature could not be supported in that existence. But if, in addition to that general activity and direction of our industry put in motion by these laws, we further consider that the incidental evils arising from them are constantly directing our attention to the proper check to population, moral restraint; and if it appears that, by a strict obedience to the duties pointed out to us by the light of nature and reason, and confirmed and sanctioned by revelation, these evils may be avoided, the objection will, I trust, be removed, and all apparent imputation on the goodness of the Deity be done away.

The heathen moralists never represented happiness as attainable on earth, but through the medium of virtue; and among their virtues prudence ranked in the first class, and by some was even considered as including every other. The Christian religion places our present as well as future happiness in the exercise of those virtues which tend to fit us for a state of superior enjoyment; and the subjection of the passions to the guidance of reason, which, if not the whole, is a principal branch of prudence, is in consequence most particularly inculcated.

If, for the sake of illustration, we might be permitted to draw a picture of society, in which each individual endeavoured to attain happiness by the strict fulfilment of those duties, which the most enlightened of the ancient philosophers deduced from the laws of nature, and which have been directly taught, and received such powerful sanctions in the moral code of Christianity, it would present a very different scene from that which we now contemplate. Every act, which was prompted by the desire of immediate gratification, but which threatened an ultimate overbalance of pain, would be considered as a breach of duty; and consequently no man, whose earnings were only sufficient to maintain two children, would put himself in a situation in which he might have to maintain four or five, however he might be prompted to it by the passion of love. This prudential restraint, if it were generally adopted, by narrowing the supply of labour in the market, would, in the natural course of things, soon raise its price. The period of delayed gratification would be passed in saving the earnings which were above the wants of a single man, and in acquiring habits of sobriety, industry and economy, which would enable him in a few years to enter into the matrimonial contract without fear of its consequences. The operation of the preventive check in this way, by constantly keeping the population within the limits of the food, though constantly following its increase, would give a real value to the rise of wages and the sums saved by labourers before marriage, very different from those forced advances in the price of labour or arbitrary parochial donations, which, in proportion to their magnitude and extensiveness, must of necessity be followed by a proportional advance in the price of provisions. As the wages of labour would thus be sufficient to maintain with decency a large family, and as every married couple would set out with a sum for contingencies, all abject poverty would be removed from society; or would at least be confined to a very few, who had fallen into misfortunes, against which no prudence or foresight could provide.

The interval between the age of puberty and the period at which each individual might venture on marriage must, according to the supposition, be passed in strict chastity; because the law of chastity cannot be violated without producing evil . . .

These considerations show that the virtue of chastity is not, as some have supposed, a forced product of artificial society; but that it has the most real and solid foundation in nature and reason; being apparently the only virtuous means of avoiding the vice and misery which result so often from the principle of population . . .

The difficulty of moral restraint will perhaps be objected to this doctrine. To him who does not acknowledge the authority of the Christian religion, I have only to say that after the most careful investigation, this virtue appears to be absolutely necessary, in order to avoid certain evils which would otherwise result from the general laws of nature. According to his own principles, it is his duty to pursue the greatest good consistent with these laws; and not to fail in this important end, and produce an overbalance of misery by a partial obedience to some of the dictates of nature, while he neglects others. The path of virtue, though it be the only path which leads to permanent happiness, has always been represented by the heathen moralists as of difficult ascent. [cf. p. 21 above.]

To the Christian I would say that the Scriptures most clearly and precisely point it out to us as our duty, to restrain our passions within the bounds of reason; and it is a palpable disobedience of this law to indulge our desires in such a manner as reason tells us will unavoidably end in misery . . .

If we could suppose such a system general, the accession of happiness to society in its internal economy would scarcely be greater than in its external relations. It might fairly be expected that war, that great pest of the human race, would, under such circumstances, soon cease to extend its ravages so widely and so frequently as it does at present.

One of its first causes and most powerful impulses was undoubtedly an insufficiency of room and food; and greatly as the circumstances of mankind have changed since it first began, the same cause still continues to operate and to produce, though in a smaller degree, the same effects.

The ambitions of princes would want instruments of destruction, if the distresses of the lower classes of people did not drive them under their standards . . .

. . . According to the genuine principles of moral science, "The method of coming at the will of God from the light of nature is, to inquire into the tendency of the action to promote or diminish the general happiness." [W. Paley, *The Principles of Moral and Political Philosophy*, 5th edn., 2 vols. (1788), I, p. 65.] There are perhaps few actions that tend so directly to diminish the general happiness, as to marry without the means of supporting children. He who commits this act, therefore, clearly offends against the will of God; and having become a burden on the society in which he lives, and plunged himself and family into a situation, in which virtuous habits are preserved with more difficulty than in any other, he appears to have violated his duty to his neighbours and to himself, and thus to have listened to the voice of passion in opposition to his higher obligations . . .

As it appears therefore, that it is in the power of each individual to avoid all the evil consequences to himself and society resulting from the principle of population, by the practice of a virtue clearly dictated to him by the light of nature, and expressly enjoined in revealed religion; and as we have reason to think, that the exercise of this virtue to a certain degree would tend rather to increase than to diminish individual happiness; we can have no reason to impeach the justice of the Deity, because his general laws make this virtue necessary, and punish our offences against it by the evils attendant upon vice, and the pains that accompany the various forms of premature death. A really virtuous society, such as I have supposed, would avoid these evils. It is the apparent object of the Creator to deter us from vice by the pains which accompany it, and to lead us to virtue by the happiness that it produces. This object appears to our conceptions to be worthy of a benevolent Creator. The laws of nature respecting population tend to promote this object. No imputation, therefore, on the benevolence of the Deity, can be founded on these laws, which is not equally applicable to any of the evils necessarily incidental to an imperfect state of existence.

39

F. W. J. Schelling, "Philosophical Investigations into the Essence of Human Freedom and Related Matters"

Free will is the war-horse of Christian theodicy, but how is the freedom to choose (or not choose) real – not just apparent – evil possible? In order for choice to be meaningful, something must be there to be chosen, but how could evil be there to be chosen in the creation of a good God *before* it is ever chosen? These questions, recognized but hardly settled by Augustine's understanding of the evil will as "defective" and Kant's idea of "radical evil," occupied the German idealist Friedrich Wilhelm Joseph Schelling (1775–1854) throughout a career which took him from being the self-proclaimed heir to Kant to being (in Paul Tillich's terms) the founder of existentialism. Pursuing what Paul Ricoeur has called the "strange experience of passivity, at the very heart of evil doing," Schelling blurred the boundary between nature and freedom ("nature is to be visible mind, mind invisible nature"). Inspired by Böhme, he postulated the ground of evil in a kind of dialectical monotheism which came close to dualism. In "Philosophical Investigations . . ." (1809), Schelling claimed to have provided the first real concept of the divine personality.

F. W. J. Schelling, "Philosophical Investigations into the Essence of Human Freedom and Related Matters," trans. Priscilla Hayden-Roy in *Philosophy of German Idealism*, ed. Ernst Behler (The German Library, vol. 23) (New York: Continuum, 1987), 217–84: 270–5.

In the divine understanding there is a system; however, God himself is not a system, but a life, and therein alone lies the answer to the question concerning the possibility of evil with reference to God, . . . All existence requires a condition in order for it to become actual, i.e., personal, existence. God's existence, too, could not be personal without such a condition, except that he has this condition within himself, not outside himself. He cannot annul this condition, for in that case he would have to annul himself; he can only overpower it through love and subordinate it to himself for his glorification. In God, too, there would be a ground of darkness if he did not integrate the condition into himself, combining himself with it as one, in absolute personality. Man never obtains control of this condition, although in evil he strives to do so; it is only loaned to him, is independent of him; thus his personality and selfhood can never rise to perfect act. This is the sadness clinging to all finite life and if in God, too, there is a condition which is at least relatively independent, then within him there is a well of sadness, which, however, never comes to actuality, but serves only for the eternal joy of overcoming. Hence the veil of despondency spread over all of nature, the deep, indestructible melancholy of all life. Joy must have sorrow, sorrow must be transfigured into joy. Hence whatever comes from this mere condition or from the ground does not come from God, even though it is necessary for his existence. Neither can it be said that evil comes from the ground, or that the will of the ground is its originator. For evil can arise only in the innermost will of one's own heart, and is never accomplished without one's own deed. The solicitation of the ground or the reaction to the supercreaturely awakens the appetite for the creaturely, that is, one's own will, but it awakens this will only so that an independent ground exist for the good, and so that it be overpowered and penetrated by the good. For aroused selfhood in itself is not evil, but only insofar as it has torn itself entirely free of its opposite, light or the universal will. But this very dissociation from the good alone is sin. Activated selfhood is necessary for the sharpness of life; without it there would be complete death, the good would slumber; for where there is no battle, there is no life. Thus the awakening of life alone is the will of the ground, not immediate evil in itself. If man's will encloses activated selfhood in love and subordinates it to light as to the general will, then actual goodness first arises thereby, having become sensitive through the sharpness within him. Thus in the good the reaction of the ground works for the good; in evil it works for evil, as Scripture says: in the pious you are pious; in the perverse, perverse. The good which is without effective selfhood is itself ineffective good. The same thing that becomes evil by the creature's will (when it tears itself free in order to be for itself), is in itself the good as long as it remains swallowed up in the good and in the ground. Only selfhood overcome, and thus retrieved from activity to potentiality, is the good; and as potential, having been overpowered by the good, it also remains in the good forever. If there were not a root of coldness in the body, warmth could not be felt. It is impossible to think of an attractive or a repellent force by itself: for upon what is the repelling force to act, if the attracting force does not make an object for it; or upon what is the attracting force to act if it does not have a repelling force within itself at the same time? Hence it is entirely correct to say dialectically that good and evil are the same thing, but viewed from different aspects; or evil in itself, i.e., viewed in the root of its identity, is the good, as, on the other hand, the good, viewed in its disunion or non-identity, is evil. For this reason the saying is also entirely correct that whoever has neither the material nor the forces for evil within himself is also incapable of the good – of which we have seen sufficient examples in our times. The passions against which our negative morality makes war are forces, each of which has a common root with its corresponding virtue. The soul of all hatred is love, and one sees in the most violent rage only the stillness that has been affected and provoked in its innermost center. In proper measure and in organic equilibrium these forces are the strength of virtue itself and its immediate instruments . . .

The arousal of the self-will occurs only so that the love within man finds a material or opposite in which it can actualize itself. To the extent that selfhood in its dissociation is the principle of evil, the ground indeed arouses the principle of evil as a possibility, but not evil itself, nor for the sake of evil. But even this arousal does not occur according to God's free will, as he does not move in the ground according to this, or to his heart, but only according to his attributes.

Thus whoever asserted that God himself willed evil would have to seek the ground of this assertion in the act of self-revelation as creation, even as it has often been supposed that he who willed the world also had to will evil. However, in that God brought the disorderly births of chaos into order and spoke his eternal unity into nature, he much rather acted against darkness, and opposed the ruleless movement of the unintelligent principle with the word as a constant center and eternal lamp. The will to creation was thus immediately but a will to give birth to light, and thereby to the good. But evil came into consideration for this will neither as a means, nor even, as Leibniz says, as a *conditio sine qua non* of the greatest possible perfection of the world. It was neither the object of divine decree, nor even less of permission. But the question why God did not prefer to forgo self-revelation altogether, since he necessarily foresaw that evil would result, at least attendantly, indeed does not deserve a reply. For this would amount to saying in order that there be no opposition to love, love itself should not be, i.e., the absolutely positive should be sacrificed for what has existence only as an opposite, and the eternal should be sacrificed for the merely temporal. We have already explained that self-revelation in God must be viewed not as an unconditional, voluntary act, but as a morally necessary act in which love and goodness have overcome absolute inwardness. Thus if God had not revealed himself for the sake of evil, evil would have triumphed over the good and love. The Leibnizian concept of evil as a *conditio sine qua non* can be applied only to the ground, so that it arouses the creaturely will (the principle of evil as possibility) as the condition under which the will of love alone can be actualized. Furthermore, we have already shown why God does not resist the will of the ground or annul it. This would amount to God annulling the condition of his existence, i.e., annulling his own personality. Thus in order for there to be no evil, there would have to be no God.

After all this the question still remains: does evil come to an end, and how? Does creation have a final intent at all, and if so, why is it not achieved immediately; why is the perfect not there from the beginning? There is no answer to this except the one already given: because God is a life, not merely a being. But all life has a fate and is subject to suffering and becoming. To this, too, God has subjugated himself freely, ever since he separated the world of light from the world of darkness in order to become personal. Being becomes sensitive to itself only in becoming. In being there is no becoming, to be sure; rather being itself is posited as eternity in becoming; but in actualization through opposition there is necessarily a becoming. Without the concept of a humanly suffering God, which is common to all the mysteries and spiritual religions of ancient times, all of history remains incomprehensible; even Scripture distinguishes periods of revelation, and posits a time in the distant future when God will be all in all, i.e., when he will be entirely actualized. The first period of creation is, as has been shown earlier, the birth of light. Light or the ideal principle is, as an eternal opposite of the dark principle, the creating word which redeems the life hidden in the ground from non-being, raising it from potential to act. Spirit rises above the word, and spirit is the first being which unites the worlds of darkness and light, subjugating both principles to itself for the sake of actualization and personality. The ground, however, reacts against this unity and asserts the initial duality, but only towards ever heightening intensification and the final division of good and evil. The will of the ground must remain in its freedom until all has been fulfilled, all has become actual. If it were subjugated before this, then good and evil together would remain hidden within it. However, the good shall be raised from darkness to actuality to dwell immortally with God;

but evil shall be separated from the good to be cast out eternally into non-being. For this is the final intent of creation: that whatever could not be for itself, should be for itself by being raised from darkness, as from a ground independent of God, into existence. Hence the necessity of birth and death. God yields the ideas, which within him were without autonomous life, to selfhood and non-being, so that by being called forth from this into life, they may be in him again as independent existences. Thus in its freedom the ground effects separation and judgment (*chrisis*), and precisely therein it effects the complete actualization of God. For evil, when it *is* entirely separated from the good, no longer *is* as evil. It had been able to act only through the (abused) good that was in it, itself being unconscious of it. In life it still enjoyed the forces of external nature with which it attempted to create, and it still participated mediately in God's goodness. But in death it is divided from all that is good, and while it remains a desire, as eternal hunger and thirst for actuality, it can never step out of potentiality. Thus its state is one of non-being, a state in which its activity, or what strives within it to be active, is constantly being consumed. Thus the restitution of evil to the good (the restoration of all things) is in nowise required for the realization of the idea of a final, comprehensive perfection, for evil is evil only insofar as it goes beyond potentiality, but when reduced to non-being, or to the state of potential, it is what it always should be: a basis, subjugated, and as such no longer in contradiction to God's holiness or love. Thus the end of revelation is the expulsion of evil from the good, the explanation of evil as complete unreality. On the other hand, the good that was raised from the ground is combined with original good in eternal unity; those born out of darkness into light join the ideal principle as limbs of its body in which is the perfectly actualized and now completely personal being.

. . . [W]hat purpose is served by that first distinction between the being insofar as it is the ground, and insofar as it exists? For either there is no common midpoint for these two – then we must declare ourselves for absolute dualism; or there is such a midpoint – and then in the final analysis the two coincide again. In this case we have one being for all opposites, an absolute identity of light and darkness, good and evil, and all the incongruous consequences which must befall every rational system, and which were detected in this system, too, some time ago.

We have already explained what we assume in the first respect: there must be a being *before* all ground and before all existence, thus before any duality at all; how can we call this anything but the original ground, or rather the *unground*? Since it precedes all opposites, these cannot be dif-

ferentiated within it or be in any way present within it. Thus it cannot
be designated as the identity of opposites, but only as their absolute *indifference*. Most people, when they come to the point where they must recognize a disappearance of all opposites, forget that these now have actually
disappeared, and they repredicate the opposites, as such, of the indifference
that had arisen precisely through their complete cessation. Indifference is
not a product of opposites, nor are they contained in it *implicite*; rather it
is a being of its own, separated from all opposition, on which all opposites are broken, which is nothing other than their very non-being, and
which therefore has no predicate except predicatelessness, without therefore being a nothing or an absurdity. Thus either they actually posit indifference in the unground preceding all ground, in which case they have
neither good nor evil . . . , and can predicate neither the one nor the other
nor both at once of the unground; or they posit good and evil, in which
case they at once posit duality as well, and thus no longer posit the
unground or indifference. Let the following commentary be made on what
was just said: real and ideal, darkness and light, or however else we wish
to designate the two principles, can never be predicated of the unground
as opposites. But nothing hinders their being predicated of it as non-
opposites, i.e., in disjunction and each *for itself*; whereby, however, this
very duality (the actual twofoldness of the principles) is posited. In the
unground itself there is nothing that would hinder this. For precisely
because the unground is related to both as total indifference, it is impartial to them. If it were the absolute identity of both, then it could only
be both *simultaneously*, i.e., both would have to be predicated of it as *opposites*, and would themselves thereby be one again. Thus from this
neither-nor, or from this indifference, duality (which is something entirely
different from opposition . . .) immediately breaks forth, and *without* indifference, i.e., *without* an unground, there would be no twofoldness of the
principles. Instead of annulling the differentiation as was supposed, the
unground much rather posits and confirms it. Far from the differentiation
between the ground and the existent being merely a logical one, or one
called in only as a stopgap and then found to be a sham again in the end,
it rather showed itself to be a very real differentiation which was first
rightly proven and fully comprehended from the highest standpoint.

   Following this dialectical discussion we thus can most definitely explain
ourselves in the following manner: the essence of the ground, as that of
the existent, can be only that which precedes a ground, thus the absolute
viewed purely and simply, the unground. However it can be this (as has
been proven) in no other way than by separating into two equally eternal
beginnings, not that it is both *simultaneously*, but that it is in both *in like*

manner, thus being the whole or its own essence in both. But the unground separates itself into the two equally eternal beginnings only in order that the two that could not be simultaneous or one in the unground as such, become one through love, i.e., it separates itself only in order that life and love may be, and personal existence.

40

John Keats, to George and Georgiana Keats, February 14 to May 8, 1819

In the year when the English Romantic poet John Keats (1795–1821) wrote his greatest poems, he also coined a phrase which has made its way into discussions of theodicy through its use by John Hick: the world as a "vale of soul-making." Keats thought the idea ancient (if not particularly Christian), but the conception of individual *personality* underlying his account of soul reveals it to be very much an idea of the early nineteenth century. (The many spelling mistakes and other oddities in the text which follows are reproduced from the original.)

The Letters of John Keats: A New Selection, ed. Robert Gittings (Oxford: Oxford University Press, 1970), 248–51.

I have been reading lately two very different books Robertson's America [William Robertson (1721–93), *The History of America*] and Voltaire's Siecle De Louis xiv It is like walking arm and arm between Pizarro and the great-little Monarch. In How lementabl[e] a case do we see the great body of the people in both instances: in the first, where Men might seem to inherit quiet of Mind from unsophisticated senses; from uncontamination of civilization; and especially from their being as it were estranged from the mutual helps of Society and its mutual injuries — and thereby more immediately under the Protection of Providence — even there they had mortal pains to bear as bad; or even worse than Baliffs, Debts and Poverties of civilised Life — The whole appears to resolve into this — that Man is originally "a poor forked creature" subject to the same mischances as the beasts of the forest, destined to hardships and disquietude of some kind or other. If he improves by degrees his bodily accommodations and comforts — at each stage, at each accent there are waiting for him a fresh set of annoyances — he is mortal and there is still a heaven with its stars abov[e] his head. The most interesting question that can come before us is, How far by the persevering endeavours of a seldom appearing Socrates Mankind may be made happy – I can imagine such happiness carried to an extreme – but what must it end in? – Death – and who could in such a case bear with death – the whole troubles of life which are now frittered away in a series of years, would the[n] be accumulated for the last days of a being who instead of hailing its approach, would leave this world as Eve left Paradise – But in truth I do not at all believe in this sort of perfectibility – the nature of the world will not admit of it – the inhabitants of the world will correspond to itself – Let the fish philosophise the ice away from the Rivers in winter time and they shall be at continual play in the tepid delight of summer. Look at the Poles and at the sands of Africa, Whirlpools and volcanoes – Let men exterminate them and I will say that they may arrive at earthly Happiness – The point at which man may arrive is as far as the paralel state in inanimate nature – For instance suppose a rose to have sensation, it blooms on a beautiful morning it enjoys itself – but there comes a cold wind, a hot sun – it cannot escape it, it cannot destroy its annoyances – they are as native to the world as itself: no more can man be happy in spite, the world[l]y elements will prey upon his nature – The common cognomen of this world among the misguided and superstitious is "a vale of tears" from which we are to be redeemed by a certain arbitary interposition of God and taken to Heaven – What a little circumscribe[d] straightened notion! Call the world if you Please "The vale of Soul-making" Then you will find out the use of the world (I am speaking now in the highest terms for human nature admitting it to be immortal which I will here take for granted for the purpose of showing a thought which has struck me concerning it) I say 'Soul making' Soul as distinguished from an Intelligence – there may be intelligences or sparks of the divinity in millions – but they are not Souls . . . till they acquire identities, till each one is personally itself. I[n]telligences are atoms of perception – they know and they see and they are pure, in short they are God – how then are Souls to be made? How then are these sparks which are God to have identity given them – so as ever to possess a bliss peculiar to each ones individual existence? How, but by the medium of a world like this? This point I sincerely wish to consider because I think it a grander system of salvation than the chyrstain religion – or rather it is a system of Spirit-creation – This is effected by three grand materials acting the one upon the other for a series of years – These three Materials are the *Intelligence* – the *human heart* (as distinguished from intelligence or Mind) and the *World* or *Elemental space* suited for the proper action of *Mind and Heart* on each other for the purpose of forming the

Soul or *Intelligence destined to possess the sense of Identity.* I can scarcely express what I but dimly perceive – and yet I think I perceive it – that you may judge the more clearly I will put it in the most homely form possible – I will call the *world* a School instituted for the purpose of teaching little children to read – I will call the *Child able to read, the Soul* made from that *school* and its *hornbook.* Do you not see how necessary a World of Pains and troubles is to school an Intelligence and make it a soul? A place where the heart must feel and suffer in a thousand diverse ways! Not merely is the Heart a Hornbook, It is the Minds Bible, it is the Minds experience, it is the teat from which the Mind or intelligence sucks its identity – As various as the Lives of Men are – so various become their souls, and thus does God make individual beings, Souls, Identical Souls of the sparks of his own essence – This appears to me a faint sketch of a system of Salvation which does not affront our reason and humanity – I am convinced that many difficulties that christians labour under would vanish before it – There is one wh[i]ch even now Strikes me – the Salvation of Children – In them the Spark or intelligence returns to God without any identity – it having had no time to learn of, and be altered by, the heart – or seat of the human Passions – It is pretty generally suspected that the chr[i]stian scheme has been coppied from the ancient persian and greek Philosophers. Why may they not have made this simple thing even more simple for common apprehension by introducing Mediators and Personages in the same manner as in the hethen mythology abstractions are personified – Seriously I think it probable that this System of Soul-making – may have been the Parent of all the more palpable and personal Schemes of Redemption, among the Zoroastrians the Christians and the Hindoos. For as one part of the human species must have their carved Jupiter; so another part must have the palpable and named Mediator and saviour, their Christ their Oromanes their Vishnu – If what I have said should not be plain enough, as I fear it may not be, I will put you in the place where I began in this series of thoughts – I mean, I began by seeing how man was formed by circumstances – and what are circumstances? – but touchstones of his heart? – and what are touch stones? – but proovings of his hearrt? – and what are proovings of his heart but fortifiers or alterers of his nature? and what is his altered nature but his soul? – and what was his soul before it came into the world and had These provings and alterations and perfectionings? – An intelligence – without Identity – and how is this Identity to be made? Through the medium of the Heart? And how is the heart to become this Medium but in a world of Circumstances? . . .

41

Georg Wilhelm Friedrich Hegel, "The Philosophical History of the World"

The German idealist Georg Wilhelm Friedrich Hegel (1770–1831) revolu-
tionized philosophy by inventing a new logic, a logic of the concrete. His
account of "identity in difference" ("the identity of identity and non-
identity"), perhaps the most radical innovation since Aristotle, is often mis-
represented. "Thesis" and "antithesis" do not lead to "synthesis," for example,
but to "mediation." They are *aufgehoben* – transcended but also preserved in
a fuller understanding, a newer, more self-conscious state of affairs which
contains both. For any pair of opposed concepts (universal and particular,
infinite and finite, freedom and nature, self and other, real and rational), you
can't have one without the other. History is the process whereby this
becomes clear, its means the "principle of negation." Opinions diverge as to
whether Hegel's philosophy takes evil seriously or not. Critics argue that by
making evil a necessary "moment," Hegel's view justifies and trivializes evil
just as (they believe) those of Augustine and Leibniz did. Defenders insist
that only Hegel's system really recognizes evil *as* evils, that is, as things to be
overcome. (The italicized sections below are Hegel's own notes for lectures he
gave in 1830; the rest comes from student notes.)

G. W. F. Hegel, *Lectures on the Philosophy of World History. Introduction: Reason in
History*, trans. H. B. Nisbet (Cambridge: Cambridge University Press, 1975),
27–43.

*. . . As already remarked, the main objection levelled at philosophy is that it imports
its own thoughts into history and considers the latter in the light of the former.
But the only thought which philosophy brings with it is the simple idea of **reason**
– the idea that reason governs the world, and that world history is therefore a
rational process. From the point of view of history as such, this conviction and*

insight is a **presupposition**. *Within philosophy itself, however, it is not a presupposition; for it is* **proved** *in philosophy by speculative cognition that reason — and we can adopt this expression for the moment without a detailed discussion of its relationship to God — is* **substance** *and* **infinite power**; *it is itself the* **infinite material** *of a natural and spiritual life, and the* **infinite form** *which activates the material content. It is* **substance**, *i.e. that through which and in which a reality has its being and subsistence; it is infinite* **power**, *for reason is sufficiently powerful to be able to create something more than just an idea, an obligation which supposedly exists in some unknown region beyond reality (or, as is more likely, only as a particular idea in the heads of a few individuals); and it is the infinite* **content**, *the essence and truth of everything itself constituting the material on which it operates through its own activity. Unlike finite actions, it does not require an external material as a condition of its operation, or outside resources from which to derive its sustenance and the objects of its activity; it is self-supporting, and is itself the material of its own operations. On the one hand, it is its own sole precondition, and its end is the absolute and ultimate end of everything; and on the other, it is itself the agent which implements and realises this end, translating it from potentiality into actuality both in the natural universe and in the spiritual world — that is, in world history. That this Idea is true, eternal, and omnipotent, that it reveals itself in the world, and that nothing is revealed except the Idea in all its honour and majesty — this, as I have said, is what philosophy has proved, and we can therefore* **posit** *it as demonstrated for our present purposes.*

. . . But we must be sure to take history as it is; in other words, we must proceed historically and empirically . . .

We can therefore lay it down as our first condition that history must be **apprehended accurately**. *But general expressions such as* **apprehend** *and* **accurately** *are not without ambiguity. Even the ordinary, run-of-the-mill historian who believes and professes that his attitude is entirely receptive, that he is dedicated to the facts, is by no means passive in his thinking, he brings his categories with him, and they influence his vision of the data he has before him. The truth is not to be found on the superficial plane of the senses; for, especially in subjects which claim a scientific status, reason must always remain alert, and conscious deliberation is indispensable. Whoever looks at the world rationally will find that it in turn assumes a rational aspect; the two exist in a reciprocal relationship.*

It is perfectly correct to say that the design of the world should be distinguishable by observation. But to recognise the universal and the rational, it is necessary to use reason too . . . But the overall content of world history is rational, and indeed has to be rational; a divine will rules supreme and is strong enough to determine the overall content. Our aim must be to discern this substance, and to do so, we must bring with us a rational consciousness. Physical perception and a finite understanding are not enough; we must see with the eye of the concept, the eye of reason, which penetrates the surface and finds its way through the complex and confusing turmoil of events . . .

The perspective adopted by the philosophical history of the world is accordingly not just one among many general perspectives, an isolated abstraction singled out at the expense of the rest. Its spiritual principle is the sum total of all possible perspectives. It concentrates its attention on the concrete spiritual principle in the life of nations, and deals not with individual situations but with a universal thought which runs throughout the whole. This universal element is not to be found in the world of contingent phenomena; it is the unity behind the multitude of particulars . . .

[By contrast, the] general faith in providence is . . . indeterminate, and lacks a determinate application to the whole, to the entire course of world events . . . The determinate aspects of providence, the specific actions it performs, constitute the providential plan (i.e. the end and means of its destiny and aims). But this plan is supposed to be hidden from our view, and we are told that it is presumptuous to try to comprehend it . . . But those who believe in providence are hostile to all attempts to apply the idea on a large scale, i.e. to any attempts to comprehend the providential plan. No-one objects to it being applied in isolated cases, and pious souls discern in numerous particular occurrences, where others see only the agency of chance, not just dispensations of God himself, but of divine providence – i.e. the ends which providence pursues by means of such dispensations. But this usually happens only in isolated instances; and when, for example, an individual in great perplexity and distress receives unexpected help, we must not hold it against him if his gratitude at once leads him to see the hand of God at work. But the design of providence in such cases is of a limited nature; its content is merely the particular end of the individual in question. In world history, however, the individuals we are concerned with are nations, totalities, states. We cannot, therefore, be content with this (if the word be permitted) trivial faith in providence, nor indeed with a merely abstract and indeterminate faith which conceives in general terms of a ruling providence but refuses to apply it to determinate reality; on the contrary, we must tackle the problem seriously. The concrete events are the ways of providence, the means it uses, the phenomena in which it manifests itself in history; they are open to our inspection, and we only have to relate them to the general principle referred to above . . .

As I have said, we are often told that it is presumptuous to try to fathom the plan of providence. This is a direct consequence of the idea (which has now become an almost universally accepted axiom) that it is impossible to obtain knowledge of God. And when theology itself is in so desperate a position, we must take refuge in philosophy if we wish to learn anything about God. Certainly, reason is often accused of arrogance in presuming to attain such knowledge. But it would be more accurate to say that true humility consists precisely in recognising and revering God in everything, especially in the theatre of world history . . . To believe that God's wisdom is not active in everything is to show humility towards the material rather than towards the divine wisdom itself . . .

It is often said that God does reveal himself, but only in nature on the one hand, and in the heart, in the feelings of men, on the other. We are usually told nowadays that this is the point at which we must draw a halt, for God is present only to our immediate consciousness or intuition. Intuition and emotion, however, are both unreflecting forms of consciousness and we must insist in reply to such arguments that man is a thinking being, for it is thought which distinguishes him from the animals. He behaves as a thinking being even when he is himself unaware of it. When God reveals himself to man, he reveals himself essentially through man's rational faculties; if he revealed himself essentially through the emotions, this would imply that he regarded man as no better than the animals, who do not possess the power of reflection – yet we do not attribute religion to the animals. In fact, man only possesses religion because he is not an animal but a thinking being. . . .

But what, we may ask, is the plan of providence in world history? Has the time come for us to understand it? . . .

God has revealed himself through the Christian religion; that is, he has granted mankind the possibility of recognising his nature, so that he is no longer an impenetrable mystery. The fact that knowledge of God is possible also makes it our duty to know him, and that development of the thinking spirit which the Christian revelation of God initiated must eventually produce a situation where all that was at first present only to the emotional and representational faculties can also be comprehended by thought . . .

It is one of the central doctrines of Christianity that providence has ruled and continues to rule the world, and that everything which happens in the world is determined by and commensurate with the divine government. This doctrine is opposed both to the idea of chance and to that of limited ends (such as the preservation of the Jewish people). Its end is the ultimate and absolutely universal end which exists in and for itself. Religion does not go beyond this general representation; it remains on the level of generality. But we must proceed from this general faith firstly to philosophy and then to the philosophy of world history – from the faith that world history is a product of eternal reason, and that it is reason which has determined all its great revolutions.

God does not wish to have narrow-minded and empty-headed children. On the contrary, he demands that we should know him; he wishes his children to be poor in spirit but rich in knowledge of him, and to set the highest value on acquiring knowledge of God. History is the unfolding of God's nature in a particular, determinate element, so that only a determinate form of knowledge is possible and appropriate to it.

The time has now surely come for us to comprehend even so rich a product of creative reason as world history. The aim of human cognition is to understand that the intentions of eternal wisdom are accomplished not only in the natural world, but also in the realm of the [spirit] which is actively present in the world. From this point of view, our investigation can be seen as a theodicy, a justification of the ways of God (such as Leibniz attempted in his own metaphysical manner, but using categories which were as yet abstract and indeterminate). It should enable us to comprehend all the ills of the world, including the existence of evil, so that the thinking spirit may be reconciled with the negative aspects of existence; and it is in world history that we encounter the sum total of concrete evil. (Indeed, there is no department of knowledge in which such a reconciliation is more urgently required than in world history, and we shall accordingly pause for a moment to consider this question further.)

A reconciliation of the kind just described can only be achieved through knowledge of the affirmative side of history, in which the negative is reduced to a subordinate position and transcended altogether. In other words, we must first of all know what the ultimate design of the world really is, and secondly we must see that this design has been realised and that evil has not been able to maintain a position of equality beside it.

42

Ralph Waldo Emerson, "The Tragic"

The eclectic thought of the American transcendentalist Ralph Waldo Emerson (1803–82) celebrates nature, innovation, and what he called "the infinitude of the private man." Combining a Stoic faith in the possibility of human self-reliance with a pantheist faith in the wisdom and solicitude of nature, Emerson's philosophy aspires for a vantage-point from which fate is seen not to crush individuals but to live in them. Suffering is an important element in Emerson's world, but at times it seems that nobody is seriously *hurt* by it. (Like Epictetus, Emerson seems to think much of suffering is in the mind.) George Santayana criticized Emerson for a mysticism that "allows his will and his conscience to be hypnotized by the spectacle of a necessary evolution, and lulled into cruelty by the pomp and music of a tragic show . . . evil is not explained, it is forgotten." The essay below was read in Boston as part of a course on "Human Life" in 1839–40.

Ralph Waldo Emerson, *Natural History of Intellect and Other Papers* [*Emerson's Works* XII] (Cambridge, Mass.: Riverside Press, 1893), 260–72.

He has seen but half the universe who has never been shewn the house of Pain. As the salt sea covers more than two-thirds of the surface of the globe, so sorrow encroaches in man on felicity. The conversation of men is a mixture of regrets and apprehensions. I do not know but the prevalent hue of things to the eye of leisure is melancholy. In the dark hours, our existence seems to be a defensive war, a struggle against the encroaching All, which threatens surely to engulf us soon, and is impatient of our short reprieve. How slender the possession that yet remains to us; how faint the animation! How the spirit seems already to contract its domain, retiring within narrower walls by the loss of memory, leaving its planted fields to erasure and annihilation. Already our own thoughts and words have an alien sound. There is a simultaneous diminution of memory and hope. Projects that once we laughed and leapt to execute, find us now sleepy and preparing to lie down in the snow. And in the serene hours we have no courage to spare. We cannot afford to let go any advantages. The riches of body or of mind which we do not need to-day, are the reserved fund against the calamity that may come to-morrow. It is usually agreed that some nations have a more sombre temperament, and one would say that history gave no record of any society in which despondency came so readily to heart as we see it and feel it in ours. Melancholy cleaves to the English mind in both hemispheres as closely as to the strings of an Aeolian harp . . . But whether we and those who are next to us are more or less vulnerable, no theory of life can have any right which leaves out of account the values of vice, pain, disease, poverty, disunion, fear and death.

What are the conspicuous tragic elements in human nature? The bitterest tragic element in life to be derived from an intellectual source is the belief in a brute Fate or Destiny; the belief that the order of nature and events is controlled by a law not adapted to man, nor man to that, but holds on its way to the end, serving him if his wishes chance to lie in the same course, crushing him if his wishes lie contrary to it, and heedless whether it serves or crushes him. This is the terrible meaning that lies at the foundation of the old Greek tragedy, and makes the Oedipus and Antigone and Orestes objects of such hopeless commiseration. They must perish and there is no overgod to stop or to mollify this hideous enginery that grinds or thunders, and snatches them up into its terrific system. The same idea makes the paralyzing terror with which the East Indian mythology haunts the imagination. The same thought is the predestination of the Turk. And universally, in uneducated and unreflecting persons on whom too the religious sentiment exerts little force, we discover traits of the same superstition: "If you baulk water you will be drowned the next time:" "if you count ten stars you will fall down dead:" "if you spill the salt;" "if your fork sticks upright in the floor;" "if you say the Lord's prayer backwards;" – and so on, a several penalty, nowise grounded in the nature of the thing, but on an arbitrary will. But this terror of contravening an unascertained and unascertainable will, cannot co-exist with reflection: it disappears with civilization, and can no more be reproduced than the fear of ghosts after childhood. It is discriminated from the doctrine of Philosophical Necessity herein: that the last is an Optimism, and therefore the suffering individual finds his good consulted in the good of all, of which he is a part. But in destiny, it is not the good of the whole or the *best will* that is enacted, but only *one particular will*. Destiny proper is not a will at all, but an immense whim; and this the only ground of terror and despair in the rational mind, and of tragedy in literature. Hence the antique tragedy, which was founded on this fate, can never be reproduced.

After reason and faith have introduced a better public and private tradition, the tragic element is somewhat circumscribed. There must always remain, however, the hindrance of our private satisfaction by the laws of the world. The law which establishes nature and the human race, continually thwarts the will of ignorant individuals, and this in the particulars of disease, want, insecurity and disunion.

But the essence of tragedy does not seem to me to lie in any list of particular evils. After we have enumerated famine, fever, inaptitude, mutilation, rack, madness and loss of friends, we have not yet included the proper tragic element, which is Terror, and which does not respect definite evils but indefinite; an ominous spirit which haunts the afternoon and the night, idleness and solitude.

A low, haggard sprite sits by our side, "casting the fashion of uncertain evils" – a sinister presentiment, a power of the imagination to dislocate things orderly and cheerful and show them in startling array. Hark! what sounds on the night wind, the cry of Murder in that friendly house; see these marks of stamping feet, of hidden riot. The whisper overheard, the detected glance, the glare of malignity, ungrounded fears, suspicions, half-knowledge and mistakes, darken the brow and chill the heart of men. And accordingly it is natures not clear, not of quick and steady perceptions, but imperfect characters from which somewhat is hidden that all others see, who suffer most from these causes. In those persons who move from the profoundest pity, tragedy seems to consist in temperament, not in events. There are people who have an appetite for grief, pleasure is not strong enough and they crave pain, mithridatic stomachs which must be fed on poisoned bread, natures so doomed that no prosperity can soothe their ragged and dishevelled desolation. They mis-hear and mis-behold, they suspect and dread. They handle every nettle and ivy in the hedge, and tread on every snake in the meadow

> "Come bad chance,
> And we add to it our strength,
> And we teach it art and length,
> Itself o'er us to advance."

Frankly, then, it is necessary to say that all sorrow dwells in a low region. It is superficial; for the most part fantastic, or in the appearance and not in things. Tragedy is in the eye of the observer, and not in the heart of the sufferer. It looks like an insupportable load under which earth moans aloud. But analyze it; it is not I, it is not you, it is always another person who is tormented. If a man says, Lo! I suffer – it is apparent that he suffers not, for grief is dumb. It is so distributed as not to destroy. That which would rend you falls on tougher textures. That which seems intolerable reproach or bereavement, does not take from the accused or bereaved man or woman appetite or sleep. Some men are above grief, and some below it. Few are capable of love. In phlegmatic natures, calamity is unaffecting, in shallow natures it is rhetorical. Tragedy must be somewhat which I can respect. A querulous habit is not a tragedy. A panic such as frequently in ancient or savage nations put a troop or an army to flight without an enemy; a fear of ghosts; a terror of freezing to death that seizes a man in a winter midnight in the moors; a fright at uncertain sounds heard by a family at night in the cellar or on the stairs, – are terrors that make the knees knock and the teeth clatter, but are no tragedy, any more than sea-sickness, which may also destroy life . . .

A man should not commit his tranquillity to things, but should keep as much as possible the reins in his own hands, rarely giving way to extreme emotions of joy or grief. It is observed that the earliest works of the art of sculpture are countenances of sublime tranquillity. The Egyptian sphinxes, which sit to-day as they sat when the Greeks came and saw them and departed, and when the Roman came and saw them and departed, and as they will still sit when the Turk, the Frenchman and the Englishman, who visit them now, shall have passed by, – "with their stony eyes fixed on the East and on the Nile," have countenances expressive of complacency and repose, an expression of health, deserving their longevity, and verifying the primeval sentence of history on the permanency of that people, "Their strength is to sit still." To this architectural stability of the human form, the Greek genius added an ideal beauty, without disturbing the seals of serenity; permitting no violence of mirth, or wrath, or suffering. This was true to human nature. For, in life, actions are few, opinions even few, prayers few; loves, hatreds, or any emissions of the soul. All that life demands of us through the greater part of the day, is an equilibrium, a readiness, open eyes and ears, and free hands. Society asks this, and truth, and love, and the genius of our life . . . If a man is centred, men and events appear to him a fair image or reflection of that which he knoweth before-hand in himself. If any perversity or profligacy break out in society, he will join the others to avert the mischief, but it will not arouse resentment or fear, because he discerns its impassable limits. He sees already in the ebullition of sin the simultaneous redress.

Particular reliefs also, fit themselves to human calamities; for the world will be in equilibrium, and hates all manner of exaggerations.

Time, the consoler, Time, the rich carrier of all change, dries the freshest tears by obtruding new figures, new costumes, new roads, on our eye, new voices on our ear. As the west wind lifts up again the heads of the wheat which were bent down and lodged in the storm, and combs out the matted and dishevelled grass as it lay in night-locks on the ground, so we let in time as a drying wind into the seed-field of thoughts which are dark and wet and low bent. Time restores to them temper and elasticity. How fast we forget the blow that threatened to cripple us. Nature will not sit still; the faculties will do somewhat; new hopes spring, new affections twine and the broken is whole again.

Time consoles, but Temperament resists the impression of pain. Nature proportions her defence to the assault. Our human being is wonderfully plastic; if it cannot win this satisfaction here, it makes itself amends by running out there and winning that. It is like a stream of water, which if dammed up on one bank, overruns the other, and flows equally at its own convenience over sand, or mud, or marble. Most suffering is only apparent. We fancy it is torture; the patient has his own compensations. A tender American girl doubts of Divine Providence whilst she reads the horrors of "the middle passage;" and they are bad enough at the mildest; but to such as she these crucifixions do not come: they come to the obtuse and barbarous, to whom they are not horrid, but only a little worse than the old sufferings. They exchange a cannibal war for the stench of the hold. They have gratifications which would be none to the civilized girl. The market-man never damned the lady because she had not paid her bill, but the stout Irishwoman has to take that twice a month. She however never feels weakness in her back because of the slave-trade. This self-adapting strength is especially seen in disease. "It is my duty," says Sir Charles Bell, "to visit certain wards of the hospital where there is no patient admitted but with that complaint which most fills the imagination with the idea of insupportable pain and certain death. Yet these wards are not the least remarkable for the composure and cheerfulness of their inmates. The individual who suffers has a mysterious counterbalance to that condition, which, to us who look upon her, appears to be attended with no alleviating circumstance." Analogous supplies are made to those individuals whose character leads them to vast exertions of body and mind. Napoleon said to one of his friends at St. Helena, "Nature seems to have calculated that I should have great reverses to endure, for she has given me a temperament like a block of marble. Thunder cannot move it; the shaft merely glides along. The great events of my life have slipped over me without making any demand on my moral or physical nature."

The intellect is a consoler, which delights in detaching or putting an interval between a man and his fortune, and so converts the sufferer into a spectator and his pain into poetry. It yields the joys of conversation, of letters and of science. Hence also the torments of life become tuneful tragedy, solemn and soft with music, and garnished with rich dark pictures. But higher still than the activities of art, the intellect in its purity and the moral sense in its purity are not distinguished from each other, and both ravish us into a region whereinto these passionate clouds of sorrow cannot rise.

43

Arthur Schopenhauer, *The World as Will and Representation*

If *optimism* is the philosophical argument that this is the best possible world, *pessimism* argues that it is the worst. Arthur Schopenhauer (1788–1860) coined the term "pessimism" (from *pessimum*, the worst). An empiricist and one of the first openly atheistic German philosophers, Schopenhauer inverted traditional arguments about the privative nature of evil: since happiness is really but the *cessation* of suffering, he argued, not pleasure but pain alone is real. Reacting with Schelling to Hegel's insistence that the world was rational, Schopenhauer argued that the world is driven by an irrational will which generates meaningless pain and hostility by the illusion of differentiation into individuals; "in the fierceness and intensity of its desires it buries its teeth in its own flesh." His philosophy alone admits "the evils of the world . . . in all their magnitude . . . because the answer to the question of their origin coincides with the answer to the question of the origin of the world." Schopenhauer's philosophy was widely read at the end of the nineteenth century, influencing thinkers from Nietzsche and Royce to Freud and Wittgenstein. The affinity Schopenhauer claimed with Buddhism is the source of the abiding misunderstanding of Buddhism as a "pessimistic" religion.

Arthur Schopenhauer, *The World as Will and Representation* II.46, 48, 49; trans. E. F. J. Payne, 2 vols. (New York: Dover, 1958), 576, 581–84, 605, 634, 643.

On the Vanity and Suffering of Life

. . . Before we state so confidently that life is desirable or merits our gratitude, let us for once calmly compare the sum of the pleasures which are in any way possible, and which a man can enjoy in his life, with the sum of the sufferings which are in any way possible, and can come to him in his life. I do not think it will be difficult to strike the balance. In the long run, however, it is quite superfluous to dispute whether there is more good or evil in the world; for the mere existence of evil decides the matter, since evil can never be wiped off, and consequently can never be balanced, by the good that exists along with or after it.

Mille piacer' non vagliono un tormento.
[a thousand pleasures do not compensate for one pain – Petrarch]

For that thousands had lived in happiness and joy would never do away with the anguish and death-agony of one individual; and just as little does my present well-being undo my previous sufferings. Therefore, were the evil in the world even a hundred times less than it is, its mere existence would still be sufficient to establish a truth that may be expressed in various ways, although always only somewhat indirectly, namely that we have not to be pleased but rather sorry about the existence of the world; that its non-existence would be preferable to its existence; that it is something which at bottom ought not to be, and so on. . . .

This world is the battle-ground of tormented and agonized beings who continue to exist only by each devouring the other. Therefore, every beast of prey in it is the living grave of thousands of others, and its self-maintenance is a chain of torturing deaths. Then in this world the capacity to feel pain increases with knowledge, and therefore reaches its highest degree in man, a degree that is the higher, the more intelligent the man. To this world the attempt has been made to adapt the system of optimism, and to demonstrate to us that it is the best of all possible worlds. The absurdity is glaring. However, an optimist tells me to open my eyes and look at the world and see how beautiful it is in the sunshine, with its mountains, valleys, rivers, plants, animals, and so on. But is the world, then, a peep-show? These things are certainly beautiful to behold, but to be them is something quite different. A teleologist then comes along and speaks to me in glowing terms about the wise arrangement by virtue of which care is taken that the planets do not run their heads against one another; that land and sea are not mixed up into pulp, but are held apart in a delightful way; also that everything is neither rigid in continual frost nor roasted with heat; likewise that, in consequence of the obliquity of the ecliptic, there is not an eternal spring in which nothing could reach maturity, and so forth. But this and everything like it are indeed mere *conditiones sine quibus non*. If there is to be a world at all, if its planets are to exist at least as long as is needed for the ray of light from a remote fixed

star to reach them, and are not, like Lessing's son, to depart again immediately after birth, then of course it could not be constructed so unskil-
fully that its very framework would threaten to collapse. But if we proceed
to the *results* of the applauded work, if we consider the *players* who act
on the stage so durably constructed, and then see how with sensibility
pain makes its appearance, and increases in proportion as that sensibility
develops into intelligence, and then how, keeping pace with this, desire
and suffering come out ever more strongly, and increase, till at last human
life affords no other material than that for tragedies and comedies, then
whoever is not a hypocrite will hardly be disposed to break out into hal-
lelujahs. The real but disguised origin of these latter has moreover been
exposed, mercilessly but with triumphant truth, by David Hume in his
Natural History of Religion . . . He also explains without reserve in the tenth
and eleventh books of his *Dialogues on Natural Religion*, with arguments
very convincing yet quite different from mine, the miserable nature of this
world and the untenableness of all optimism; here at the same time he
attacks optimism at its source . . .

But against the palpably sophistical proofs of Leibniz that this is the best
of all possible worlds, we may even oppose seriously and honestly the proof
that it is the worst of all possible worlds. For possible means not what we
may picture in our imagination, but what can actually exist and last. Now
this world is arranged as it had to be if it were to be capable of continuing with great difficulty to exist; if it were a little worse, it would be no
longer capable of continuing to exist. Consequently, since a worse world
could not continue to exist, it is absolutely impossible; and so this world
itself is the worst of all possible worlds. For not only if the planets ran
their heads against one another, but also if any one of the actually occurring perturbations of their course continued to increase, instead of being
gradually balanced again by the others, the world would soon come to an
end. Astronomers know on what accidental circumstances – in most cases
on the irrational relation to one another of the periods of revolution –
all this depends. They have carefully calculated that it will always go on
well, and consequently that the world can also last and go on. Although
Newton was of the opposite opinion, we will hope that the astronomers
have not miscalculated, and consequently that the mechanical perpetual
motion realized in such a planetary system will also not, like the rest, ultimately come to a standstill. Again, powerful forces of nature dwell under
the firm crust of the planet. As soon as some accident affords these free
play, they must necessarily destroy that crust with everything living on it.

This has occurred at least three times on our planet, and will probably occur even more frequently. The earthquake of Lisbon, of Haiti, the destruction of Pompeii are only small, playful hints at the possibility. An insignificant alteration of the atmosphere, not even chemically demonstrable, causes cholera, yellow fever, black death, and so on, which carry off millions of people; a somewhat greater alteration would extinguish all life. A very moderate increase of heat would dry up all rivers and springs. The animals have received barely enough in the way of organs and strength to enable them with the greatest exertion to procure sustenance for their own lives and food for their offspring. Therefore, if an animal loses a limb, or even only the complete use of it, it is in most cases bound to perish. Powerful as are the weapons of understanding and reason possessed by the human race, nine-tenths of mankind live in constant conflict with want, always balancing themselves with difficulty and effort on the brink of destruction. Thus throughout, for the continuance of the whole as well as for that of every individual being, the conditions are sparingly and scantily given, and nothing beyond these. Therefore the individual life is a ceaseless struggle for existence itself, while at every step it is threatened with destruction. Just because this threat is so often carried out, provision had to be made, by the incredibly great surplus of seed, that the destruction of individuals should not bring about that of the races, since about these alone is nature seriously concerned. Consequently, the world is as bad as it can possibly be, if it is to exist at all. Q.E.D.

On the Doctrine of the Denial of the Will to Live

Man has his existence and being either with his will, in other words, with his consent, or without it; in the latter case such an existence, embittered by inevitable sufferings of many kinds, would be a flagrant injustice. The ancients, particularly the Stoics, and also the Peripatetics and Academics, laboured in vain to prove that virtue is enough to make life happy; experience loudly cried out against this. Although they were not clearly aware of it, what was really at the root of the attempt of those philosophers was the assumed *justice* of the case; he who was *without guilt* ought to be free from suffering, and hence happy. But the serious and profound solution of the problem is to be found in the Christian doctrine that works do not justify. Accordingly, although a man has practised all justice and philanthropy, consequently the *agathon, honestum,* he is still not *culpa omni carens* [free from all guilt] as Cicero imagines (*Tusc.,* V.1); but *el delito mayor del hombre es haber nacido* (Man's greatest offence is that he was born) as the poet Calderon, inspired by Christianity, has expressed it from a knowledge far profounder than was possessed by those wise men. Accordingly, that man comes into the world already involved in guilt can appear absurd only to the person who regards him as just having come from nothing, and as the work of another. Hence in consequence of this guilt, which must therefore have come from his will, man rightly remains abandoned to physical and mental sufferings, even when he has practised all those virtues, and so he is *not* happy . . . However, as St. Paul (Rom. iii.21 *seqq.*), Augustine, and Luther teach, works cannot justify, since we all are and remain essentially sinners. This is due in the last resort to the fact that, since *operari sequitur esse* [What we do follows from what we are], if we acted as we ought to act, we should also necessarily be what we ought to be. But then we should not need any *salvation* from our present condition, and such salvation is represented as the highest goal not only by Christianity, but also by Brahmanism and Buddhism (under the name expressed in English by *final emancipation*); in other words, we should not need to become something quite different from, indeed the very opposite of, what we are. However, since we are what we ought *not* to be, we also necessarily do what we ought *not* to do. We therefore need a complete transformation of our nature and disposition, i.e., the new spiritual birth, regeneration, as the result of which salvation appears. Although the guilt lies in conduct, in the *operari*, yet the root of the guilt lies in our *essentia et existentia*, for the *operari* necessarily proceeds from these . . . Accordingly, original sin is really our only true sin. Now it is true that the Christian myth makes original sin arise only after man already existed, and for this purpose ascribes to him, *per impossibile*, a free will; it does this, however, simply as a myth. The innermost kernel and spirit of Christianity is identical with that of Brahmanism and Buddhism; they all teach a heavy guilt of the human race through its existence itself, only Christianity does not proceed in this respect directly and openly, like those more ancient religions. It represents the guilt not as being established simply by existence itself, but as arising through the act of the first human couple. This was possible only under the fiction of a *liberum arbitrium indifferentiae* [free decision of the will not influenced in any direction], and was necessary only on account of the Jewish fundamental dogma, into which that doctrine was here to be implanted. According to the truth, the very origin of man himself is the act of his free will, and is accordingly identical with the Fall, and therefore the original sin, of which all others are the result, appeared already with man's *essentia* and *existentia*; but the fundamental dogma of Judaism did not admit of such an explanation. Therefore Augustine taught in his books *De Libero Arbitrio* that only as Adam before the Fall was man guiltless and had a free will, whereas for ever after he is involved in the necessity of sin. The law . . . in the biblical sense, always demands that we should change our conduct, while our essential nature would remain unchanged. But since this is impossible, Paul says that no one is justified before the law; we can be transferred from the state of sinfulness into that of freedom and salvation only by the new birth or regeneration in Jesus Christ, in consequence of the effect of grace, by virtue of which a new man arises, and the old man is abolished (in other words, a fundamental change of disposition). This is the Christian myth with regard to ethics. But of course Jewish theism, on to which the myth was grafted, must have received marvellous additions in order to attach itself to that myth. Here the fable of the Fall presented the only place for the graft of the old Indian stem. It is to be ascribed just to this forcibly surmounted difficulty that the Christian mysteries have obtained an appearance so strange and opposed to common sense. Such an appearance makes proselytizing more difficult; on this account and from an inability to grasp their profound meaning, Pelagianism, or present-day rationalism, rises up against them, and tries to explain them away by exegesis, but in this way it reduces Christianity to Judaism.

However, to speak without myth; as long as our will is the same, our world cannot be other than it is. It is true that all men wish to be delivered from the state of suffering and death; they would like, as we say, to attain to eternal bliss, to enter the kingdom of heaven, but not on their own feet; they would like to be carried there by the course of nature. But this is impossible; for nature is only the copy, the shadow, of our will. Therefore, of course, she will never let us fall and become nothing; but she cannot bring us anywhere except always into nature again. Yet everyone experiences in his own life and death how precarious it is to exist as a part of nature. Accordingly, existence is certainly to be regarded as an error or mistake, to return from which is salvation; it bears this character throughout. Therefore it is conceived in this sense by the ancient Samana religions, and also by real and original Christianity, although in a roundabout way. Even Judaism itself contains the germ of such a view, at any rate in the Fall of man; this is its redeeming feature. Only Greek paganism and Islam are wholly optimistic; therefore in the former the opposite tendency had to find expression at least in tragedy. In Islam, however, the most modern as well as the worst of all religions, this opposite tendency appeared as *Sufism*, that very fine phenomenon which is entirely Indian in spirit and origin, and has now continued to exist for over a thousand years. In fact, nothing else can be stated as the aim of our existence except the knowledge that it would be better for us not to exist . . .

The Road to Salvation

There is only one inborn error, and that is the notion that we exist in order to be happy. It is inborn in us, because it coincides with our existence itself, and our whole being is only its paraphrase, indeed our body its monogram. We are nothing more than the will-to-live, and the successive satisfaction of all our willing is what we think of through the concept of happiness.

So long as we persist in this inborn error, and indeed even become confirmed in it through optimistic dogmas, the world seems to us full of contradictions. For at every step, in great things as in small, we are bound to experience that the world and life are certainly not arranged for the purpose of containing a happy existence . . .

. . . [S]uffering is the process of purification by which alone man is in most cases sanctified, in other words, led back from the path of error of the will-to-live. Accordingly, the salutary nature of the cross and of suffering is so often discussed in Christian devotional books, and in general the cross, an instrument of suffering not of doing, is very appropriately the symbol of the Christian religion. In fact, even the Preacher, Jewish indeed but very philosophical, rightly says: "Sorrow is better than laughter" (Eccles. vii.3) . . .

The current and peculiarly Protestant view that the purpose of life lies solely and immediately in moral virtues, and hence in the practice of justice and philanthropy, betrays its inadequacy by the fact that so deplorably little real and pure morality is to be found among men. I do not wish to speak of lofty virtue, noble-mindedness, generosity, and self-sacrifice, which are hardly ever met with except in plays and novels, but only of those virtues which are everyone's duties . . . If, on the other hand, we put this purpose in the complete reversal of this nature of ours . . . , a reversal brought about by suffering, the matter assumes a different aspect, and is brought into agreement with what actually lies before us. Life then presents itself as a process of purification, the purifying lye of which is pain . . .

44

Charles Darwin, to Asa Gray, May 22, 1860

The 1859 *Origin of Species by Means of Natural Selection* by English naturalist Charles Darwin (1809–82) painted a picture of waste and endless violence in nature, but this was not what bothered his contemporaries about it. They were used to sublime conceptions of God and his awe-inspiring ways. Half a century had passed since Malthus had argued that competition to the death among his creations was "worthy of a benevolent Creator." (See p. 240 above.) In 1850, Tennyson could suggest (admittedly in an elegy) that "Man"

> . . . trusted God was love indeed
> And love Creation's final law –
> Tho' Nature, red in tooth and claw
> With ravine, shrieked against his creed –

and still become the friend of the Queen. Overlooking the centrality of chance to the processes Darwin had described, thinkers like the American botanist Asa Gray (1810–88) argued that the process of natural selection must be directed by God – a view John Dewey memorably called "design on the installment plan." Prudent scientist, Darwin did not comment on the theological implications of his theory.

The Life and Letters of Charles Darwin, ed. Francis Darwin, 2 vols. (New York: D. Appleton, 1919), II.105–6.

With respect to the theological view of the question. This is always painful to me. I am bewildered. I had no intention to write atheistically. But I own that I cannot see as plainly as others do, and as I should wish to do, evidence of design and beneficence on all sides of us. There seems to me too much misery in the world. I cannot persuade myself that a beneficent and omnipotent God would have designedly created the Ichneumonidae with the express intention of their feeding within the living bodies of Caterpillars, or that a cat should play with mice. Not believing this, I see no necessity in the belief that the eye was expressly designed. On the other hand, I cannot anyhow be contented to view this wonderful universe, and especially the nature of man, and to conclude that everything is the result of brute force. I am inclined to look at everything as resulting from designed laws, with the details, whether good or bad, left to the working out of what we may call chance. Not that this notion *at all* satisfies me. I feel most deeply that the whole subject is too profound for the human intellect. A dog might as well speculate on the mind of Newton. Let each man hope and believe what he can. Certainly I agree with you that my views are not at all necessarily atheistical. The lightning kills a man, whether a good one or bad one, owing to the excessively complex action of natural laws. A child (who may turn out an idiot) is born by the action of even more complex laws, and I can see no reason why a man, or other animal, may not have been aboriginally produced by other laws, and that all these laws may have been expressly designed by an omniscient Creator, who foresaw every future event and consequence. But the more I think the more bewildered I become; as indeed I probably have shown by this letter.

45

John Stuart Mill, *An Examination of Sir William Hamilton's Philosophy*

As scientific knowledge of the morally indifferent workings of nature grew, certainty about God and his attributes receded. One way of defending theism in this case was to argue that the divine attributes, being infinite, are unthinkable to mortal men. In 1865, the empiricist political economist, logician, and political radical John Stuart Mill (1806–73) provided a memorable critique of this view, in his long discussion of the Kantianized Scottish common-sense philosophy of Sir William Hamilton and his Oxford disciple Henry Longueville Mansel. Mill himself favored a Comtian "Religion of Humanity" over "supernatural" religions. "One only form of belief in the supernatural . . . stands wholly clear both of intellectual contradiction and of moral obliquity," Mill wrote in a essay of the 1850s published posthumously, "that which, resigning irrevocably the idea of an omnipotent creator, regards Nature and Life not as the expression throughout of the moral character and purpose of the Deity, but as the product of a struggle between contriving goodness and an intractable material, as was believed by Plato, or a Principle of Evil, as was the doctrine of the Manichaeans . . . A virtuous human being assumes in this theory the exalted character of a fellow-labourer with the Highest."

John Stuart Mill, *An Examination of Sir William Hamilton's Philosophy, and of The Principal Philosophical Questions Discussed in his Writings*, ed. J. M. Robson (Toronto: University of Toronto Press, 1979), 100–4.

The fundamental property of our knowledge of God, Mr. Mansel says, is that we do not and cannot know him as he is in himself: certain persons, therefore, whom he calls Rationalists, he condemns as unphilosophical, when they reject any statement as inconsistent with the character of God.

This is a valid answer, as far as words go, to some of the later Transcendentalists – to those who think that we have an intuition of the Divine Nature; though even as to them it would not be difficult to show that the answer is but skin-deep. But those "Rationalists" who hold, with Mr. Mansel himself, the relativity of human knowledge, are not touched by his reasoning. We cannot know God as he is in himself (they reply); granted: and what then? Can we know man as he is in himself, or matter as it is in itself? We do not claim any other knowledge of God than such as we have of man or of matter. Because I do not know my fellow-men, nor any of the powers of nature, as they are in themselves, am I therefore not at liberty to disbelieve anything I fear respecting them as being inconsistent with their character? I know something of Man and Nature, not as they are in themselves, but as they are relative to us; and it is as relative to us, and not as he is in himself, that I suppose myself to know anything of God. The attributes which I ascribe to him, as goodness, knowledge, power, are all relative. They are attributes (says the rationalist) which my experience enables me to conceive, and which I consider as proved, not absolutely, by an intuition of God, but phaenomenally, by his action on the creation, as known through my senses and my rational faculty. These relative attributes, each of them in an infinite degree, are all I pretend to predicate of God. When I reject a doctrine as inconsistent with God's nature, it is not as being inconsistent with what God is in himself, but with what he is as manifested to us. If my knowledge of him is only phaenomenal, the assertions which I reject are phaenomenal too. If those assertions are inconsistent with my relative knowledge of him, it is no answer to say that all my knowledge of him is relative. That is not more a reason against disbelieving an alleged fact as unworthy of God, than against disbelieving another alleged fact as unworthy of Turgot, or of Washington, whom I also do not know as Noumena, but only as Phaenomena.

There is but one way for Mr. Mansel out of this difficulty, and he adopts it. He must maintain, not merely that an Absolute Being is unknowable in himself, but that the Relative attributes of an Absolute Being are unknowable likewise. He must say that we do not know what Wisdom, Justice, Benevolence, Mercy, are, as they exist in God. Accordingly he does say so. The following are his direct utterances on the subject: as an implied doctrine, it pervades his whole argument.

It is a fact which experience forces upon us, and which it is useless, were it possible, to disguise, that the representation of God after the model of the highest human morality which we are capable of conceiving, is not sufficient to account for all the phenomena exhibited by the course of his natural providence. The infliction of physical suffering, the permission of moral evil, the adversity of the good, the prosperity of the wicked, the crimes of the guilty involving the misery of the innocent, the tardy appearance and partial distribution of moral and religious knowledge in the world – these are facts which no doubt are reconcilable, we know not how, with the Infinite Goodness of God, but which certainly are not to be explained on the supposition that its sole and sufficient type is to be found in the finite goodness of man.

In other words, it is necessary to suppose that the infinite goodness ascribed to God is not the goodness which we know and love in our fellow-creatures, distinguished only as infinite in degree, but is different in kind, and another quality altogether. When we call the one finite goodness and the other infinite goodness, we do not mean what the words assert, but something else: we intentionally apply the same name to things which we regard as different.

Accordingly Mr. Mansel combats, as a heresy of his opponents, the opinion that infinite goodness differs only in degree from finite goodness. The notion "that the attributes of God differ from those of man in degree only, not in kind, and hence that certain mental and moral qualities of which we are immediately conscious in ourselves, furnish at the same time a true and adequate image of the infinite perfections of God," (the word *adequate* must have slipped in by inadvertence, since otherwise it would be an inexcusable misrepresentation) he identifies with "the vulgar Rationalism which regards the reason of man, in its ordinary and normal operation, as the supreme criterion of religious truth." And in characterizing the mode of arguing of this vulgar Rationalism, he declares its principles to be, that "all the excellences of which we are conscious in the creature, must necessarily exist in the same manner, though in a higher degree, in the Creator. God is indeed more wise, more just, more merciful, than man; but for that very reason, his wisdom and justice and mercy must contain nothing that is incompatible with the corresponding attributes in their human character." It is against this doctrine that Mr. Mansel feels called on to make an emphatic protest.

Here, then, I take my stand on the acknowledged principle of logic and of morality, that when we mean different things we have no right to call them by the same name, and to apply to them the same predicates, moral and intellectual. Language has no meaning for the words Just, Merciful, Benevolent, save that in which we predicate them of our fellow-creatures; and unless that is what we intend to express by them, we have no business to employ the words. If in affirming them of God we do not mean to affirm these very qualities, differing only as greater in degree, we are neither philosophically nor morally entitled to affirm them at all. If it be said that the qualities are the same, but that we cannot conceive them as they are when raised to the infinite, I grant that we cannot adequately conceive them in one of their elements, their infinity. But we can conceive them in their other elements, which are the very same in the infinite as in the finite development. Anything carried to the infinite must have all the properties of the same thing as finite, except those which depend upon the finiteness. Among the many who have said that we cannot conceive infinite space, did any one ever suppose that it is *not* space? that it does not possess all the properties by which space is characterized? Infinite Space cannot be cubical or spherical, because these are modes of being bounded: but does any one imagine that in ranging through it we might arrive at some region which was not extended; of which one part was not outside another; where, though no Body intervened, motion was impossible; or where the sum of two sides of a triangle was less than the third side? The parallel assertion may be made respecting infinite goodness. What belongs to it either as Infinite or as Absolute I do not pretend to know; but I know that infinite goodness must be goodness, and that what is not consistent with goodness, is not consistent with infinite goodness. If in ascribing goodness to God I do not mean what I mean by goodness; if I do not mean the goodness of which I have some knowledge, but an incomprehensible attribute of an incomprehensible substance, which for aught I know may be a totally different quality from that which I love and venerate – and even must, if Mr. Mansel is to be believed, be in some important particulars opposed to this – what do I mean by calling it goodness? and what reason have I for venerating it? If I know nothing about what the attribute is, I cannot tell that it is a proper object of veneration. To say that God's goodness may be different in kind from man's goodness, what is it but saying with a slight change of phraseology, that God may possibly not be good? To assert in words what we do not think in meaning, is as suitable a definition as can be given of a moral falsehood, . . . Besides, suppose that certain unknown attributes are ascribed to the Deity in a religion the external evidence of which are so conclusive to my mind, as effectually to convince me that it comes from God. Unless I believe God to possess the same moral attributes which I find, in however inferior a degree, in a good man, what ground of assurance have I of God's veracity? All trust in a Revelation presupposes a conviction that God's attributes are the same, in all but degree, with the best human attributes.

If, instead of the "glad tidings" that there exists a Being in whom all the excellences which the highest human mind can conceive, exist in a degree inconceivable to us, I am informed that the world is ruled by a being whose attributes are infinite, but what they are we cannot learn, nor what are the principles of his government, except that "the highest human morality which we are capable of conceiving" does not sanction them; convince me of it, and I will bear my fate as I may. But when I am told that I must believe this, and at the same time call this being by the names which express and affirm the highest human morality, I say in plain terms that I will not. Whatever power such a being may have over me, there is one thing which he shall not do: he shall not compel me to worship him. I will call no being good, who is not what I mean when I apply that epithet to my fellow-creatures; and if such a being can sentence me to hell for not so calling him, to hell will I go.

Neither is this to set up my own limited intellect as a criterion of divine or of any other wisdom. If a person is wiser and better than myself, not in some unknown and unknowable meaning of the terms, but in their known human acceptation, I am ready to believe that what this person thinks may be true, and that what he does may be right, when, but for the opinion I have of him, I should think otherwise. But this is because I believe that he and I have at bottom the same standard of truth and rule of right, and that he probably understands better than I the facts of the particular case. If I thought it not improbable that his notion of right might be my notion of wrong, I should not defer to his judgment. In like manner, one who sincerely believes in an absolutely good ruler of the world, is not warranted in disbelieving any act ascribed to him, merely because the very small part of its circumstances which we can possible know does not sufficiently justify it. But if what I am told respecting him is of a kind which no facts that can be supposed added to my knowledge could make me perceive to be right; if the alleged ways of dealing with the world are such as no imaginable hypothesis respecting things known to him and unknown to me, could make consistent with the goodness and wisdom which I mean when I use the terms, but are in direct con-tradiction to their signification; then, if the law of contradiction is a law of human thought, I cannot both believe these things, and believe that God is a good and wise being. If I call any being wise or good, not meaning the only qualities which the words import, I am speaking insin-cerely; I am flattering him by epithets which I fancy that he likes to hear, in the hope of winning him over to my own objects. For it is worthy of remark that the doubt whether words applied to God have their human signification, is only felt when the words relate to this moral attributes; it is never heard of in regard to his power. We are never told that God's omnipotence must not be supposed to mean an infinite degree of the power we know in man and nature, and that perhaps it does not mean the he is able to kill us, or consign us to eternal flames. The Divine Power is always interpreted in a completely human signification, but the Divine Goodness and Justice must be understood to be such only in an unintelligible sense. Is it unfair to surmise that this is because those who speak in the name of God, have need of the human conception of power, since an idea which can overawe and enforce obedience must address itself to real feelings; but are content that his goodness should be conceived only as something inconceivable, because they are so often required to teach doctrines respecting him which conflict irreconcilably with all goodness that we can conceive?

46

Fyodor Dostoyevsky,
The Brothers Karamazov

Some of the most powerful arguments ever made about the challenge innocent suffering poses to belief in God are made by the atheist Ivan Karamazov in Fyodor Mikhaylovich Dostoyevsky's last novel. But the pious
Dostoyevsky (1821–81) no more intended Ivan and his "Grand Inquisitor"
to eclipse the rest of the world of *The Brothers Karamazov* than Milton
intended his Satan to be the star of *Paradise Lost*. Ivan's arguments seem
irrefutable – especially because Ivan's saintly brother Alexei (or Alyosha)
never tries to refute them. Alyosha's is a Christianity not of reasoned argument but of humility and action, a religion articulated famously by his
teacher Zosima in the sublimely unreasonable claim, "everyone is responsible for everyone and everything." The author of Ivan's defiant challenge and
Alyosha's silent response was an important inspiration for atheists like Freud
and Camus, no less than for religious thinkers like Berdyayev, Barth, Soelle,
and Levinas. (The selection below begins in the middle of an impassioned
speech of Ivan's.)

Fyodor Dostoyevsky, *The Brothers Karamazov*, V.iv ("Rebellion"); trans. Constance Garnett (New York: The Modern Library, n.d.), 246–7, 250–5.

". . . I meant to speak of the suffering of mankind generally, but we had
better confine ourselves to the sufferings of the children. That reduces the
scope of my argument to a tenth of what it would be. Still we'd better
keep to the children, though it does weaken my case. But, in the first
place, children can be loved even at close quarters, even when they are
dirty, even when they are ugly (I fancy, though, children never are ugly).
The second reason why I won't speak of grown-up people is that, besides

being disgusting and unworthy of love, they have a compensation – they've eaten the apple and know good and evil, and they have become 'like god.' They go on eating it still. But the children haven't eaten anything, and are so far innocent. Are you fond of children, Alyosha? I know you are, and you will understand why I prefer to speak of them. If they, too, suffer horribly on earth, they must suffer for their fathers' sins, they must be punished for their fathers, who have eaten the apple; but that reasoning is of the other world and is incomprehensible for the heart of man here on earth. The innocent must not suffer for another's sins, and especially such innocents! You may be surprised at me, Alyosha, but I am awfully fond of children, too. And observe, cruel people, the violent, the rapacious, the Karamazovs are sometimes very fond of children . . .

"I've collected a great, great deal about Russian children, Alyosha. There was a little girl of five who was hated by her father and mother, 'most worthy and respectable people, of good education and breeding.' You see, I must repeat again, it is a peculiar characteristic of many people, this love of torturing children, and children only. To all other types of humanity these torturers behave mildly and benevolently, like cultivated and humane Europeans; but they are very fond of tormenting children, even fond of children themselves in that sense. It's just their defencelessness that tempts the tormentor, just the angelic confidence of the child who has no refuge and no appeal, that sets his vile blood on fire. In every man, of course, a demon lies hidden – the demon of rage, the demon of lustful heat at the screams of the tortured victim, the demon of lawlessness let off the chain, the demon of diseases that follow on vice, gout, kidney disease, and so on.

"This poor child of five was subjected to every possible torture by those cultivated parents. They beat her, thrashed her, kicked her for no reason till her body was one bruise. Then, they went to greater refinements of cruelty – shut her up all night in the cold and frost in a privy, and because she didn't ask to be taken up at night (as though a child of five sleeping its angelic, sound sleep could be trained to wake and ask), they smeared her face and filled her mouth with excrement, and it was her mother, her mother did this. And that mother could sleep, hearing the poor child's groans! Can you understand why a little creature, who can't even understand what's done to her, should beat her little aching heart with her tiny fist in the dark and the cold, and weep her meek unresentful tears to dear, kind God to protect her? Do you understand that, friend and brother, you pious and humble novice? Do you understand why this infamy must be and is permitted? Without it, I am told, man could not have existed on earth, for he could not have known good and evil. Why should he know that diabolical good and evil when it costs so much? Why, the whole world of knowledge is not worth that child's prayer to 'dear, kind God'! I say nothing of the sufferings of grown-up people, they have eaten the apple, damn them, and the devil take them all! But these little ones! I am making you suffer, Alyosha, you are not yourself. I'll leave off if you like."

"Never mind. I want to suffer too," muttered Alyosha.

"One picture, only one more, because it's so curious, so characteristic, and I have only just read it in some collection of Russian antiquities. I've forgotten the name. I must look it up. It was in the darkest days of serfdom at the beginning of the century, and long live the Liberator of the People! There was in those days a general of aristocratic connections, the owner of great estates, one of those men – somewhat exceptional, I believe, even then – who, retiring from the service into a life of leisure, are convinced that they've earned absolute power over the lives of their subjects. There were such men then. So our general, settled on his property of two thousand souls, lives in pomp, and domineers over his poor neighbours as though they were dependents and buffoons. He has kennels of hundreds of hounds and nearly a hundred dog-boys – all mounted, and in uniform. One day a serf boy, a little child of eight, threw a stone in play and hurt the paw of the general's favourite hound. 'Why is my favourite dog lame?' He is told that the boy threw a stone that hurt the dog's paw. 'So you did it.' The general looked the child up and down. 'Take him.' He was taken – taken from his mother and kept shut up all night. Early that morning the general comes out on horseback, with the hounds, his dependents, dog-boys, and huntsmen, all mounted around him in full hunting parade. The servants are summoned for their edification, and in front of them all stands the mother of the child. The child is brought from the lock-up. It's a gloomy cold, foggy autumn day, a capital day for hunting. The general orders the child to be undressed; the child is stripped naked. He shivers, numb with terror, not daring to cry. . . . 'Make him run,' commands the general. 'Run! Run!' shout the dog-boys. The boy runs. . . . 'At him!' yells the general, and he sets the whole pack of hounds on the child. The hounds catch him, and tear him to pieces before his mother's eyes! . . . I believe the general was afterwards declared incapable of administering his estates. Well – what did he deserve? To be shot? To be shot for the satisfaction of our moral feelings? Speak, Alyosha!"

"To be shot," murmured Alyosha, lifting his eyes to Ivan with a pale, twisted smile.

"Bravo!" cried Ivan delighted. "If even you say so . . . You're a pretty monk! So there is a little devil sitting in your heart, Alyosha Karamazov! . . ."

"Listen! I took the case of children only to make my case clearer. Of the other tears of humanity with which the earth is soaked from its crust

to its centre, I will say nothing. I have narrowed my subject on purpose.
I am a bug, and I recognise in all humility that I cannot understand why
the world is arranged as it is. Men are themselves to blame, I suppose; they
were given paradise, they wanted freedom, and stole fire from heaven,
though they knew they would become unhappy, so there is no need to
pity them. With my pitiful, earthly, Euclidian understanding, all I know is
that there is suffering and that there are none guilty; that cause follows
effect, simply and directly; that everything flows and finds its level – but
that's only Euclidian nonsense, I know that and I can't consent to live by
it! What comfort is to me that there are none guilty and that cause follows
effect simply and directly, and that I know it – I must have justice, or I
will destroy myself. And not justice in some remote infinite time and space,
but here on earth, and that I could see myself. I have believed in it. I want
to see it, and if I am dead by then, let me rise again, for if it all happens
without me, it will be too unfair. Surely I haven't suffered, simply that I,
my crimes and my sufferings, may manure the soil of the future harmony
for somebody else. I want to see with my own eyes the hind lie down
with the lion and the victim rise up and embrace his murderer. I want to
be there when every one suddenly understands what it has all been for.
All the religions of the world are built on this longing, and I am a believer.
But then there are the children, and what am I to do about them? That's
a question I can't answer. For the hundredth time I repeat, there are
numbers of questions, but I've only taken the children, because in their
case what I mean is so unanswerably clear. Listen! If all must suffer to pay
for the eternal harmony, what have children to do with it, tell me, please?
It's beyond all comprehension, why they should suffer, and why they
should pay for the harmony. Why should they, too, furnish material to
enrich the soil for the harmony of the future? I understand solidarity in
sin among men. I understand solidarity in retribution, too; but there can
be no such solidarity with children. And if it is really true that they must
share responsibility for all their fathers' crimes, such a truth is not of this
world and is beyond my comprehension. Some jester will say, perhaps, that
the child would have grown up and have sinned, but you see he didn't
grow up, he was torn to pieces by the dogs, at eight years old. Oh, Alyosha,
I am not blaspheming! I understand, of course, what an upheaval of the
universe it will be, when everything in heaven and earth blends in one
hymn of praise and everything that lives and has lived cries aloud: 'Thou
art just, O Lord, for Thy ways are revealed.' When the mother embraces
the fiend who threw her child to the dogs, and all three cry aloud with
tears, 'Thou are just, O Lord!' then, of course, the crown of knowledge

will be reached and all will be made clear. But what pulls me up here is that I can't accept that harmony. And while I am on earth, I make haste to take my own measures. You see, Alyosha, perhaps it really may happen that if I live to that moment, or rise again to see it, I, too, perhaps, may cry aloud with the rest, looking at the mother embracing the child's torturer, 'Thou art just, O Lord!' but I don't want to cry aloud then. While there is still time, I hasten to protect myself and so I renounce the higher harmony altogether. It's not worth the tears of that one tortured child who beat itself on the breast with its little fist and prayed in its stinking outhouse, with its unexpiated tears to 'dear, kind God'! It's not worth it, because those tears are unatoned for. They must be atoned for, or there can be no harmony. But how? How are you going to atone for them? Is it possible? By their being avenged? But what do I care for avenging them? What do I care for a hell for oppressors? What good can hell do, since those children have already been tortured? And what becomes of harmony, if there is hell? I want to forgive. I want to embrace. I don't want more suffering. And if the sufferings of children go to swell the sum of sufferings which was necessary to pay for truth, then I protest that the truth is not worth such a price. I don't want the mother to embrace the oppressor who threw her son to the dogs! She dare not forgive him! Let her forgive him for herself, if she will, let her forgive the torturer for the immeasurable suffering of her mother's heart. But the sufferings of her tortured child she has no right to forgive; she dare not forgive the torturer, even if the child were to forgive him! And if that is so, if they dare not forgive, what becomes of harmony? Is there in the whole world a being who would have the right to forgive and could forgive? I don't want harmony. From love for humanity I don't want it. I would rather be left with the unavenged suffering. I would rather remain with my unavenged suffering and unsatisfied indignation, even if I were wrong. Besides, too high a price is asked for harmony; it's beyond our means to pay so much to enter on it. And so I hasten to give back my entrance ticket, and if I am an honest man I am bound to give it back as soon as possible. And that I am doing. It's not God that I don't accept, Alyosha, only I most respectfully return Him the ticket."

"That's rebellion," murmured Alyosha, looking down.

"Rebellion? I am sorry you call it that," said Ivan earnestly. "One can hardly live in rebellion, and I want to live. Tell me yourself, I challenge you – answer. Imagine that you are creating a fabric of human destiny with the object of making men happy in the end, giving them peace and rest at last, but that it was essential and inevitable to torture to death only one tiny creature – that baby beating its breast with its fist, for instance – and to found that edifice on its unavenged tears, would you consent to be the architect on those conditions? Tell me, and tell the truth."

"No, I wouldn't consent," said Alyosha softly.

"And can you admit the idea that men for whom you are building it would agree to accept their happiness on the foundation of the unexpiated blood of a little victim? And accepting it would remain happy for ever?"

"No, I can't admit it. Brother," said Alyosha suddenly, with flashing eyes, "you said just now, is there a being in the whole world who would have the right to forgive and could forgive? But there is a Being and He can forgive everything, all and for all, because He gave His innocent blood for all and everything. You have forgotten Him, and on Him is built the edifice, and it is to Him they cry aloud, 'Thou art just, O Lord, for Thy ways are revealed!'"

"Ah! the One without sin and His blood! No, I have not forgotten Him; on the contrary I've been wondering all the time how it was you did not bring Him in before, for usually all arguments on your side put Him in the foreground . . ."

47

Friedrich Nietzsche,
On the Genealogy of Morality

The German philologist and cultural critic Friedrich Nietzsche (1844–1900) is famous for "philosophizing with a hammer," but the hammer he had in mind, he explained, was like a tuning fork. Tapping at the ideals of western culture, he found most of them hollow, expressions of individual and social malaise. None proved hollower than God ("God is dead, and we have killed him": high time to create new gods) and prevalent views of good and evil. Influenced by Schelling and Schopenhauer, the sickly Nietzsche had no illusions about the prevalence of suffering in human life. With Spinoza and Emerson, however, he thought it could be affirmed, criticizing Schopenhauer's ascetic ideal of world-rejection as the clearest instance of the nihilist pessimism which underlies the pieties of modern democratic civilization. Moving beyond judgments of the value of life, the Nietzschean "free spirit" creates values, and in anticipation of the Overman, wills the whole of which he is a part. "Have you ever said Yes to a single joy?" Nietzsche's Zarathustra asks; "O my friends, then you said Yes to all woe. All things are entangled, ensnared, enamored; if you ever wanted one thing twice, if you ever said, 'You please me, happiness! Abide, moment!' then you wanted all back. All anew, all eternally, all entangled, ensnared, enamored – oh, then you loved the world."

Friedrich Nietzsche, *On the Genealogy of Morality: A Polemic*, trans. Maudemarie Clark and Alan J. Swensen (Indianapolis: Hackett, 1998), 2–3, 12, 14–21, 117.

Preface

3. Given a skepticism that is characteristic of me, to which I reluctantly admit – for it is directed towards *morality*, towards everything on earth that has until now been celebrated as morality – a skepticism that first appeared so early in my life, so spontaneously, so irrepressibly, so much in contradiction to my environment, age, models, origins, that I almost have the right to call it my "*a priori*" – it was inevitable that early on my curiosity and my suspicion as well would stop at the question: *what*, in fact, is the *origin* of our good and evil? In fact, the problem of the origin of evil haunted me as a thirteen-year-old lad: at an age when one has "half child's play, half God in one's heart," I devoted my first literary child's play to it, my first philosophic writing exercise – and as to my "solution" to the problem back then, well, I gave the honor to God, as is fitting, and made him the *father* of evil. Was *this* what my "a priori" wished of me? that new, immoral, at least immoralistic "a priori" and the, alas! so anti-Kantian, so mysterious "categorical imperative" speaking through it, to which I have since increasingly lent my ear, and not just my ear? . . . Fortunately I learned early on to distinguish theological from moral prejudice and no longer sought the origin of evil *behind* the world. A little historical and philological schooling, combined with an innate sense of discrimination in all psychological questions, soon transformed my problem into a different one: under what conditions did man invent those value judgments good and evil? *and what value do they themselves have*? Have they inhibited or furthered human flourishing up until now? Are they a sign of distress, of impoverishment, of the degeneration of life? Or, conversely, do they betray the fullness, the power, the will of life, its courage, its confidence, its future? – In response I found and ventured a number of answers; I distinguished ages, peoples, degrees of rank among individuals; I divided up my problem; out of the answers came new questions, investigations, conjectures, probabilities: until I finally had a land of my own, a ground of my own, an entire unspoken growing blossoming world, secret gardens as it were, of which no one was permitted even an inkling . . . O how we are *happy*, we knowers, provided we simply know how to be silent long enough! . . .

First Treatise: "Good and Evil," "Good and Bad"

. . .

4. – The pointer to the *right* path was given to me by the question: what do the terms coined for "good" in the various languages actually mean

from an etymological viewpoint? Here I found that they all lead back to the *same conceptual transformation* – that everywhere the basic concept is "noble," "aristocratic" in the sense related to the estates, out of which "good" in the sense of "noble of soul," "high-natured of soul," "privileged of soul" necessarily develops: a development that always runs parallel to that other one which makes "common," "vulgar," "base" pass over finally into the concept "bad." The most eloquent example of the latter is the German word "*schlecht*" [bad] itself: which is identical with "*schlicht*" [plain, simple] – compare "*schlechtweg*," "*schlechterdings*" [simply or downright] – and originally designated the plain, the common man, as yet without a suspecting sideward glance, simply in opposition to the noble one. Around the time of the Thirty-Years' War, in other words late enough, this sense shifts into the one now commonly used. – With respect to morality's genealogy this appears to me to be an essential insight; that it is only now being discovered is due to the inhibiting influence that democratic prejudice exercises in the modern world with regard to all questions of origins. And this influence extends all the way into that seemingly most objective realm of natural science and physiology, as I shall merely hint at here. But the nonsense that this prejudice – once unleashed to the point of hate – is able to inflict, especially on morality and history, is shown by Buckle's notorious case; the plebeianism of the modern spirit, which is of English descent, sprang forth there once again on its native ground, vehemently like a muddy volcano and with that oversalted, overloud, common eloquence with which until now all volcanoes have spoken. – . . .

6. To this rule that the concept of superiority in politics always resolves itself into a concept of superiority of soul, it is not immediately an exception (although it provides occasion for exceptions) when the highest caste is at the same time the *priestly* caste and hence prefers for its collective name a predicate that recalls its priestly function. Here, for example, "pure" and "impure" stand opposite each other for the first time as marks of distinction among the estates; and here, too, one later finds the development of a "good" and a "bad" in a sense no longer related to the estates. Incidentally, let one beware from the outset of taking these concept "pure" and "impure" too seriously, too broadly, or even too symbolically: rather all of earlier humanity's concepts were initially understood in a coarse, crude, superficial, narrow, straightforward, and above all *unsymbolic* manner, to an extent that we can hardly imagine. The "pure one" is from the beginning simply a human being who washes himself, who forbids himself certain foods that bring about skin diseases, who doesn't sleep with the dirty women of the baser people, who abhors blood – nothing more, at least not much more! On the other hand the entire nature of an essen-

tially priestly aristocracy admittedly makes clear why it was precisely here that the valuation opposites could so soon become internalized and heightened in a dangerous manner; and indeed through them gulfs were finally torn open between man and man across which even an Achilles of free-spiritedness will not be able to leap without shuddering. From the beginning there is something *unhealthy* in such priestly aristocracies and in the habits ruling there, ones turned away from action, partly brooding, partly emotionally explosive, habits that have as a consequence the intestinal disease and neurasthenia that almost unavoidably clings to the priests of all ages; but what they themselves invented as a medicine against this diseasedness of theirs – must we not say that in the end it has proved itself a hundred times more dangerous in its aftereffects than the disease from which it was to redeem them? Humanity itself still suffers from the aftereffects of these priestly cure naïvetés! Think, for example, of certain dietary forms (avoidance of meat), of fasting, of sexual abstinence, of the flight "into the wilderness" . . . : in addition, the whole anti-sensual metaphysics of priests, which makes lazy and overrefined, their self-hypnosis after the manner of the fakir and Brahmin – brahma used as glass pendant and *idée fixe* – and the final, only too understandable general satiety along with its radical cure, *nothingness* (or God – the longing for a *unio mystica* with God is the longing of the Buddhist for nothingness, Nirvana – and nothing more!). With priests *everything* simply becomes more dangerous, not only curatives and healing arts, but also arrogance, revenge, acuity, excess, love, lust to rule, virtue, disease; – though with some fairness one could also add that it was on the soil of this *essentially dangerous* form of human existence, the priestly form, that man first became *an interesting animal*, that only here did the human soul acquire *depth* in a higher sense and become *evil* – and these are, after all, the two basic forms of the previous superiority of man over other creatures! . . .

8. – But you don't understand that? You don't have eyes for something that has taken two thousand years to achieve victory? . . . There is nothing to wonder at in this: all *lengthy* things are difficult to see, to see in their entirety. *This* however is what happened: out of the trunk of that tree of revenge and hate, Jewish hate – the deepest and most sublime hate, namely an ideal-creating, value-reshaping hate whose like has never before existed on earth – grew forth something just as incomparable, a *new love*, the deepest and most sublime of all kinds of love: – and from what other trunk could it have grown? . . . But by no means should one suppose it grew upwards as, say, the true negation of that thirst for revenge, as the opposite of Jewish hate! No, the reverse is the truth! This love grew forth

out of it, as its crown, as the triumphant crown unfolding itself broadly and more broadly in purest light and sunny fullness, reaching out, as it were, in the realm of light and of height, for the goals of that hate – for victory, for booty, for seduction – with the same drive with which the roots of that hate sunk themselves ever more thoroughly and greedily down into everything that had depth and was evil. This Jesus of Nazareth, as the embodied Gospel of Love, this "Redeemer" bringing blessedness and victory to the poor, the sick, the sinners – was he not precisely seduction in its most uncanny and irresistible form, the seduction and detour to precisely those *Jewish* values and reshapings of the ideal? Has not Israel reached the final goal of its sublime desire for revenge precisely via the detour of this "Redeemer," this apparent adversary and dissolver of Israel? Does it not belong to the secret black art of a truly *great* politics of revenge, of a far-seeing, subterranean, slow-working and precalculating revenge, that Israel itself, before all the world, should deny as its mortal enemy and nail to the cross the actual tool of its revenge, so that "all the world," namely all the opponents of Israel, could take precisely this bait without thinking twice? And, out of all sophistication of the spirit, could one think up any more *dangerous* bait? Something that in its enticing, intoxicating, anesthetizing, destructive power might equal that symbol of the "holy cross," that gruesome paradox of a "god on the cross," that mystery of an inconceivable, final, extreme cruelty and self-crucifixion of God *for the salvation of man?* . . . What is certain, at least, is that *sub hoc signo* Israel, with its revenge and revaluation of all values, has thus far again and again triumphed over all other ideals, over all more noble ideals. —

10. The slave revolt in morality begins when *ressentiment* itself becomes creative and gives birth to values: the *ressentiment* of beings denied the true reaction, that of the deed, who recover their losses only through an imaginary revenge. Whereas all noble morality grows out of a triumphant yes-saying to oneself, from the outset slave morality says "no" to an "outside," to a "different," to a "not-self": and *this* "no" is its creative deed. This reversal of the value-establishing glance – this necessary direction toward the outside instead of back onto oneself – belongs to the very nature of *ressentiment*: in order to come into being, slave-morality always needs an opposite and external world; it needs, psychologically speaking external stimuli in order to be able to act at all, – its action is, from the ground up, reaction. The reverse is the case with the noble manner of valuation: it acts and grows spontaneously, it seeks out its opposite only in order to say "yes" to itself still more gratefully and more jubilantly – its negative concept "low" "common" "bad" is only an after-birth, a pale con-

trast-image in relation to its positive basic concept, saturated through and through with life and passion: "we noble ones, we good ones, we beautiful ones, we happy ones!" When the noble manner of valuation lays a hand on reality and sins against it, this occurs relative to the sphere with which it is *not* sufficiently acquainted, indeed against a real knowledge of which it rigidly defends itself: in some cases it forms a wrong idea of the sphere it holds in contempt, that of the common man, of the lower people; on the other hand, consider that the affect of contempt, of looking down on, of the superior glance – assuming that it does *falsify* the image of the one held in contempt – will in any case fall far short of the falsification with which the suppressed hate, the revenge of the powerless, lays hand on its opponent – in effigy, of course. Indeed there is too much carelessness in contempt, too much taking-lightly, too much looking away and impatience mixed in, even too much of a feeling of cheer in oneself, for it to be capable of transforming its object into a real caricature and monster. Do not fail to hear the almost benevolent nuances that, for example, the Greek nobility places in all words by which it distinguishes the lower people from itself; how they are mixed with and sugared by a kind of pity, considerateness, leniency to the point that almost all words that apply to the common man ultimately survive as expressions for "unhappy" "pitiful" (compare *deilos, deilaios, poneros, mochtheros*, the latter two actually designating the common man as work-slave and beast of burden) – and how, on the other hand, to the Greek ear "bad" "low" "unhappy" have never ceased to end on the same note, with a tone color in which "unhappy" predominates: this as inheritance of the old, nobler aristocratic manner of valuation that does not deny itself even in its contempt (let philologists be reminded of the sense in which *oizyros, anolbos, tlemon, dystychein, xymphora* are used). The "well-born" simply *felt* themselves to be the "happy"; they did not first have to construct their happiness artificially by looking at their enemies, to talk themselves into it, to *lie themselves into it* (as all human beings of *ressentiment* tend to do); and as full human beings, overloaded with power and therefore *necessarily* active, they likewise did not know how to separate activity out from happiness, – for them being active is of necessity included in happiness (whence *eu prattein* takes its origins) – all of this very much in opposition to "happiness" on the level of the powerless, oppressed, those festering with poisonous and hostile feelings, in whom it essentially appears as narcotic, anesthetic, calm, peace, "Sabbath," relaxation of mind and stretching of limbs, in short, *passively*. While the noble human being lives with himself in confidence and openness (*gennaios* "noble-born" underscores the nuance "sincere" and probably also "naive") the human being of *ressentiment* is neither sincere, nor naive, nor honest and frank with himself. His soul *looks obliquely* at things; his spirit loves hiding places, secret passages and back-doors, everything hidden strikes him as *his* world, *his* security, *his* balm; he knows all about being silent, not forgetting, waiting, belittling oneself for the moment, humbling oneself. A race of such human beings of *ressentiment* in the end necessarily becomes *more prudent* than any noble race, it will also honor prudence in an entirely different measure: namely as a primary condition of existence. With noble human beings, in contrast, prudence is likely to have a refined aftertaste of luxury and sophistication about it: – here it is not nearly as essential as the complete functional reliability of the regulating *unconscious* instincts of even a certain imprudence, for example the gallant making-straight-for it, be it toward danger, be it toward the enemy, or that impassioned suddenness of anger, love, reverence, gratitude, and revenge by which noble souls in all ages have recognized each other. For the *ressentiment* of the noble human being, when it appears in him, runs its course and exhausts itself in an immediate reaction, therefore it does not *poison* – on the other hand it does not appear at all in countless cases where it is unavoidable in all the weak and powerless. To be unable for any length of time to take his enemies, his accidents, his *misdeeds* themselves seriously – that is the sign of strong, full natures in which there is an excess of formative reconstructive, healing power that also makes one forget (a good example of this from the modern world is Mirabeau, who had no memory for insults and base deeds committed against him and who was only unable to forgive because he – forgot). Such a human is simply able to shake off with a single shrug a collection of worms that in others would dig itself in; here alone is also possible – assuming that it is at all possible on earth – the true "*love* of one's enemies." What great reverence for his enemies a noble human being has! – and such reverence is already a bridge to love . . . After all, he demands his enemy for himself, as his distinction; he can stand no other enemy than one in whom there is nothing to hold in contempt and a very great deal to honor! On the other hand, imagine "the enemy" as the human being of *ressentiment* conceives of him – and precisely here is his deed, his creation: he has conceived of "the evil enemy," "*the evil one*," and this indeed as the basic concept starting from which he now also thinks up, as reaction and counterpart, a "good one" – himself! . . .

Third Treatise: What Do Ascetic Ideals Mean?

. . .

28. If one disregards the ascetic ideal: man, the *animal* man, has until now had no meaning. His existence on earth contained no goal; "to what end

man at all?" – was a question without answer; the *will* for man and earth
was lacking; behind every great human destiny a still greater "for nothing!"
resounded as refrain. Precisely this is what the ascetic ideal means: that
something *was lacking*, that an enormous void surrounded man – he did
not know how to justify, to explain, to affirm himself; he *suffered* from the
problem of his meaning. He suffered otherwise as well, he was for the
most part a diseased animal: but the suffering itself was not his problem,
rather that the answer was missing to the scream of his question: "*to what
end* suffering?" Man, the bravest animal and the one most accustomed to
suffering, does *not* negate suffering in itself: he *wants* it, he even seeks it
out, provided one shows him a meaning for it, a *to-this-end* of suffering.
The meaninglessness of suffering, not the suffering itself, was the curse
that thus far lay stretched out over humanity – *and the ascetic ideal offered
it a meaning!* Thus far it has been the only meaning; any meaning is better
than no meaning at all; in every respect the ascetic ideal has been the
"*faute de mieux*" *par excellence* there has been thus far. In it suffering was
interpreted; the enormous emptiness seemed filled; the door fell shut to all
suicidal nihilism. The interpretation – there is no doubt – brought new
suffering with it, deeper, more inward, more poisonous, gnawing more at
life: it brought all suffering under the perspective of *guilt* . . . But in spite
of all this – man was *rescued* by it, he had a *meaning*, he was henceforth
no longer like a leaf in the wind, a plaything of nonsense, "without-sense,"
now he could *will* something – no matter for the moment in what direction, to what end, with what he willed: *the will itself was saved.* One simply
cannot conceal from oneself *what* all the willing that has received its direction from the ascetic ideal actually expresses: this hatred of the human, still
more of the animal, still more of the material, this abhorrence of the senses,
of reason itself, this fear of happiness and of beauty, this longing away from
all appearance, change, becoming, death, wish, longing itself – all of this
means – let us dare to grasp this – a *will to nothingness*, an aversion to life,
a rebellion against the most fundamental presuppositions of life; but it is
and remains a *will!* . . . And, to say again at the end what I said at the
beginning: man would much rather will *nothingness* than *not* will . . .

48

Gerard Manley Hopkins, "Thou Art Indeed Just, Lord"

The work of the English Jesuit poet Gerard Manley Hopkins (1844–89), a convert to Catholicism, was not published until 1918. Hopkins' experiments with prosody were revolutionary; the sentiment expressed in the poem below (dating from 1889) is as old as the Psalms.

The Norton Anthology of English Literature, gen. ed. M. H. Abrams, 6th edn. (New York: W. W. Norton, 1993), II.1553.

Justus quidem tu es, Domine, si disputem tecum; verumtamen
justa loquar ad te: Quare via impiorum prosperatur? &c.*

Thou art indeed just, Lord, if I contend
With thee; but, sir, so what I plead is just.
Why do sinners' ways prosper? and why must
Disappointment all I endeavour end?

Wert thou my enemy, O thou my friend,
How wouldst thou worse, I wonder, than thou dost
Defeat, thwart me? Oh, the sots and thralls of lust
Do in spare hours more thrive than I that spend,

---

* [Righteous art thou, O Lord, when I plead with thee: yet let me talk with thee/of thy judgments: Wherefore doth the way of the wicked prosper? – Jer. 12:1.

Sir, life upon thy cause. See, banks and breaks
Now, leavèd how thick! lacèd they are again
With fretty chervil, look, and fresh wind shakes

Them; birds build – but not I build; no, but strain,
Time's eunuch, and not breed one work that wakes,
Mine, O thou lord of life, send my roots rain.

49

Josiah Royce,
"The Problem of Job"

The Californian philosopher Josiah Royce (1855–1916) was the main American exponent of idealism at the turn of the twentieth century. While profoundly influenced by Hegel's thought, Royce was haunted by pessimism: Schopenhauer is the "phantom ship of post-Kantian idealism," he wrote, a thinker "we can neither afford to lose nor be willing in all things to follow." Royce's idealism is unusually attentive to the struggles of individual selves to make sense of their lives in the face of tragedy. He proposed that any theodicy must pass this test: would it console a mourner at a funeral? In "The Problem of Job" (1898), he argues that only his brand of idealism consoles, because only it accepts the sufferer's *experience* of evil; other views either deny the reality of the evil, or make it the sufferer's fault. Royce's theodicy, which forms a bridge from Schelling and Hegel to process thought, was criticized by his friend and Harvard colleague William James as a demoralizing and disempowering monism (a "block universe") which justifies evil by making it necessary. (As we will see, James thought that metaphysical pluralism is the best response to evil, precisely because it gives it no abiding meaning.)

Josiah Royce, "The Problem of Job," in *Studies of Good and Evil* (New York: D. Appleton & Co., 1906 [1898]), 1–28: 13–23.

[Philosophical idealism] first frankly admits that Job's problem is, upon Job's presuppositions, simply and absolutely insoluble. Grant Job's own presupposition that God is a being other than this world, that he is its external creator and ruler, and then all solutions fail. God is then either cruel or helpless, as regards all real finite ill of the sort that Job endures. Job, moreover, is right in demanding a reasonable answer to his question. The only possible answer is, however, one that undertakes to develop what I hold to be the immortal soul of the doctrine of the divine atonement. The answer to Job is: God is not in ultimate essence another being than yourself. He is the Absolute Being. You truly are one with God, part of his life. He is the very soul of your soul. And so, here is the first truth: When you suffer, *your sufferings are God's sufferings*, not his external work, not his external penalty, not the fruit of his neglect, but identically his own personal woe. In you God himself suffers, precisely as you do, and has all your concern in overcoming this grief.

The true question then is: Why does God thus suffer? The sole possible, necessary, and sufficient answer is, Because without suffering, without ill, without woe, evil, tragedy, God's life could not be perfected. This grief is not a physical means to an external end. It is a logically necessary and eternal constituent of the divine life. It is logically necessary that the Captain of your salvation should be perfect through suffering. No outer nature compels him. He chooses this because he chooses his own perfect selfhood. He is perfect. His world is the best possible world. Yet all its finite regions know not only of joy but of defeat and sorrow, for thus alone, in the completeness of his eternity, can God in his wholeness be triumphantly perfect.

. . . In the absolute oneness of God with the sufferer, in the concept of the suffering and therefore triumphant God, lies the logical solution of the problem of evil. The doctrine of philosophical idealism . . . maintains that there is in the universe but one perfectly real being, namely, the Absolute, that the Absolute is self-conscious, and that his world is essentially in its wholeness the fulfillment *in actu* of an all-perfect ideal. We ourselves exist as fragments of the absolute life, or better, as partial functions in the unity of the absolute and conscious process of the world. On the other hand, our existence and our individuality are not illusory, but are what they are in an organic unity with the whole life of the Absolute Being . . .

In endeavoring to grapple with the theoretical problem of the place of evil in a world that, on the whole, is to be conceived, not only as good, but as perfect, there is happily one essentially decisive consideration concerning good and evil which falls directly within the scope of our own human experience, and which concerns matters at once familiar and momentous as well as too much neglected in philosophy. When we use such words as good, evil, perfect, we easily deceive ourselves by the abstract meanings which we associate with each of the terms taken apart from the other. We forget the experiences from which the words have been abstracted. To these experiences we must return whenever we want really to comprehend the words. If we take the mere words, in their abstraction, it is easy to say, for instance, that if life has any evil in it at all, it must needs not be so perfect as life would be were there no evil in it whatever. Just so, speaking abstractly, it is easy to say that, in estimating life, one has to set the good over against the evil, and to compare their respective sums. It is easy to declare that, since we hate evil, wherever and just so far as we recognize it, our sole human interest in the world must be furthered by the removal of evil from the world. And thus viewing the case, one readily comes to say that if God views as not only good but perfect a world in which we find so much evil, the divine point of view must be very foreign to ours, so that Job's rebellious pessimism seems well in order . . . Shocked, however, by the apparent impiety of this result, some teachers, considering divine matters, still misled by the same one-sided use of words, have opposed one falsely abstract view by another, and have strangely asserted that the solution must be in proclaiming that since God's world, the real world, in order to be perfect, must be without evil, what we men call evil must be a mere illusion – a mirage of the human point of view – a dark vision which God, who sees all truth, sees not at all . . .

[The] essentially pernicious view . . . that all evil is *merely* an illusion and that there is no such thing in God's world . . . is often advanced as an idealistic view, but that, in my opinion, it is false idealism. Good idealism it is to regard all finite experience as an appearance, a hint, often a very poor hint, of deeper truth. Good idealism it is to admit that man can err about truth that lies beyond his finite range of experience. And very good idealism it is to assert that all truth, and so all finite experience, exists in and for the mind of God, and nowhere outside of or apart from God. But it is not good idealism to assert that any facts which fall within the range of finite experience are, even which they are experienced, mere illusions. God's truth is inclusive, not exclusive. What you experience God experiences. The difference lies only in this, that God sees in unity what you see in fragments. For the rest, if one said, "The source and seat of evil is only the error of mortal mind," one would but have changed the name of one's problem. If the evil were but the error, the error would still be the evil, and altering the name would not have diminished the horror of the evil of this finite world.

. . . A sound idealism says, whatever we experience is a fragment, and, as far as it goes, a genuine fragment of the truth of the divine mind. With this principle before us, let us consider directly our own experiences of good and of evil, to see whether they are as abstractly opposed to each other as the mere words often suggest . . .

By good, as we mortals experience it, we mean something that, when it comes or is expected, we actively welcome, try to attain or keep, and regard with content. By evil in general, as it is in our experience, we mean whatever we find in any sense repugnant and intolerable. I use the words repugnant and intolerable because I wish to indicate that words for evil frequently, like the words for good, directly refer to our actions as such. Commonly and rightly, when we speak of evil, we make reference to acts of resistance, of struggle, of shrinking, of flight, of removal of ourselves from a source of mischief – acts which not only follow upon the experience of evil, but which serve to define in a useful fashion what we mean by evil. The opposing acts of pursuit and of welcome define what we mean by good . . . To shun, to flee, to resist, to destroy, are our primary attitudes towards ill; the opposing acts are our primary attitudes towards the good . . .

But man is a very complex creature. He has many organs. He performs many acts at once, and he experiences his performance of these acts in one highly complex life of consciousness . . . [H]e can at the same time shun one object and grasp at another. In this way he can have at once present to him a consciousness of good and a consciousness of ill . . .

Now it is easy to say that such states of inner tension, where our conscious lives are full of a warfare of the self with itself, are contradictory or absurd states. But it is easy to say this only when you dwell on the words and fail to observe the facts of experience. As a fact, not only our lowest but our highest states of activity are the ones which are fullest of this crossing, conflict, and complex interrelation of loves and hates, of attractions and repugnances . . . I maintain that this organization of life by virtue of the tension of manifold impulses and interests is not a mere accident of our imperfect human nature, but must be a type of the organization of every rational life. There are good and bad states of tension, there are conflicts that can only be justified when resolved into some higher form of harmony. But I insist that, in general, the only harmony that can exist in the realm of the spirit is the harmony that we possess when we thwart the present but more elemental impulse for the sake of the higher unity of experience; as when we rejoice in the endurance of the tragedies of life, because they show us the depth of life, or when we know that it is better to have loved and lost than never to have loved at all, or when we possess a virtue in the moment of victory over the tempter. And the reason why this is true lies in the fact that the more one's experience fulfills ideals, the more that experience presents to one, not of ignorance, but of triumphantly wealthy acquaintance with the facts of manifold, varied and tragic life, full of tension and thereby of unity. Now this is an universal and not merely human law. It is not those innocent of evil who are fullest of the life of God, but those who in their own case have experienced the triumph over evil . . .

Generalizing the lesson of experience we may then say: It is logically impossible that a complete knower of truth should fail to know, to experience, to have present to his insight, the fact of actually existing evil. On the other hand, it is equally impossible for one to know a higher good than comes from the subordination of evil to good in a total experience . . . Now this law, this form of the knowledge of the good, applies as well to the existence of moral as to that of sensuous ill. If moral evil were simply destroyed and wiped away from the external world, the knowledge of moral goodness would also be destroyed. For the love of moral good is the thwarting of lower loves for the sake of the higher organization. What is needed, then, for the definition of the divine knowledge of a world that in its wholeness is perfect, is not a divine knowledge that shall ignore, wipe out and utterly make naught the existence of any ill, whether physical or moral, but a divine knowledge to which shall be present that love of the world as a whole which is fulfilled in the endurance of physical ill, in the subordination of moral ill, in the thwarting of impulses which survive even when subordinated, in the acceptance of repugnances which are still eternal, in the triumph over an enemy that endures even through its eternal defeat, and in the discovery that the endless tension of the finite world is included in the contemplative consciousness of the repose and harmony of eternity. To view God's nature thus is to view his nature as the whole idealistic theory views him, not as the Infinite One beyond the finite imperfections, but as the being whose unity determines the very constitution, the lack, the tension, and relative disharmony of the finite world.

The Twentieth Century

50

William James, *The Varieties of Religious Experience*

American philosopher and psychologist William James (1842–1910) gave his famous *Pragmatism* the subtitle, "A new name for some old ways of thinking." His pioneering work in the psychology of religion, presented as Gifford Lectures in Edinburgh 1901–2, likewise presented a new way of making sense of an old observation – that what people believe in their religious lives seems to be a matter less of reasons and arguments than of individual temperament. James described his aims in the *Varieties* as being two: "first, to defend . . . 'experience' against 'philosophy' as being the real backbone of the world's religious life . . . and second, to make the hearer or reader believe, what I myself invincibly do believe, that although all the special manifestations of religion may have been absurd (I mean its creeds and theories), yet the life of it as a whole is mankind's most important function." James's generally celebratory account of the diversity of religious tempers in *Varieties* occasionally gives way to comparative judgments, but his larger point is that the religious life of humanity is strengthened by its multiplicity.

William James, *The Varieties of Religious Experience: A Study in Human Nature* (Harmondsworth: Penguin, 1982 [facsimile reprint of 1902 edition]), 127–35, 142–5, 156–7, 162–5.

At our last meeting, we considered the healthy-minded temperament, the temperament which has a constitutional incapacity for prolonged suffering, and in which the tendency to see things optimistically is like a water of crystallization in which the individual's character is set. We saw how this temperament may become the basis for a peculiar type of religion, a religion in which good, even the good of this world's life, is regarded as the essential thing for a rational being to attend to. This religion directs him to settle his scores with the more evil aspects of the universe by systematically declining to lay them to heart or make much of them, by ignoring them in his reflective calculations, or even, on occasion, by denying outright that they exist. Evil is a disease; and worry over disease is itself an additional form of disease, which only adds to the original complaint. Even repentance and remorse, affections which come in the character of ministers of good, may be but sickly and relaxing impulses. The best repentance is to up and act for righteousness, and forget that you ever had relations with sin.

Spinoza's philosophy has this sort of healthy-mindedness woven into the heart of it, and this has been one secret of its fascination. He whom Reason leads, according to Spinoza, is led altogether by the influence over his mind of good. Knowledge of evil is an "inadequate" knowledge, fit only for slavish minds. So Spinoza categorically condemns repentance. When men make mistakes, he says, –

"One might perhaps expect gnawings of conscience and repentance to help to bring them on the right path, and might thereupon conclude (as every one does conclude) that these affections are good things. Yet when we look at the matter closely, we shall find that not only are they not good, but on the contrary deleterious and evil passions. For it is manifest that we can always get along better by reason and love of truth than by worry of conscience and remorse. Harmful are these and evil, inasmuch as they form a particular kind of sadness; and the disadvantages of sadness," he continues, "I have already proved, and shown that we should strive to keep it from our life. Just so we should endeavor, since uneasiness of conscience and remorse are of this kind of complexion, to flee and shun these states of mind." [*Tract on God, Man, and Happiness*, Bk. ii, ch. x]

Within the Christian body, for which repentance of sins has from the beginning been the critical religious act, healthy-mindedness has always come forward with its milder interpretation. Repentance according to such healthy-minded Christians means *getting away from* the sin, not groaning and writhing over its commission. The Catholic practice of confession and absolution is in one of its aspects little more than a systematic method of keeping healthy-mindedness on top. By it a man's accounts with evil are periodically squared and audited, so that he may start the clean page with no old debts inscribed. Any Catholic will tell us how clean and fresh and free he feels after the purging operation. Martin Luther by no means belonged to the healthy-minded type in the radical sense in which we have discussed it, and he repudiated priestly absolution for sin. Yet in this matter of repentance he had some very healthy-minded ideas, due in the main to the largeness of his conception of God . . .

Now in contrast with such healthy-minded views as these, if we treat them as a way of deliberately minimizing evil, stands a radically opposite view, a way of maximizing evil, if you please so to call it, based on the persuasion that the evil aspects of our life are of its very essence, and that the world's meaning most comes home to us when we lay them most to heart. We have now to address ourselves to this more morbid way of looking at the situation . . .

If we admit that evil is an essential part of our being and the key to the interpretation of our life, we load ourselves down with a difficulty that has always proved burdensome in philosophies of religion. Theism, whenever it has erected itself into a systematic philosophy of the universe, has shown a reluctance to let God be anything less than All-in-All. In other words, philosophic theism has always shown a tendency to become pantheistic and monistic, and to consider the world as one unit of absolute fact; and this has been at variance with popular or practical theism, which latter has ever been more or less frankly pluralistic, not to say polytheistic, and shown itself perfectly well satisfied with a universe composed of many original principles, provided we be only allowed to believe that the divine principle remains supreme, and that the others are subordinate. In this latter case God is not necessarily responsible for the existence of evil; he would only be responsible if it were not finally overcome. But on the monistic or pantheistic view, evil, like everything else, must have its foundation in God; and the difficulty is to see how this can possibly be the case if God be absolutely good. This difficulty faces us in every form of philosophy in which the world appears as one flawless unit of fact. Such a unit is an *Individual*, and in it the worst parts must be as essential as the best, must be as necessary to make the individual what he is; since if any part whatever in an individual were to vanish or alter, it would no longer be *that* individual at all. The philosophy of absolute idealism, so vigorously represented both in Scotland and America to-day, has to struggle with this difficulty quite as much as scholastic theism struggled in its time; and although it would be premature to say that there is no speculative issue whatever from the puzzle, it is perfectly fair to say that there is no clear or easy issue, and that the only *obvious* escape from paradox here is to cut loose from the monistic assumption altogether, and to allow the world to have existed from its origin in pluralistic form, as an aggregate or collection of higher and lower things and principles, rather than an absolutely unitary fact. For then evil would not need to be essential; it might be, and may always have been, an independent portion that had no rational or absolute right to live with the rest, and which we might conceivably hope to see got rid of at last.

Now the gospel of healthy-mindedness, as we have described it, casts its vote distinctly for this pluralistic view. Whereas the monistic philosopher finds himself more or less bound to say, as Hegel said, that everything actual is rational, and that evil, as an element dialectically required, must be pinned in and kept and consecrated and have a function awarded to it in the final system of truth, healthy-mindedness refuses to say anything of the sort. Evil, it says, is emphatically irrational, and *not* to be pinned in, or preserved, or consecrated in any final system of truth. It is a pure abomination to the Lord, an alien unreality, a waste element, to be sloughed off and negated, and the very memory of it, if possible, wiped out and forgotten. The ideal, so far from being co-extensive with the whole actual, is a mere *extract* from the actual, marked by its deliverance from all contact with this diseased, inferior, and excrementitious stuff . . .

On the whole, the Latin races have leaned more towards the former way of looking upon evil, as made up of ills and sins in the plural, removable in detail; while the Germanic races have tended rather to think of Sin in the singular, and with a capital S, as of something ineradicably ingrained in our natural subjectivity, and never to be removed by any superficial piecemeal operations. These comparisons of races are always open to exception, but undoubtedly the northern tone in religion has inclined to the more intimately pessimistic persuasion, and this way of feeling, being the more extreme, we shall find by far the more instructive for our study . . .

The early Greeks are continually held up to us in literary works as models of the healthy-minded joyousness which the religion of nature may engender. There was indeed much joyousness among the Greeks – Homer's flow of enthusiasm for most things that the sun shines upon is steady. But even in Homer the reflective passages are cheerless, and the moment the Greeks grew systematically pensive and thought of ultimates, they became unmitigated pessimists.* [*. . . The difference between Greek pessimism and the oriental and modern variety is that the Greeks had not made the discovery that the pathetic mood may be idealized, and figure as a higher form of sensibility. Their spirit was still too essentially masculine for pessimism to be elaborated or lengthily dwelt on in their classic literature. They would have despised a life set wholly in a minor key, and summoned it to keep within the proper bounds of lachrymosity. The discovery that the enduring emphasis, so far as this world goes, may be laid on its pain and failure, was reserved for races more complex, and (so to speak) more feminine than the Hellenes had attained to being in the classic period.

But all the same was the outlook of those Hellenes blackly pessimistic.] The jealousy of the gods, the nemesis that follows too much happiness, the all-encompassing death, fate's dark opacity, the ultimate and unintelligible cruelty, were the fixed background of their imagination. The beautiful joyousness of their polytheism is only a poetic modern fiction. They knew no joys comparable in quality of preciousness to those which we shall erelong see that Brahmans, Buddhists, Christians, Mohammedans, twice-born people whose religion is non-naturalistic, get from their several creeds of mysticism and renunciation.

Stoic insensibility and Epicurean resignation were the farthest advance which the Greek mind made in that direction. The Epicurean said: "Seek not to be happy, but rather to escape unhappiness; strong happiness is always linked with pain; therefore hug the safe shore, and do not tempt the deeper raptures. Avoid disappointment by expecting little, and by aiming low; and above all do not fret." The Stoic said: "The only genuine good that life can yield a man is the free possession of his own soul; all other goods are lies." Each of these philosophies is in its degree a philosophy of despair in nature's boons. Trustful self-abandonment to the joys that freely offer has entirely departed from both Epicurean and Stoic; and what each proposes is a way of rescue from the resultant dust-and-ashes state of mind. The Epicurean still awaits results from economy of indulgence and damping of desire. The Stoic hopes for no results, and gives up natural good altogether. There is dignity in both these forms of resignation. They represent distinct stages in the sobering process which man's primitive intoxication with sense-happiness is sure to undergo. In the one the hot blood has grown cool, in the other it has become quite cold; and although I have spoken of them in the past tense, as if they were merely historic, yet Stoicism and Epicureanism will probably be to all time typical attitudes, marking a certain definite stage accomplished in the evolution of the world-sick soul. They mark the conclusion of what we call the once-born period, and represent the highest flights of what twice-born religion would call the purely natural man – Epicureanism, which can only by great courtesy be called a religion, showing his refinement, and Stoicism exhibiting his moral will. They leave the world in the shape of an unreconciled contradiction, and seek no higher unity. Compared with the complex ecstasies which the supernaturally regenerated Christian may enjoy, or the oriental pantheist indulge in, their receipts for equanimity are expedients which seem almost crude in their simplicity.

Please observe, however, that I am not yet pretending finally to *judge* any of these attitudes. I am only describing their variety.

The securest way to the rapturous sorts of happiness of which the twice-born make report has as an historic matter of fact been through a more radical pessimism than anything that we have yet considered. We have seen how the lustre and enchantment may be rubbed off from the goods of nature. But there is a pitch of unhappiness so great that the goods of nature may be entirely forgotten, and all sentiment of their existence vanish from the mental field. For this extremity of pessimism to be reached, something more is needed than observation of life and reflection upon death. The individual must in his own person become the prey of a pathological melancholy. As the healthy-minded enthusiast succeeds in ignoring evil's very existence, so the subject of melancholy is forced in spite of himself to ignore that of all good whatever: for him it may no longer have the least reality. Such sensitiveness and susceptibility to mental pain is a rare occurrence where the nervous constitution is entirely normal; one seldom finds it in a healthy subject even where he is the victim of the most atrocious cruelties of outward fortune. So we note here the neurotic constitution, of which I said so much in my first lecture, making its active entrance on our scene, and destined to play a part in much that follows . . .

When disillusionment has gone as far as this, there is seldom a *restitutio ad integrum*. One has tasted of the fruit of the tree, and the happiness of Eden never comes again. The happiness that comes, when any does come, and often enough it fails to return in an acute form, though its form is sometimes very acute, – is not the simple ignorance of ill, but something vastly more complex, including natural evil as one of its elements, but finding natural evil no such stumbling-block and terror because it now sees it swallowed up in supernatural good. The process is one of redemption, not of mere reversion to natural health, and the sufferer, when saved, is saved by what seems to him a second birth, a deeper kind of conscious being than he could enjoy before . . .

Arrived at this point, we can see how great an antagonism may naturally arise between the healthy-minded way of viewing life and the way that takes all this experience of evil as something essential. To this latter way, the morbid-minded way, as we might call it, healthy-mindedness pure and simple seems unspeakably blind and shallow. To the healthy-minded way, on the other hand, the way of the sick soul seems unmanly and diseased. With their grubbing in rat-holes instead of living in the light; with their manufacture of fears, and preoccupation with every unwholesome kind of misery, there is something almost obscene about these children of wrath and cravers of a second birth. If religious intolerance and hanging and burning could again become the order of the day, there is little doubt that, however it may have been in the past, the healthy-minded would at present show themselves the less indulgent party of the two.

In our own attitude, not yet abandoned, of impartial onlookers, what are we to say of this quarrel? It seems to me that we are bound to say that morbid-mindedness ranges over the wider scale of experience, and that its survey is the one that overlaps. The method of averting one's attention from evil, and living simply in the light of good is splendid as long as it will work. It will work with many persons; it will work far more generally than most of us are ready to suppose; and within the sphere of its successful operation there is nothing to be said against it as a religious solution. But it breaks down impotently as soon as melancholy comes; and even though one be quite free from melancholy one's self, there is no doubt that healthy-mindedness is inadequate as a philosophical doctrine, because the evil facts which it refuses positively to account for are a genuine portion of reality; and they may after all be the best key to life's significance, and possibly the only openers of our eyes to the deepest levels of truth . . .

It may indeed be that no religious reconciliation with the absolute totality of things is possible. Some evils, indeed, are ministerial to higher forms of good; but it may be that there are forms of evil so extreme as to enter into no good system whatsoever, and that, in respect of such evil, dumb submission or neglect to notice is the only practical resource. This question must confront us on a later day. But provisionally, and as a mere matter of program and method, since the evil facts are as genuine parts of nature as the good ones, the philosophic presumption should be that they have some rational significance, and that systematic healthy-mindedness, failing as it does to accord to sorrow, pain, and death any positive and active attention whatever, is formally less complete than systems that try at least to include these elements in their scope.

The completest religions would therefore seem to be those in which the pessimistic elements are best developed. Buddhism, of course, and Christianity are the best known to us of these. They are essentially religions of deliverance: the man must die to an unreal life before he can be born into the real life. In my next lecture, I will try to discuss some of the psychological conditions of this second birth.

51

W. E. B. Du Bois,
"A Litany at Atlanta"

On the night of September 22, 1906, "two years of vituperation and tra-
duction of the Negro race by the most prominent candidates for governer-
ship, together with a bad police system" led to a night of terror in Atlanta,
Georgia. A murderous white mob tore through the city, pillaging offices and
businesses in search of blacks, leaving two dozen dead. "A Litany at Atlanta,"
written by the African American social scientist, cultural critic, and civil
rights leader W. E. B. Du Bois (1868–1963) as he hurried home to his family
in Atlanta after the "race riot," marks a turning point in his thought. Making
brilliant and subversive use of biblical language, it conveys the explosive ener-
gies communal religious ritual can channel.

W. E. B. Du Bois, "A Litany at Atlanta," *The Independent* 61 (Oct. 11, 1906):
856–8, repr. in *W. E. B. Bu Bois: A Reader*, ed. David Levering Lewis (New
York: Henry Holt, 1995), 441–4.

O Silent God, Thou whose voice afar in mist and mystery hath left our
ears a-hungered in these fearful days –
Hear us, good Lord!

Listen to us, Thy children: our faces dark with doubt, are made a mockery
in Thy Sanctuary. With uplifted hands we front Thy Heaven, O God,
crying:
We beseech Thee to hear us, good Lord!

We are not better than our fellows, Lord; we are but weak and human
men. When our devils do deviltry, curse Thou the doer and the deed:
curse them as we curse them, do to them all and more than ever they
have done to innocence and weakness, to womanhood and home.
Have mercy upon us, miserable sinners!

And yet, whose is the deeper guilt? Who made these devils ? Who nursed them in crime and fed them on injustice? Who ravished and debauched their mothers and their grandmothers? Who bought and sold their crime and waxed fat and rich on public iniquity?

Thou knowest, good God!

Is this Thy Justice, O Father, that guile be easier than innocence and the innocent crucified for the guilt of the untouched *guilty?*   *Christ*

Justice, O Judge of men!

Wherefore do we pray? Is not the God of the Fathers dead ? Have not seers seen in Heaven's halls Thine hearsed and lifeless form stark amidst the black and rolling smoke of sin, where all along bow bitter forms of endless dead?

Awake; Thou that sleepest!

Thou art not dead, but flown afar, up hills of endless light, thru blazing corridors of suns, where worlds do swing of good and gentle men, of women strong and free – far from the cozeage, black hypocrisy, and chaste prostitution of this shameful speck of dust!

Turn again, O Lord; leave us not to perish in our sin!

From lust of body and lust of blood
Great God, deliver us!

From lust of power and lust of gold,
Great God, deliver us!

From the leagued lying of despot and of brute,
Great God, deliver us!

A city lay in travail, God our Lord, and from her loins sprang twin Murder and Black Hate. Red was the midnight; clang, crack, and cry of death and fury filled the air and trembled underneath the stars where church spires pointed silently to Thee. And all this was to sate the greed of greedy men who hide behind the veil of vengeance!

Bend us Thine ear, O Lord!

In the pale, still morning we looked upon the deed. We stopped our ears and held our leaping hands, but they – did they not wag their heads and leer and cry with bloody jaws: *Cease from Crime!* The word was mockery, for thus they train a hundred crimes while we do cure one.

Turn again our captivity, O Lord!

Behold this maimed and broken thing, dear God; it was an humble black
man, who toiled and sweat to save a bit from the pittance paid him.
They told him: *Work and Rise!* He worked. Did this man sin? Nay, but
some one told how someone said another did – one whom he had
never seen nor known. Yet for that man's crime this man lieth maimed
and murdered, his wife naked to shame, his children, to poverty and
evil.

   Hear us, O heavenly Father!

Doth not this justice of hell stink in Thy nostrils, O God? How long shall
the mounting flood of innocent blood roar in Thine ears and pound in
our hearts for vengeance? Pile the pale frenzy of blood-crazed brutes,
who do such things, high on Thine altar, Jehovah Jireh, and burn it in
hell forever and forever!

   Forgive us, good Lord; we know not what we say!

Bewildered we are and passion-tost, mad with the madness of a mobbed
and mocked and murdered people; straining at the armposts of Thy
throne, we raise our shackled hands and charge Thee, God, by the bones
of our stolen fathers, by the tears of our dead mothers, by the very
blood of Thy crucified Christ: *What meaneth this?* Tell us the Plan; give
us the Sign!

   Keep not Thou silent, O God!

Sit no longer blind, Lord God, deaf to our prayer and dumb to our dumb
suffering. Surely Thou too are not white, O Lord, a pale, bloodless,
heartless thing?

   Ah! Christ of all the Pities!

Forgive the thought! Forgive these wild blasphemous words! Thou art still
the God of our black fathers and in Thy soul's soul sit some soft dark-
enings of the evening, some shadowings of the velvet night.
But whisper – speak – call, great God, for Thy silence is white terror to
our hearts! The way, O God, show us the way and point us the path!
Whither? North is greed and South is blood; within, the coward, and
without, the liar. Whither? To death?

   Amen! Welcome dark sleep!

Whither? To life? But not this life, dear God, not this. Let the cup pass
from us, tempt us not beyond our last strength, for there is that clam-
oring and clawing within, to whose voice we would not listen, yet
shudder lest we must, and it is red, Ah! God! It is a red and awful shape.

   Selah!

In yonder East trembles a star.
Vengeance is mine; I will repay, saith the Lord!

Thy Will, O Lord, be done!
Kyrie Eleison!

Lord, we have done these pleading, wavering words.
We beseech Thee to hear us, good Lord!

We bow our heads and hearken soft to the sobbing of women and little children.
We beseech Thee to hear us, good Lord!

Our voices sink in silence and in night.
Hear us, good Lord!

In night, O God of a godless land!
Amen!

In silence, O Silent God.
Selah!

Done at Atlanta, in the Day of Death, 1906.

52

Thomas Hardy,
"Before Life and After"

The world of the novels and poems of English writer Thomas Hardy (1840–1928) is a bleak world of meaningless "hap." In this poem, published in 1909, Hardy subversively uses the psalmist's cry – "How long, Lord!" – to articulate a pessimism worthy of Schopenhauer.

The Complete Poetical Works of Thomas Hardy, ed. Samuel Hynes, vol. 1 (Oxford: Clarendon, 1982), 333.

A time there was – as one may guess
And as, indeed, earth's testimonies tell –
Before the birth of consciousness,
When all went well.

None suffered sickness, love or loss,
None knew regret, starved hope, or heart-burnings;
None cared whatever crash or cross
Brought wrack to things.

If something ceased, no tongue bewailed,
If something winced and waned, no heart was wrung;
If brightness dimmed, and dark prevailed,
No sense was stung.

But the disease of feeling germed
And primal rightness took the tinct of wrong;
Ere nescience shall be reaffirmed
How long, how long?

53

Hermann Cohen,
Religion of Reason
out of the Sources of Judaism

The German Jewish philosopher Hermann Cohen (1842–1918) understood religion as an ethical universalism which arises out of the encounter with the suffering other. Cohen's *Religion of Reason out of the Sources of Judaism* (published in 1919) presents Jewish tradition as the kernel of the understanding of "ethical monotheism" he had developed as one of the leading reinterpreters of the philosophy of Kant: the role of the human individual is analogous to Israel's role among the nations. This leads to a powerful universalization of the "suffering servant." The nations will become aware of true religion only by witnessing the suffering of the stateless people of Israel – Israel is "the sacrificial victim," suffering "the martyrdom of monotheism." Just so, each of us must learn to see the suffering of others as vicarious and prophetic. As responding to suffering is an infinite task, Cohen rejects the question of the justice of the distribution of happiness and suffering: "all measuring and comparing of the inner *dignity* of man with the outward appearance of his earthly lot is futile and meaningless, shortsighted and deluded."

Hermann Cohen, *Religion of Reason out of the Sources of Judaism*, trans. Simon Kaplan (New York: Frederick Ungar, 1972), 226–30.

17. Pessimism laments the sum total of human existence. Moreover, pantheism puts on a mask of wisdom when it finds all this perfectly in order, because, in relation to the cruel necessity of natural laws, all moral as well as aesthetic distinctions are nothing but isolated individualizations (modes) of thinking. From this point of view the individual phenomenon has its value in itself: it cannot be excelled by any other. This is the wisdom of

the fool lamenting the suffering of man. But monotheism must consider suffering, ordained to man by God, differently.

In the divine order of the world there is only good and bad. "Woe to them, who say to the good bad and to the light darkness." [Isa. 5:20] If the Second Isaiah draws the defiant conclusion that God also "creates evil" (Isa. 45:7), we have rather substituted ill . . . for this evil. What man calls ill because it hurts him, this is in truth not ill but happens for his own good. *Suffering is the punishment that man demands inexorably of himself for himself.*

With regard to the suffering of one's fellowman, one is not entitled to interpret his suffering as punishment that befalls him because of his sin. For one has to discover and affirm one's fellowman through compassion. For oneself, on the contrary, one cannot waive punishment. Hence, suffering is proper to oneself: one considers it a punishment that one has to demand for oneself and for which one calls and appeals.

18. It would be an immoral *confidence in God* if man were to expect forgiveness merely because of God's goodness and if he would not rather establish this confidence upon his own confession of sin along with the declaration of his readiness to accept punishment. He himself has to recognize that he deserves and is in need of punishment. Deeming oneself deserving of punishment manifests itself in the acknowledgment of suffering as a necessary step in the self-development of man.

19. The morality of pantheism is based on the principle of the instinct for *self-preservation*. In pantheism the natural instinct for life becomes the foundation of morality. Life demands preservation. The preservation of the elemental power of life is the elemental right of man. The instinct for the preservation of life establishes the *identity of might and right*; but the self that this instinct tries to preserve is the natural being, the biological creature.

20. Religion does not recognize such a notion of an isolated creature who exists merely to stay alive. For religion, the self exists only in the correlation with God, within which alone the correlation of man to man comes to be. I am not permitted to explain the suffering of my fellowman as punishment. I am in no way interested in his possible guilt. Perhaps he suffers for my guilt. One may confidently ascribe such intimate effects to the correlation of man with man. My own self, on the contrary, with all its hidden motives, becomes a necessary problem to me, and when I come so far in the solution of this problem that I have gained self-recognition of my sin and achieved confession of it, I am not even yet at the end of the road, until the confession has as its consequence the acknowledgment of suffering as the just punishment. For the affirmation

of my self, for the preservation of my self, I may not be satisfied merely with my trust in God's forgiveness.

The confession of sin, despite it all, would be merely a formality if the declaration of my willingness to suffer did not confirm it. *Suffering is related not so much to sin as to its forgiveness*, and to redemption, insofar as the latter is dependent on self-sanctification. Self-sanctification culminates in the insight into the necessity of suffering and in the voluntary self-sacrifice of submission to the suffering of punishment.

21. It is Maimonides' profound idea that Job also is a prophet, that suffering is a genuine form of prophecy. [cf. pp. 92, 94 above.] Through this idea he interprets the meaning of this prophetic, didactic poem, in which suffering as a form of prophecy is incorporated into the theodicy of the organization of the moral world. Suffering is not a defect, no dysteleology, but an independent link in the moral system and, thus, full of purpose.

Job's friends are not right when they wish to console him in his suffering by reminding him of his sin. His friends should have acknowledged him as a prophet who could instruct them about the value of suffering. Job is a prophet from whom his friends should have learned that suffering is a force in God's plan of salvation. This plan however, is obscured and dissipated unless the sufferer is considered as suffering for the sake of others. It is obscured if one thinks erroneously that suffering and punishment are related as cause and effect.

On the other hand, Job himself does not lack the deeper insight that he is in need of suffering and deserves to pass through it, though not so much as a single individual but as a self in its correlation with God. Our routine thinking of sin and punishment, of punishment and suffering, as cause and effect should cease. God makes this moral of the fable known at the end of the poem. At the same time in God's justification of Job it is explained that Job suffers for the sake of his own justification.

What God proclaims to be the meaning of the entire poem is expressed negatively in Job's conviction, in which he rejects sin as the cause of his suffering. He is a prophet, and as such the symbol of humanity. But insofar as he is aware of his prophetic position, he needs to recognize the cause of his suffering in order to preserve his self. Job has had earthly enjoyment and possessions in abundance, and after he has lost them they are given back to him. Is there anything that could give his life more value when he has already participated in all wisdom and piety? Are prosperity and earthly self-esteem the highest things for human self-consciousness? Is not the moral economy of the world deficient precisely in that the prophet is needed for the world? Job points to this deficiency in his lamentations. And he bases his suffering on the need for his prophecy.

But that which the world is in need of, the prophet, in the first instance, is in need of for himself. However, the need of the human self seems to recede in the consciousness of the prophet. This difficulty exists for the *self-awareness of the prophet* in general, and it is indeed not lacking in Job's case. The ambiguity in Job's suffering therefore remains: as a prophet he suffers for others, but he himself remains a man and, as such, is in need of suffering for his own self.

22. The value of the biblical poem is limited to the refutation of the prejudice that there is a causal relation between sin and suffering; it rather introduces suffering, as do all the other prophetic writings, into the working of the theodicy of the moral world. However, the Day of Atonement does not pursue such a poetic solution of the riddle of the world. Its task is to affirm and preserve, in spite of sin, the self-awareness of the I of the individual in his correlation with God. The Day of Atonement therefore puts suffering into an immediate relation to the individual's own problem.

Jewish piety accordingly recognizes suffering as a step to redemption. Suffering is indeed not longed for as in ascetic mysticism, but it is validated in *prayer* by the entreaty for liberation from and protection against it in all detail. The *fast* on the Day of Atonement is the symbol of this understanding of the necessary value of suffering.

Suffering may be the common lot of men. Nevertheless, it must first of all become the *watchword* for the I. I am not merely an organism. Eudaemonism cannot become the key to my being. The blind alternation of pleasure and pain cannot regulate my moral life. Only a certain permanency of suffering gives my existence its correct meaning. My suffering is not an effect but an end for my self, or, possibly, only a means to this, my final end . . .

24. This suffering within the human race has been primarily the suffering of *Israel*. This is the ancient theme that resounds through all the prophets, the psalms, and the entire literature that follows. We shall see later how the highest figure of monotheism, the Messiah himself, is transfigured through this suffering so that he suffers for mankind. And as he himself is only a symbol for Israel, so Israel suffers for the peoples who do not accept the unique God.

This is precisely the theodicy, the moral that the story of Job is meant to teach us. Is not the people of Israel itself in need of suffering and of the recognition of its obligation to suffer? If this were not the case, Israel, too, could not be redeemed. This is the highest meaning of the Day of Atonement, that repentance is in earnest only in the recognition and taking upon oneself of suffering.

Israel stands, as everywhere, simply as the symbol of the individual. Since Ezekiel, every one has become "a soul," and since that time the soul no longer means merely life and person, but the self that strengthens itself in self-responsibility. One measure of this self-responsibility is the acknowledgment of the value of suffering. It cannot be ignored, it cannot be eliminated. It is the precondition for the individual who is conscious of himself. And from the individual it is transferred to the people.

What other people, what other religious community is there whose distinctive mark in history is such martyrdom? As a Job it wanders through world history. And always and everywhere the surrounding contemporary world destroys itself through the self-righteousness with which it interprets for itself Israel's suffering as the result of Israel's unworthiness. When will the time dawn in which the peril of this self-righteousness will be recognized? . . .

25. Other systems of faith made the mistake of thinking that suffering is not a means but a final end. Thus it became possible to represent the divine itself as suffering, as human suffering. Although in this idea the end of the redemption of men is seen along with and beyond suffering, yet the redeemer himself must take this suffering upon himself. And through this idea, suffering becomes and is the end. Moreover, there is a corrupting attraction in the idea that suffering is a divine end in itself.

Nonetheless, this idea is false. Only morality itself, only the correlation of God and man can be an end in itself. Everything else in morality, everything else in religion, is accessory and a means to this unique end. Therefore, suffering also can only be a means. And the end itself, which is redemption, cannot be thought of in isolation from its means; both have to cooperate in order to achieve the end. Hence, redemption and not suffering is the final meaning of life. In order to consummate redemption man and God cooperate; in this the correlation of man and God receives its highest confirmation.

54

Sigmund Freud,
The Future of an Illusion

Sigmund Freud (1856–1939), the founder of psychoanalysis, was also a cultural critic of great power. Influenced by Schopenhauer's pessimism as well
as by Nietzsche's genealogies, Freud's writings have profoundly shaped contemporary understandings of the etiology of human evil. In the discussion
of religion below, Freud suggests that it is a mark of immaturity to see the
irrationality of human experience as *remediable*: the challenge is to live
without illusions, without consolation. *The Future of an Illusion* is one of
Freud's more optimistic works; in *Civilization and its Discontents*, written three
years later (1930), he seems no longer to think human beings can achieve
the reconciliation with the demands of civilization which would allow them
to live without illusions.

Sigmund Freud, *The Future of an Illusion*, trans. James Strachey (New York:
Norton, 1961), 38–42.

[W]e turn our attention to the psychical origin of religious ideas. These,
which are given out as teachings, are not precipitates of experience or
end-results of thinking: they are illusions, fulfilments of the oldest, strongest
and most urgent wishes of mankind. The secret of their strength lies in
the strength of those wishes. As we already know, the terrifying impression of helplessness in childhood aroused the need for protection – for
protection through love – which was provided by the father; and the
recognition that this helplessness lasts throughout life made it necessary to
cling to the existence of a father, but this time a more powerful one. Thus
the benevolent rule of a divine Providence allays our fear of the dangers
of life; the establishment of a moral world-order ensures the fulfilment of
the demands of justice, which have so often remained unfulfilled in human

civilization; and the prolongation of earthly existence in a future life provides the local and temporal framework in which these wish-fulfilments shall take place. Answers to the riddles that tempt the curiosity of man, such as how the universe began or what the relation is between body and mind, are developed in conformity with the underlying assumptions of this system. It is an enormous relief to the individual psyche if the conflicts of its childhood arising from the father-complex – conflicts which it has never wholly overcome – are removed from it and brought to a solution which is universally accepted.

When I say that these things are all illusions, I must define the meaning of the word. An illusion is not the same thing as an error; nor is it necessarily an error. Aristotle's belief that vermin are developed out "of dung" (a belief to which ignorant people still cling) was an error; so was the belief of a former generation of doctors that *tabes dorsalis* is the result of sexual excess. It would be incorrect to call these errors illusions. On the other hand, it was an illusion of Columbus's that he had discovered a new sea-route to the Indies. The part played by his wish in this error is very clear. One may describe as an illusion the assertion made by certain nationalists that the Indo-Germanic race is the only one capable of civilization; or the belief, which was only destroyed by psycho-analysis, that children are creatures without sexuality. What is characteristic of illusions is that they are derived from human wishes. In this respect they come near to psychiatric delusions. But they differ from them, too, apart from the more complicated structure of delusions. In the case of delusions, we emphasize as essential their being in contradiction with reality. Illusions need not necessarily be false – that is to say, unrealizable or in contradiction to reality. For instance, a middle-class girl may have the illusion that a prince will come and marry her. This is possible; and a few such cases have occurred. That the Messiah will come and found a golden age is much less likely. Whether one classifies this belief as an illusion or as something analogous to a delusion will depend on one's personal attitude . . . Thus we call a belief an illusion when a wish-fulfilment is a prominent factor in its motivation, and in doing so we disregard its relations to reality, just as the illusion itself sets no store by verification.

Having thus taken our bearings, let us return once more to the question of religious doctrines. We can now repeat that all of them are illusions and insusceptible of proof. No one can be compelled to think them true, to believe in them. Some of them are so improbable, so incompatible with everything we have laboriously discovered about the reality of the world, that we may compare them – if we pay proper regard to the psychological differences – to delusions. Of the reality value of most of them we cannot judge; just as they cannot be proved, so they cannot be refuted. We still know too little to make a critical approach to them. The riddles of the universe reveal themselves only slowly to our investigation; there are many questions to which science to-day can give no answer. But scientific work is the only road which can lead us to a knowledge of reality outside ourselves. It is once again merely an illusion to expect anything from intuition and introspection; they can give us nothing but particulars about our own mental life, which are hard to interpret, never any information about the questions which religious doctrine finds it so easy to answer. It would be insolent to let one's own arbitrary will step into the breach and, according to one's personal estimate, declare this or that part of the religious system to be less or more acceptable. Such questions are too momentous for that; they might be called too sacred.

At this point one must expect to meet with an objection. "Well then, if even obdurate sceptics admit that the assertions of religion cannot be refuted by reason, why should I not believe in them, since they have so much on their side – tradition, the agreement of mankind, and all the consolations they offer?" Why not, indeed? Just as no one can be forced to believe, so no one can be forced to disbelieve. But do not let us be satisfied with deceiving ourselves that arguments like these take us along the road of correct thinking. If ever there was a case of a lame excuse we have it here. Ignorance is ignorance; no right to believe anything can be derived from it. In other matters no sensible person will behave so irresponsibly or rest content with such feeble grounds for his opinions and for the line he takes. It is only in the highest and most sacred things that he allows himself to do so. In reality these are only attempts at pretending to oneself or to other people that one is still firmly attached to religion, when one has long since cut oneself loose from it. Where questions of religion are concerned, people are guilty of every possible sort of dishonesty and intellectual misdemeanour. Philosophers stretch the meaning of words until they retain scarcely anything of their original sense. They give the name of "God" to some vague abstraction which they have created for themselves; having done so they can pose before all the world as deists, as believers in God, and they can even boast that they have recognized a higher, purer concept of God, notwithstanding that their God is now nothing more than an insubstantial shadow and no longer the mighty personality of religious doctrines. Critics persist in describing as "deeply religious" anyone who admits to a sense of man's insignificance or impotence in the face of the universe, although what constitutes the essence of the religious attitude is not this feeling but only the next step after it, the reaction to it which seeks a remedy for it. The man who goes no further, but humbly acquiesces in the small part which human beings play in the great world – such a man is, on the contrary, irreligious in the truest sense of the word.

To assess the truth-value of religious doctrines does not lie within the scope of the present enquiry. It is enough for us that we have recognized them as being, in their psychological nature, illusions. But we do not have to conceal the fact that this discovery also strongly influences our attitude to the question which must appear to many to be the most important of all. We know approximately at what period and by what kind of men religious doctrines were created. If in addition we discover the motives which led to this, our attitude to the problem of religion will undergo a marked displacement. We shall tell ourselves that it would be very nice if there were a God who created the world and was a benevolent Providence, and if there were a moral order in the universe and an after-life; but it is a very striking fact that all this is exactly as we are bound to wish it to be. And it would be more remarkable still if our wretched, ignorant and downtrodden ancestors had succeeded in solving all these difficult riddles of the universe.

55

Martin Heidegger,
An Introduction to Metaphysics

One of the greatest philosophers of the twentieth century, the German phe-
nomenologist and existentialist Martin Heidegger (1889–1976) thought that
the western metaphysical tradition from Plato to Nietzsche had misconstrued
the most fundamental of questions. Beneath inquiry into the nature and
meaning of *beings* ("essents" in the 1930 lecture below) lies the deeper question of the *Being* of beings. The issue had resurfaced in Leibniz's question,
"why is there something rather than nothing at all?" (Leibniz's traditional
religious answer – a good God will create a world because being is itself
good – was, Heidegger thought, insufficient.) Heidegger's discussion below
suggests a stark choice of faith *or* philosophy, with the question of "Being"
in principle inaccessible to the former. What about the questions surrounding evils – their nature, their place in or in opposition to the order of the
world? Heidegger never discusses evil (although his student Hannah Arendt's
controversial category of the "banality" of evil, explored in her *Eichmann in
Jerusalem*, is as Heideggerian as it is Kantian); is this because it is a problem
only for faith?

Martin Heidegger, *An Introduction to Metaphysics*, trans. Ralph Manheim (New
Haven: Yale University Press, 1959), 1–8.

Why are there essents rather than nothing? That is the question. Clearly
it is no ordinary question. "Why are there essents, why is there anything
at all, rather than nothing?" – obviously this is the first of all questions,
though not in a chronological sense. Individuals and peoples ask a good
many questions in the course of their historical passage through time. They
examine, explore and test a good many things before they run into the

question "Why are there essents rather than nothing?" Many men never encounter this question, if by encounter we mean not merely to hear and read about it as an interrogative formulation but to ask the question, that is, to bring it about, to raise it, to feel its inevitability.

And yet each of us is grazed at least once, perhaps more than once, by the hidden power of this question, even if he is not aware of what is happening to him. The question looms in moments of great despair, when things tend to lose all their weight and all meaning becomes obscured. Perhaps it will strike but once like a muffled bell that rings into our life and gradually dies away. It is present in moments of rejoicing, when all the things around us are transfigured and seem to be there for the first time, as if it might be easier to think they are not than to understand that they are and are as they are. The question is upon us in boredom, when we are equally removed from despair and joy and everything about us seems so hopelessly commonplace that we no longer care whether anything is or is not – and with this the question "Why are there essents rather than nothing?" is evoked in a particular form.

But this question may be asked expressly, or, unrecognized as a question, it may merely pass through our lives like a brief gust of wind; it may press hard upon us, or, under one pretext or another, we may thrust it away from us and silence it. In any case it is never the question that we ask first in point of time.

But it is the first question in another sense – in regard to rank. This may be clarified in three ways. The question "Why are there essents rather than nothing?" is first in rank for us first because it is the most far reaching, second because it is the deepest, and finally because it is the most fundamental of all questions.

It is the widest of all questions. It confines itself to no particular essent of whatever kind. The question takes in everything, and this means not only everything that is present in the broadest sense but also everything that ever was or will be. The range of this question finds its limit only in nothing, in that which simply is not and never was. Everything that is not nothing is covered by this question, and ultimately even nothing itself; not because it is something, since after all we speak of it, but because it is nothing. Our question reaches out so far that we can never go further. We do not inquire into this and that, or into each essent in turn, but from the very outset into the essent as a whole, or, as we say for reasons to be discussed below: into the essent as such in its entirety.

This broadest of questions is also the deepest: Why are there essents . . . ? Why, that is to say, on what ground? from what source does the essent derive? on what ground does it stand? The question is not concerned with particulars, with what essents are and of what nature at any time, here and there, with how they can be changed, what they can be used for, and so on. The question aims at the ground of what is insofar as it is. To seek the ground is to try to get to the bottom; what is put in question is thus related to the ground . . . [T]he ground in question must account for the being of the essent as such. This question "why" does not look for causes that are of the same kind and on the same level as the essent itself. This "why" does not move on any one plane but penetrates to the "underlying" ["zu-grunde" liegend] realms and indeed to the very last of them, to the limit; turning away from the surface, from all shallowness, it strives toward the depths; this broadest of all questions is also the deepest.

Finally, this broadest and deepest question is also the most fundamental. What do we mean by this? If we take the question in its full scope, namely the essent as such in its entirety, it readily follows that in asking this question we keep our distance from every particular and individual essent, from every this and that. For we mean the essent as a whole, without any special preference . . . [W]e must avoid singling out any special, particular essent, including man. For what indeed is man? Consider the earth within the endless darkness of space in the universe. By way of comparison it is a tiny grain of sand; between it and the next grain of its own size there extends a mile or more of emptiness; on the surface of this grain of sand there lives a crawling, bewildered swarm of supposedly intelligent animals, who for a moment have discovered knowledge. And what is the temporal extension of a human life amid all the millions of years? Scarcely a move of the second hand, a breath. Within the essent as a whole there is no legitimate ground for singling out this essent which is called mankind and to which we ourselves happen to belong.

But whenever the essent as a whole enters into this question, a privileged, unique relation arises between it and the act of questioning. For through this questioning the essent as a whole is for the first time opened up as such with a view to its possible ground, and in the act of questioning it is kept open. In relation to the essent as such in its entirety the asking of the question is not just any occurrence within the realm of the essent, like the falling of raindrops for example. The question "why" may be said to confront the essent as a whole, to break out of it, though never completely. But that is exactly why the act of questioning is privileged. Because it confronts the essent as a whole, but does not break loose from it, the content of the question reacts upon the questioning itself. Why the why? What is the ground of this question "why" which presumes to ask after the ground of the essent as a whole? Is the ground asked for in this why not merely a foreground – which would imply that the sought-for ground is again an essent? Does not the "first" question nevertheless come first in view of the intrinsic rank of the question of being and its modulations?

To be sure, the things in the world, the essents, are in no way affected by our asking of the question "Why are there essents rather than nothing?" Whether we ask it or not, the planets move in their orbits, the sap of life flows through plant and animal.

But if this question is asked and if the act of questioning is really carried out, the content and the object of the question react inevitably on the act of questioning. Accordingly this questioning is not just any occurrence but a privileged happening that we call an *event* . . .

[I]f we decline to be taken in by surface appearances we shall see that this question "why," this question as to the essent as such in its entirety, goes beyond any mere playing with words, provided we possess sufficient intellectual energy to make the question actually recoil into its "why" – for it will not do so of its own accord. In so doing we find out that this privileged question "why" has its ground in a leap through which man thrusts away all the previous security, whether real or imagined, of his life. The question is asked only in this leap; it *is* the leap; without it there is no asking. What "leap" means here will be elucidated later. Our questioning is not yet the leap; for this it must undergo a transformation; it still stands perplexed in the face of the essent. Here it may suffice to say that the leap in this questioning opens up its own source – with this leap the question arrives at its own ground. We call such a leap, which opens up its own source, the original source or origin [Ur-sprung], the finding of one's own ground. It is because the question "Why are there essents rather than nothing?" breaks open the ground for all authentic questions and is thus at the origin [Ursprung] of them all that we must recognize it as the most fundamental of all questions . . .

In this threefold sense the question is the first in rank – first, that is, in the order of questioning within the domain which this first question opens, defining its scope and thus founding it. Our question is the question of all authentic questions, i.e. of all self-questioning questions, and whether consciously or not it is necessarily implicit in every question. No questioning and accordingly no single scientific "problem" can be fully intelligible if it does not include, i.e. ask, the question of all questions . . .

Anyone for whom the Bible is divine revelation and truth has the answer to the question "Why are there essents rather than nothing?" even before it is asked: everything that is, except God himself, has been created by Him. God himself, the increate creator, "is." One who holds to such faith can in a way participate in the asking of our question, but he cannot

really question without ceasing to be a believer and taking all the consequences of such a step. He will only be able to act "as if" . . . On the
other hand a faith that does not perpetually expose itself to the possibility of unfaith is no faith but merely a convenience: the believer simply
makes up his mind to adhere to the traditional doctrine. This is neither
faith nor questioning, but the indifference of those who can busy themselves with everything, sometimes even displaying a keen interest in faith
as well as questioning.

What we have said about security in faith as one position in regard to
the truth does not imply that the biblical "In the beginning God created
heaven and earth" is an answer to our question. Quite aside from whether
these words from the Bible are true or false for faith, they can supply no
answer to our question because they are in no way related to it. Indeed,
they cannot even be brought into relation with our question. From the
standpoint of faith our question is "foolishness."

Philosophy is this very foolishness. A "Christian philosophy" is a round
square and a misunderstanding. There is, to be sure, a thinking and questioning elaboration of the world of Christian experience, i.e. of faith. That
is theology. Only epochs which no longer fully believe in the true greatness of the task of theology arrive at the disastrous notion that philosophy can help to provide a refurbished theology if not a substitute for
theology, which will satisfy the needs and tastes of the time. For the original Christian faith philosophy is foolishness. To philosophize is to ask "Why
are there essents rather nothing?" Really to ask the question signifies: a
daring attempt to fathom this unfathomable question by disclosing what
it summons us to ask, to push our questioning to the very end. Where
such an attempt occurs there is philosophy . . .

56

W. H. Auden,
"Musée des Beaux Arts"

?

This famous poem by the Catholic English poet W. H. Auden (1907–73), composed as Europe headed toward war in September 1938, is one of several poems which explore the world's indifference to and unwillingness to recognize suffering.

W. H. Auden, *Selected Poems*, new edition, ed. Edward Mendelson (New York: Vintage, 1979), 79–80.

About suffering they were never wrong,
The Old Masters: how well they understood
Its human position; how it takes place
While someone else is eating or opening a window or just
                                     walking dully along;
How, when the aged are reverently, passionately waiting
For the miraculous birth, there always must be
Children who did not specially want it to happen, skating
On a pond at the edge of the wood:
They never forgot
That even the dreadful martyrdom must run its course
Anyhow in a corner, some untidy spot
Where the dogs go on with their doggy
                              life and the torturer's horse
Scratches its innocent behind on a tree.
In Brueghel's *Icarus*, for instance: how everything turns away
Quite leisurely from the disaster; the ploughman may
Have heard the splash, the forsaken cry,
But for him it was not an important failure; the sun shone

As it had to on the white legs disappearing into the green
Water; and the expensive delicate ship that must have seen
Something amazing, a boy falling out of the sky
Had somewhere to get to and sailed calmly on.

57

C. S. Lewis, "Animal Pain"

The continued appeal of Augustinian Christianity is proved by the enduring popularity of the apologetic works of the English medievalist and
novelist Clive Staples Lewis (1898–1963). A convert to Christianity in
adulthood, Lewis never downplayed what he saw as the irreconcilability of
a traditional Christian worldview and the values of modern, scientific
culture. Lewis thought the "problem of pain" a problem *only* for religious
people: if you have no reason to expect moral order in experience, you
should not be disappointed by apparent disorder. Lewis accounts for human
pain in terms of "the old Christian doctrine of being made 'perfect through
suffering' [Heb. ii.10]." Indeed, he does this so thoroughly that the question
turns around: if pain is necessary medicine for sinful souls, "the real problem
is not why some humble, pious, believing people suffer, but why some do
not." None of these arguments applies to the suffering of animals, however,
and if Lewis's speculations below are unconvincing, they at least have the
rare virtue of taking the problem seriously.

C. S. Lewis, *The Problem of Pain* (New York: Collier, 1962 [1940]), 129–36,
138–43.

And whatsoever Adam called every living creature, that was the name thereof.

Genesis ii:19

To find out what is natural, we must study specimens which retain their nature
and not those which have been corrupted.

Aristotle, Politics, I.v.5

. . . The problem of animal suffering is appalling; not because the animals
are so numerous (for, as we have seen, no more pain is felt when a million

suffer than when one suffers) but because the Christian explanation of human pain cannot be extended to animal pain. So far as we know beasts are incapable either of sin or virtue: therefore they can neither deserve pain nor be improved by it. At the same time we must never allow the problem of animal suffering to become the centre of the problem of pain; not because it is unimportant – whatever furnishes plausible grounds for questioning the goodness of God is very important indeed – but because it is outside the range of our knowledge. God has given us data which enable us, in some degree, to understand our own suffering: He has given us no such data about beasts. We know neither why they were made nor what they are, and everything we say about them is speculative. From the doctrine that God is good we may confidently deduce that the *appearance* of reckless divine cruelty in the animal kingdom is an illusion, and the fact that the only suffering we know at first hand (our own) turns out not to be a cruelty will make it easier to believe this. After that, everything is guess-work . . .

. . . [T]hree questions arise. There is, first, the question of fact; what do animals suffer? There is, secondly, the question of origin; how did disease and pain enter the animal world? And, thirdly, there is the question of justice; how can animal suffering be reconciled with the justice of God?

1. In the long run the answer to the first question is, We don't know; but some speculations may be worth setting down. We must begin by distinguishing among animals: . . . Clearly in some ways the ape and man are much more like each other than either is like the worm . . . At some point, however (though where, we cannot say), sentience almost certainly comes in, for the higher animals have nervous systems very like our own. But at this level we must still distinguish sentience from consciousness . . . Suppose that three sensations follow one another – first A, then B, then C. When this happens to you, you have the experience of passing through the process ABC. But note what this implies. It implies that there is something in you which stands sufficiently outside A to notice A passing away, and sufficiently outside B to notice B now beginning and coming to fill the place which A has vacated; and something which recognises itself as the same through the transition from A to B and B to C, so that it can say "I have had the experience ABC." Now this something is what I call Consciousness or Soul, and the process I have just described is one of the proofs that the soul, though experiencing time, is not itself completely "timeful." The simplest experience of ABC as a succession demands a soul which is not itself a mere succession of states, but rather a permanent bed along which these different portions of the stream of sensation

roll, and which recognises itself as the same beneath them all. Now it is almost certain that the nervous system of one of the higher animals presents it with successive sensations. It does not follow that it has any "soul," anything which recognises itself as having had A, and now having B, and now marking how B glides away to make room for C. If it had no such "soul," what we call the experience ABC would never occur . . . Such sentience without consciousness, I admit, we cannot imagine: not because it never occurs in us, but because, when it does, we describe ourselves as being "unconscious." . . .

At least a great deal of what appears to be animal suffering need not be suffering in any real sense. It may be we who have invented the "sufferers" by the "pathetic fallacy" of reading into the beast a self for which there is no real evidence.

2. The origin of animal suffering could be traced, by earlier generations, to the Fall of man – the whole world was infected by the uncreating rebellion of Adam. This is now impossible, for we have good reason to believe that animals existed long before men. Carnivorousness, with all that it entails, is older than humanity. Now it is impossible at this point not to remember a certain sacred story which, though never included in the creeds, has been widely believed in the Church and seems to be implied in several Dominican, Pauline, and Johannine utterances – I mean the story that man was not the first creature to rebel against the Creator, *Satan* but that some older and mightier being long since became apostate and is now the emperor of darkness and (significantly) the Lord of this world . . .

It seems to me, therefore, a reasonable supposition, that some mighty created power had already been at work for ill on the material universe, or the solar system, or, at least, the planet Earth, before ever man came on the scene: and that when man fell, someone had, indeed, tempted him. This hypothesis is not introduced as a general "explanation of evil": it only gives a wider application to the principle that evil comes from the abuse of free will. If there is such a power, as I myself believe, it may well have corrupted the animal creation before man appeared. The intrinsic evil of the animal world lies in the fact that animals, or some animals, live by destroying each other. That plants do the same I will not admit to be an evil. The Satanic corruption of the beasts would therefore be analogous, in one respect, to the Satanic corruption of man. For one result of man's fall was that his animality fell back from the humanity into which it had been taken up but which could no longer rule it. In the same way, animality may have been encouraged to slip back into behaviour proper to vegetables . . . If it offends less, you may say that the "life-force" is corrupted, where I say that living creatures were corrupted by an evil angelic being . . .

If this hypothesis is worth considering, it is also worth considering whether man, at his first coming into the world, had not already a redemptive function to perform. Man, even now, can do wonders to animals: my cat and dog live together in my house and seem to like it. It may have been one of man's functions to restore peace to the animal world, and if he had not joined the enemy he might have succeeded in doing so to an extent now hardly imaginable.

3. Finally, there is the question of justice. We have seen reason to believe that not all animals suffer as we think they do: but some, at least, look as if they had selves, and what shall be done for these innocents? And we have seen that it is possible to believe that animal pain is not God's handiwork but begun by Satan's malice and perpetuated by man's desertion of his post: still, if God has not caused it, He has permitted it, and, once again, what shall be done for these innocents? . . .

. . . The error we must avoid is that of considering them in themselves. Man is to be understood only in his relation to God. The beasts are to be understood only in their relation to man and, through man, to God. Let us here guard against one of those untransmuted lumps of atheistical thought which often survive in the minds of modern believers. Atheists naturally regard the existence of man and the other animals as a mere contingent result of interacting biological facts; and the taming of an animal by a man as a purely arbitrary interference of one species with another. The "real" or "natural" animal to them is the wild one, and the tame animal is an artificial or unnatural thing. But a Christian must not think so. Man was appointed by God to have dominion over the beasts, and everything a man does to an animal is either a lawful exercise, or a sacrilegious abuse, of an authority by divine right. The tame animal is therefore, in the deepest sense, the only "natural" animal – the only one we see occupying the place it was made to occupy, and it is on the tame animal that we must base all our doctrine of beasts. Now it will be seen that, in so far as the tame animal has a real self or personality, it owes this almost entirely to its master. If a good sheepdog seems "almost human" that is because a good shepherd has made it so . . . you must not think of a beast by itself, and call that a personality and then inquire whether God will raise and bless that. You must take the whole context in which the beast acquires its selfhood – namely "The-goodman-and-the-goodwife-ruling-their-children-and-their-beasts-in-the-good-homestead." That whole context may be regarded as a "body" in the Pauline (or a closely sub-Pauline) sense; and how much of that "body" may be raised along with the goodman and the goodwife, who can predict? . . .

[A] future happiness connected with the beast's present life simply as a compensation for suffering – so many millenniums in the happy pastures paid down as "damages" for so many years of pulling carts – seems a clumsy assertion of Divine goodness. We, because we are fallible, often hurt a child or an animal unintentionally, and then the best we can do is to "make up for it" by some caress or tit-bit. But it is hardly pious to imagine omniscience acting in that way – as though God trod on the animals' tails in the dark and then did the best He could about it! In such a botched adjustment I cannot recognise the master-touch; whatever the answer is, it must be something better than that.

58

Simone Weil, "The Love of God and Affliction"

The phenomenology of *malheur* (the English "affliction" does not capture its sense of inevitability and doom) of French social activist, philosopher, and mystic Simone Weil (1909–43) puts the lie to sanguine views of the edifying character of suffering. Weil led a life of self-sacrificing political work and, after a conversion experience in 1938, developed a powerful mystical philosophy that combined arguments from ancient thought (especially Plato and the Stoics) and Hinduism with Christian language and imagery. (The essay below is at heart a meditation on the cross.) Weil thought most people are defenseless before *malheur* – especially in the modern west. Unless we retrieve resources to help us find God in our own powerlessness, *malheur* will simply destroy us, body and soul.

Simone Weil, "The Love of God and Affliction," in *Waiting for God*, trans. Emma Craufurd (New York: Harper & Row, 1951), 117, 119–22, 123–9, 132, 134–5.

In the realm of suffering, affliction is something apart, specific, and irreducible. It is quite a different thing from simple suffering. It takes possession of the soul and marks it through and through with its own particular mark, the mark of slavery. Slavery as practiced by ancient Rome is only an extreme form of affliction. The men of antiquity, who knew all about this question, used to say: "A man loses half his soul the day he becomes a slave."

Affliction is inseparable from physical suffering and yet quite distinct . . .

There is not real affliction unless the event that has seized and uprooted a life attacks it, directly or indirectly, in all its parts, social, psychological, and physical. The social factor is essential. There is not really affliction unless there is social degradation or the fear of it in some form or another.

There is both continuity and the separation of a definite point of entry, as with the temperature at which water boils, between affliction itself and all the sorrows that, even though they may be very violent, very deep and very lasting, are not affliction in the strict sense. There is a limit; on the far side of it we have affliction but not on the near side. This limit is not purely objective; all sorts of personal factors have to be taken into account. The same event may plunge one human being into affliction and not another.

The great enigma of human life is not suffering but affliction. It is not surprising that the innocent are killed, tortured, driven from their country, made destitute, or reduced to slavery, imprisoned in camps or cells, since there are criminals to perform such actions. It is not surprising either that disease is the cause of long sufferings, which paralyze life and make it into an image of death, since nature is at the mercy of the blind play of mechanical necessities. But it is surprising that God should have given affliction the power to seize the very souls of the innocent and to take possession of them as their sovereign lord. At the very best, he who is branded by affliction will keep only half his soul.

As for those who have been struck by one of those blows that leave a being struggling on the ground like a halfcrushed worm, they have no words to express what is happening to them. Among the people they meet, those who have never had contact with affliction in its true sense can have no idea of what it is, even though they may have suffered a great deal. Affliction is something specific and impossible to describe in any other terms, as sounds are to anyone who is deaf and dumb. And as for those who have themselves been mutilated by affliction, they are in no state to help anyone at all, and they are almost incapable of even wishing to do so. Thus compassion for the afflicted is an impossibility. When it is really found we have a more astounding miracle than walking on water, healing the sick, or even raising the dead.

Affliction constrained Christ to implore that he might be spared, to seek consolation from man, to believe he was forsaken by the Father. It forced a just man to cry out against God, a just man as perfect as human nature can be, more so, perhaps, if Job is less a historical character than a figure of Christ. "He laughs at the affliction of the innocent!" [Job 9:23] This is not blasphemy but a genuine cry of anguish. The Book of Job is a pure marvel of truth and authenticity from beginning to end. As regards affliction, all that departs from this model is more or less stained with falsehood.

Affliction makes God appear to be absent for a time, more absent than a dead man, more absent than light in the utter darkness of a cell. A kind of horror submerges the whole soul. During this absence there is nothing to love. What is terrible is that if, in this darkness where there is nothing to love, the soul ceases to love, God's absence becomes final. The soul has to go on loving in the emptiness, or at least to go on wanting to love, though it may only be with an infinitesimal part of itself. Then, one day, God will come to show himself to this soul and to reveal the beauty of the world to it, as in the case of Job. But if the soul stops loving it falls, even in this life, into something almost equivalent to hell.

That is why those who plunge men into affliction before they are prepared to receive it kill their souls. On the other hand, in a time such as ours, where affliction is hanging over us all, help given to souls is effective only if it goes far enough really to prepare them for affliction. That is no small thing.

Affliction hardens and discourages us because, like a red hot iron, it stamps the soul to its very depths with the scorn, the disgust, and even the self-hatred and sense of guilt and defilement that crime logically should produce but actually does not. Evil dwells in the heart of the criminal without being felt there. It is felt in the heart of the man who is afflicted and innocent. Everything happens as though the state of soul suitable for criminals had been separated from crime and attached to affliction; and it even seems to be in proportion to the innocence of those who are afflicted.

If Job cries out that he is innocent in such despairing accents, it is because he himself is beginning not to believe in it; it is because his soul within him is taking the side of his friends. He implores God himself to bear witness, because he no longer hears the testimony of his own conscience; it is no longer anything but an abstract, lifeless memory for him . . .

One can only accept the existence of affliction by considering it at a distance.

God created through love and for love. God did not create anything except love itself, and the means to love. He created love in all its forms. He created beings capable of love from all possible distances. Because no other could do it, he himself went to the greatest possible distance, the infinite distance. This infinite distance between God and God, this supreme tearing apart, this agony beyond all others, this marvel of love, is the crucifixion. Nothing can be further from God than that which has been made accursed.

This tearing apart, over which supreme love places the bond of supreme union, echoes perpetually across the universe in the midst of the silence, like two notes, separate yet melting into one, like pure and heart-rending harmony. This is the Word of God. The whole creation is nothing but its vibration. When human music in its greatest purity pierces our soul, this is what we hear through it. When we have learned to hear the silence, this is what we grasp more distinctly through it . . .

Men struck down by affliction are at the foot of the Cross, almost at the greatest possible distance from God. It must not be thought that sin is a greater distance. Sin is not a distance, it is a turning of our gaze in the wrong direction.

It is true that there is a mysterious connection between this distance and an original disobedience. From the beginning, we are told, humanity turned its gaze away from God and walked in the wrong direction for as far as it could go. That was because it could walk then. As for us, we are nailed down to the spot, only free to choose which way we look, ruled by necessity. A blind mechanism, heedless of degrees of spiritual perfection, continually tosses men about and throws some of them at the very foot of the Cross. It rests with them to keep or not to keep their eyes turned toward God through all the jolting. It does not mean that God's Providence is lacking. It is in his Providence that God has willed that necessity should be like a blind mechanism.

If the mechanism were not blind there would not be any affliction. Affliction is anonymous before all things; it deprives its victims of their personality and makes them into things. It is indifferent; and it is the coldness of this indifference – a metallic coldness – that freezes all those it touches right to the depths of their souls. They will never find warmth again. They will never believe any more that they are anyone . . .

Lovers or friends desire two things. The one is to love each other so much that they enter into each other and only make one being. The other is to love each other so much that, with half the globe between them, their union will not be diminished in the slightest degree. All that man vainly desires here below is perfectly realized in God. We have all those impossible desires within us as a mark of our destination, and they are good for us when we no longer hope to accomplish them.

The love between God and God, which in itself is God, is this bond of double virtue: the bond that unites two beings so closely that they are no longer distinguishable and really form a single unity and the bond that stretches across distance and triumphs over infinite separation. The unity of God, wherein all plurality disappears, and the abandonment, wherein

Christ believes he is left while never ceasing to love his Father perfectly, these are two forms expressing the divine virtue of the same Love, the Love that is God himself.

God is so essentially love that the unity, which in a sense is his actual definition, is the pure effect of love. Moreover corresponding to the infinite virtue of unification belonging to this love, there is the infinite separation over which it triumphs, which is the whole creation spread throughout the totality of space and time, made of mechanically harsh matter and interposed between Christ and his Father.

As for us men, our misery gives us the infinitely precious privilege of sharing in this distance placed between the Son and his Father. This distance is only separation, however for those who love. For those who love, separation, although painful, is a good, because it is love. Even the distress of the abandoned Christ is a good. There cannot be a greater good for us on earth than to share in it. God can never be perfectly present to us here below on account of our flesh. But he can be almost perfectly absent from us in extreme affliction. This is the only possibility of perfection for us on earth. That is why the Cross is our only hope. "No forest bears such a tree, with such blossoms, such foliage, and such fruit."

This universe where we are living, and of which we form a tiny particle, is the distance put by Love between God and God. We are a point in this distance. Space, time, and the mechanism that governs matter are the distance. Everything that we call evil is only this mechanism. God has provided that when his grace penetrates to the very center of a man and from there illuminates all his being, he is able to walk on the water without violating any of the laws of nature. When, however, a man turns away from God, he simply gives himself up to the law of gravity. Then he thinks that he can decide and choose, but he is only a thing, a stone that falls. If we examine human society and souls closely and with real attention, we see that wherever the virtue of supernatural light is absent, everything is obedient to mechanical laws as blind and as exact as the laws of gravitation. To know this is profitable and necessary. Those whom we call criminals are only tiles blown off a roof by the wind and falling at random. Their only fault is the initial choice by which they became such tiles.

The mechanism of necessity can be transposed to any level while still remaining true to itself. It is the same in the world of pure matter, in the animal world, among nations, and in souls. Seen from our present standpoint, and in human perspective, it is quite blind. If, however, we transport our hearts beyond ourselves, beyond the universe, beyond space and time to where our Father dwells, and if from there we behold this mechanism, it appears quite different. What seemed to be necessity becomes obedience. Matter is entirely passive and in consequence entirely obedient to God's will. It is a perfect model for us. There cannot be any being other than God and that which obeys God. On account of its perfect obedience, matter deserves to be loved by those who love its Master, in the same way as a needle, handled by the beloved wife he has lost, is cherished by a lover. The beauty of the world gives us an intimation of its claim to a place in our heart. In the beauty of the world brute necessity becomes an object of love. What is more beautiful than the action of gravity on the fugitive folds of the sea waves, or on the almost eternal folds of the mountains?

The sea is not less beautiful in our eyes because we know that sometimes ships are wrecked by it. On the contrary, this adds to its beauty. If it altered the movement of its waves to spare a boat, it would be a creature gifted with discernment and choice and not this fluid, perfectly obedient to every external pressure. It is this perfect obedience that constitutes the sea's beauty.

All the horrors produced in this world are like the folds imposed upon the waves by gravity. That is why they contain an element of beauty. Sometimes a poem, such as the *Iliad*, brings this beauty to light.

Men can never escape from obedience to God. A creature cannot but obey. The only choice given to men, as intelligent and free creatures, is to desire obedience or not to desire it . . .

Joy and suffering are two equally precious gifts both of which must be savored to the full, each one in its purity, without trying to mix them. Through joy, the beauty of the world penetrates our soul. Through suffering it penetrates our body . . . On the plane of physical sensibility, suffering alone gives us contact with that necessity which constitutes the order of the world, for pleasure does not involve an impression of necessity. It is a higher kind of sensibility, capable of recognizing a necessity in joy, and that only indirectly through a sense of beauty. In order that our being should one day become wholly sensitive in every part to this obedience that is the substance of matter, in order that a new sense should be formed in us to enable us to hear the universe as the vibration of the word of God, the transforming power of suffering and of joy are equally indispensable . . .

But affliction is not suffering. Affliction is something quite distinct from a method of God's teaching . . .

When we hit a nail with a hammer, the whole of the shock received by the large head of the nail passes into the point without any of it being lost, although it is only a point. If the hammer and the head of the nail were infinitely big it would be just the same. The point of the nail would transmit this infinite shock at the point to which it was applied.

Extreme affliction, which means physical pain, distress of soul, and social degradation, all at the same time, is a nail whose point is applied at the very center of the soul, whose head is all necessity spreading throughout space and time.

Affliction is a marvel of divine technique. It is a simple and ingenious device which introduces into the soul of a finite creature the immensity of force, blind, brutal, and cold. The infinite distance separating God from the creature is entirely concentrated into one point to pierce the soul in its center.

The man to whom such a thing happens has no part in the operation. He struggles like a butterfly pinned alive into an album. But through all the horror he can continue to want to love. There is nothing impossible in that, no obstacle, one might almost say no difficulty. For the greatest suffering, so long as it does not cause the soul to faint, does not touch the acquiescent part of the soul, consenting to a right direction.

It is only necessary to know that love is a direction and not a state of the soul. If one is unaware of this, one falls into despair at the first onslaught of affliction.

He whose soul remains ever turned toward God though the nail pierces it finds himself nailed to the very center of the universe. It is the true center; it is not in the middle; it is beyond space and time; it is God. In a dimension that does not belong to space, that is not time, that is indeed quite a different dimension, this nail has pierced cleanly through all creation, through the thickness of the screen separating the soul from God.

59

C. G. Jung, *Aion*

The analytic psychology of Carl Gustav Jung (1875–1961) seeks wholeness, the integration of antitheses as individuals achieve harmony between the conscious and unconscious and "come to selfhood." In the context of a discussion of Christ as a symbol of the self in *Aion* (1951), Jung launched an extended attack on the doctrine of evil as privation, a view he thought gave the very real power of evil free rein in human life. "As long as Satan is not integrated, the world is not healed and man is not saved," he told Mircea Eliade in 1952; "But Satan represents evil, and how can evil be integrated? There is only one possibility: to assimilate it, that is to say, raise it to the level of consciousness. This is done by means of a very complicated symbolic process which is more or less identical with the psychological process of individuation."

C. G. Jung, *Aion: Researches into the Phenomenology of the Self*, 2nd edn., trans. R. F. C. Hull (Bollingen Series XX) (Princeton: Princeton University Press, 1959), 41–3, 53–5, 61–2.

[74] There can be no doubt that the original Christian conception of the *imago Dei* embodied in Christ meant an all embracing totality that even includes the animal side of man. Nevertheless the Christ-symbol lacks wholeness in the modern psychological sense, since it does not include the dark side of things but specifically excludes it in the form of a Luciferian opponent. Although the exclusion of the power of evil was something the Christian consciousness was well aware of, all it lost in effect was an insubstantial shadow, for, through the doctrine of the *privatio boni* first propounded by Origen, evil was characterized as a mere diminution of good and thus deprived of substance. According to the teachings of the

Church, evil is simply "the accidental lack of perfection." This assumption resulted in the proposition "omne bonum a Deo, omne malum ab homine." Another logical consequence was the subsequent elimination of the devil in certain Protestant sects.

[75] Thanks to the doctrine of the *privatio boni*, wholeness seemed guaranteed in the figure of Christ. One must, however take evil rather more substantially when one meets it on the plane of empirical psychology. There it is simply the opposite of good. In the ancient world the Gnostics, whose arguments were very much influenced by psychic experience, tackled the problem of evil on a broader basis than the Church Fathers. For instance, one of the things they taught was that Christ "cast off his shadow from himself." If we give this view the weight it deserves, we can easily recognize the cut-off counterpart in the figure of Antichrist. The Antichrist develops in legend as a perverse imitator of Christ's life. He . . . follows in Christ's footsteps like a shadow following the body. This complementing of the bright but one-sided figure of the Redeemer – we even find traces of it in the New Testament – must be of especial significance. And indeed, considerable attention was paid to it quite early.

[76] If we see the traditional figure of Christ as a parallel to the psychic manifestation of the self, then the Antichrist would correspond to the shadow of the self, namely the dark half of the human totality, which ought not to be judged too optimistically. So far as we can judge from experience, light and shadow are so evenly distributed in man's nature that his psychic totality appears, to say the least of it, in a somewhat murky light. The psychological concept of the self, in part derived from our knowledge of the whole man, but for the rest depicting itself spontaneously in the products of the unconscious as an archetypal quaternity bound together by inner antinomies, cannot omit the shadow that belongs to the light figure, for without it this figure lacks body and humanity. In the empirical self, light and shadow form a paradoxical unity. In the Christian concept, on the other hand, the archetype is hopelessly split into two irreconcilable halves, leading ultimately to a metaphysical dualism – the final separation of the kingdom of heaven from the fiery world of the damned.

[77] For anyone who has a positive attitude towards Christianity the problem of the Antichrist is a hard nut to crack. It is nothing less than the counterstroke of the devil, provoked by God's Incarnation; for the devil attains his true stature as the adversary of Christ, and hence of God, only after the rise of Christianity, while as late as the Book of Job he was still one of God's sons and on familiar terms with Yahweh. Psychologically the case is clear, since the dogmatic figure of Christ is so sublime and spot-

less that everything else turns dark beside it. It is, in fact, so one-sidedly perfect that it demands a psychic complement to restore the balance. This inevitable opposition led very early to the doctrine of the two sons of God, of whom the elder was called Satanael. The coming of the Antichrist is not just a prophetic prediction – it is an inexorable psychological law whose existence, though unknown to the author of the Johannine Epistles, brought him a sure knowledge of the impending enantiodromia . . .

[97] Psychology does not know what good and evil are in themselves; it knows them only as judgments about relationships. "Good" is what seems suitable, acceptable, or valuable from a certain point of view; evil is its opposite. If the things we call good are "really" good, then there must be evil things that are "real" too. It is evident that psychology is concerned with a more or less subjective judgment, i.e., with a psychic antithesis that cannot be avoided in naming value relationships: "good" denotes something that is not bad, and "bad" something that is not good. There are things which from a certain point of view are extremely evil, that is to say dangerous. There are also things in human nature which are very dangerous and which therefore seem proportionately evil to anyone standing in their line of fire. It is pointless to gloss over these evil things, because that only lulls one into a sense of false security. Human nature is capable of an infinite amount of evil, and the evil deeds are as real as the good ones so far as human experience goes and so far as the psyche judges and differentiates between them. Only unconsciousness makes no difference between good and evil. Inside the psychological realm one honestly does not know which of them predominates in the world. We hope, merely, that good does – i.e., what seems suitable to us. No one could possibly say what the general good might be. No amount of insight into the relativity and fallibility of our moral judgment can deliver us from these defects, and those who deem themselves beyond good and evil are usually the worst tormentors of mankind, because they are twisted with the pain and fear of their own sickness.

[98] Today as never before it is important that human beings should not overlook the danger of the evil lurking within them. It is unfortunately only too real, which is why psychology must insist on the reality of evil and must reject any definition that regards it as insignificant or actually non-existent . . . My criticism of the *privatio boni* holds only so far as psychological experience goes. From the scientific point of view, the *privatio boni*, as must be apparent to everyone, is founded on a *petitio principii*, where what invariably comes out at the end is what you put in at the beginning. Arguments of this kind have no power of conviction. But the fact that such arguments are not only used but are undoubtedly

believed is something that cannot be disposed of so easily. It proves that there is a tendency, existing right from the start, to give priority to "good," and to do so with all the means in our power, whether suitable or unsuitable. So if Christian metaphysics clings to the *privatio boni*, it is giving expression to the tendency always to increase the good and diminish the bad. The *privatio boni* may therefore be a metaphysical truth. I presume to no judgment on this matter. I must only insist that in our field of experience white and black, light and dark, good and bad, are equivalent opposites which always predicate one another.

[99] This elementary fact was correctly appreciated in the so-called Clementine Homilies, a collection of Gnostic-Christian writings dating from about AD 150. The unknown author understands good and evil as the right and left hand of God, and views the whole of creation in terms of syzygies, or pairs of opposites. In much the same way the follower of Bardesanes, Marinus, sees good as "light" and pertaining to the right hand, and evil as "dark" and pertaining to the left hand. The left also corresponds to the feminine. Thus in Irenaeus (*Adv. haer.*, I, 30, 3), Sophia Prounikos is called Sinistra. Clement finds this altogether compatible with the idea of God's unity. Provided that one has an anthropomorphic God-image – and every God-image is anthropomorphic in a more or less subtle way – the logic and naturalness of Clement's view can hardly be contested. At all events this view, which may be some two hundred years older than the quotations given above, proves that the reality of evil does not necessarily lead to Manichaean dualism and so does not endanger the unity of the God-image. As a matter of fact, it guarantees that unity on a plane beyond the crucial difference between the Yahwistic and the Christian points of view. Yahweh is notoriously unjust, and injustice is not good. The God of Christianity, on the other hand, is *only* good. There is no denying that Clement's theology helps us to get over this contradiction in a way that fits the psychological facts . . .

[113] I have gone into the doctrine of the *privatio boni* at such length because it is in a sense responsible for a too optimistic conception of the evil in human nature and for a too pessimistic view of the human soul. To offset this, early Christianity, with unerring logic, balanced Christ against an Antichrist. For how can you speak of "high" if there is no "low," or "right" if there is no "left," of "good" if there is no "bad," and the one is as real as the other? Only with Christ did a devil enter the World as the real counterpart of God, and in early Jewish-Christian circles Satan, as already mentioned, was regarded as Christ's elder brother.

[114] But there is still another reason why I must lay such critical stress on the *privatio boni*. As early as Basil we meet with the tendency to

attribute evil to the disposition of the soul, and at the same time to give it a "non-existent" character. Since, according to this author, evil originates in human frivolity and therefore owes its existence to mere negligence, it exists, so to speak, only as a by-product of psychological oversight, and this is such a *quantité négligeable* that evil vanishes altogether in smoke. Frivolity as a cause of evil is certainly a factor to be taken seriously, but it is a factor that can be got rid of by a change of attitude. We can act differently, if we want to. Psychological causation is something so elusive and seemingly unreal that everything which is reduced to it inevitably takes on the character of futility or of a purely accidental mistake and is thereby minimized to the utmost. It is an open question how much of our modern undervaluation of the psyche stems from this prejudice. This prejudice is all the more serious in that it causes the psyche to be suspected of being the birthplace of all evil. The Church Fathers can hardly have considered what a fatal power they were ascribing to the soul. One must be positively blind not to see the colossal role that evil plays in the world. Indeed, it took the intervention of God himself to deliver humanity from the curse of evil, for without his intervention man would have been lost. If this paramount power of evil is imputed to the soul, the result can only be a negative inflation – i.e., a daemonic claim to power on the part of the unconscious which makes it all the more formidable. This unavoidable consequence is anticipated in the figure of the Antichrist and is reflected in the course of contemporary events . . .

60

The "Serenity Prayer"

Probably the only selection in this reader to grace refrigerator doors and websites, the "Serenity Prayer" is a staple of contemporary religious and therapeutic culture. Its evolution provides a good illustration of the way powerful religious ideas and texts spread – and change.

The first version below is the work of the mid-twentieth-century American Protestant theologian Reinhold *Niebuhr* (1892–1971). Niebuhr apparently used it in a sermon during the Second World War, first publishing it in a newspaper column in 1951. Niebuhr reported that he was asked if he had found it in *Marcus Aurelius*. Marcus Aurelius was the most famous student of *Epictetus*, the starting point of whose work is the importance of distinguishing those things under our control from those which aren't. (See p. 23 above.)

The second version, which asks for "courage to change the things we can" rather than "the courage to change what should be changed," is sometimes called the AA Prayer. *Alcoholics Anonymous* apparently encountered it in a newspaper obituary in 1942. "Never had we seen so much of AA in so few words." The prayer was included in all AA mailings for the next several years, and "with amazing speed the Serenity Prayer came into general use and took its place alongside our two other favorites, the Lord's Prayer and the Prayer of St. Francis."

At some point, the AA Prayer was extended into the third version below, which replaces the first-person plural with the first-person singular, and Christianizes it in a distinctively Evangelical idiom.

Richard Wightman Fox, *Reinhold Niebuhr: A Biography* (New York: Pantheon, 1985), 290; *Alcoholics Anonymous Comes of Age: A Brief History of A. A.* (New York: Alcoholics Anonymous Publishing, Inc., 1957), 196; and http://Open-Mind.org/Serenity.htm.

God, give us the serenity to accept what cannot be changed.
Give us the courage to change what should be changed.
Give us the wisdom to distinguish one from the other.

★ ★ ★ ★ ★ ★ ★

God grant us the serenity to accept the things we cannot change,
courage to change the things we can,
and wisdom to know the difference.

★ ★ ★ ★ ★ ★ ★

God, grant me the Serenity to accept the things I cannot change
Courage to change the things I can
and Wisdom to know the difference.
Living one day at a time,
Enjoying one moment at a time;
Accepting hardship as the pathway to peace.
Taking, as He did, this sinful world as it is, not as I would have it.
Trusting that He will make all things right if I surrender to His will.
That I may be reasonably happy in this life,
And supremely happy with Him forever in the next.
Amen.

61

Karl Barth, "God and Nothingness"

The Swiss Protestant theologian Karl Barth (1886–1968) attacked the very project of theodicy. Barth's Christocentric "dialectical theology," announced in the *Commentary on the Epistle to the Romans* (1919) and elaborated in the uncompleted *Church Dogmatics* (1932–67), argues that all man-made understandings of the world are false. Existentialists like Heidegger and Sartre sensed the problem, but not its solution: we can only know ourselves as sinful, and this only through Christ, who defeated evil: "the incarnation of the Word of God was obviously not necessary merely to reveal the goodness of God's creation." Evil, which Barth defines as *das Nichtige* (barely translatable as "nothingness"), is neither the Creator nor the creation; arising with creation, it is what God does not choose. Not just nonbeing, it constitutes an incomprehensible menace to creation. Christian tradition's awareness of *das Nichtige* was lost when Leibniz left *corruptio* and *conversio boni* (the aspects Ricoeur called "anti-gnostic Gnosis") out of the Augustinian idea of *privatio boni*; it is lost also in any effort to demythologize Satan and his demons. Enlightenment theodicy and liberal theology blind us to evil by confusing it with the "negative side" of creation. (It may be easier to read the second selection first.)

Karl Barth, *Church Dogmatics* III/3, § 50.1–2; trans. G. W. Bromily and R. J. Ehrlich (Edinburgh: T. & T. Clarke, 1960), 289–97.

The Problem of Nothingness

There is opposition and resistance to God's world-dominion. There is in world-occurrence an element, indeed an entire sinister system of elements, which is not comprehended by God's providence . . . , and which is not therefore preserved, accompanied, nor ruled by the almighty action of God like creaturely occurrence. It is an element to which God denies the benefit of His preservation, concurrence and rule, of His fatherly lordship and which is itself opposed to being preserved, accompanied and ruled in any sense, fatherly or otherwise. There is amongst the objects of God's providence an alien factor. It cannot escape God's providence but is comprehended by it. The manner, however, in which this is done is highly peculiar . . . It is distinct from that in which God's providence rules the creature and creaturely occurrence. The result is that the alien factor can never be considered or mentioned together in the same context as other objects of God's providence. Thus the whole doctrine of God's providence must be investigated afresh. This opposition and resistance, this stubborn element and alien factor may be provisionally defined as nothingness . . .

It would be comparatively easy to understand and state the doctrine of God's providence if it involved no more than the relationship between the lordship of God and creaturely occurrence as such . . . There would be no difficulty if only creaturely occurrence, though ruled by God, did not also stand under the determination of this alien factor, of nothingness. There would be no difficulty if only a careful consideration of this factor which also determines creaturely activity were not absolutely unavoidable if the doctrine of God's providence is not to ignore its most urgent question and to desist from giving its most important answer. Perpendicular lines from above can render it in some measure intelligible and clear, as we have already demonstrated, what takes place between God the Creator and the creature as God's royal dominion on the one side, and creaturely existence, life and occurrence under this dominion on the other. "Of him and through him, and to him are all things: to whom be glory for ever. Amen" (Rom. 11:36) . . . With regard to the good Creator and Lord, and the creature created good by Him, it could indeed be developed in straight (or apparently straight) lines. The truth of this scriptural saying must stand. Yet what does "of him, through him, and to him" mean in view of the fact that "all things," i.e., man first, but through him and for him all things, are also affected by nothingness, being enmeshed in and bound up with it, sharing its nature, bearing its marks, and in some degree, directly or indirectly, actively or passively, overtly or covertly, being involved in the existence and operation of this alien factor? . . . Does not even the best which emerges from God's Word concerning His lordship over the creature remain unsaid if it is not also stated from the particular standpoint that it also belongs to the existence of life and activity of the creature to be involved in nothingness, and always to be partly determined by it in its present form? . . .

In this instance, however, we do not make any advance by drawing straight lines from above, i.e., by thinking and speaking in direct statements concerning the action of the Creator on and with His creature . . . [T]he peculiar factor now to be considered is that between the Creator and the creature, or more exactly the creaturely sphere under the lordship of the Creator, there is that at work which can be explained neither from the side of the Creator nor from that of the creature, neither as the action of the Creator nor as the life-act of the creature, and yet which cannot be overlooked or disowned but must be reckoned with in all its peculiarity. The simple recognition that God is Lord over all must obviously be applied to this third factor as well. Where would be the real situation of the real man or the real way of real trust of the real Christian, where would be the decisive truth and power of the doctrine of God's providence, if the knowledge that He is Lord over all were not applied especially to this element? But if God's lordship is applicable here too, how are we to avoid error on the one side or the other? We stray on the one side if we argue that this element of nothingness derives from the positive will and work of God as if it too were a creature, and that the Creator Himself and His lordship are responsible for its nothingness, the creature being exonerated from all responsibility for its existence, presence and activity. But we go astray on the other side if we maintain that it derives solely from the activity of the creature, in relation to which the lordship of God can only be a passive permission and observation, an ineffectual foreknowledge and a subsequent attitude. In the one case, the obvious error is to misinterpret the fact that God is Lord, to fail to understand that for that reason His lordship cannot be affected by nothingness. In the other case, the error is to misinterpret the meaning of lordship, namely, that God rules in sublime and unlimited majesty over every sphere, and therefore over that of nothingness as well. But how is it possible to avoid the one error without falling into the other? How can justice be done both to the holiness and to the omnipotence of God when we are faced by the problem of nothingness? How can the simple recognition that God is Lord over all be applied to this sphere? . . .

Yet it is also possible to go astray here in an entirely different manner. For it is clearly wrong to apply the basic recognition of God's lordship in such a way that nothingness in its relation of opposition and resistance to God's world-dominion assumes the form of a monster which, vested with demonic qualities, inspires fear and respect instead of awakening the Easter

joy that even in all its power as sin and evil it is no more than the nothingness which as such is already judged in Jesus Christ and can therefore
injure but no longer kill or destroy. Again, it is no less clearly wrong if
this victorious might of faith is treated as if it were a principle at our own
disposal, or if it is forgotten that the victory over nothingness can be ours
only through hope in Jesus Christ, or if we think and speak of this adversary, who was certainly not defeated by us, in any other way than in the
fear of God and the seriousness of faith. We describe the same dilemma
when we say that in considering the manner in which God disposes even
of nothingness, letting it have its course and yet overruling it for good,
there is the danger either of an uneasy, bleak and sceptical overestimating
of its power in relation to God, or of an easy, comfortable and dogmatic
underestimation of its power in relation to us. How are we to avoid both
an easy pessimism on the one side and a no less easy optimism on the
other? How are we to think and speak of God's lordship even over
nothingness with the necessary confidence and yet also the required
humility, the required humility and yet also the necessary confidence? . . .

It may be said at least that it can be so only as we soberly acknowledge that we have here an extraordinarily clear demonstration of the necessary brokenness of all theological thought and utterance. There is no
theological sphere where this is not noticeable. All theology is *theologia
viatorum*. It can never satisfy the natural aspiration of human thought
and utterance for completeness and compactness. It does not exhibit its
object but can only indicate it, and in so doing it owes the truth to the
self-witness of the theme and not to its own resources. It is broken thought
and utterance to the extent that it can progress only in isolated thoughts
and statements directed from different angles to the one object. It can
never form a system, comprehending and as it were "seizing" the object.
That is true of all theological assertions. It is true even of the perpendicular lines from above in which we have developed the general doctrine
of God's providence with regard to the relationship between the good
Creator and His good creature. But if we failed to see this there and elsewhere, here at last we must surely see and acknowledge that our knowledge is piece-work, and that only as such can it stand and make sense in
relation to its theme. But why is this true here, and therefore universally?
The reason is obvious. The existence, presence and operation of nothingness, which we are here concerned to discuss, are also objectively the break
in the relationship between Creator and creature. The existence, presence,
and operation of nothingness are not only the frontier which belongs to
the nature of this relationship on both sides and which is grounded in the

goodness of the Creator and that of the Creature. They are also the break which runs counter to the nature of this relationship, which is compatible with neither the goodness of the Creator nor that of the creature and which cannot be derived from either side but can only be regarded as hostility in relation to both. We are not now dealing with the break itself, but with God's relation to it, with His providence and the extent to which it comprehends this break as well. In this context, however, this break is our particular concern. For theology as a human activity, and under the presuppositions of the present dispensation knows its object solely under the shadow of this break. Objectively, it must always receive it from beyond this break. Hence it cannot even be aware of its object without also being aware of this break. And this means that theological thought and utterance must always be broken. Not even objectively is the relationship between Creator and creature a system. It is always disrupted by this alien element. Hence there can be no system in the subjective knowledge of this relationship, and therefore in theology. Does not this emerge with particular clarity when we have to deal specifically with God's providence in its relation to the nothingness with which His creature is involved? Here if anywhere it is imperative that theology, which is also a creaturely activity should acknowledge that it is bound up with nothingness, and cannot and must not try to escape it. Here if anywhere theology as the subjective reproduction of objective reality ought not to impose or simulate a system. Here especially theology must set an example for its procedure generally, corresponding to its object in broken thoughts and utterance . . .

This does not mean, of course, that we ought not to proceed here and everywhere with the greatest intellectual probity and with rigorous logic and objectivity. Here however – and not only here, but here with particular urgency by reason of the particular aspect of the theological object – the meaning of objectivity is that we must be prepared simply and without diminution to accept and take into account, each in its own place and manner, all the conflicting claims: the claim that God's holiness and omnipotence should be equally respected; the claim that we should think and speak of this matter with joy and also with seriousness; the claim that the power of nothingness should be rated as low as possible in relation to God and as high as possible in relation to ourselves. If we do this, it does not mean that we shall be led to a system nor to the complete and compact sequence of thoughts and statements yielded by a principle. On the contrary, the break itself and as such will be reproduced and reflected in our knowledge and its presentation; and not only the break, but in, with and above it the history in which it is after all – for God is Lord – no more than an alien, disruptive and retarding moment – the history of the Creator's dealings with His creature, of the doing of His will as it was in His counsel and as it will finally be fulfilled. This history, in the course of which this break occurs, is the object of theology. Theology is the record of this history. Hence it must consider all those claims in their place and manner. It must not be intent on unifications or mediations which are not to be found in the history. It must not degenerate into a system. It must always be related to that history. It must always be a report. It must not strain after completeness and compactness. Its aim must simply be to make the right report. This is the general and formal answer to the question how the simple recognition of God's universal lordship is rightly to be applied in view of the presence of nothingness as opposition and resistance to that lordship . . .

The Misconception of Nothingness

. . . It is true that in creation there is not only a Yes but also a No; not only a height but also an abyss; not only clarity but also obscurity; not only progress and continuation but also impediment and limitation; not only growth but also decay; not only opulence but also indigence; not only beauty but also ashes; not only beginning but also end; not only value but also worthlessness. It is true that in creaturely existence, and especially in the existence of man, there are hours, days and years both bright and dark, both success and failure, laughter and tears, youth and age, gain and loss, birth and sooner or later its inevitable corollary, death. It is true that individual creatures and men experience these things in most unequal measure, their lots being assigned by a justice which is curious or very much concealed. Yet it is irrefutable that creation and creature are good even in the fact that all that is exists in this contrast and antithesis. In all this, far from being null, it praises its Creator and Lord even on its shadowy side, even in the negative aspect in which it is so near to nothingness. If He Himself has comprehended creation in its totality and made it His own in His Son, it is for us to acquiesce without thinking that we know better, without complaints, reproach or dismay. For all that we can tell, may not His creatures praise Him more mightily in humility than in exaltation, in need than in plenty, in fear than in joy, on the frontier of nothingness than when wholly oriented on God? . . . [I]f there may also be praise of God from the abyss, the night and misfortune, and perhaps even from the darkest abyss, the darkest night and the greatest misfortune, why should we doubt the hidden justice which apportions the distinctions and contrasts to ourselves and others? . . . We aspire to be Christians, and no doubt in some small measure we are, but is it not strange that only in our few better moments can we make anything either theoretically or practically of the truth that the creation of God in both its aspects, even the negative, is His good creation?

62

John Hick, "The 'Vale of Soul-Making' Theodicy"

Evil and the God of Love by the English theologian and philosopher of religion John Hick (1922–) is the most influential recent study of theodicy and its history. In response to critiques of theodicy like Barth's, Hick argues that the problem of theodicy is "unavoidable . . . in virtue of the nature of the world and of the essential character of the Christian understanding of God." Following the Christian existentialist Gabriel Marcel, Hick distinguishes between the "mystery" of evil "to be encountered and lived through" by sufferers, and the "problem" of evil confronting spectators. "It is true that the intellectual problem, which invites rational reflection, is distinct from the experienced mystery, which must be faced in the actual business of living, and that to a certain extent the one excludes the other from our attention. But it does not at all follow from this that the intellectual problem of evil is a false or an unreal problem, or that our obligation to grapple with it is in any degree lessened." Hick's own theodicy builds on the "Irenaean" tradition he describes below, but does not aspire to be more than "negative": "The aim of a Christian theodicy must . . . be the relatively modest and defensive one of showing that the mystery of evil, largely incomprehensible though it remains, does not render irrational a faith that has arisen, not from the inferences of natural theology, but from participation in a stream of religious experience which is continuous with that recorded in the Bible."

John Hick, *Evil and the God of Love*, rev. edn. (New York: Harper SanFrancisco, 1977 [1966]), 253–61.

. . . As well as the "majority report" of the Augustinian tradition, which has dominated Western Christendom, both Catholic and Protestant, since the time of Augustine himself, there is the "minority report" of the Irenaean tradition. This latter is both older and newer than the other, for it goes back to St. Irenaeus and others of the early Hellenistic Fathers of the Church in the two centuries prior to St. Augustine, and it has flourished again in more developed forms during the last hundred years.

Instead of regarding man as having been created by God in a finished state, as a finitely perfect being fulfilling the divine intention for our human level of existence, and then falling disastrously away from this, the minority report sees man as still in process of creation. Irenaeus himself expressed the point in terms of the (exegetically dubious) distinction between the "image" and the "likeness" of God referred to in Genesis i. 26: "Then God said, Let us make man in our image, after our likeness." His view was that man as a personal and moral being already exists in the image, but has not yet been formed into the finite likeness of God. By this "likeness" Irenaeus means something more than personal existence as such; he means a certain valuable quality of personal life which reflects finitely the divine life. This represents the perfecting of man, the fulfilment of God's purpose for humanity, the "bringing of many sons to glory" [Heb. 2:10], the creating of "children of God" who are "fellow heirs with Christ" of his glory [Rom. 8:17].

And so man, created as a personal being in the image of God, is only the raw material for a further and more difficult stage of God's creative work. This is the leading of men as relatively free and autonomous persons, through their own dealings with life in the world in which He has placed them, towards that quality of personal existence that is the finite likeness of God. The features of this likeness are revealed in the person of Christ, and the process of man's creation into it is the work of the Holy Spirit. In St. Paul's words, "And we all, with unveiled faces, beholding the glory of the Lord, are being changed into his likeness . . . from one degree of glory to another; for this comes from the Lord who is the Spirit" [2 Cor. 3:18], or again, "For God knew his own before ever they were, and also ordained that they should be shaped to the likeness of his Son" [Rom. 8:29; cf. Eph. 2:21, 3:16; Col. 2:19; 1 Jn. 3:2; 2 Cor. 4:16]. In Johannine terms, the movement from the image to the likeness is a transition from one level of existence, that of animal life (*Bios*), to another and higher level, that of eternal life (*Zoe*), which includes but transcends the first. And the fall of man was seen by Irenaeus as a failure within the second phase of this creative process, a failure that has multiplied the perils and complicated the route of the journey in which God is seeking to lead mankind.

In the light of modern anthropological knowledge some form of two-stage conception of the creation of man has become an almost unavoidable Christian tenet. At the very least we must acknowledge as two distinguishable stages the fashioning of *homo sapiens* as a product of the long evolutionary process, and his sudden or gradual spiritualization as a child of God. But we may well extend the first stage to include the development of man as a rational and responsible person capable of personal relationship with the personal Infinite who has created him. This first stage of the creative process was, to our anthropomorphic imaginations, easy for divine omnipotence. By an exercise of creative power God caused the physical universe to exist, and in the course of countless ages to bring forth within it organic life, and finally to produce out of organic life personal life; and when man had thus emerged out of the evolution of the forms of organic life, a creature had been made who has the possibility of existing in conscious fellowship with God. But the second stage of the creative process is of a different kind altogether It cannot be performed by omnipotent power as such. For personal life is essentially free and self-directing. It cannot be perfected by divine fiat, but only through the uncompelled responses and willing co-operation of human individuals in their actions and reactions in the world in which God has placed them. Men may eventually become the perfected persons whom the New Testament calls "children of God", but they cannot be created ready-made as this.

The value-judgement that is implicitly being invoked here is that one who has attained to goodness by meeting and eventually mastering temptations, and thus by rightly making responsible choices in concrete situations, is good in a richer and more valuable sense than would be one created *ab initio* in a state either of innocence or of virtue. In the former case, which is that of the actual moral achievements of mankind, the individual's goodness has within it the strength of temptations overcome, a stability based upon an accumulation of right choices, and a positive and responsible character that comes from the investment of costly personal effort. I suggest, then, that it is an ethically reasonable judgement, even though in the nature of the case not one that is capable of demonstrative proof, that human goodness slowly built up through personal histories of moral effort has a value in the eyes of the Creator which justifies even the long travail of the soul-making process.

The picture with which we are working is thus developmental and teleological. Man is in process of becoming the perfected being whom God is seeking to create. However, this is not taking place – it is important to add – by a natural and inevitable evolution, but through a hazardous adventure in individual freedom. Because this is a pilgrimage within the life of each individual, rather than a racial evolution, the progressive fulfilment of God's purpose does not entail any corresponding progressive improvement in the moral state of the world. There is no doubt a development in man's ethical situation from generation to generation through the building of individual choices into public institutions, but this involves an accumulation of evil as well as of good. It is thus probable that human life was lived on much the same moral plane two thousand years ago or four thousand years ago as it is today. But nevertheless during this period uncounted millions of souls have been through the experience of earthly life, and God's purpose has gradually moved towards its fulfilment within each one of them, rather than within a human aggregate composed of different units in different generations.

If, then, God's aim in making the world is "the bringing of many sons to glory", that aim will naturally determine the kind of world that He has created. Antitheistic writers almost invariably assume a conception of the divine purpose which is contrary to the Christian conception. They assume that the purpose of a loving God must be to create a hedonistic paradise; and therefore to the extent that the world is other than this, it proves to them that God is either not loving enough or not powerful enough to create such a world. They think of God's relation to the earth on the model of a human being building a cage for a pet animal to dwell in. If he is humane he will naturally make his pet's quarters as pleasant and healthful as he can. Any respect in which the cage falls short of the veterinarian's ideal, and contains possibilities of accident or disease, is evidence of either limited benevolence or limited means, or both. Those who use the problem of evil as an argument against belief in God almost invariably think of the world in this kind of way. David Hume, for example, speaks of an architect who is trying to plan a house that is to be as comfortable and convenient as possible. If we find that "the windows, doors, fires, passages, stairs, and the whole economy of the building were the source of noise, confusion, fatigue, darkness, and the extremes of heat and cold" we should have no hesitation in blaming the architect. It would be in vain for him to prove that if this or that defect were corrected greater ills would result: "still you would assert in general, that, if the architect had had skill and good intentions, he might have formed such a plan of the whole, and might have adjusted the parts in such a manner, as would have remedied all or most of these inconveniences" [*Dialogues concerning Natural Religion*, xi].

But if we are right in supposing that God's purpose for man is to lead him from human *Bios*, or the biological life of man, to that quality of *Zoe*, or the personal life of eternal worth, which we see in Christ, then the question that we have to ask is not, Is this the kind of world that an all-powerful and infinitely loving being would create as an environment for his human pets? or, Is the architecture of the world the most pleasant and convenient possible? The question that we have to ask is rather, Is this the kind of world that God might make as an environment in which moral beings may be fashioned, through their own free insights and responses, into "children of God"?

Such critics as Hume are confusing what heaven ought to be, as an environment for perfected finite beings, with what this world ought to be, as an environment for beings who are in process of becoming perfected. For if our general conception of God's purpose is correct the world is not intended to be a paradise, but rather the scene of a history in which human personality may be formed towards the pattern of Christ. Men are not to be thought of on the analogy of animal pets, whose life is to be made as agreeable as possible, but rather on the analogy of human children, who are to grow to adulthood in an environment whose primary and overriding purpose is not immediate pleasure but the realizing of the most valuable potentialities of human personality.

Needless to say, this characterization of God as the heavenly Father is not a merely random illustration but an analogy that lies at the heart of the Christian faith. Jesus treated the likeness between the attitude of God to man, and the attitude of human parents at their best towards their children, as providing the most adequate way for us to think about God. And so it is altogether relevant to a Christian understanding of this world to ask, How does the best parental love express itself in its influence upon the environment in which children are to grow up? I think it is clear that a parent who loves his children, and wants them to become the best human beings that they are capable of becoming, does not treat pleasure as the sole and supreme value. Certainly we seek pleasure for our children, and take great delight in obtaining it for them; but we do not desire for them unalloyed pleasure at the expense of their growth in such even greater values as moral integrity, unselfishness, compassion, courage, humour, reverence for the truth, and perhaps above all the capacity for love. We do not act on the premise that pleasure is the supreme end of life; and if the development of these other values sometimes clashes with the provision of pleasure, then we are willing to have our children miss a certain amount of this, rather than fail to come to possess and to be possessed by the finer and more precious qualities that are possible to the human personality. A child brought up on the principle that the only or the supreme value is pleasure would not be likely to become an ethically mature adult or an attractive or happy personality. And to most parents it seems more important to try to foster quality and strength of character in their children than to fill their lives at all times with the utmost possible degree of pleasure. If, then, there is any true analogy between God's purpose for his human creatures, and the purpose of loving and wise parents for their children, we have to recognize that the presence of pleasure and the absence of pain cannot be the supreme and overriding end for which the world exists. Rather, this world must be a place of soul-making. And its value is to be judged, not primarily by the quantity of pleasure and pain occurring in it at any particular moment, but by its fitness for its primary purpose, the purpose of soul-making.

In all this we have been speaking about the nature of the world considered simply as the God-given environment of man's life. For it is mainly in this connection that the world has been regarded in Irenaean and in Protestant thought. But such a way of thinking involves a danger of anthropocentrism from which the Augustinian and Catholic tradition has generally been protected by its sense of the relative insignificance of man within the totality of the created universe. Man was dwarfed within the medieval world-view by the innumerable hosts of angels and archangels above him – unfallen rational natures which rejoice in the immediate presence of God, reflecting His glory in the untarnished mirror of their worship. However, this higher creation has in our modern world lost its hold upon the imagination. Its place has been taken, as the minimizer of men, by the immensities of outer space and by the material universe's unlimited complexity transcending our present knowledge . . . [T]he truth that was symbolized for former ages by the existence of the angelic hosts is today impressed upon us by the vastness of the physical universe, countering the egoism of our species by making us feel that this immense prodigality of existence can hardly all exist for the sake of man – though, on the other hand, the very realization that it is not all for the sake of man may itself be salutary and beneficial to man!

However, instead of opposing man and nature as rival objects of God's interest, we should perhaps rather stress man's solidarity as an embodied being with the whole natural order in which he is embedded. For man is organic to the world; all his acts and thoughts and imaginations are conditioned by space and time; and in abstraction from nature he would cease to be human. We may, then, say that the beauties and sublimities and powers, the microscopic intricacies and macroscopic vastnesses, the wonders and the terrors of the natural world and of the life that pulses through it, are willed and valued by their Maker in a creative act that embraces man together with nature. By means of matter and living flesh God both builds a path and weaves a veil between Himself and the creature made in His image. Nature thus has permanent significance; for God has set man in a creaturely environment, and the final fulfilment of our nature in relation to God will accordingly take the form of an embodied life within "a new heaven and a new earth" [Rev. 21:1]. And as in the present age man moves slowly towards that fulfilment through the pilgrimage of his earthly life, so also "the whole creation" is "groaning in travail", waiting for the time when it will be "set free from its bondage to decay" [Rom. 8:21–2].

And yet however fully we thus acknowledge the permanent significance and value of the natural order, we must still insist upon man's special character as a personal creature made in the image of God; and our theodicy must still centre upon the soul-making process that we believe to be taking place within human life.

This, then, is the starting-point from which we propose to try to relate the realities of sin and suffering to the perfect love of an omnipotent Creator. And as will become increasingly apparent, a theodicy that starts in this way must be eschatological in its ultimate bearings. That is to say, instead of looking to the past for its clue to the mystery of evil, it looks to the future, and indeed to that ultimate future to which only faith can look. Given the conception of a divine intention working in and through human time towards a fulfilment that lies in its completeness beyond human time, our theodicy must find the meaning of evil in the part that it is made to play in the eventual outworking of that purpose; and must find the justification of the whole process in the magnitude of the good to which it leads. The good that outshines all ill is not a paradise long since lost but a kingdom which is yet to come in its full glory and permanence.

63

William R. Jones,
Is God a White Racist?

It is often asserted that theodicy is the Achilles' heel of liberation theology: that God should be on the side of the poor or oppressed does not yet explain why there is poverty or oppression in the first place. The black religious humanist William R. Jones (1933–) forced this question in the context of Black theology in America. Influenced by the existentialists Sartre and Camus, Jones argued that if we judge God's character as we judge human character – "as the sum of His acts" – we cannot escape the question whether God is a white racist (or, after the Holocaust, an anti-Semite). Jones' argument is not that God *is* a white racist, but that any effort to understand African Americans as a chosen people will founder on the shoals of theodicy. If liberation is worth pursuing, Jones argues, we may have to place the "functional ultimacy of wo/man" above such tenets of theism as divine benevolence.

William R. Jones, *Is God a White Racist? A Preamble to Black Theology* (Boston: Beacon, 1998 [1973]), 20–3.

I have attempted thus far to show that the multievidentiality of suffering, in part, forces consideration of the question, Is God a white racist? At this juncture it is necessary to enlarge; the complex of categories that generates the issue of divine racism. The concept of ethnic suffering, the correlate of divine racism, will be our immediate focus.

Four essential features constitute ethnic suffering: (a) maldistribution, (b) negative quality, (c) enormity, and (d) noncatastrophic character. By accenting the ethnic factor I wish to call attention to that suffering which is maldistributed; it is not spread, as it were, more or less randomly and impartially over the total human race. Rather, it is concentrated in a particular ethnic group. My concern in utilizing the concept of ethnic suffering is to accentuate the fact that black suffering is balanced by white non-suffering instead of white suffering. Consequently, black suffering in particular and ethnic suffering in general raise the issue of the scandal of particularity.

John Bowker makes the cogent observation that the problem of the maldistribution of suffering is central in the Old Testament. "The problem in Scripture," he contends, "is not why suffering exists, but why it afflicts some people and not others. The problem is not the fact of suffering, but its distribution." Ethnic suffering underlines and gives emphasis to the same notion.

If we differentiate between positive and negative suffering, ethnic suffering in my stipulative definition would be a subclass of negative suffering. It describes a suffering without essential value for man's salvation or well-being. It leads away from, rather than toward, one's highest good. In contrast, certain advocates of types of asceticism, for instance, would regard suffering positively, as something to be actively pursued.

A third feature of ethnic suffering is its enormity, and here the reference is to several things: There is the factor of numbers, but numbers in relation to the total class, i.e., the number of suffering Jews or blacks in comparison with the total number of Jews or blacks. The factor of numbers raises the issue of divine racism at the point where the level of suffering and death makes the interpretation of genocide feasible.

Enormity also designates suffering unto death. Ethnic suffering reduces the life expectancy or anticipates the immediate death of the individual. The importance of this feature is that it nullifies various explanations of suffering and thereby narrows the spectrum of possible theodicies. Suffering unto death, for instance, negates any interpretation of pedagogical suffering; i.e., we learn from a burn to avoid fire. This makes little sense if the learning method destroys the learner. Suffering as a form of testing is also contradicted if the amount and severity of the suffering are incommensurate with the alleged purpose. It is for this reason that Rabbi Richard Rubenstein, for instance, denies that the horror of the suffering of Jews at Auschwitz could ever be likened to the testing of Job.

The final feature to be discussed is the non-catastrophic aspect. Ethnic suffering does not strike quickly and then leave after a short and terrible siege. Instead, it extends over long historical eras. It strikes not only the father but the son, the grandson, and the great-grandson. In short, non-catastrophic suffering is transgenerational.

When these aspects of ethnic suffering are connected, one is not tempted to account for their presence on the grounds of the operation of indifferent and impersonal laws of nature. Rather, one is more inclined to explain its causal nexus in terms of purpose and consequently person. This, too, is but a short step to seeing God as perhaps that person.

It is my contention that the peculiarities of black suffering make the question of divine racism imperative; it is not my position that the special character of black suffering answers the question. What I do affirm is that black theology, precisely because of the prominence of ethnic suffering in the black experience, cannot operate as if the goodness of God for all mankind were a theological axiom.

With the foregoing analysis of ethnic suffering as a background, it is now possible to restate certain aspects of the biblical understanding of suffering. Of special importance in this respect is the connection between the exaltation-liberation event and the catastrophic feature of ethnic suffering. The suffering-servant model, in my view, demands the category of catastrophic suffering; unrelieved suffering or transgenerational suffering appears to contradict it. The interval between Cross and Resurrection was by no means a millennium. Indeed it would be an interesting and rewarding study to examine the duration of suffering in biblical thought when the suffering is not the result of divine disfavor.

A final observation about the limitations of the category of ethnic suffering: The reader, and surely the critic, may sense that ethnic suffering is a self-negating concept. It is possible to argue that ethnic classification is arbitrary and reflects only the operation of human classification. Accordingly it is possible to divide mankind into a mind-boggling variety of ethnic groups to the point where the particularity presupposed in ethnic suffering becomes meaningless. That is, the framework of ethnic suffering permits one to raise the question, Is God a sexist, anti-Semite, anti-German, anti-Watusi? This is a just criticism and one which should be advanced if the critic thinks it has merit.

Allowing for this problem, the concept, I feel, still warrants consideration. Where one makes the class division is unimportant; nor is it crucial how often the division is made. As long as one is willing to isolate and identify a specific group and demonstrate that it receives a preponderance of suffering in comparison with members outside the class, the issue of the partiality of ultimate reality can be raised . . .

64

Dorothee Soelle, "A Critique of Christian Masochism"

Kenneth Surin has argued that Christian theodicy must be "practical" rather than "theoretical"; his first example is the theology of the cross of German Lutheran activist and theologian Dorothee Soelle (1929–). "In the face of suffering," Soelle asserts, "you are either with the victim or the executioner" – there is no third option. The position of the spectator – the theorist or theodicist – is no different from that of the "executioner." Alyosha Karamazov's silent suffering with others is preferable to Ivan's desire to "give back my entrance ticket" (see p. 281 above), even if it is motivated by love of his fellow human beings. Indeed, unless we think of God, too, as suffering with the sufferer, we think of him as an executioner. Soelle cites Dietrich Bonhoeffer's famous claim that "man is challenged to participate in the sufferings of God at the hands of a godless world."

Dorothee Soelle, *Suffering*, trans. Everett R. Kalin (Philadelphia: Fortress, 1975), 15–23, 25–7.

Dimensions of Affliction

. . . In a certain sense all affliction has an anachronistic character: tuberculosis among the Indians in Argentina as well as the landscape of Vietnam, made to look as barren as the moon. It is not our time, this time of affliction – it can't be true! "Our senses attach all the scorn, all the revulsion, all the hatred that our reason attaches to crime, to affliction" [says Simone Weil]. Gratuitous solidarity with the afflicted changes nothing; precise knowledge that such suffering could be avoided becomes our defense against addressing it. Only our own physical experience and our own experience of social helplessness and threat compel us "to recognize the presence of affliction." Our experience of anachronistic suffering, that objectively need no longer exist, alters even our understanding of time. It strips us of all superiority that grows out of feeling of progress and puts us in the same time-frame with the one who is suffering anachronistically. We can only help sufferers by stepping into their time-frame. Otherwise we would only offer condescending charity that reaches down from on high.

The recognition of the three dimensions of suffering – physical, psychological, and social – is fundamental for probing the problem more deeply. [See p. 334 above.] The unity of the three dimensions can be demonstrated by means of many texts and testimonies, best perhaps by means of those psalms that belong to the genre of so-called individual psalms of lament (for example, Pss. 16, 22, 73, 88, 116). The elements of lament keep recurring: illness and physical pain in which people find themselves crushed and dried up; physical and psychological symptoms of dissolution which are often depicted with words like "pour out, empty"; abandonment by friends, neighbors, and intimates; imprisonment in pain so that one no longer has time or place to experience personal or corporate salvation; being in the sphere of death, in its grasp. Suffering, as it appears in the lament, threatens every dimension of life: time to await what is promised, freedom of movement and opportunity for development, vital association with others, food and health and living space as one's share of the land of promise. This kind of suffering has social dimensions – isolation, loneliness, ostracism – as well as physical . . .

The story of Jesus' passion is in this sense a narrative about suffering. It is falsified whenever it is robbed of one of its dimensions, as has happened in various epochs of church history and art history. It is the story of a man whose goal is shattered. But this despair over his own cause would be incomplete – and below the level of other human suffering – without the physical and social experience the story describes. Without blood, sweat, and tears, without the threat and experience of torture, it would remain on a purely spiritual level. And the disintegration of his company of followers is part of this experience of suffering, for Jesus is denied, betrayed, and abandoned by his friends.

Unconditional Submission

In Christian literature on suffering these three dimensions, especially the social one, are more or less suppressed. Religious pamphlets on suffering proceed from several common fundamental motifs:

Affliction comes from God's hand. The connection between sin and sickness is recognized far too little. Sin is the deepest and most essential root of sickness. The person who is sick fails to recognize this essential cause of sickness and attributes his suffering to "external circumstances, to natural causes." Full health will be realized in the age to come. Sickness is a splendid opportunity to grow and mature inwardly. Don't you feel how God is at work in you precisely while you are sick? The grace that is operative as one suffers is more valuable than physical healing. Affliction is a means of training used by God's salutary love.

It is possible to summarize two tendencies that appear in the material presented in this study. One is the vindication of divine power through human powerlessness . . .

Corresponding to this tendency is the other, on the human side, to push for a willingness to suffer, which is called for as a universal Christian attitude . . . Why God sends affliction is no longer asked. It is sufficient to know he causes it. In this way one represses all other causes of suffering, particularly the social causes, and doesn't deal rationally with the actual causes . . .

Often, however, this purely individualistic view sidesteps reality because it overlooks other people involved in the situation. However we understand Christ's injunction, "Do not resist evil" (Matt. 5:39), it is not intended to apply to evil that is destroying others. Jesus criticized with extreme harshness those who make others suffer and lead astray "the little ones"; a millstone is to be hung around their necks (Matt. 18:6). It is really not enough for a person to transform his own suffering "into a positive element of his own self-fulfilment." . . .

Almost all Christian interpretations, however, ignore the distinction between suffering that we can and cannot end. And, by referring to the universality of sin, they deny the distinction, in a marriage involving guilt, for instance, between the guilty and the innocent party.

To that extent the Christian interpretations of suffering sketched here amount to a recommendation of masochism . . .

There have been innumerable religious attempts to explain suffering. The difficulty here lies less in the existential interpretation that people give to their pain than in the later theological systematization, which has no use for suffering that hasn't been named and pigeonholed. Thus, for example, in the Old Testament suffering is divided into "suffering that punishes, trains, tests and serves." The fact that in some Old Testament passages it is Yahweh himself who injured, wounded, imperiled, and caused illness is systematized into the proposition that all pain comes from God. In late Judaism an expiatory force is ascribed to suffering, which helps people obtain forgiveness for their sins. A distinction is made between cultic means of atonement, such as sacrifice, attendance at the temple, and blood-offerings, and noncultic means, such as repentance, suffering, and death. Suffering, and here one speaks principally of sickness, poverty, and childlessness, is considered to have greater expiatory force than sacrifice, because suffering affects the person himself in a direct way and not just his property and possessions. Suffering imparts to the pious person the sure hope that his guilt is thereby atoned for and that in the life to come he will receive only reward for his good deeds. The ungodly, on the other hand, who are already rewarded here for their few good deeds, have only punishment to await beyond the grave. Thereby the old doctrine of ret-ribution – sin is followed by suffering – has been reversed: atonement results from suffering. To be sure, the structure of a calculable equalization is retained, in fact sharpened.

But these divisions and interpretations, as well as others, fall to pieces in the face of actual experiences. Affliction strikes even the pious. How can it be punishment in that case? The training value of suffering is neg-ligible. The reaction to the real or imagined creator of suffering is pic-tured in the Old Testament itself as wrath, ill temper. Suffering produces fruits like curses, imprecations, and prayers for vengeance more readily than reform and insight. Suffering causes people to experience helplessness and fear; indeed intense pain cripples all power to resist and frequently leads to despair. It is precisely the Old Testament that corrects again and again theological theories based on the premise that God sends suffering. "For affliction does not come from the dust, nor does trouble sprout from the ground; much more people bring trouble on themselves as the sparks fly upward" (Job 5:6f.) . . .

Theological Sadism

It is not difficult to criticize Christian masochism, since it has so many features that merit criticism: the low value it places on human strength; its veneration of one who is neither good nor logical but only extremely powerful; its viewing of suffering exclusively from the perspective of endurance; and its consequent lack of sensitivity for the suffering of others.

Nevertheless this masochism of the pious is not the worst thing imag-inable. For it offered a kind of help for people, as an existential stance, just in those periods in which the possibilities for lessening suffering were not highly developed. Libidinal impulses are, to be sure, perverted by this stance, but they are not destroyed.

The picture changes as soon as theologians, in a kind of overly-rigorous application of the masochistic approach, sketch in as a companion piece a sadistic God. The libidinal and flexible impulses of pious sufferers are now sadistically fixed by the theologians, who make the wrath of God their essential motif. The God who produces suffering and causes affliction becomes the glorious theme of a theology that directs our attention to the God who demands the impossible and tortures people . . . The existential experience developed in mysticism that God is with those who suffer is replaced by a theological system preoccupied with judgment day. The situation is not viewed from the standpoint of the sufferer; rather it is through God's eyes that things are seen and, above all, judged . . .

The justice of the modern objection against this God is shown by suffering, the suffering of the innocent. And it must be added that in comparison with the enormity of human suffering, all are "innocent." There is misery that totally exceeds every form of guilt; for all guilt put together it would be "too much." . . .

Any attempt to look upon suffering as caused directly or indirectly by God stands in danger of regarding him as sadistic. Therefore it also seems to me problematic to ask, "What is the cause of the suffering of the God who suffers with imprisoned, persecuted and murdered Israel," or whether Christ suffered merely because of "human injustice and human wickedness." Jürgen Moltmann has repeated the attempt to show that Jesus suffers "at God's hands," that God causes suffering and crucifies – at least in the case of this one person. On the one hand, Moltmann has carved out the figure of the "crucified God," the "suffering, poor, defenseless Christ," and criticized the ancient ideal of an apathetic God by portraying God as the "God of the poor, the peasants and the slaves," who suffers "in us, where love suffers." But this intention, this passion for suffering, is weakened and softened through the theological system that transmits it. God is not understood only or even primarily as the loving and suffering Christ. He is simultaneously supposed to occupy the position of the ruling, omnipotent Father. Moltmann attempts to develop a "theology of the cross" from the perspective of the one who originates and causes suffering. This correlates with an understanding of suffering as a process within the Trinity, whereby "one of the persons of the Trinity" underwent suffering while another person of the Trinity was the very one who caused it. An example of this kind of theology is instructive: What happened here is what Abraham did not need to do to Isaac (cf. Rom. 8:32): Christ was quite deliberately abandoned by the Father to the fate of death: God subjected him to the power of corruption, whether this be called man or death. To express the idea in its most acute form, one might say in the words of the dogma of the early church: the first person of the Trinity casts out and annihilates the second . . .

[T]heological sadism . . . school[s] people in thought patterns that regard sadistic behavior as normal, in which one worships, honors, and loves a being whose "radicality," "intentionality," and "greatest sharpness" is that he slays. The ultimate conclusion of theological sadism is worshiping the executioner.

65

Emmanuel Levinas, "Useless Suffering"

The Lithuanian-born Jewish philosopher Emmanuel Levinas (1906–95) studied with Husserl and Heidegger in Germany before moving to France, where he spent the rest of his life. Most of Levinas's family in Eastern Europe was killed in the Shoah. His works span – and call into question – the historic divide between "Judaism" and "philosophy." Like Schelling, Levinas argued that evil – understood as suffering – destroys the possibility of all philosophy in the conventional mode, not excluding Heidegger's "fundamental ontology." The centerpiece of Levinas's work was his phenomenology of the "face-to-face" encounter, where the Other puts me in question. Radically reinterpreting the asymmetry between the way we should regard our own suffering and the suffering of others (something we have seen already in Dostoyevsky and Cohen), Levinas argues that not ontology is fundamental but ethics. The implications of this argument for theodicy are explored in the difficult essay below.

Emmanuel Levinas, "Useless Suffering," trans. Richard Cohen, in *The Provocation of Levinas: Rethinking the Other*, eds. Robert Bernasconi and David Wood (London: Routledge, 1988), 156–67.

Phenomenology

Suffering is surely a *given* in consciousness, a certain "psychological content," like the lived experience of colour, of sound, of contact, or like any sensation. But in this "content" itself, it is in-spite-of-consciousness, unassumable. It is unassumable and "unassumability." "Unassumability" does

not result from the excessive intensity of a sensation, from some sort of
quantitative "too much," surpassing the measure of our sensibility and our
means of grasping and holding. It results from an excess, a "too much"
which is inscribed in a sensorial content, penetrating as suffering the
dimensions of meaning which seem to be opened and grafted on to it.
For the Kantian "I think" which is capable of reuniting and embracing
the most heterogeneous and disparate givens into order and meaning
under its *a priori* forms – it is as if suffering were not only a *given* refrac-
tory to synthesis, but the *way* in which the refusal opposed to the assem-
bling of givens into a meaningful whole is opposed to it: suffering is at
once what disturbs order and this disturbance itself. It is not only the consciousness of rejection or a symptom of rejection, but this rejection itself:
a backwards consciousness, "operating" not as "grasp" but as revulsion. It
is a modality, or the categorial ambiguity of quality and modality. Taken
as an "experienced" content, the denial and refusal of meaning which
is imposed as a sensible quality is the *way* in which the unbearable is
precisely not borne by consciousness, the way this not-being-borne is,
paradoxically, itself a sensation or a given. This is a quasi-contradictory
structure, but a contradiction which is not formal like that of the dialectical tension between the affirmative and the negative which arises for the
intellect; it is a contradiction by way of sensation the plaintiveness of pain,
hurt [*mal*].

Suffering, in its hurt and its in-spite-of-consciousness, is passivity. Here,
"taking cognizance" is no longer, properly speaking, a taking; it is no
longer *the performance of an act of consciousness*, but, in its adversity, a submission; and even a submission to the submitting, since the "content" of
which the aching consciousness is conscious is precisely this very adversity of suffering, its hurt. But, here again, this *passivity* – in the sense of a
modality – signifies as a *quiddity*, and perhaps as the place where passivity
signifies originally, independent of its conceptual opposition to activity.
The latter is an abstraction made from its psycho-physical and psycho-
physiological conditions; in its pure phenomenology, the passivity of
suffering is in no way the reverse side of activity, as an effect would still
be correlative to its cause, or as a sensorial receptivity would be correlative to the "Obstance" of the object which affects and impresses it.
The passivity of suffering is more profoundly passive than the receptivity
of our senses, which is already the activity of welcome, and straight away
becomes perception. In suffering sensibility is a vulnerability, more passive
than receptivity; it is an ordeal more passive than experience. It is precisely
an evil. It is not, to tell the truth, through passivity that evil is described,
but through evil that suffering is understood. Suffering is a pure under-

going. It is not matter of a passivity which would degrade man by striking a blow against his freedom. Pain would limit such freedom to the
point of compromising self-consciousness, permitting man the identity of
a thing only in the passivity of the submission. The evil which rends the
humanity of the suffering person, overwhelms his humanity otherwise than
non-freedom overwhelms it: violently and cruelly, more irremissibly than
the negation which dominates or paralyzes the act in non-freedom. What
counts in the non-freedom or the undergoing of suffering is the concreteness of the *not* looming as a hurt more negative than any apophantic *not*. This negativity of evil is, probably, the source or kernel of all
apophantic negation. The *not* of evil is negative right up to non-sense. All
evil refers to suffering. It is the *impasse* of life and being, their absurdity,
where pain does not come, somehow innocently, "to colour" consciousness with affectivity. The evil of pain, the harm itself, is the explosion and
most profound articulation of absurdity.

Thus the least one can say about suffering is that in its own phenom-
enality, intrinsically, it is useless, "for nothing." Doubtlessly this basic
sense-lessness that the analysis seems to suggest is confirmed by empirical
situations of pain, where pain somehow remains undiluted and isolates
itself in consciousness, or absorbs the rest of consciousness. It would suffice,
for example, to extract from the medical journals certain cases of persistent or obstinate pain, the neuralgias and the intolerable lumbagos resulting from lesions of the peripheral nerves, and the tortures which are
experienced by certain patients stricken with malignant tumours. Pain can
become the central phenomenon of the diseased state. These are the
"pain-illnesses" where the integration of other psychological states does
not bring any relief but where, on the contrary, anxiety and distress add
to the cruelty of the hurt. But one can go further – and doubtless thus
arrive at the essential facts of pure pain – by evoking the "pain-illnesses"
of beings who are psychically deprived, backward, handicapped, in their
relational life and in their relationships to the Other, relationships where
suffering, without losing anything of its savage malignancy, no longer
covers up the totality of the mental and comes across novel lights within
new horizons. These horizons none the less remain closed to the men-
tally deficient, except that in their "pure pain" they are projected into them
to expose them to me, raising the fundamental ethical problem which pain
poses "for nothing": the inevitable and preemptory ethical problem of the
medication which is my duty. Is not the evil of suffering – extreme passivity, impotence, abandonment and solitude – also the unassumable and
thus the possibility of a half opening, and, more precisely, the possibility
that wherever a moan, a cry, a groan or a sigh happen there is the

original call for aid, for curative help, for help from the other ego whose alterity, whose exteriority promises salvation? It is the original opening toward what is helpful, where the primordial, irreducible, and ethical, anthropological category of the medical comes to impose itself – across a demand for analgesia, more pressing, more urgent in the groan than a demand for consolation or a postponement of death. For pure suffering, which is intrinsically meaningless and condemned to itself without exit, a beyond takes shape in the inter-human. It is starting from such situations – we say in passing – that medicine as technique, and consequently the general technology it presupposes, the technology so easily exposed to the attacks of "right-thinking" rigour, does not merely originate in the so-called "will to power." This bad will is perhaps only the price which must sometimes be paid by the elevated thought of a civilization called to nourish persons and to lighten their sufferings. This elevated thought is the honour of a still uncertain and blinking modernity coming at the end of a century of nameless sufferings, but in which the suffering of suffer-ing, the suffering for the useless suffering of the other person, the just suf-fering in me for the unjustifiable suffering of the Other, opens upon suffering the ethical perspective of the inter-human. In this perspective a radical difference develops between *suffering in the Other*, which for me is unpardonable and solicits me and calls me, and suffering *in me*, my own adventure of suffering, whose constitutional or congenital uselessness can take on a meaning, the only meaning to which suffering is susceptible, in becoming a suffering for the suffering – be it inexorable – of someone else. It is this attention to the Other which, across the cruelties of our century – despite these cruelties, because of these cruelties – can be affirmed as the very bond of human subjectivity, even to the point of being raised to a supreme ethical principle – the only one which it is not possible to contest – a principle which can go so far as to command the hopes and practical discipline of vast human groups. This attention and this action are so imperiously and directly incumbent on people – on their selves – that it makes waiting for the saving actions of an all-powerful God impossible without degradation. To be sure, consciousness of this inescapable obligation makes the idea of God more difficult, but it also makes it spiritually closer than confidence in any kind of theodicy.

Theodicy

In the ambiguity of suffering which the above phenomenological essay brings out, its modality also shows the content or sensation that con-sciousness "supports." This adversity-to-all-harmony, as quiddity, enters into conjunction with other "contents" which it disturbs, to be sure, but where it is given reasons or produces a reason. Already within an isolated consciousness, the pain of suffering can take on the meaning of a pain which merits and hopes for reward, and so lose, it seems, in diverse ways, its modality of uselessness. Is it not meaningful as a means with an end in view, when it tallies with the effort which leads to a work or in the fatigue which results from it? One can discover in it a biological finality: the role of an alarm signal manifesting itself for the preservation of life against the cunning dangers which menace life in illness; "He that increaseth knowledge increaseth sorrow," says Ecclesiastes (1:18), where suffering appears at the very least as the price of reason and of spiritual refinement. It would also temper the individual's character. It would be necessary to the teleology of community life, where social unrest awakens a useful attention to the health of the collective body. The social utility of suffering is necessary to the pedagogic function of Power in education, discipline and repression. Is not fear of punishment the beginning of wisdom? Is it not believed that sufferings, submitted to as sanctions, regenerate the enemies of society and man? This political teleology is founded, to be sure, on the value of existence, on the perseverance of society and the individual in being, on their successful health as the supreme and ultimate end.

But the unpleasant and gratuitous non-sense of pain already pierces beneath the reasonable forms which the social "uses" of suffering assume. These, in any case, do not make the torture which strikes the psychically handicapped and isolates them in their pain any less scandalous. But behind the rational administration of pain in sanctions distributed by human courts, immediately dressing up dubious appearances of repression, the arbitrary and strange failure of justice amidst wars, crimes and the oppression of the weak by the strong, rejoins, in a sort of fatality, the useless sufferings which spring from natural plagues as if effects of an ontological perversion. Beyond the fundamental malignity of suffering itself, revealed in its phenomenology, does not human experience in history attest to a malice and a bad will?

Western humanity has none the less sought for the meaning of this scandal by invoking the proper sense of a metaphysical order, an ethics, which is invisible in the immediate lessons of moral consciousness. This is a kingdom of transcendent ends, willed by a benevolent wisdom, by the absolute goodness of a God who is in some way defined by this super-natural goodness; or a widespread, invisible goodness in Nature and History, where it would command the paths which are, to be sure, painful, but which lead to the Good. Pain is henceforth meaningful, subordinated in one way or another to the metaphysical finality envisaged by faith or by a belief in progress. These beliefs are presupposed by theodicy! Such is the grand idea necessary to the inner peace of souls in our distressed world. It is called upon to make sufferings here below comprehensible. These will make sense by reference to an original fault or to the congenital finitude of human being. The evil which fills the earth would be explained in a "plan of the whole"; it would be called upon to atone for a sin, or it would announce, to the ontologically limited consciousness, compensation or recompense at the end of time. These supra-sensible perspectives are invoked in order to envisage in a suffering which is essentially gratuitous and absurd, and apparently arbitrary, a signification and an order.

Certainly one may ask if theodicy, in the broad and narrow senses the term, effectively succeeds in making God innocent, or in saving morality in the name of faith, or in making suffering – and this is the true intention of the thought which has recourse to theodicy – bearable. By underestimating its temptation one could, in any case, misunderstand the profundity of the empire which theodicy exerts over humankind, and the *epoch-making* character – or the *historical* character, as one says today – of its entry into thought. It has been, at least up to the trials of the twentieth century, a component of the self-consciousness of European humanity. It persisted in watered-down form at the core of atheist progressivism, which was confident, none the less, in the efficacy of the Good which is immanent to being, called to visible triumph by the simple play of the natural and historical laws of injustice, war, misery and illness. As providential, Nature and History furnished the eighteenth and nineteenth centuries with the norms of moral consciousness. They are associated with many essentials of the deism of the age of Enlightenment. But theodicy – ignoring the name that Leibniz gave to it in 1710 – is as old as a certain reading of the Bible. It dominated the consciousness of the believer who explained his misfortunes by reference to the Sin, or at least by reference to his sins. In addition to the Christians' well-established reference to Original Sin, this theodicy is in a certain sense implicit in the Old Testament, where the drama of the Diaspora reflects the sins of Israel. The wicked conduct of ancestors, still non-expiated by the sufferings of exile, would explain to the exiles themselves the duration and the harshness of this exile.

The End of Theodicy

Perhaps the most revolutionary fact of our twentieth-century consciousness – but it is also an event in Sacred History – is that of the destruction of all balance between the explicit and implicit theodicy of Western thought and the forms which suffering and its evil take in the very unfolding of this century. This is the century that in has known two world wars, the totalitarianisms of right and left, Hitlerism and Stalinism, Hiroshima, the Gulag, and the genocides of Auschwitz and Cambodia. This is the century which is drawing to a close in the haunting memory of the return of everything signified by these barbaric names: suffering and evil are deliberately imposed, yet no reason sets limits to the exasperation of a reason become political and detached from all ethics.

Among these events the Holocaust of the Jewish people under the reign of Hitler seems to us the paradigm of gratuitous human suffering, where evil appears in its diabolical horror. This is perhaps not a subjective feeling. The disproportion between suffering and every theodicy was shown at Auschwitz with a glaring, obvious clarity. Its possibility puts into question the multi-millennial traditional faith. Did not the word of Nietzsche on the death of God take on, in the extermination camps, the signification of a quasi-empirical fact? Is it necessary to be surprised, then, that this drama of Sacred History has had among its principal actors a people which, since forever, has been associated with this history, whose collective soul and destiny would be wrongly understood as limited to any sort of nationalism, and whose gesture, in certain circumstances, still belongs to Revelation – be it as apocalypse – which "provokes thought" from philosophers or which impedes them from thinking?

Here I wish to evoke the analysis which the Canadian Jew, the philosopher Emil Fackenheim, of Toronto, has made of this catastrophe of the human and the divine, in his work, and notably in his book *God's Presence in History*:

The Nazi Genocide of the Jewish people has no precedent within Jewish history. Nor . . . will one find a precedent outside Jewish history . . . Even actual cases of genocide, however, still differ from the Nazi holocaust in at least two respects. Whole peoples have been killed for "rational" (however horrifying) ends such as power, territory, wealth . . . The Nazi murder . . . was annihilation for the sake of annihilation, murder for the sake of murder, evil for the sake of evil. Still more incontestably unique than the crime itself is the situation of the victims. The Albigensians died for their faith, believing unto death that God needs martyrs. Negro Christians have been murdered for their race, able to find comfort in a faith not at issue. The more than one million Jewish children murdered in the Nazi holocaust died neither because of their faith, nor despite their faith, nor for reasons unrelated to the Jewish faith [but] because of the Jewish faith of their great-grandparents [who brought] up Jewish children. [*God's Presence in History: Jewish Affirmations and Philosophical Reflections after Auschwitz* (New York: New York University Press, 1970), 69–70]

The inhabitants of the Eastern European Jewish communities constituted the majority of the six million tortured and massacred; they represented the human beings least corrupted by the ambiguities of our world, and the million infants killed had the innocence of infants. Theirs is the death of martyrs, a death given in the torturers' unceasing destruction of the dignity which belongs to martyrs. The final act of this destruction is accomplished today in the posthumous denial of the very fact of martyrdom by the would-be "revisers of history." This would be pain in its undiluted malignity, suffering for nothing. It renders impossible and odious every proposal and every thought which would explain it by the sins of those who have suffered or are dead. But does not this end of theodicy, which obtrudes itself in the face of this century's inordinate distress, at the same time in a more general way reveal the unjustifiable character of suffering in the other person, the scandal which would occur by my justifying my neighbour's suffering? So that the very phenomenon of suffering in its uselessness is, in principle, the pain of the Other. For an ethical sensibility – confirming itself, in the inhumanity of our time, against this inhumanity – the justification of the neighbour's pain is certainly the source of all immorality. Accusing oneself in suffering is undoubtedly the very turning back of the ego to itself. It is perhaps thus; and the for-the-other – the most upright relation to the Other – is the most profound adventure of subjectivity, its ultimate intimacy. But this intimacy can only be discreet. It could not be given as an example, or be narrated as an edifying discourse. It could not be made a prediction without being perverted.

The philosophical problem, then, which is posed by the useless pain which appears in its fundamental malignancy across the events of the twentieth century, concerns the meaning that religiosity and the human morality of goodness can still retain after the end of theodicy. According to the philosopher we have just quoted, Auschwitz would paradoxically entail a revelation of the very God who nevertheless was silent as Auschwitz: a commandment of faithfulness. To renounce after Auschwitz this God absent from Auschwitz – no longer to assure the continuation of Israel – would amount to finishing the criminal enterprise of National-Socialism, which aimed at the annihilation of Israel and the forgetting of the ethical message of the Bible, which Judaism bears, and whose multi-millennial history is concretely prolonged by Israel's existence as a people. For if God was absent in the extermination camps, the devil was very obviously present in them. From whence, for Emil Fackenheim comes the obligation for Jews to live and to remain Jews, in order not to be made accomplices of a diabolical project. The Jew, after Auschwitz, is pledged to his faithfulness to Judaism and to the material and even political conditions of its existence.

This final reflection of the Toronto philosopher, formulated in terms which render it relative to the destiny of the Jewish people, can be given a universal signification. From Sarajevo to Cambodia humanity has witnessed a host of cruelties in the course of a century when Europe, in its "human sciences," seemed to reach the end of its subject, the humanity which, during all these horrors, breathed – already or still – the fumes of the crematory ovens of the "final solution" where theodicy abruptly appeared impossible. Is humanity, in its indifference, going to abandon the world to useless suffering, leaving it to the political fatality – or the drifting – of the blind forces which inflict misfortune on the weak and conquered, and which spare the conquerors, whom the wicked must join? Or, incapable of adhering to an order – or to a disorder – which it continues to think diabolic, must not humanity now, in a faith more difficult than ever, in a faith without theodicy, continue Sacred History; a history which now demands even more of the resources of the self in each one, and appeals to its suffering inspired by the suffering of the other person, to its compassion which is a non-useless suffering (or love), which is no longer suffering "for nothing," and which straightaway has a meaning? At the end of the twentieth century and after the useless and unjustifiable pain which is exposed and displayed therein without any shadow of a consoling theodicy, are we not all pledged – like the Jewish people to their faithfulness – to the second term of this alternative? This is a new modality in the faith of today, and also in our moral certainties, a modality quite essential to the modernity which is dawning.

The Inter-human Order

To envisage suffering, as I have just attempted to do, in the interhuman perspective – that is, as meaningful in me, useless in the Other – does not consist in adopting a relative point of view on it, but in restoring it to the dimensions of meaning outside of which the immanent and savage concreteness of evil in a consciousness is but an abstraction. To think suffering in an inter-human perspective does not amount to seeing it in the coexistence of a multiplicity of consciousnesses, or in a social determinism, accompanied by the simple knowledge that people in society can have of their neighbourliness or of their common destiny. The inter-human perspective can subsist, but can also be lost, in the political order of the City where the Law establishes mutual obligations between citizens. Properly speaking, the inter-human lies in a non-indifference of one to another, in a responsibility of one for another. The inter-human is prior to the reciprocity of this responsibility, which inscribes itself in impersonal laws, and becomes superimposed on the pure altruism of this responsibility inscribed in the ethical position of the self as self. It is prior to every contact which would signify precisely the moment of reciprocity where it can, to be sure, continue, but where it can also attenuate or extinguish altruism and disinterestedness. The order of politics – postethical or pre-ethical – which inaugurates the "social contract" is neither the sufficient condition nor the necessary outcome of ethics. In its ethical position, the self is distinct from the citizen born of the City, and from the individual who precedes all order in his natural egoism, from whom political philosophy, since Hobbes, tries to derive – or succeeds in deriving – the social or political order of the City.

The inter-human lies also in the recourse that people have to one another for help, before the marvellous alterity of the Other has been banalized or dimmed in a simple exchange of courtesies which become established as an "inter-personal commerce" of customs. We have spoken of this in the first paragraph of this study. These are expressions of a properly ethical meaning, distinct from those which the *self* and *other* acquire in what one calls the state of Nature or civil society. It is in the inter-human perspective of *my* responsibility for the other person, without concern for reciprocity, in my call to help him gratuitously, in the asymmetry of the relation of *one* to the *other*, that we have tried to analyze the phenomenon of useless suffering.

66

Nel Noddings, *Women and Evil*

The American ethicist and philosopher of education Nel Noddings (1929–) is one of the founders of the "ethics of care." Building on Rosemary Radford Ruether's and Mary Daly's critiques of traditional Christianity, Noddings argues that traditional theodicies are "suffused with male interests and conditioned by masculine experience." She bases her own view of evil on a not uncontroversial phenomenology of "women's experience" (not the experience of all women, but the experience of the "responsibility for caring, maintaining, and nurturing" which has traditionally fallen to women in most societies). What we fear as evil, she concludes, is really "pain, separation and helplessness": traditional religious practices and theodicies don't just misdescribe these evils, but add to them. What we need is a "morality of evil" (a phrase Noddings takes from C. G. Jung), "a carefully thought out plan by which to manage the evil in ourselves, in others, and in whatever deities we posit."

Nel Noddings, *Women and Evil* (Berkeley: University of California Press, 1989), 17, 19–20, 24–5, 118–20, 229–30.

Evil and Ethical Terror

The Augustinian tradition provided the main line of thinking on theodicy, but the Greek Epicureans had already posed the problem as a trilemma in response to Stoic attempts at theodicy: if God could have prevented evil and did not, he is malevolent; if God would have prevented evil but could not, he is impotent; if God could not and would not, why call him God? The answer might be political. An all-good, all-powerful authority was thought to have considerably more clout than a loving, fallible parent-figure. Augustine followed the path of the Stoics . . .

When we look at evil from the perspective of women's experience – through the eyes of people who bear and raise children, try to maintain a comfortable and stable home, feed and nurture the hungry and developing – we find much more wrong with the Augustinian theodicy. First, it requires something like the Adamic myth, some account of the first sin, to hold it up. When the Adamic myth combines with Augustine's pronouncements on original sin, the burden on women becomes enormous, as we will see. But not only women have suffered. Ricoeur says: "The harm that has been done to souls, during the centuries of Christianity, first by literal interpretation of the story of Adam, and then by confusion of this myth, treated as history, with later speculations, principally Augustinian, about original sin, will never be adequately told."

Second, it is not just eternal damnation that raises questions about the goodness of the God who decrees it. The problem of suffering is by no means adequately treated, and I will turn to that discussion shortly. Third, the explanation of suffering as retribution for sin sets the investigation of evil on the wrong track. This is a large part of the perversion Mary Daly, Rosemary Ruether, and other feminists condemn. The raw terror of natural evil is turned prematurely and arbitrarily into *ethical* terror, the fear of incurring the father-God's wrath. Our thinking, then, is distracted from the loving parent's attitude that would relieve and eliminate suffering to a long and perhaps hopeless quest to be justified in God's sight. In accepting this quest, we too often do harm to one another . . .

Fourth, the image of God created in this long chain of arguments in theodicy has greatly favored his omnipotence and omniscience. Hence the religious tradition has blinded us ethically. Since God, who clearly has the knowledge and power to do otherwise, inflicts or allows the greatest of suffering, the infliction of pain cannot be a *primary* ethical abuse. Since God hides himself from us, the neglect of a loving personal relation cannot be a primary evil, and the responsibility for remaining in contact falls to the weak and dependent. Since God presents the world to us in impenetrable mystery, there is precedent for mystification, and the dependent and powerless must learn to trust authority. These will be the great themes of evil from the perspective of women's experience . . .

The most prominent, but deeply flawed, solution to the problem of suffering lies in the concept of soul making. [See Hick, pp. 357–61 above.] This idea, central to the Irenaean theodicy, echoes in Kant and in modern writers like C. S. Lewis. Ricoeur says of Kant that he understood "the fall, free and fated, of man as the painful road of all ethical life that is of an adult character and on an adult level." This view helps explain why Kant felt that it was not our duty to contribute to another's moral perfection:

It is contradictory to say that I make another person's *perfection* my end and consider myself obliged to promote this. For the *perfection* of another man, as a person, consists precisely of *his own* power to adopt his end in accordance with his own concept of duty; and it is self-contradictory to demand that I do (make it my duty to do) what only the other person himself can do. [*Metaphysics of Morals*, part 2, *The Doctrine of Virtue*, trans. Mary J. Gregor (New York: Harper & Row, 1964), 44–5]

Kant's ethical perspective is consistent with his religious (or metaphysical) perspective. God leaves us free to choose our moral course, and we in turn have no obligation to promote the moral perfection of our fellows. Life is a painful and lonely struggle designed to "make souls." In the Christian design faith may lighten the struggle, but the suffering is no less real. Instead of concentrating on the alleviation and possible elimination of suffering, Christians are urged to find meaning in it. C. S. Lewis, for example, said of his wife's relentless pain from cancer: "But is it credible that such extremities of torture should be necessary for us? Well, take your choice. The tortures occur. If they are unnecessary, then there is no God or a bad one. If there is a good God, then these tortures are necessary. For no even moderately good Being could possibly inflict or permit them if they weren't."

Completely immersed in a strict monotheism, Lewis fails to appreciate the possibilities in a fallible god – one who controls just so much and is perhaps still struggling toward an ethical vision. This sort of god – lovable and understandable to women – may be unattractive to many men because he cannot make absolute claims on us for worship, obedience, and authority, or if he makes such claims, we might be justified in challenging him and even charging the claim to his wicked or unfinished side. A fallible god shakes the entire hierarchy and endangers men in their relations to women, children, animals, and the whole living environment . . .

Toward a Phenomenology of Evil

We may recall Simone Weil's comment that real evil is "gloomy, monotonous, barren, boring," whereas imaginary evil is "romantic and varied." In describing pain, separation, and helplessness as the trinity of elemental evils, we feel none of the excitement conveyed by stories of devils, witches, demons, spells, and possession. Evil does not have a stomach-turning stench, nor does it signal its presence with palpable cold and darkness. We do not fall into it haplessly, nor does it entrap (possess) us. Rather, we often act willfully in complicity with it.

If we set aside the myths and stories that have fascinated us for so long, we see that our sense of evil is activated when we become aware that something is harming or threatening to harm us or others. Too often we move directly from this awareness to a judgment that the thing or event itself is evil, or we ignore the actual evil in the event and move to some abstract entity or alien other that is said to be responsible for it. We make mistakes in locating and labeling evil.

The most basic form of evil seems to be pain. Physical pain, when it does not promise a better end state (right here on earth), is an evil we should avoid or relieve. Separation is evil because of the deep psychic pain it causes, and the fear of separation makes human beings vulnerable to all sorts of further evils. Helplessness too is associated with psychic pain, and we must consider its deliberate infliction a great moral evil.

But what should we say about the traditional senses of evil – its filth, ugliness, power, craftiness, stench? What should we do with the familiar categories of defilement, shame, guilt, terror, anger, obsession? What should we say about vice? We can discuss each, I think, within the perspective of women's experience.

What is filthy and ugly is not some bodily function or contamination by some unseen entity of great power. It is, rather, the harm that we do to one another and our fearful refusal to alleviate great pain when we encounter it. From this perspective a woman who is raped is not defiled but hurt, wounded. The man who rapes her is the one defiled; it is he who is dirty, unclean, sullied, dishonored . . . The pain and terror that a woman experiences in rape compound the shame that a cruel society makes her feel about her body and who should have access to it. In the act itself she suffers the physical pain of violence and the psychic pain of helplessness, but both become infinitely worse if she must also fear separation from those who should love and support her. It is not sex that is filthy, then, but the infliction of pain and the use of physical force to satisfy selfish purposes.

Shame, an affect associated with the public disclosure of errors, faults, relations, or evil acts, seems to be part of our fear of separation. When we are ashamed, we fear the loss of esteem of those whom we regard as important. Unlike guilt, shame is pressed on us by the opinions of others. Guilt and shame do not necessarily go together. One may suffer public shame and escape a feeling of guilt entirely, or one may escape shame and suffer deeply from inner guilt. To shame another is to inflict deep psychic pain, and we must ask ourselves whether some good is likely to accrue to the one shamed in our act of public disclosure. Sometimes, of course, we must disclose the wrongdoings of another publicly, but shame is not the aim in such cases. Indeed, one who is likely to feel shame can usually be persuaded by other means.

Guilt is also associated with evil and is an important affect to understand in a morality of evil. In particular we have to understand that guilt can be healthy if it leads to restitution. If we can undo an act or soften it or make up for it, we can relieve our guilt and at the same time help heal the separation that occurs when we wrong another. This is another area in which the traditional view has led us astray. Doing penance for wrong acts does not necessarily address the victim's pain; making restitution, giving an apology, and asking forgiveness of the one wronged are more effective in avoiding evil. As we will see, guilt is a powerful precursor of scapegoating. When we have hurt another person, it is comforting to convince ourselves that he or she deserved it.

Anger too is associated with evil. Indeed, anger is a popular theme with feminists, many of whom call on women to feel and express rage at their long years of exploitation and oppression. Women who resist this move sometimes encounter suspicion within feminist circles. Judith Stacey, for example, considers the recent work of Betty Friedan and Jean Elshtain to be "conservative" precisely because it takes the anger out of sexual politics; both look toward a reconciliation with men and an effort to promote the well-being of all human beings, not just women. To be sure, Stacey does not oppose making the world a better place for all people, and she agrees with Friedan and Elshtain that feminism must pay more attention to the needs of children. What Stacey fears is that "social feminism" as Elshtain (and many women before her) described it will encourage women to abandon sexual politics. What we need, Stacey believes, is a passionate sense of being wronged if our society is ever to be a just one for women.

Mary Daly also speaks of rage and the necessity to maintain it. From the standpoint I have taken, however, rage seems to be counterindicated. Rage creates separation and causes new pain. It is yet another example of risking the actual commission of evil in well-intentioned efforts to overcome it. As we examine several great evils in the following chapters, we may find effective alternatives to rage . . .

Educating for a Morality of Evil

. . . Early on I rejected the notion held long ago by Socrates and recently by Hannah Arendt that evil is simply the absence of knowledge or good. Evil is a real presence, and moral evil is often the result of trying to do something either genuinely thought to be good or rationalized layer on layer in gross bad faith. Evil is thus intimately bound up in disputes over good. Nor do I believe that evil is necessarily ugly or that people cannot think on that which is ugly . . . Although Sartre was technically right when he said that we cannot sustain a choice to do evil for its own sake (we do evil mainly in opposition to some perceived evil and therefore choose something we rationalize as right or good), this only points up the power of mystification and repression. We cannot think for long on our own evil motives, so we think about obedience, the knowledge to be gained, the cause to be won, and the safety of our lives, and we evaluate all these as good. But this slippery bit of thinking comes into question when we regard evil as relational and positively real. When we acknowledge that pain, separation, and helplessness are the basic states of consciousness associated with evil and that moral evil consists in inducing, sustaining, or failing to relieve these conditions, we can no longer ignore that we *do* think on and intend evil when we perform such acts. Just as disease is real and not just an illusion or absence of health, evil is real, and to control it we need to understand it and accept that the tendency toward it dwells in all of us.

If we believe this, a primary purpose of education should be to reduce pain, separation, and helplessness by encouraging people to explore the nature of evil and commit themselves to continue the search for understanding. Further, faced with the temptation or apparent need to do something evil, appropriately educated people should ask themselves: Is there a different way to accomplish my goal? Is the goal *itself* evil or tainted with evil? What good am I trying to achieve? Thinking this way should govern our political and social relations as well as our personal lives. Because such thinking requires analytical skill, all students need practice in considering their lives philosophically. And because we should not reduce such consideration to a purely contemplative state divorced from action, philosophy *becomes* largely as John Dewey advised − philosophy of education, that is, philosophy of life. An important purpose of education should be to combat mystification . . .

Index

Texts by our author are identified in **bold**.

Scripture Index

Ephesians
  2:21, 356
  3:16, 356

Colossians
  2:19, 356

1 Timothy
  5:21, 143

2 Timothy
  4:4, 136

Hebrews
  2:10, 356, 329
  12:7, xxii

James
  5:10, 103

1 John
  3:2, 356

Revelation
  2:7, 131
  21:1, 36

Made in the USA
Middletown, DE
15 January 2017